Peak Vitality

Raising the Threshold of Abundance in
Our Material, Spiritual and Emotional Lives

edited by

JEANNE M. HOUSE

associate editors
Courtney Arnold
Dawson Church
Randy Peyser
Barbara Stahura

www.PeakVitality.org

Elite Books
Santa Rosa, CA 95403
www.EliteBooksOnline.com

Library of Congress Cataloging-in-Publication Data:

Peak Vitality: raising the threshold of abundance in our material, spiritual and emotional lives / edited by Jeanne M. House.

p. cm.

Includes bibliographical references.

ISNB 978-1-60070-013-2

1. Health. 2. World health. 3. Humanity.　　　1. House, Jeanne

362.1 – jh

2008

Cover art by Shiloh McCloud. To order a print, see www.WisdomHouseCatalog.com
Copyedited by Stephanie Marohn and Melissa Mower
Typeset by Maria Ayala Cirner
Printed in USA by Bang Printing
10 9 8 7 6 5 4 3 2 1

CONTENTS

Part Four: Creating Vibrant Relationships

Part Five: Living on a Small Planet

Part Six: New Medicine, New Psychology

Part Seven: Breaking Through Your Barriers

Part Eight: Dancing With the Universe

JAMES STROHECKER

High-Level Wellness

W hat comes to mind when you hear the words "Peak Vitality"? Do you envision someone who is buzzing with so much energy that she can't sit still? Do you think of someone who is in a perpetual state of peak performance? Or do you see someone who always seems to have all the energy he needs to live a fulfilling life, and who seems to be in a state of balance and is fully present?

Where does our energy come from? Do we get it from an outside source? Do we generate it? Or is it always present and available at the core of our being?

My personal experience is that all three are true.

Energy from Our Environment

There are some fundamental things we need to do to maintain a state of "energy homeostasis" with our physical environment. We need to bring in energy every day. If our intake of oxygen through breathing or nutrients through eating is deficient, our energy level will not be optimal; we are not doing the minimum necessary to maintain the human operating system on a physical level. Metabolically speaking, air and nutrients are two of our primary sources of energy. The quality of the energy we bring into our system through our breathing and eating is critical to sustaining our energy level.

James Strohecker, an e-health pioneer and wellness visionary, communicates fundamental principles of wellness from the world's great traditions into mainstream cultural awareness. He is president and cofounder of HealthWorld Online (www.Healthy.net), the world's first Internet network for wellness and complementary/alternative medicine, and cocreator of the Wellness Inventory assessment and life-balance program (www.WellPeople. com). He was cofounder of the first business-to-business Internet network for the natural products industry. He has coauthored five books, including *Natural Healing for Depression* (Perigee, 1999).

Just as important, however, is how we manage our energy throughout the day. If we expend more energy than we take in, we will likely be tired at the end of the day. Many of us push ourselves to exhaustion before we are willing to get into bed at night. We have exhausted our energy supply. And each night we attempt to regenerate our energy supply during sleep, although this regeneration is becoming increasingly difficult in our modern society. We have a hard time turning off our minds at night for a variety of reasons, and a high percentage of us are sleep deprived, unable to get a sufficient amount of sleep and "recharge our batteries" on a regular basis.

What follows is an endless loop of exhaustion and the need to stimulate our tired minds and bodies "back to our senses" so we can make it through the day. One of our favorite ways to do this is caffeine—stimulating our adrenals into overdrive to give us a burst of energy. But as we all know, that stimulation comes at a price; over time, we can exhaust our adrenal glands and then experience a sense of fatigue that never seems to leave us.

Generating Internal Energy

Many ancient disciplines focused on developing our full human potential, such as yoga, qigong, and shamanic practices from many traditions, teach us methods of generating energy and allowing our vital energy to circulate more freely throughout the body. Breathing practices are usually central to these methods. Yogic breathing practices (*pranayama*—regulation of the vital force) are becoming increasingly well known, and are commonly taught in yoga classes.

Many of these breathing practices are designed to create a balanced flow of vital energy. When our breathing rhythm becomes balanced, our mind and emotions are more centered and less reactive, our senses are calm, and our entire system becomes more relaxed. At the same time, when we reach this balance point and state of deep relaxation, we often experience a higher degree of vitality and well-being.

These disciplines also emphasize building or cultivating energy by not dissipating energy throughout the day in our daily activities. So much of our energy is dissipated through anxiety, worry, repetitive negative thinking, and the myriad actions we take based on these mental and emotional states.

Innate Energy

Do we bring in all of our energy from the outer environment or do we maintain our own core of innate energy? These same ancient disciplines are based on the concept that innate potential energy is dormant and in need of activation.

Certain yogic traditions from India refer to *kundalini*, a Sanskrit term for our latent, potential spiritual energy, figuratively described as a coiled serpent at the base of the spine. When activated and sustained through spiritual practices, under the guidance of a master, this spiritual energy vitalizes the body, mind, and emotions and enables us to experience our potential as human beings more deeply. This can include a more profound sense of Self, deeper/heightened states of awareness/consciousness, and energy levels that can be difficult to contain, as they stretch the limits of our "human operating system" (body, mind, and emotions).

In Chinese medicine, "prenatal *qi*" is the vital force that we bring into the world when we are born. According to some experts in Chinese Medicine, we are born with enough prenatal qi to live for five hundred years. This prenatal qi is like "an energy savings account" to which we cannot make a deposit; we can use but cannot add to our store of prenatal qi. Considering a "normal" lifespan of one hundred years, we are using up our prenatal qi five times faster than is necessary, needlessly expending our core energy.

How do we keep from depleting our core innate energy, our prenatal qi? The answer in the ancient Chinese tradition is to generate additional internal energy to supplement your innate energy, or in the language of that tradition, cultivate postnatal qi. This is the qi or energy you can derive from the food you eat, the water you drink, and the air you breathe. The practice of qigong is a time-tested method for generating more energy (postnatal qi) and maintaining your energy in a healthy balance. Qigong is becoming increasingly popular worldwide. Tai chi (taiji) is one form of qigong. It reminds us that by stilling the mind, cultivating positive emotion, and developing a deeper and more balanced breathing rhythm, we not only generate and access deeper levels of energy, but we better manage our energy as well.

Wellness Energy System

The Wellness Energy System, envisioned in the mid-1970s by wellness pioneer John W. Travis, MD, MPH, provides an excellent model for determining our overall state of vitality, health, and well-being at any point in time and how to manage our energy. This systemic view acts as an organizing principle to bring clarity and deeper understanding to your personal life and experience.

According to Dr. Travis, "We are energy transformers. All our life processes, including health and illness depend on how we manage energy. Putting together a person's energy inputs and outputs we have the complete wellness energy system." These twelve life processes are the basis of the Wellness Inventory, an online assessment and life-balance program based on Dr. Travis's work. He created the original Wellness Inventory assessment in 1975 for his Wellness Resource Center in Mill Valley, California, the first Wellness Center in the United States.

The representation of the Wellness Energy System in the wellness wheel is like a mandala of the whole person (your whole being) — a map of your experience — your behavior, attitudes, and beliefs. You can also look at the wheel as a dynamic system of interdependent elements, each connected to, affected by, and influencing the other eleven elements. If you look at the wheel, you see the whole-person perspective and the interdependence of the twelve life processes.

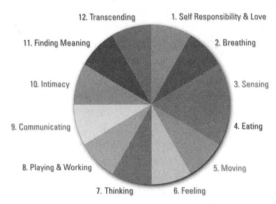

© 2002, John W. Travis and Healthworld Online

This wellness model helps you appreciate your personal wellness activities, attitudes, and beliefs from the perspective of how each activity affects the whole person. It also reveals how you can bring more of yourself as a whole person — in body, mind, and spirit — to each of your wellness activities.

Assessing Your Wellness

Here is an excerpt from the Wellness Inventory for assessing yourself in three key areas of wellness. The three areas chosen are the three key energy inputs in the Wellness Energy System: Breathing, Sensing, and Eating.

In each section, ask yourself the following two questions regarding each wellness statement. Your choices for answers are in *italics*. You don't need to write down your answers. Just pay attention to the process of contemplating each statement and your two answers.

1) How true is the statement for me today?

Yes /Always/Usually

Often

Sometimes/Maybe

Occasionally

No/Never/Hardly ever

2) How satisfied am I with my answer to the statement? (Would I prefer to have had a higher wellness score?)

Satisfied with my score

Moderately desire higher score

Strongly desire higher score

Breathing

- I use my breath as a tool for centering and increasing mental clarity on a regular basis.
- When I am feeling stressed, I take a little time to do some slow, deep breathing to calm myself and reduce my anxiety.
- I regularly practice breathing exercises to help generate internal energy.

Sensing

- I use soothing and enchanting music and sounds to create a relaxing and healing environment.
- I receive a full-body massage or other soothing touch on a regular basis to enhance my state of well-being.
- I am comfortable with solitude and silence.

Eating

- I allow myself to experience a moment of gratitude before I start eating a meal.
- I approach meals mindfully, eating slowly and chewing my food thoroughly to ensure optimal digestion, assimilation, and nourishment.

- When possible, I eat my meals in a relaxed, nurturing environment.

As this is just a mini-assessment with a few statements, we will not ask you to score or rate your responses. Simply reflect on your responses and note the increased awareness of possibilities for meaningful change in your life. That is what you can gain here.

What is common to all of the statements is that a positive response to the first question indicates a movement toward increasing your level of vitality and well-being. Answering the second question with "moderately or strongly desire a higher score" indicates willingness and motivation to change and to improve, again moving you in the direction of peak vitality or high-level wellness.

Exploring Possibilities for Greater Energy in Your Life

Where do you go from here? You have assessed yourself in three key areas of the Wellness Energy System. Did this experience awaken a sense of greater possibilities in enhancing the primary energy inputs in your life—Breathing, Sensing, and Eating? What are some of the actions and attitudes you can begin to integrate into your life to increase both the quantity and quality of energy in these three key inputs?

Breathing with Awareness

Breathing is the most fundamental of the energy inputs. There is no physiological function more vital than breathing, as it brings in life-giving oxygen, producing energy in our cells, and removes the by-product, carbon dioxide, from the body. Without breathing, life as we know it would last for but a few minutes. And, as discussed earlier, breathing practices play a central role in many ancient and modern traditions of spirituality and human development as well as energy generation. Calm, balanced breathing tends to heighten sensory awareness, promotes mental clarity, and helps support a more balanced emotional state.

There are literally thousands of breathing practices and exercises. Where do you start?

I recommend simply observing your breathing at different times during the day. Simple awareness of how you are breathing at different times and under different circumstances can go a long way toward shifting how you breathe.

- If you feel stressed or anxious, notice how you are breathing.

- If you have been on your computer for hours and are tiring, notice how you are breathing.
- When you are feeling really good, notice how you are breathing.

Most of us are totally unaware of our breathing. The idea that our breathing can influence our state of vitality and well-being is foreign to most of us; it is rarely emphasized in our culture. Yet it is such a fundamental skill that it should be taught in kindergarten and elementary school as a key life skill, a key to optimal functioning of the human operating system.

Sensing with Awareness

We take in our environment through our five senses—seeing, hearing, tasting, smelling, and touching. Without these sense impressions, life as we know it on Earth would not exist. The senses bring in the information that enables our mind to create its own map of reality. Yet most of us are not aware of our sensing. Like breathing, it is part of our operating system, something we do all day long without thinking. Over time, however, we can become desensitized due to sensory overload or to pain, abuse, or trauma, which can cause us to shut down. Or we become overly sensitive to sounds, light, smells, and other sensory stimuli. This can interfere with our functioning in the world and our energy level.

Again, like breathing, simple awareness of the senses is the doorway to using your senses to support your personal growth and energy levels. Here is an idea for bringing your awareness back to your senses.

Take a walk in nature, in a local park, or in your neighborhood.

On your walk on one day, focus your awareness on your sense of seeing. Survey your entire visual field. Take in everything around you. Notice the sky, the clouds, the trees, the flowers, the people, the animals, the buildings — everything around you. Are you taking in more visual input than normal? What would you normally see taking this same walk? Where is your attention normally? Is it on the environment around you, or in your thoughts?

On your walk the next day, do the same process but focus instead on your sense of hearing. Notice all of the sounds you normally filter out — people's voices, car radios, motorcycles, a distant lawnmower, a dog barking, crickets chirping, or birds singing.

A deeper sensory awareness and engagement is associated with increased learning and heightened levels of performance. As with breathing, ancient and modern transformational practices such as yoga and qigong deeply engage our senses to help generate higher levels of energy and awareness.

Eating with Awareness

We are constantly inundated with recommendations about our diet. What to eat, what to avoid—and the landscape is constantly changing. A few simple guidelines could probably be agreed on: Eat a balanced diet with the maximum of fresh whole foods when possible. Eat nutrient-dense foods. Eat organic produce when possible, to minimize your exposure to chemical fertilizers, pesticides, and other environmental contaminants. Support your local farmers and shop at farmer's markets when possible.

We rarely hear, though, about *how* we eat. What is your state of mind when you eat?

What is your emotional state? This has a big impact on what you choose to eat, how fast you eat, and how much you eat. We are told not to eat too much if we don't want to gain weight. There is another perspective, however.

The ancient science of yoga was very practical about how much to eat. The yogic texts recommend leaving your stomach one-third empty after a meal to allow for the circulation of *prana* or vital energy. Yogis noticed that when you fill your stomach to capacity, you need to divert a greater amount of energy to the process of digestion, and may actually feel heavy and lethargic—hardly the outcome one would expect from a healthy meal!

> *Try this experiment in awareness around eating. Chew each bite of food thoroughly, twenty to twenty-five times. At first this may seem like torture. You realize that when you are stressed, you have a tendency to chew, chew, chew, swallow, before your food has been fully masticated. Chewing is the first stage of digestion. By fully chewing your food, the next stage of digestion in the stomach is greatly facilitated and assimilation in the intestines is greatly enhanced.*

In addition to improved assimilation, there is another bonus: You tend to eat less when you chew thoroughly and eat more slowly. And this may actually help you live longer! Research into longevity has shown that the two factors that have a real impact on longevity are caloric restriction (eating less) and lowering core body temperature (achieved through meditation, breathing, and deep relaxation).

There are some practices that can make it easier to eat more mindfully and more slowly. Eating, like breathing, is one of our most important activities, and one that deserves every bit of mindfulness we can bring to it. Yet we often approach eating as if it were just another one of our multitasking activities during the day. When we are able to slow down and actually sit down to enjoy a meal, and take a brief moment to feel gratitude for the food we are about to consume, it is much easier to eat more deliberately, eat less, and enjoy and appreciate what we eat much more. We also get the bonus of fully breathing between each bite and chewing. Imagine that!

Choice and Self-Responsibility

Awareness is the first step in creating lifestyle change, which is why I refer to Breathing with Awareness, Sensing with Awareness, and Eating with Awareness. With awareness, we can observe our current behavior, as well as possibilities for new behavior. The keyword here is *possibilities*.

Frequently, we do not attempt to change because we don't believe that change is an option. We have always done things the same way — that's just the way we are. As we become aware of new possibilities, we also become aware that we have *choices*. As we become aware of our choices, we see that by being self-responsible we can make the choices that are likely to bring the most benefit into our lives.

We tend to look at choices and actions as needing to be on a larger and more dramatic scale if they are to create change in our lives. I believe this is partly a cultural phenomenon and partly our belief that we need a large goal to motivate us. And we often later discover that the large changes are not sustainable and slide back into our old behaviors.

Small Steps—Creating Sustainable Lifestyle Change

A key to creating sustainable lifestyle change is to focus on small steps for continuous improvement. As a member of a highly goal-oriented society, this may seem counterintuitive to you, but this strategy of incremental change can remake the fabric of your life and lead to major lifestyle change.

Our desire to achieve a higher level of wellness and vitality is a lifelong journey composed of many small choices that present themselves every day of our lives. At first glance, this approach may seem to require a great deal of patience, but it is a highly effective strategy. Large, ambitious steps toward lifestyle change may inspire and motivate the individual at first, but they can raise a great deal of resistance to change that may eventually sabotage any positive gains made. This constantly occurs in attempts to diet, lose weight, and maintain an exercise regimen.

Returning to the whole-person model embodied in the wellness wheel and its twelve dimensions, the small-step strategy begins to make sense. When you look at yourself as a whole person, and see how one dimension affects the others, you begin to understand the wisdom of this approach, and how powerful small steps can be in your life.

Discovering Where You Are Most Motivated to Change

When you self-assessed yourself in Breathing, Sensing, and Eating earlier, you were asked how satisfied you were with each answer. If you answered, "I strongly desire a higher score," this typically indicates greater motivation to change. As you discover (through an assessment such as the Wellness Inventory or through self-inquiry) the areas of your life in which you are most motivated to change, you can then begin the process of creating small action steps for sustainable lifestyle change.

What might this look like in your everyday life? Here are some suggestions for action steps for breathing, sensing, and eating. See if you can come up with steps that reflect your own life and experiences.

Action Steps for Breathing

- Take a one-minute breathing break every afternoon at the same time to relax and re-center.
- Put a note on your computer or refrigerator to remind yourself: BREATHE.
- Take a moment to notice your breathing whenever you feel stressed.

Action Steps for Sensing

- Get a massage once a month.
- Take a soothing hot bath by candlelight, adding essential oils for fragrance.
- Play your favorite relaxing/healing music as you prepare to go to bed.

Action Steps for Eating

- Place a large glass of water next to your computer at the beginning of the day.

- When you sit down for a meal, take a couple of deep breaths to center and relax yourself before starting to eat.

- Make your lunch a priority and schedule a regular time to eat, just as you would schedule a business meeting.

Maintaining Positive Feeling

American culture has tended to place far more emphasis on the power of thoughts, beliefs, and attitudes in achieving goals than on the power of positive emotion. Often motivation to change is fueled by self-criticism, shame, judgment, and other limiting, negative emotions and attitudes that do not lay a solid foundation for the change process. Learning to focus on what you do want in your life, rather than on what you don't want, opens the door to new possibilities. Energy follows thought, and energy also follows emotion. The choice of where you direct your energy is yours. If you focus your energy in a negative or self-limiting direction, your energy will run in circles and dissipate. By focusing in the direction of where you want to go in your life, with positive emotion, your energy and level of vitality and inspiration can grow.

The practice of gratitude is a wonderful means of cultivating positive emotion. By beginning to practice feeling gratitude for what you currently have in your life, you free up a tremendous amount of energy that is normally dissipated in worry, anxiety, and fear. You also create a positive feeling state that is a much stronger foundation from which to begin moving toward what you want in your life. A positive feeling state, with an inspired heart and a clear mind, is the perfect starting place for moving toward creating a higher level of well-being in your life through the small choices you make on a daily basis.

High-Level Wellness and Peak Vitality as an Ongoing Orientation

If you are highly motivated to create sustainable lifestyle change and experience a higher level of vitality and well-being, you might consider engaging a wellness coach. A coach acts as your partner and helps to empower you in finding your own answers and supports you in realizing your desired goals. A good wellness coach understands that you are the ultimate expert in your own life. By asking the appropriate questions, your coach can help you discover solutions that are right for you and keep you focused on and accountable to your wellness action plan and on the road to high-level wellness and peak vitality.

Wellness is an ongoing, lifelong journey. Every day, you can improve the quality of your life and level of personal well-being through your small lifestyle choices, as well as choices regarding your emotional responses and attitudes. You can orient yourself toward a higher level of vitality, health, and well-being, or you can live day by day, never investing in your wellness. If you choose the latter, one day you will discover that your "wellness savings account" is empty; you are exhausted, depleted, and have driven yourself to a poor state of health.

Just as we save for retirement, let's also make regular deposits to a "wellness savings account" through life-affirming wellness practices and positive lifestyle choices. Life without energy is not the life we want. Our lives continue to blossom and develop even greater depth and meaning as we age. Choose to live well!

How Best to Utilize This Book

Using the Wellness Wheel (Wellness Energy System) as an "organizing principle," you can see that the approaches to peak vitality from the experts in this book address one or more of the twelve key life processes. In fact, from the perspective of the Wellness Wheel, the book itself becomes a mandala for peak vitality. Look at the chapters in this book as an expression of the whole person, as well as an expression of the personal journey to higher levels of awareness and vitality.

Whether a chapter addresses the dimension of *Finding Meaning* ("Living Consistent with Your Values," "Personal Mythology and Wellness"), the dimension of *Transcending* ("Hardwired for Bliss," "Rituals for Rebirth"), the dimension of *Feeling* ("Breaking the Blame Box," "Emotional Freedom Techniques"), or any of the other twelve dimensions, it can act as a gateway to the next stage of your journey to a higher level of personal well-being.

As my dear friend and associate Bobbie Burdett likes to say, "It doesn't matter where you enter the wheel. What is important, however, is that you enter the wheel." As each of the twelve dimensions is part of the larger whole, each is connected to the other eleven dimensions. In the same way, you can look at this book as another tool to help you reclaim your innate wholeness.

As a new awareness is awakened by reading a specific chapter, you may then find yourself drawn to another chapter and then yet another—as if you are stringing your own personal strand of pearls. You may find that the perspectives of your chosen chapters are taking you on a journey around the Wellness Wheel. Go with your own personal flow. Follow your own heart and mind. Be curious. Explore. Absorb. Integrate. Allow your new awareness to inspire positive changes in your life, changes that allow you to experience your wholeness more deeply. Wholeness is the basis of a deeper sense of well-being and vitality.

Most of all, approach the book with a sense of gratitude. There are many treasures here to explore, treasures offered by some of our greatest contemporary luminaries. Allow your curiosity and your passion to open the doors that are right for you now, at this moment in your life.

PART ONE

Presence in Your Body

MEHMET OZ

YOU:
The Vibrant Human

Doctors will be the first ones to tell you that they can't keep you from getting heart disease, or put sunblock on your nose before a noontime run, or snatch the third Twinkie out of your paw before you torpedo it down your throat.

But you can.

You can control your health destiny. Just look at the way Lance Armstrong has done it. In 1996, the champion cyclist had tests that revealed advanced testicular cancer that had spread to his lungs and brain. With a far less than 50 percent chance of survival, Armstrong endured surgeries and an aggressive form of chemotherapy to treat his cancer. Armstrong was left weak—yet determined. Combined with medical treatments, Armstrong's own willpower and the support of the people around him gave him the strength to fight, to beat cancer, to become the record-breaking six-time Tour de France champion, and most important, to inspire, help, and motivate millions of other people (just look at all those yellow LIVESTRONG wristbands!). One of the great many lessons we've learned from Armstrong is that while you can't always control what happens to you (no matter how fit you are), there are some things you can control: your attitude, your determination, and—what serves as the crux of this book—your willingness to take your health into your own hands and know as much about your body as possible.

Now, in no way are we endorsing that you order a box of scalpels

Mehmet Oz, MD, is Professor of Cardiac Surgery at Columbia University, and is a founder of the Complementary Medicine Program at New York-Presbyterian Hospital. He has authored more than 350 original publications and books. His most recent is *You: Staying Young: The Owner's Manual for Extending Your Warranty* (Free Press, 2007), co-written with Michael Roizen. Oz serves on the Trustees Advisory Council of the One Voice Movement, a non-profit organization that strives to empower moderate Israelis and Palestinians to take a more assertive role in resolving the conflict. He appears on many media shows each year.

and remove suspect-looking moles from your arm or schedule a self-performed colonoscopy after the kids go to bed. (Even we don't do *that*.) We all need doctors. The point is that the power you have to control your health destiny is real—and it's in your hands, not someone else's.

If you make five—just five—adjustments to your life, you can have a dramatic effect on your life expectancy and the quality of your life. The five things are: controlling your blood pressure; avoiding cigarettes; exercising thirty minutes a day; controlling stress; and following an easy-to-love healthy diet.

Whether you look at clocks, calendars, or hourglasses, time doesn't stop. It ticks and tocks at the same pace day after day, minute after minute, second after second. Everyone ages at the same rate with birthdays every year—that's your calendar age. But you have the power to turn your clock faster or slower with the lifestyle choices you make regarding what you do with your body and what you put into it. For example, a fifty-year-old who douses her lungs with nicotine and builds her food pyramid with chopped liver and sausage actually may have the body of a sixty-five-year-old because of the destruction she's doing, while a fifty-year-old who eats well, stays away from toxins, and takes care of her body with moderate physical activity could have the body and health of a thirty-six-year-old.

To show you the power you have, consider this: You control more than 70 percent of how well and how long you live. By the time you reach fifty your lifestyle dictates 80 percent of how you age; the rest is controlled by inherited genetics.

Of course, we can't stop aging. That's because our bodies are continually aged by the environment through oxidation or other processes within your body. Oxidation, which is a lot like the rusting of your house's foundation or pillars, is a natural, important process that's a by-product of the proper functioning of your body. But when too much oxidation occurs, it puts you at a higher risk of aging—or rusting—of your body. It's why so many foods that are good for us are antioxidants—foods that slow the oxidation process. We do not know that the antioxidant property of these foods is responsible for the health benefits you get from them. But what we do know is that there are three main factors in age-related disease that you can control—and by controlling them, you slow the aging process. From a purely scientific perspective, we don't really know what causes aging, but we do know what makes us feel old before age one hundred, and that's age-related disease. So we can tell you 80 percent of how to stop these three factors in age-related disease. They are:

- Aging of your heart and blood vessels (responsible for things like strokes, heart attacks, memory loss, and impotence, when arteries cut off nutrient-rich blood to important organs)

- Aging of your immune system (which leads to autoimmune diseases, infection, and cancer)

- Aging caused by environmental or social issues (accidents and social factors like stress are very powerful factors that contribute to aging)

YOU Are on Your Way to Living with More Vitality

Flipping through the newspaper, you can read about all kinds of news — whether it's about international conflicts or another celebrity breakup. But sometimes, at least to us, it seems that the only health news that gets attention is the bad news. Every time you turn the page, you read a stat or a story that is depressing: There's another famous case of Alzheimer's. Diabetes rates are skyrocketing. Americans are fatter than an A-lister's wallet. The effect? Eventually, it seems so depressing that you avoid health news and information the way polar bears avoid Fiji. Yes, we have some serious health problems to address, but they are only one side of the story.

For starters, look at the average life expectancy: forty-seven in 1900, and nearly eighty in 2000. A lot of credit for these extra thirty-three years goes to public health and organized medicine. So statistics show that we're going to live long. Maybe the most impressive statistics are these: While the rest of the world thinks we have the corner on obesity, there may be signs we're changing. From 1966 to 1996, the number of Americans who engaged in regular physical activity decreased by 1 percent every year. But from 1996 to 2002, the amount of physical activity grew 1 percent every year. Smoking prevalence has decreased from 50 percent of the adult population in 1970 to 27 percent in 2000. And the people with high blood pressure who went untreated fell from 80 percent in 1970 to 43 percent in 2000.

Even corporate America is catching on: General Mills broadcast that it will stop selling cereal that isn't whole grain, and Wal-Mart is reported to have told food companies it would no longer distribute foods with evil trans fats — an important signal to food manufacturers that we can demand healthier products.

What does this all mean? Although we're not perfect, we are making progress — by increasing activity, squashing cigarettes, and changing our diets. And that points to the fact that the person who has the most say over how well you age isn't us or even your regular doctors. It's the one who has five fingers on either side of this book.

GAY HENDRICKS

Eating for Vibrance

T his is probably the first and only time in my writing career that I'll use three exclamation points in a row, but in this case I think they're warranted:

Imagine eating in such a way that you always feel a glow of vibrance inside!

Imagine always feeling a steady, harmonious sense of well-being in the depths of yourself!

Imagine not having to worry about your weight!

If you'd told me ten years ago that these things were possible, I would have thought you were joking. If you'd told me that a way of eating could make me feel harmonious and vital, I would have thought you'd gone around the bend. Now, though, I've enjoyed those benefits for several years and watched many others attain them, too. The good news is that it's possible, and the best news is…it's not all that hard.

Like the Zen story says, though, you have to pour out the old tea in the cup before you fill it up with the fresh.

So…

I'm going to ask you to do something bold. For the time being, I want you to put aside everything you know about nutrition. That's what I had to do before I could finally open myself to the breakthrough that made vibrant-eating possible.

Gay Hendricks, PhD, is author and co-author of twenty-five books in conscious relationship, conscious business, and body-mind transformation. Included are such enduring bestsellers as *Conscious Loving* (Bantam, 1992), *Conscious Breathing* (Bantam, 1995), and *Conscious Living* (HarperSanFrancisco, 2001). Before founding his own institute, he was Professor of Counseling for twenty-one years at the University of Colorado. Over the past 24 years, he and his wife Kathlyn have raised two children, accumulated a million frequent flyer miles and appeared on more than 500 radio and television programs. Visit www.hendricks.com.

Begin with a simple question, the same one I had in mind when I began my quest for vibrance. The question is: How can I eat so that I feel vibrant all the time?

There was a time that I used to feel bad most of the time, simply because of what I ate. When I was in my early twenties, I weighed over three hundred pounds, compared to the 180 or so I weigh now in my fifties. I'm 6'1", so when I weighed three hundred pounds I looked like a sumo wrestler instead of a halfback. I'd been taken to weight specialists galore as a kid, but nothing had ever worked in the long term. Being a smart kid, I also knew everything there was to know about calorie counts and fat grams. I just hadn't been able to put any of this knowledge to use.

When I was 24, I decided to take responsibility for losing the weight, no matter what it required. For a year, I alternated back and forth between eating a fruit-and-vegetable diet and a high-protein diet. When I would get sick of meat and fish, I would eat fruits and vegetables for a couple of weeks. When I started to cringe at the thought of an apple or a piece of broccoli, I would go back to burgers and fish for a while. By the end of the year, I had dropped a hundred pounds. But, oh, that last twenty pounds! I hovered around 200 for years. Occasionally I would get down into the 180s, but then my weight would creep back up over 200 again.

Bill Cosby once observed that when he turned 40, his body stopped producing lean meat. I can relate. In my forties, my weight began creeping up, and as I neared 50 I was pushing 230 pounds. That's when I had my "vibrance" breakthrough. I formed *my* big question: What would it take to feel vibrant all the time? This question led me to focus on food: How and what could I eat so that I felt vibrant all the time? The question paid off beyond my wildest dreams and resulted in the exciting discoveries I'll soon share with you. It took four years to test and refine our findings on several hundred people. During these four years, I became my own best customer. I'm happy to report that those 50 extra pounds (the weight of ten Manhattan phone books!) are gone now. It took me until my fifties, but I finally figured out how to keep the weight off without dieting.

How to Eat for Vibrance

It's done by focusing on the *feeling* of vibrance.

I invite you now to let go of all the knowledge stored in your attic about what and how to eat. For the time being, set aside information about such things as fat grams and protein requirements and food combining. I even ask you to do the unthinkable: Set aside any prejudice against what one nutritionist called the "evil white powder," referring not to cocaine but to sugar. For the time being, let's focus exclusively on the feeling of vibrance.

Our questions will be: *What* can I eat to feel vibrant all the time? *How* can I eat to feel vibrant all the time?

Here's what my colleagues and I discovered:

There are no universal vibrance-foods. Your personal vibrance-foods must be tailored to your body, using a very simple testing procedure you'll learn in this chapter.

While there are no universal vibrance-foods, we discovered about twenty-five foods that come close. These are foods that nearly always produced vibrance in the several hundred people in our study.

There is a simple secret to knowing when to stop eating. If you master this secret, you can eat practically anything and feel vibrant.

Focusing on the feeling of vibrance is helpful in losing weight. Focusing on losing weight is not helpful in learning to feel vibrant.

Here are the specifics of how to do it.

First, discover your "vibrance-foods." If you put some attention on it, the process of discovering your vibrance-foods will take a week or so. Once you identify your vibrance-foods, you can move as fast as you want toward vibrance. If you want to take it easy, gradually begin to favor more vibrance-foods in your diet. If you want to feel vibrant right away, eat nothing but vibrance-foods for three days or so.

What Are Vibrance-Foods?

Have you noticed that sometimes you feel sluggish or off-center after you eat? Believe it or not, people have told me they always feel that sluggish, off-center feeling after they eat! They thought it was normal and that everybody felt that way. It's definitely not. It's a symptom of eating something that's not a vibrance-food for you.

By contrast, you may have noticed that sometimes you feel fine after you eat. You feel pleasant sensations in your stomach and intestines, and you feel a calm and energized sense of well-being as you move through your activities. That sensation tells you that you've eaten vibrance-food.

Here's the specific definition of vibrance-food: Any food that is making you feel energetic, clear, and steady an hour after eating it. It's important to draw the one-hour time-distinction. The reason: Many foods are designed to make you feel zippy and cheerful right away. Foods with high doses of sugar, fat, salt, and refined flour fire up your system for a half-hour or so after you eat them. After thirty minutes, those same zippy foods start to make you feel foggy, run-down, and often grouchy. As that sludgy feeling settles in, guess what your body begins to crave. Another zippy food! If this sounds suspiciously like how an addictive drug works, you've caught on to a big secret. It's the key to the spectacular success of the corporate Twinkie-machine. They sell legal addictions. Discovering your vibrance-foods is a two-step process.

Step one: Eat a food you like.

Step two: Notice your body-sensations 45 to 60 minutes later.

The key is to notice how you feel about an hour after you eat the food. If you feel clear, energetic, and harmonious, you ate a vibrance-food. If you don't, you didn't. It's all about getting that vibrant feeling and keeping it.

Testing yourself an hour or so later is important for another reason. We found, through experimentation, that if you feel vibrant after an hour, you're highly likely to feel vibrant for several more hours after that. That's definitely not true for non-vibrance foods. When you eat something that's a non-vibrance food for you, you won't feel vibrant an hour later and you won't feel vibrant for the next few hours, either.

To give you an example of how this works, let me contrast two very different foods. The first one tests as a vibrance-food for over 90 percent of the people we've researched. The second one tests as a non-vibrance food for over 90 percent of them. In other words, the two foods are at opposite ends of the vibrance-spectrum for most of us.

Our first food will be a large organically grown Fuji apple, providing approximately 100 calories. Nine out of ten people, according to our studies, will feel vibrant an hour after eating a Fuji apple, especially if it's organically grown. (I'll have more to say on the "organic" issue later.)

Our second food will be two large medjool dates, totalling approximately 100 calories. Nine out of ten people will not feel vibrant an hour after eating two large medjool dates. There's nothing wrong with dates—its just that they are so loaded with sugar that they out-score table sugar on the glycemic index (more of this index later, too).

Here's what you would see, if you were watching over our shoulders as we conduct a vibrance-testing session. Ten hungry people each eat a Fuji apple at noon. A second group often, also hungry, eats two large medjool dates apiece. At one o'clock, they give themselves a vibrance rating on a 1-10 scale. It measures physical energy, mental clarity, and emotional harmony.

The Fuji group will rate themselves high on the scale, while the medjool group will rate themselves low. If you look at the two groups closely, you wouldn't need a rating-scale to figure out which ones ate a vibrance-food. The date-eaters look a little fatigued. Even though they move more sluggishly, they also look antsy. The apple-eaters look peppy but relaxed.

Everybody's still hungry, though, so we test them on another pair of foods. This time, one group eats a bowl of crispy rice cereal, the kind that entertains you with the famous snapping, crackling sound effects. The second group gets a bowl of buckwheat cereal. Everybody gets the same calorie amount, the same amount of low-fat milk, and a spoonful of fructose on the top. (I'll explain about the fructose later.) An hour later, the crispy-rice group gives themselves a vibrance rating averaging 4.5 on the 10-point scale. The buckwheat group gives themselves a rating of 8.2. For most of the people we've tested, buckwheat is a vibrance-food. Crispy rice cereal isn't.

The Premier Vibrance–Foods

Before I give you our High-Vibrance list of foods, I need to say a word about portions. Practically any food will make you feel non-vibrant if you eat too much of it. Interestingly enough even non-vibrance foods won't make you feel off-center if you eat a small enough amount. For example, more than two medjool dates makes nine out of ten people we've tested feel non-vibrant an hour later. However, if you nibble half of a medjool date, you probably would not feel sluggish or foggy an hour later. There's a simple way to figure out how much to eat. We teach it to people in our program, and they've found it uniformly useful:

Some foods are one-hand foods.

Others are two-hand foods.

Think of the amount of nuts you could hold in one cupped hand without any of them spilling over. That's a one-hand amount. A small hamburger patty also would fit on the palm of one hand. It might be a little messy, but you could hold it in one cupped hand, so it also qualifies as a one-hand food. It would be hard to hold two hamburger patties side by side in one cupped hand.

If you held out your two hands, cupped together, I could put at least a cup of steamed rice in them without any spilling over, and maybe even two cups. That would be a two-hand amount.

Okay, got the trick?

Here are the punch lines:

- Don't eat more than a one-hand amount of meat or fish. Only one-hand amounts of meat and fish (about five or six ounces after cooking) make people feel vibrant. If ten people eat a typical "restaurant portion" of meat and fish (a half-pound or more), nine of them won't feel vibrant an hour later. We found this to be true even if they are eating a meat or fish that usually tests "vibrant" for them in a smaller, one-hand portion.

- Don't eat more cooked grain than you can hold in two hands. Two-hand portions of cooked grains make people feel vibrant — more doesn't. Eat more than about two cupped hands of grain at a time, and you probably won't feel vibrant later.

High-Vibrance Foods

The following foods produced high-vibrance rating in 90 percent of people tested. An asterisk (*) marks a food that only tested "vibrant" if it was organically grown.

Fruit

Apples*, particularly Fuji, gala, golden delicious, and braeburn
Blueberries*
Plums
Cherries*
Nectarines

Vegetables

Lightly cooked greens, such as kale, spinach, bok choy, collards
Green beans*
Salad greens*
Soybeans (steamed or boiled in the style called *edamame* in Japanese restaurants)
Bean sprouts

Grains

Oatmeal*
Cream of buckwheat
Oat bran*
Kamut
Rye

Dairy

Kefir and some yogurts
Butter (small amounts)

Fish

    Salmon
    Halibut
    Sea bass
    Sardines, drained of oil

Meat

    Lamb
    Venison

Nuts

    Almonds*
    Peanuts*

Oils

    Olive
    Flax
    Bran
    Grapeseed

So, don't expect perfection from yourself. Vibrance-eating is not about doing it right all the time. It's about feeling vibrant, then blowing it, then remembering to eat so you feel vibrant again. Gradually you'll become accustomed, as I did, to feeling vibrant. Your body will gravitate more toward vibrance-foods and less toward the beckoning seductions of the false-vibrance family. One day you'll probably wake up and realize you've been eating vibrance-foods consistently for a long time. You realize you've been feeling great for a long time without even thinking about it. That's what happened for me, and it was well worth the effort to get there.

In the meantime, how about tuning in right now to find out if you are hungry? If you are, treat yourself to a vibrance-food. And notice how good you're still feeling an hour from now.

Enjoy!

Maureen Whitehouse

True Beauty

"I" was suspended. I found myself not only out of my body, but also out of my senses, experiencing what I can only describe as free-falling upwards, directly into the Heart of God. As my body lay motionless for the next few hours, my heart traversed typically inaccessible realms in a wordless, resting peace. The last thing I recall is being wrapped in what felt like a soft down comforter of love while a bright, white quiet overcame me. The world stood in a stillness so deep that it defies all definition. However I can say what it felt like afterwards: as though an Almighty One took a match and set me on fire.

I had been a fashion model for quite a few years. I'd made it past the ingénue phase of my career, when I'd strutted my stuff on Madison and Seventh Avenues and traveled the world. Now I was known as *the* quintessential "young mom" to the best advertising agencies and photographers in Boston. I was in high demand not only because of my "look" as the well-put-together and successful girl-next-door type, but also my reputation as great on a set with animals and kids.

That was my career. At home, I was an equally unparalleled success—lovely house, expansive, organic gardens complete with Zen waterfalls, captivatingly bright and gorgeous children, a devoted and handsome husband, and the coolest, best-behaved dog ever. I designed and sewed my own curtains, cooked gourmet organic meals from scratch. We even had a white-picket fence that I'd painted

Maureen Whitehouse, author of *E³ The Transformational Triad* (Axiom, 2004), *Soul-Full Eating* (Axiom, 2007), and *True Beauty* (Axiom, 2008), has helped thousands of people—from CEOs to artists, students, and prison inmates—to radically shift their perception of challenge, transition, and change. An international model, actress, reporter, and talk show host, Maureen experienced a profound awakening in 1996 and has since lived her life helping others to realize their full potential. When not lecturing, counseling clients, or writing books, she travels widely, leading Miracle Journeys to sacred sites. www.ExperienceAxiom.com.

myself! Suffice it to say that, on the home front, I could outdo Martha Stewart any day.

Yet each morning when I awoke to our typical family routine, I suffered a numbing, nameless pang. Not loud or strong enough to make me actually stop, but evident enough to make me go, go, go incessantly forward into my life with an insatiable hunger to satisfy and fill the ever-present void I felt inside. Although on the outside my life looked great, I was in a perpetual state of condemnation, judging myself and the world around me in defensiveness against my fear that no matter what I did or how well I performed in life, I could *never* be good enough.

Sure, my image to the world was nearly flawless, but when I stood in front of the mirror all I saw was one big mistake. My classic Volvo looked fabulous on the outside — unless you took a closer look inside and saw me behind the wheel, enraged and indiscriminately giving the finger to anyone who even remotely got in my way. And of course the house was immaculate. To keep up my meticulous maven image I'd frantically and fanatically clean it at even the slightest hint that guests might drop by to visit — most especially my parents. I was a perpetual performance queen both on and off the set!

Perhaps the pain was more acute because each time I felt the emptiness I'd simultaneously berate myself for being such an ingrate. After all, I was living the American Dream to the hilt. For God's sake, I'd bared my pearly whites time and time again on the very commercials that sold this American dream to millions of others.

And God Laughed

So I plodded on, not knowing how or what more I could do to "fix it." Years were spent in self-inquiry, spiritual practice, and pointed forgiveness work. Finally I realized it was time to give up the losing battle with myself. I was exhausted, and I could no longer keep up the image of impeccability. The way I had lived just made no sense — I was "done."

To my surprise, I found this notion of "being done" amazingly liberating. I could actually forgive and forget my past, relax, and exhale for what felt like the first time in my life! I actually felt what it was like to just *be* with myself without the nagging sense of performance anxiety.

The night after this realization I fell asleep quickly, but at 3:00 AM I spontaneously awoke. It wasn't a frenzied middle-of-the-night awakening, however; I felt that same sense of peace I'd had earlier in the day. So I began to pray, and this prayer was a petition. But before

I had a chance to complete the request, my mind stopped — utterly and completely — and I remained in that breathless state of suspended animation for hours...

Along with my next graspable thought came my first breath. I gasped in the staggering truth of the realization that *there is no judgment to God*. On the heels of this revelation, my entire life flashed before me. I was presented with every situation in which I had found forgiveness difficult, in intricate detail. But instead of experiencing the intense emotional ego-pain I had the first time around, this time I saw each scenario bathed in the ecstasy of genuine laughter — a booming, benevolent chuckle surrounding each and every one of the situations. And although I was entirely aware that God was beyond name or form, it was as if "He" were saying to me, "Now you see how I see."

I was experiencing "Judgment Day," but not in the way that we are taught to fear it. Instead, I was being afforded the Divine opportunity to clearly see how I had judged all of the grace that had been showered upon me in my life. I saw that this grace continually encircles and permeates each and every one of our lives. Through my ego's eyes, I had interpreted so much of this symmetry wrongly. I had made the all-too-human mistake of judging perfection using limited notions begotten by fear (such as my "I'll never be good enough" syndrome). Paradoxically, in my newly enlightened state, I was unable to judge my own judgments. I was unable to find anything worthy of disparagement. Within this space of clarity, I tangibly felt and saw that I had been safe all along, and I actually found the distortions of my ego to be hysterically funny.

Lifting the Veil

It seemed so ludicrous to me that all along, through the veil of illusion, my own judgment and fear had caused me to misinterpret the poetry of my life as pain. And in that realization I found the most profound and absolute liberation. My one prevailing thought was that everything is okay. It had *always* been okay. In fact, not only was it okay, it was perfect!

I became instantaneously aware that I was — that we all are — the essence of God on this earth. We are limitless, all-powerful, omniscient co-creators. It became perfectly clear to me that I had experienced all of my life until that moment as a voyeur, as a sleep-walker blundering through a mysteriously beautiful and perfectly orchestrated existence. All my past discords and ego-driven reactions were rooted in the dream interpretation I had been giving to everything. I saw that no matter what I'd thought, nothing but total perfection lay before me, behind me, and in me, at each and every moment of my life.

At 7:00 AM I was back in my body, lying in bed, wondering if I had the wherewithal to pull off a typical day of getting the kids off to school and tending to the normal routine. Still shaking and on fire from the experience, I went into the bathroom and turned on the faucet to splash some water on my face, hoping to ground myself a bit. When I looked up into the mirror, what I saw had the opposite effect. It nearly blew me away. I saw the most astonishingly beautiful sight I had ever seen.

I saw myself without a physical body. I saw myself as a living Soul—entirely filled with Light. *I was astounding.* It took everything in me to remain on my feet, while my eyes, which were like golden orbs emitting a soft and fiery love, blazed away at me from within this brilliant form. *How had I forgotten this?* I marveled. My wonder climbed as I realized this beauty is not just me; it is everyone else as well. As a fashion model, I worked with some of the most impeccably perfect people on the face of this earth, and not one of them came close to touching the magnificence of the reflection I saw in the mirror that morning.

For the next three days, my eyes were fully opened to the miraculous in all things. Blades of grass shone like emeralds; birds sang as though an entire orchestra was contained in their throat. Watching a crippled young girl in her wheel chair, her arms twisted, I saw in her a sense of poise and elegance I'd have never perceived before. I viewed the world as our souls know it—seeing that behind everything that is apparently ordinary looms the immanent, the stupendous, and the glorious.

Picking up my daughters at their elementary school, I actually saw love greeting love as children ran towards their mothers and fathers. Even at places like the grocery store and K-mart, the mundane was revealed as miraculous. I was astounded by the orchestration required to get all those objects into the space they occupied on the shelves, just so the customer now buying them, totally unaware of the magnificence of this event, could have them. I saw people pass on the sidewalk and in the parking lot completely oblivious to the fact that they were at the exact right place at the exact right time. Yet an instantaneous view of heaven was available to them if only they were present enough, and grateful enough, to see it—to notice the present perfection.

After all of those years of seeking, I realized we are put on this earth to liberate our souls: to see the heaven surrounding us. To step out of the whirlpool of life into the wide ocean and to bring our brilliant Being to the surface. There was no turning back for me. I no longer saw myself chained to a routine existence. And what had changed in my life? Nothing at all...except *my perceptions*.

Seeing the Miraculous Everyday

From these experiences, I've learned that we don't need to leave our typical lives to find heaven. In fact, the most profound and powerful spiritual revelations can be found right smack in the midst of our everyday lives. When we can unearth the Divine in the down and dirty doldrums and see the miraculous in the mundane, it's those realizations that follow us most poignantly into the next moment and the next, transforming our perceptions of life as we know it. Then we see that in each and every person a God walks on Earth, veiled by fleshy form that has a desirous nature and a limited mind which primarily hinders and imprisons, but which finally releases and liberates. We are just temporarily prey to the illusions of the senses.

When I began to write my book, *Soul-Full Eating*, I realized what a powerful path to self-actualization choosing, preparing, and eating food could be. Meals are a profound and accessible way to recognize the Divine countless times a day — via the food we eat. *And we all eat!* It is a common denominator for all people on Earth. What a revelation it is to experience the notion that what and how we consume food can actually precipitate our being consumed by the Divine.

A Soul-fullness Exercise

I begin the "diet" section of my True Beauty workshops without saying a word. Instead, I hand each of the participants three raisins. Then I tell them to imagine that they have never seen such a food before. They are to experience them anew, or as Zen Buddhists call it, with a "beginner's mind."

You can get three raisins now and try this Zen mindfulness meditation, which first became popularized by the renowned meditation teacher Jon Kabat-Zinn, PhD. Here's how I take people through the exercise:

Taking the first raisin, begin to examine it carefully — touch it, feel it, roll it in the palm of your hand. How does it feel, smell, and look? Then lick the raisin; how does it taste? When you have fully considered this, put it in your mouth, but don't chew it. Let it sit there, allowing your tongue to explore it. Notice what your tongue does — how it reacts to this "object." Now roll it all around your mouth with your tongue. Be aware of your tongue as well as of the raisin. Notice any new observations or realizations about this object. Now allow your teeth to touch it and slowly begin to chew. Try to consciously chew it until you no longer can, until it turns completely to liquid. Then, and only then, swallow it.

Now, take the second raisin. Explore it in the same way—very deeply, slowly, and consciously. Note how this experience differs, and how it is the same, as the first.

Finally, take the third raisin and do the same—proceeding even more slowly and mindfully. Try to find anything in or about the raisin you may have missed the first two times, remembering that no matter how similar these objects appear to be, they are all unique and have some differentiating qualities about them.

After this "raisin meditation," I ask people to comment on their experiences. Here are some of their responses:

"I never knew you could hear a raisin!"

"I usually eat these by the handful and barely taste one."

"Raisins have belly-buttons!"

I am always amazed to find that each time a group does this, someone, somehow, comes up with something entirely new about raisins. This is usually inspired by a flash of insight, or a reckoning about something they have been missing in their own lives on many levels. People have made comments such as:

"I realized I could learn to like and actually savor something I thought I had no affinity or liking for," and

"I tasted a medley of flavors when, before this, I had labeled raisins as having only one taste."

All of these insights can be metaphors for how we live, how closely our relationship with food mirrors our relationship with life. What did you discover if you did the exercise as you read through it?

Even a food as simple as a raisin, when consumed with mindfulness and gratitude, can open a person's mind and heart to wonder. That is, it can if they eat it deliberately, using all five of their senses, and then begin to tangibly experience what is often considered miraculous as their sixth-sense takes over and revelation after revelation begins to dawn. Only then is it seen that a tiny, seemingly insignificant dried fruit is part of a much greater whole; it was actually once an intricate part of an entire vine, and just like our bodies, it contains all of the earth's elements in it—the minerals, air, water, and the fire of the sun. A seemingly uneventful repast can be experienced as awe-inspiring.

Unveiling the Soul

Since discovering the existence of this miraculous, unseen "golden thread" that weaves through all of our lives, I've taught many people how to unearth their soul and live as fully realized human-beings via a process I call the E³ Transformational Triad. Three steps help my clients to *embrace, embody* and then *expand* the miraculous in their lives in a concrete, experiential way. Via this threefold path of miracle mindedness, miracle matrixing, and miracle mastery, they mentally cross over the "line" that divides heaven as something separate from life here on Earth. Through this they realize, just as I did, that our individual lives offer each one of us our very own unique, efficient, and miraculous way to recognize the Divine and then share that recognition. This is key to happiness because our soul yearns to share its being, just as its creator originally did with us!

Once we own our identities as miracle masters, we naturally become channels for service, which is a brilliant situation for our planet. We realize that if we work together in groups of souls, we can accomplish much more. The aggregation of the group carries the individuals to greater heights than would ever be possible alone. Then a flood of power can be collectively released to uplift humanity and help ameliorate the unsatisfying conditions of a needy world. And what do miracle masters do exactly? Well, to them, it feels as though they are doing nothing more than having fun doing whatever is in front of them *extremely well*, from the heart, and with no agenda while sharing their joy exponentially with others. The battle-less cry here is: *"Creativity not conflict!"* Obstacles no longer appear to be formidable roadblocks but are instead seen as opportunities to unleash unlimited potential. To miracle masters, the recognition of the part as whole, and of the whole in every part is perfectly natural, for that's the way a soul thinks and what is natural to our soul is natural to us.

Why wouldn't you want to live that way? You are *a soul.* You came to Earth to gift the world. That is fact. You arrived fully when you breathed your first breath. You will leave with your last. Everything in between those breaths—all the rest of your time here—is left up to you and your free will.

But here's a word of advice. No matter what it is that you choose to do, you will not, and cannot, be truly happy if you are out of step with the Divine and unconscious of your own inherent goodness. By focusing on your connection to the whole of life, you naturally fall into step—without effort, strife, or strain.

Feeding Your Soul, Changing the World

The soul in its own nature is group consciousness; it is not ruled by individual ambitions or interests. It is not at all interested in the aims of personality but, rather, in the expression of its *soul power*, *soul relationships*, and *soul purpose*. To a liberated soul, the focus of any activity becomes contribution, not acquisition—of being verses having.

We are now entering into a new era on Earth, one in which humanity is beginning to wake up from the separating dream of selfishness. We are just beginning to realize that both heaven and hell have always existed, not "somewhere out there," but right here, within every one of us. It's up to each individual to choose whether it's heaven or hell that we manifest and experience in our lives.

This planet is currently being faced with many challenges: terrorism, global-warming, pollution, starvation, disease, homelessness, natural disasters, and weapons of destruction in the hands of fearful and power-hungry leaders, to name but a few. To me, each of these has a human, not a divine, origin. Take a deep breath and a small step back into your soul, and you will see that it is our incessant movement and unceasing hunger that keeps so many people experiencing themselves in the "wrong place at the wrong time" (which is hell, by the way), grabbing for all of the alluring things that promise an ever-evasive brand of happiness. That is what keeps this ball of confusion in motion. But at the same time, our frenetic energies are affecting everything—that is how powerful we are. Only we humans can stop the inhumanity!

The wounds of this world are gaping now, far too big for Band-Aids and far too evident to ignore. But that's all right because now we can see more clearly that change is necessary. What we are experiencing is a divine wake-up call. It's time *now* to stop being so blindly selfish, to stop creating and consuming so many products that absolutely do not contribute to our well-being or survival, which even harm and endanger our lives. We can learn from our mistakes and reclaim our power on an individual and collective level. We can begin to be gentle with one another, consume responsibly in harmony with the laws of love, and come together to co-create a new Earth.

The challenges are great and many, but the simplest of actions can effect tremendous change. When you begin to see the entire world on your plate each and every time you eat—when you see how your choices affect you and the world—you automatically align with a deeper truth and commit to consciousness. Love yourself and everything you consume and then pass this consciousness on to another, one blessed plate-full at a time. What an example!

Extend your commitment by keeping soul-full lifestyle practices in mind: Stop buying products that harm or endanger lives! Carefully review what it is that you support with your dollars, your energy, and your time. Be congruent with your beliefs, words, and actions and vow to support only those services that bless the family of humanity and help build a kinder, better, and safer world. These are the keys to miracle mindedness, matrixing, and mastery! And always remember that *you* are the one person who can make a difference when you raise up your voice in conviction and become a living example of the power of love. Just start where you are today, with something as simple as the next meal you eat or your next trip to the grocery store. Revolution never begins on a grandiose scale, but rather with one person's simple willingness to show up, to lovingly and authentically live the life that unfolds before them. That is the opportunity available to you right now.

SERVAAS MES

Self Hidden in Present Time

"**W**hy do your people steal cars?" I asked Chief George. He isn't really a chief, but everybody always calls him that. Chief George is a wise man, his face weathered by long harsh winters, his body weathered by the laws of the land, and his mind sharpened by the experience of life. He has seen it all. He doesn't like watching TV. He prefers talking to people. During the cold winter months, he admits that he sleeps inside the house with a brand new electric blanket that keeps him warm. Westernization does have its advantages, so why not use it?

Chief George looked me in the eye and replied, "My people don't care about cars the way you do. We come into town during the week, often hitchhiking, spend time together, and go back home the same way. Not all of us have cars. We share. Unfortunately, our children don't have patience anymore to wait for their friends, so they take the first car they see. They drive it home and park it on the road. Somebody will bring the car back to town, you know. Maybe the next day. Or the day after. The white man calls it stealing, but it is really sharing." Then he leaned forward and said, "My friend, cars are made out of metal. Metal comes out of the earth . . . and the earth belongs to all of us."

He leaned back to observe my reaction. I knew exactly what he was saying but also knew that a philosophy like that has no place in Western society. That is not the point, however. The point is that a

Servaas Mes, a pioneer in the field of somatics and integral somatology, is the creator and teacher of Somatic Conditioning Fitness classes. He and his wife, Beverly Davies-Mes, are the directors of the Somatic Health Center (www.somatichealthcenter.com) in St. Helena, California, and are involved on an international level in expanding the frontiers of rehabilitation, health, fitness, and overall human potential. Servaas is also on the faculty of the Institute for Holistic Healing Studies at San Francisco State University and developed a postgraduate Somatic Rehabilitation program for physical therapists in the Netherlands.

person can breathe vitality into a lifeless object like a car by having a dialogue with it as if it is a living entity that belongs to the ecological life cycle of planet Earth. The little girl who communicates with her dolls as if they are truly alive or whose house of blocks becomes her new home is doing the same. As children, these processes of thought and behavior are simply part of our lives, but this earthy philosophy is foreign to most adults in our commercialized Western society.

In Native American tradition, the people did not write their history in books; they transferred their stories orally to whoever was present to listen. They lived closely with and respected the creatures of land, sea, and air — the bear, the moose, the whale, the raven. They related to the weather as a living entity by dancing with the rain and singing with the wind. But times have changed. This centuries-old wisdom about how to live life in harmony with Mother Earth has been lost in the technological revolution. Our current generation is more interested in cars, iPods, and the Internet than in spending time with the elders and learning about life the way it was. Instead of learning how to communicate with nature, we communicate most often with things. A cell phone suddenly has more importance and emotional value than a cat, shooting a gun is now for pleasure instead of survival, and television has replaced the wise words of the elderly.

Emotional Materialism

Our materialism has reached the level of emotional attachment to objects. This is different from according vitality to an inanimate object; it is looking for fulfillment through possession of material goods. At the same time that we are seeking emotional satisfaction from mass-produced objects that have no uniqueness, we are engaging in its emotional reverse: the objectification of living beings. The level of aggression and violence in our society is evidence of this objectification. Individuals can only engage in senseless behavior like bullying, violence, rape, and murder if they have objectified their victims. We are not objects that are disposable. We are somatic beings, meaning we are body, mind, and spirit: organisms that can laugh and cry; sense and move; eat, digest, and defecate; think, process, and create new thoughts; and love, be loved, and make love. Objectification of living beings sabotages communication with both self and other. Our materialistic behavioral patterns — turning objects into sources of fulfillment, and living beings into objects — have distracted us from paying attention to our inner world.

Living life in this way has caught up with us. In the rapidly advancing technological revolution, human health is showing significant signs of breaking down. Symptoms of overload are everywhere and we don't allow ourselves enough time to process and recuperate. Serious health problems directly attributable to a change in lifestyle have become the norm: cardiovascular disease, high blood pressure, impotence, depression, AIDS, cancer in its many forms, chronic fatigue syndrome, diabetes, Parkinson's disease, premature aging, back pain, and other stress-related conditions. The medical establishment does not have a firm and confident philosophy or treatment plan for any of these problems. It has not evolved to address the changes in human behavior brought on by the technological revolution and approaches treatment much as before. This explains why we often don't have an answer as to how to treat the serious diseases that are now common. This explains as well the enormous interest in complementary medicine; everybody is looking for an answer.

How can we assess the situation of our world and slow down the information so that its weaknesses become visible? Is there a way we can continue to enjoy the benefits of our technological world without all the health risks and the sacrifice of our well-being? What will humans know about health and wellness fifty years from now, a hundred years from now, or two hundred years from now? How will we understand and treat physical, emotional, energetic, and somatic diseases? Some of us are slowing down now to try and answer these questions.

Present Time: The Somatic Experience

I am lying on the treatment table in the office of a somatic practitioner and his soft warm voice guides me through very gentle movements that feel wonderful. We begin with my right leg, making different moves in all directions with my foot, ankle, knee, and hip. Some with a lot of guidance and resistance, some with hardly any. My practitioner and I are both involved in this dance-like process of movement that creates a sensation of completeness in my leg.

Then I rest and integrate. My brain had to concentrate on my movements and now, looking back, I am surprised by what occurred. The bodywork invited me to return to my innate intelligence of movement and behavior. The unique movements we did bypassed all my unconscious patterns of guarding and fear and opened up the true organic intelligence of my physical movements. By moving consciously in present time, the deep unwanted tightness in my body was immediately addressed and I could feel it melt.

The soft warm voice starts speaking again and invites me now to spend a moment sensing, feeling, and experiencing my legs. Do they feel the same at this moment? If not, what is different?

I turn within, and experience sensations I have never felt before. Even though on my life path I have practiced yoga, energy work, and meditation, this is a much deeper experience that truly blends my consciousness with my body. My left leg feels dead and heavy, lifeless, without any incentive to move. It feels lethargic, stagnant, and numb. This sensation is so strong and awkward that I feel my mind wandering to my other leg. Even the mind wants to take the path of least resistance! I resist and have to concentrate to keep my focus from drifting to my right leg. Strange, my right leg is the one that should feel useless, weak, and heavy because that is how it has felt since an injury many years ago. Here in present time, however, the sensations I feel in my right and left leg are different and totally intriguing. This must be what present time feels like when you experience your body from within, I tell myself. And how is it that my legs feel so different from each other? Which one is truly me? Am I the one that feels lifeless or am I the one that feels light, strong, grounded, and happy? Here I am in present time, not only observing the ridiculous irony of the mind-body split, but at the same moment, I am witnessing clearly the almost confusing sensation of a split between the left and right sides of my body.

The body doesn't lie. The warm voice explains that the type of inner awareness I am experiencing is called "somatic." Credit for the term and the process goes to the late Thomas Hanna, a philosopher from California and author of the groundbreaking *Bodies in Revolt*, published in 1969. In this book, Hanna defined the soma, the living body, as "the body experienced from within." Everything that is you can be seen as the soma. It is the full integration of mind and body; the full integration of left and right; the full integration of past, present, and future; and the full integration of function and structure. Spirit and soul are part of the soma, too. The soma can sense and move, breathe and think, and is designed to grow and evolve. The further we travel in time, the further we can evolve our internal and external capacities of being human and live up to our somatic potential.

The Hidden First Person

The soft voice speaks of somatics and integral somatology, the field that studies the human body from all perspectives: a subjective (first-person) perspective, an intersubjective (second-person) perspective, and an objective (third-person) perspective. The focus on the first-person experience led to the realization of a relatively unexplored dimension of human consciousness: the somatic "hidden first-person" experience. Accessing this realm of consciousness often creates an immediate change in perception of how one moves through the world. True understanding of this hidden first-person perspective adds a pulse, a heartbeat, to any philosophical model of human existence. The field of somatology can be used to explain many aspects of life — health, fitness, behavior, philosophy, politics, relationships, religion, sex — through its model of perspective, that is, how we relate to people, events, and things in a first-, second-, or third-person perspective and decide our motions and our emotions accordingly. Balance of perspective promotes good health, communication, leadership, creativity, and compassion, whereas dysfunction in perspective can result in health issues, arguments and conflicts, a sense of numbness, and difficulty in adopting self-responsibility.

The somatic model counteracts the negative energetic and behavioral components that the technological revolution has introduced into our lives by returning attention to the self, to first-person experience. The somatic model is also far more complete than our current medical model because it studies the human body from more than just the objective (third-person) perspective. Adding the information from the first-person, the hidden first-person, and the second-person experience, this new model can confidently predict, prevent, treat, and resolve many health issues that are plaguing our society. Taught in one-on-one sessions or group classes, it educates people *somatically* about the presence of their soma in time, healing many physical ailments while also setting a new motivation and intention for living life in the future.

Somatic therapy moves you into present time, the time zone where it becomes easy to be mindful and creative, to move forward, and to let go of any attachments to the past. This often results in a more independent and self-regulating being who is able to communicate more organically with the self and others.

Not many people have actually studied this characteristic of the human being, the soma, the warm voice of the practitioner continues. Due to its subjectivity, it is not something you can learn from a book. Like life, you have to experience it.

I check in with myself again. My left side still has no desire to move. It feels like there is just nothing there. No life force, no prana, no chi, no vitality. The more I concentrate on this bizarre sensation of nothingness, the more I am fascinated by its emotional character. Maybe I should refer to it as "non-emotional" character because it feels so lifeless. Besides the physical sensations of my left leg feeling shorter, tighter, heavier, and denser than my other leg, I can now also clearly sense a change in its behavior. My left leg used to be my leading leg, my dominant leg, the one that could do everything better than my other leg, and here it is, telling me the opposite. There is no sensation of warmth. My leg feels cold and frozen in time. What happened to the inner fire? Even though I am breathing, my leg isn't. How can I be living up to my potential if parts of me are not contributing to my fullness? What about our purpose on this planet? Is the purpose for my right leg different than for my left leg? Does my mind have a different purpose from my body?

At this moment, my right leg feels full of energy, like a battery that is fully charged, ready to move forward. I can also sense a deep level of relaxation in my right leg that I have never sensed before. All the usual tension that has been protecting my leg since its injury has now spontaneously disappeared and been replaced by a sensation of confidence. My right leg feels brave and has the urge to move forward into the future, which is such a contrast to how it has been, holding on to traumatic memories and attachments of the past. My mind suddenly remembers the hard scar that is so numb that it doesn't like to be touched. I touch the scar and find that it no longer resists me. My leg is breathing again and ready to evolve into even deeper sensations of completeness.

Doesn't everybody's pain-body crave to become alive again? Deep inside, I have been longing for this moment, but I never knew how to get there. I concentrate on the positive messages of love and generosity within me and realize that I am fulfilling my long-awaited dream of completeness, of being One. Truly being in present time is more profound than anything I have ever experienced. With all my studies in mindfulness, I thought I was living my life consciously, but this is a different level of experiencing myself. This moment of internal perception is an experience of total bliss, a deep integral connection with myself. My thoughts and observations have become very clear and are without judgment. My inquiry into my own Being is effortless, my wandering mind playfully scanning the internal landscape of living cells inside my body. It feels exceptionally good. This moment of self-experience, this moment of experiencing the "hidden first person," is the somatic moment.

The somatic moment is observing the self in a positive way, without any self-destructive thoughts. Why is it that we mostly talk about our bodies when they are hurting, when they are in fear, pain, or numbness? Why do we hardly ever talk about the beautiful sensations that bring us more into present time, such as warmth, love, compassion, generosity, and creativity? I think of what it would be like if my whole body felt like my right leg feels, of how it would be to live in a body that truly experiences present time. Would I still complain? Would I still travel through life at a speed I can barely manage? What would happen to my stress level? I can see that somatic therapy, this educational bodywork I am doing, offers a way to reverse unconscious habituated patterns of holding that most of us don't even sense or feel. The therapy turns *somatic amnesia* into *somatic freedom*.

By moving into the landscape of internal perception, I found endless information about myself. We can all access this deeper realm of consciousness, which is different from just sensing ourselves from a first-person perspective. In many of us, this hidden first person is the one who lives an invisible and undetectable life behind the fog of neural overload. It is a consciousness hidden behind our subjective first-person perspective and it only becomes visible with focused intention. It is a deeper layer of awareness that creates a much more profound experience than just a sensation we feel and take note of. With this awareness, we sense and move in present time while creating a fascinating internal awakening. The awareness is different from that experienced in meditation, yoga, Pilates, tai chi, qigong, or any other mindful experience. It is a specific type of awareness that grows and evolves when put into practice, and it empowers and completes our Being.

The Missing Component

"Consciousness is contagious," the soft warm voice continues. "Having gone through this (ongoing) process myself, I can only encourage you to do the same. You will learn to direct your awareness into places where you never thought you'd be and you will travel to places you never knew existed. All within yourself—physically, mentally, emotionally, and somatically! This inquiry into the Self unfolds through dedicated practice of your own movement potential. You have to create the time and the environment to experience your own inner landscape. The stronger your internal consciousness becomes, the stronger your whole body will feel. It will make it easier to understand yourself and to understand others. You will begin to live your potential as well as guide others toward theirs."

We live in a time of change and are at the beginning of a new era, one founded on an integral model of medicine, philosophy, bodywork, health and wellness, and fitness. This new model is organized around our hidden somatic consciousness, which directs our subjective, intersubjective, and objective perspectives on life. This model provides us with significant information about the functioning of the human body and guides us immediately toward better decisions about our health and health problems. It is powerful because it creates a new language that can be understood globally.

Being Green

The current technological revolution is rapidly changing into a green technological revolution in which we are invited to question our external choices. What is still missing is the somatic component, the component that not only thinks green about our environment, but also thinks green about our own Being. This first-person consciousness, developed by exploration of the hidden first person, will help us in every move we take, every decision we make, and every thought we create.

The only thing you need is *the will to improve,* the warm soft voice explains, referring to the awakening of the first-person responsibility. Our session continues and we work my left leg, my arms, my shoulder blades, my head and neck, and my torso. My whole body is waking up, leaving behind the compensatory holding patterns of my previous injuries. A stream of consciousness is starting to flow throughout my entire body. It feels really good. At the end, we do a few moves that integrate several full body movement patterns. It feels like coming home within my own body. When I check in again, I can feel that my ability to perceive myself as well as the world has increased tremendously. The future can come to me now, moment after moment, truth after truth, all in present time.

Maybe *that* is what Chief George meant…

JOHN SPENCER ELLIS

Fitness Boot Camp

CHAPTER 5

E very person has the capacity for optimal wellness. The ability to self-heal is inherent in everyone. It is your job to uncover all the tools and methods available to optimize your wellness.

The word "vitality" comes from the Latin root *vita,* meaning "life." An offshoot of the word "vitality" is "vital force," which is also known as *chi, ki, prana,* or, simply, "energy." So if life revolves around energy, then creating, maintaining, and balancing your body's energy is crucial for a life full of happiness and unlimited joy. Over time, vitality has come to mean living life at a higher level. Peak vitality, then, is taking life to the *highest* level. Achieving peak vitality requires wellness.

What is wellness? If you ask ten people who strive for wellness, each will return with his or her own definition. An Olympic athlete enjoys a high level of fitness but may, at the same time, have bone demineralization, overuse injuries, depression, and sleep apnea. Fitness alone does not equal wellness, and, without wellness, peak vitality is absent. Health can be defined as "an absence of disease processes in the body," but this is likewise not wellness. People can be fit, eat only healthful foods, and be disease free but still lack wellness. They may not get quality sleep and, as a result, suffer from fatigue, experience accidents, and be slow to recover.

So how do you know that your life and wellness are in balance? You pause and analyze what you know to be missing and consider how you might be overindulging.

John Spencer Ellis is the creator of a fitness program enjoyed by more than one million people worldwide each week. The CEO of NESTA (National Exercise & Sports Trainers Association) and the Spencer Institute for Life Coaching, he holds degrees in health science, business, marketing, and education, as well as fifteen professional certifications. He completed doctoral level studies in naturopathy, has a second-degree black belt in kung fu, and completed the Ironman triathlon. He created fitness programs used by Cirque du Soleil and the U.S. Secret Service, and is a frequent radio and TV guest. www.JohnSpencerEllis.com.

❧

Physical Wellness

Often when people visit a medical doctor for a checkup or a lifestyle-related ailment such as stress or low-back pain due to obesity, the doctor advises them to exercise, but gives no details about how to proceed. When you get such advice, what is your next step? Your body must have strength, flexibility, endurance, and balance to increase your physical wellness. In most cases, any exercise is better than being totally sedentary, but to be highly effective and optimal, exercise must have structure. The components of structure are frequency, intensity, duration, and mode of exercise. The details of these four factors are determined by your exercise history, health history, and personal goals.

Exercise frequency is the number of exercise sessions completed per week, month, or year. The *intensity* of exercise can be defined as a percentage of maximum heart rate, percentage of a one-repetition maximum (1RM), or rate of perceived exertion (RPE). RPE is a scale that goes from one to ten, one being very easy or light and ten being heavy or very difficult. The *duration* of an exercise session is based on factors such as the volume of work to be completed in that session, the focus of that particular session, and types of exercises. If you rest less between exercises, sets, or drills, it will increase your intensity due to lack of recovery time, but it will also decrease the duration of your training session. Different *modes* of exercise can be classified as: strength training, cardiovascular exercise, flexibility training, and mind-body.

Here are some general rules for creating an exercise program. First, seek a medical doctor's clearance. Second, be honest with yourself about your overall commitment, availability, and goals. Keep in mind that if you feel you don't have the energy to exercise, you'll be given more energy by the exercise itself. Your goals need to be realistic and include immediate, intermediate, and long-term desired outcomes. Your journey to wellness and vitality will also have these milestones.

Strength training benefits can be realized from two to three sessions per week of just thirty minutes each. Always rest at least forty-eight hours between weight-training sessions if you are exercising the same body part in each session.

Flexibility training can be structured, as in yoga, or less formal, as in a general flexibility class at your local health club. It is a time to ask your body for permission to relax and be present at that very moment and it teaches you how to carry that into all aspects of your life.

Mind-body exercise can be integrated throughout your day.

Meditation or guided imagery practice can improve mental clarity, assist in recovery from cancer, ease labor pains, and even aid in digestion when done after a meal.

Passive forms of attaining physical wellness can be included to enhance your results in aesthetic change and physical functionality. Passive forms of physical wellness include all modalities in which the individual is not actively involved in the movement or treatment. Examples of passive treatments include chiropractic, massage, acupuncture, and acupressure. These passive forms of wellness all have one thing in common: They are designed to improve your body's functionality and energy. When your body's energy pathways are open and free-flowing, you feel and function at a peak level.

Active forms of physical wellness burn more calories and teach you the motor patterns and breathing techniques needed to accomplish that exercise. In passive forms of physical wellness, the modalities are applied to you. You can learn body awareness and sensitivity in either, but passive modalities don't train the body to understand how, why, and when the body should move in certain patterns.

Wellness and Complementary Medicine

There is more cancer in the world today than at any time in history. There are more types of cancers and more people with cancer than ever before. Modern science and Western medicine have improved the likelihood of surviving cancer, but they have done nothing or very little to stop cancer from growing in the first place. Western medicine is reactive, not proactive. To stop the epidemic of cancer, we must create an internal environment in which cancer cannot thrive. A first step in this is to rid our immediate external environment of as many toxins, chemicals, herbicides, and pesticides as we can.

A second step is to use complementary medicine to enhance the body's ability to regulate blood sugar, improve posture, strengthen the immune system, speed recovery from exercise and illness, enhance body awareness, and relieve stress. I touch briefly on four of these techniques here, but I encourage you to research all complementary wellness modalities and find the ones that suit your needs and preferences.

One wellness-promoting modality is chiropractic, which is based on the premise that a well-aligned spine frees the body's energy. There are dozens of techniques, and each school offers a slightly different approach to aligning the spine, making joints more mobile, and restoring proper posture. Some chiropractors include massage therapy, exercises, hot and cold packs, and various electronic muscle stimulations to enhance the benefits of the chiropractic adjustment. Other doctors do what is called "straight chiropractic." In other words, they adjust the spine (or joint) and send you on your way. Chiropractic is often more successful at eliminating musculoskeletal pain than invasive surgery is.

Another modality, naturopathic medicine (or naturopathy) has been in existence in various forms for hundreds of years and is gaining popularity in the United States. It combines lifestyle counseling, nutrition, exercise, herbs, homeopathy, and stress management. Naturopathic training varies according to whether the practitioner will be a "traditional naturopath" or a licensed naturopathic physician. Traditionalists may study neurolinguistic programming (NLP), hypnosis, aromatherapy, life coaching, and/or personal training. A licensed naturopathic doctor studies the same sciences and courses as a medical doctor for the first two years of school and then studies acupuncture, massage, nutritional medicine, chelation therapy, biofeedback, and/or environmental health.

Massage therapy is one of the most widely used complementary wellness tools. There are hundreds of massage styles and techniques, ranging from sports massage to pregnancy massage, from Swedish to Hawaiian, from therapeutic body massage to scalp, foot, and even ear massage. I am still astonished when I speak to people and they tell me they have never experienced a professional massage. It is truly one of the greatest treats you can provide for yourself. The documented health benefits of massage are wide ranging. They include stress relief, injury prevention, injury recovery, eased childbirth, reduction of pain, and reduction of gastrointestinal problems. Massage has also been shown to help manage migraine headaches, fibromyalgia, neuropathy, Epstein-Barr virus, and even cancer recovery.

Wellness and Nutrition

Food is energy. Proper foods give you optimal energy—that's all! Food is not meant to replace a lost love, fulfill a need, or keep you company in front of the TV. It's true that food is frequently a centerpiece for gatherings. This, in no way, means that the food is the reason for the gathering, or that you must eat all or most of the food that was prepared for that gathering. Instead of associating food with joy, happiness, sadness, celebration, or even anger, associate food with making you strong, healthy, and full of energy. Just by changing your thinking, you will start to make better food choices.

Move toward an organic diet. Since 1945, more than eighty

thousand chemicals have been added to our environment. Many chemicals end up in our food supply through irrigation, pesticides, herbicides, urban runoff, packaging, and cross-contamination. In addition to being healthier to eat, organic foods are brighter in color, more flavorful and are approaching the same cost as conventionally farmed foods. It is equally important to buy from local growers. There are simply not enough checks and balances to ensure that organic foods grown in other countries are truly organic.

Eat whole foods. Processed foods lack important fiber and the processing exposes more of the food's surface to oxygen, which rapidly reduces the food's nutrient density. Processing also usually involves the addition of chemicals to enhance flavor, shelf life, or color. Remember, if something is added to a food to improve its shelf life, that same ingredient will reduce your shelf life. Some people argue that these additives are so minute that they cannot have a serious biological effect. In rebuttal, I say that it is not a matter of the volume ingested per sitting. Toxicity takes place over time as your tissues absorb and store unhealthy elements.

Nutrigenomics is the science of how food communicates with your genes. Some foods, such as soft drinks (diet or not), fast foods, and most candy, express or "turn on" genes that cause inflammation, a reduction in energy, irritation, chronic disease, and auto-immune disorders. On the contrary, wild Alaskan salmon, flaxseed and flaxseed oil, organic berries, spinach, broccoli, green tea, and the spices cayenne, ginger, and cinnamon express genes that reduce inflammation, increase metabolism and energy, and improve body system functions such as digestion and elimination.

The Role of Nutritional Supplements

If you lived in a toxin-free environment, always slept eight hours a night, had little or no stress, and ate only organic foods, you would not need to take nutritional supplements. Please remember the name: *supplement*. This means that they are taken "in addition to," not "instead of" a proper and, it is to be hoped, organic diet. Eating poorly and thinking that supplements will magically mitigate all the adverse effects of a lackluster diet is foolish. I strongly urge you to investigate the efficacy of various nutritional supplements and nutraceuticals (substances in foods and plants that have medicinal effects). A short list of items I encourage you to research is: lycopene, omega-3 essential fatty acid, spirulina, wheat grass, glutamine, saw palmetto berries, and milk thistle. There are many others that can dramatically improve your health. Please remember, megadoses of vitamins and minerals are frequently not needed and, in some cases, are toxic. As a general rule, use time release supplements when available and take your supplements with some food in your stomach. The reason for the latter is that food stimulates acid in your stomach, which helps break down the supplements and makes them more absorbable.

Wellness Talk

We have the ability to improve our health and increase our energy simply by our words. We have developed some interesting ways to describe health conditions and challenges. As an educator, I have observed countless individuals limit their potential for optimal health by their existing language, especially their internal dialogue (self-talk). Examples include: "I'm just fat," "It's just my genetics," and "I come from a fat family." Outwardly, we say things like "the fight against obesity," "the struggle to be thin," and "the battle of the bulge." And, of course, there is our societal favorite: "The war on drugs." None of these fights have produced positive results. When we use verbiage, either internal or external, that is negative, we get negative results. Tell yourself and others exactly the health and wellness you deserve, instead of what you are trying to avoid.

Health and wellness enhancement is easily attained with positive and empowering language patterns. Decide now that you will state your health desires in the form of positive and empowering statements. Remind yourself on a regular basis that you are grateful for your health and you are continually moving toward even greater health. If you find yourself slipping into your old habits, quickly rephrase in a powerful and positive way.

Another technique is to scan your body with your mind. Start at the head and move downward. Each time you breathe inward, ask yourself how you feel at that level of your body. If you get to an area of your body that doesn't feel as well as you'd like, start asking questions. How did this imbalance occur? What tools do I have to get back in balance? What have I learned? How will I stay in balance while moving forward, and enjoy the process? You can see how the questioning becomes progressively more positive. This is essential.

Wellness and Sleep

Sleep is more than getting your required number of hours each night. Quality sleep includes your sleep environment and rituals leading up to the sleep itself. Your sleep environment must be dark to experience the deepest levels of sleep. This is so because the pineal gland in the center of your brain senses, via the retina of the eye, the onset and degree of darkness. When this detection occurs, the hormone melatonin is released. Melatonin has important effects on circadian rhythms, which are your body's twenty-four hour cycles. Melatonin has been reported to have significant effects on reproduction, recovery, immune health, and overall wellness. The deepest levels of sleep cannot be reached without proper release of melatonin. Therefore, keep your sleep environment as dark as possible. Your bedroom should also be free from electronics, televisions, and other distractions.

To improve the quality and depth of your sleep, a ritual is required. How do you prepare for sleep? Do you just fall into bed and go to sleep immediately? If you do, you are likely overtired. It should take a few minutes to settle in and begin the sleep process. I would like to share a skill I learned in my hypnosis training. Hypnosis requires progressive relaxation. We'll just take it a step further and fall asleep. First, stand at the edge of your bed and walk twenty steps away from it. I do this process down my stairs. Now you have a starting point for your progression toward sleep. Each night, when you step on that space, you begin counting backward from twenty to zero as you move toward and into bed. When you take a deep inhalation and exhalation at zero, you will be tucked under the covers. On the way, each step slows your body and prepares you for deep sleep. Over time, you won't need to count. Simply stepping into that twenty-step space will begin your relaxation process. Other rituals to enhance sleep include taking a shower, an aromatherapy bath, candles, gentle yoga, and meditation.

Rituals to avoid include late evening exercise, alcohol consumption, and TV. Sometimes people feel they have no other time to exercise, so late evening is better than no exercise at all. Exercising too late in the day can interrupt your circadian rhythms and make it challenging to fall asleep. On a side note, people who exercise in the morning tend to be more dedicated to their exercise program over an extended period of time. Alcohol consumption before bed can disturb sleep, especially later in the night, and television is too engaging to be used as a ritual for promoting sleep. In addition, when you fall asleep with the TV on, its light decreases melatonin secretion.

I strongly suggest staying away from prescription sleep medications. They can be highly addictive and have numerous side effects that can be worse than lacking sleep. Instead, I encourage you to learn about the following natural and safe alternatives: GABA (gamma-aminobutyric acid), L-theanine, melatonin, velvet bean (*Mucuna pruriens)*, valerian, chamomile, and passionflower.

Information on sleep would be incomplete without discussing napping. There are different theories as to whether people need to nap. One theory states that if we get enough quality sleep at night, there is no need to nap. The other theory is that a nap can be greatly beneficial to overall wellness. One thing is certain. If you do nap during the day, it needs to be short in duration. During the course of each day, your body goes through various levels of energy and temperature change. When you sleep too long during the day, it interrupts the appropriate temperature decline in the evening that enables deep sleep. Learning meditation and practicing it for twenty minutes each day can have similar or even better benefits than napping, and will not disrupt quality sleep at night.

Stress Management

I did not call this section "stress elimination," because we live on planet Earth. Stress occurs and our body responds accordingly. Wellness depends on how we choose to interpret the stress in our lives and on having the tools to manage it effectively. Some stress is good. The "butterflies" that some performers feel before a public production help them attain a peak state. For others, feeling "ready to perform" for a written exam can help increase performance. Again, it's a matter of identification of the feelings and management of them. It's a matter of stimulus and response.

Life Balance

For most of us, life balance is the most challenging component of attaining optimal wellness. Start by asking yourself, "What can I eliminate that isn't working for me?" It could be a poorly planned business venture, an ill-fated relationship, or even too much exercise, which is sapping your energy. Maybe you are too focused on your family's needs, and not your own. Creating life balance is about being honest with yourself. It's often necessary to pause, step back, and view your life from a third-person perspective. Now that you are removed, at least for a period of time, what is glaringly obvious that you must change to enhance the overall balance in your life? At this time, if you were your own life coach, what would you immediately modify, omit, or enhance?

One of the best times to do this "balance assessment" is when you are on vacation. There are far fewer distractions, a reduction in stress, and perhaps greater access to massage, exercise classes, and time for contemplative walks. I learned an important skill from my yoga instructor, Erich Schiffmann. He says to pause, be in the now, and wait for the inner cue to begin. When your mind and body are ready, ask yourself for permission to move, think, ponder, experience, and understand the message your body is giving you. It is this pause between stimulus and response that allows you to make better decisions, which ultimately leads to a more balanced life. This in return leads to optimal wellness. When in doubt, pause.

Putting It All Together

When developing your wellness and vitality plan, you need to address the cause and effect of any previous or current condition. Take into account the specific physical, emotional, spiritual, and mental signs. Wellness is a way of life. It is always being aware of how the things you do, say, eat, and surround yourself with affect your well-being, energy, and vitality. Wellness is about pausing, if only for a moment, and determining if what you are about to do is in the best interests of your mind and body.

Listening to your body is essential. Learning to listen takes time. Practicing various mind-body modalities will enhance your ability to listen and then understand how to respond to what your body is saying. Treat yourself to a variety of treatments ranging from massage to facials to various water therapies. If these treatments are new to you, a great surprise awaits.

If you have not practiced many of the wellness concepts discussed in this chapter, it is unlikely you are actually well. This is a bold statement, right? But keep in mind that if you have never really felt well, and I mean unstoppable, you have no contrast by which to understand that your health and wellness may only be at a level of mediocrity.

You deserve to be well and full of energy. Life can only be experienced at the highest level when your body is performing at a peak level. In closing, I want to present you with two options for success. Option number one is gradual integration of various modalities into your daily routine. For example, it may just start with organic food. The following week, you can add massage therapy. Progressively add positive practices until you have attained the correct balance for wellness without it becoming a chore. The other option is a massive shift in your daily and weekly routine. You make a clear and decisive change that includes mind, body, and spirit. If you choose the latter path, it is important to be intelligent about it and progressive in adding physical activity.

Wellness is a choice. Choose to live a healthy life full of bliss. Peak vitality can only be attained when your body systems are operating at the highest levels. Embrace the opportunity to take your body and your energy to these levels. You will amaze yourself with what is possible.

Mariel Hemingway

Healthy Living from the Inside Out

Sometimes life's major revelations come in such quiet moments, you almost miss them. Two years ago I was traveling down a quiet country road in the middle of New Zealand's South Island after a long, cold day on the set of an action movie. The gray springtime light was finally fading to darkness, and I was quietly thrilled to be in the car's passenger seat with the heat blasting at my feet, after a morning of shooting water scenes in the frigid ocean and an afternoon of throwing kung fu kicks on dry land. I was thinking about the healthy dinner I planned to cook and how I'd use my quiet night alone to rest and recharge when a hesitant voice from the driver's side broke the silence.

"Um, Mariel? Can I ask you a question?" It was Anna, the foxy nineteen-year-old local whose job as production assistant kept her racing around on my tail from dawn to dusk.

"Absolutely," I said.

"Well," she hesitated, as if slightly embarrassed, "the rest of the crew and I are wondering something. How is it that at the end of the day you're the only person on set who isn't exhausted and cranky, who isn't clutching a coffee cup and eating cookies to keep going, and isn't getting sick?" She sneezed, then added in the most diplomatic way she could, "You're so much older—I mean, we're twenty years younger than you, at least. And you have three times our energy."

Mariel Hemingway's career emerged from the shadows of her sister Margaux and her grandfather Ernest when she starred as a teen love interest in Woody Allen's movie *Manhattan*. After receiving an Oscar nomination for her natural, relaxed performance, she followed with the risky role of a lesbian athlete in *Personal Best*. She took her business sense a step further as the executive producer of *The Suicide Club* and the owner of a New York eatery, Sam's Place. She is the author of *Healthy Living from the Inside Out* (HarperCollins, 2007). More at www.Mariel-Hemingway.com.

The question surprised me. For most of the two decades that I'd worked in the entertainment industry, I'd always been something of the kook on set — the health nut with the funny habits. I'd get teased for doing Sun Salutations during the long waits for my scenes or for bringing big vats of whey protein powder to the catering table at lunch. (Lovingly teased, I should add, but teased nonetheless.) Or the fact that I meditated daily and would wake up before our early call times to do it — that was doubly weird to most. Although I almost never talk about my practices, little clues to my lifestyle would pop up here and there, always setting me slightly apart. Anything smacking of what I call the yogic attitude — creating calm from the inside out through food, exercise, and quiet contemplation — was more or less not cool.

Yet here I was, after a good twenty years of following these lifestyle practices, suddenly finding that the very people who used to giggle at me were now coming to me with questions. Once Anna broke the ice, more curious inquiries followed. "How can I eat in a way that makes me feel better?" "Why am I so tired even when I get enough sleep?" "What will help get rid of this awful stomachache I get every time I'm anxious?"

Movie sets have traditionally been far from health conscious. Working long hours under significant amounts of stress and often eating on the fly, people do what they can to stay alert all day and calm under pressure. Caffeine, sugar, cigarettes, and occasional tantrums to let off steam are the standard methods of self-maintenance, and half the time you survive by knowing that if you hang on a bit longer, you can fall apart when the job's done. In other words, it's a microcosm of society at large. So when my Down-Under colleagues started asking about my simple, preventive methods for keeping my body boosted, my mind calm, and my spirits high, it set me thinking.

If the veteran lighting guys with the Teflon stomachs are inquiring about my cod liver oil and the college-age interns want to know how long I meditate, I'll bet a pretty wide cross section of people are seeking the same thing: to learn how to slow down, take stock of how they feel, and take back some control of their health and of their lives.

I believe we all have the same problems; they just come in different wrapping paper. And the more I talk to people, not just on movie sets but also to my friends, colleagues, and even my children's acquaintances, the more it's clear that below the surface of our very different appearances, lifestyles, and interests lie some universal concerns. At the start of the twenty-first century, the desire to stay well and find some kind of inner peace is becoming more urgent. The rapid and often relentless pace of life has delivered unprecedented opportunity, but it's also brought on exhaustion, and what many of us want most is to redress the imbalance. We want to feel more rested and restored and to reconnect with lives that seem to be getting away from us. Above all, we want to learn how to live in balance: to be less susceptible to stress and sickness and to have health and peace of mind as the norm, not the exception, in our lives.

Almost every part of life now exists in a more accelerated form than ever before: food is faster, travel is quicker, and communication is more or less instant. Our environments are crowded with noise media, and technology; "stuff" fills every corner of our homes (much of which, not surprisingly, becomes rapidly obsolete). We confront so many situations in the course of a day that we never get a chance to process everything before the next morning comes. Meanwhile, many of us feel a lingering undertow of frustration that makes it hard to find satisfaction in our present lives. It's as if a perpetual refrain is echoing in the backs of our minds: What else should I be doing? What's out there that might be better than this?

Partly, we bring the situation upon ourselves. The pressures to do more and achieve more with our time seem to grow every year, and we keep signing up for more. Work has become more intense, with jobs demanding more hours, more responsibilities, and more results. Yet we expect more of ourselves on the home front as well. Women in particular expect our relationships to be blissful and passionate, our homes to be immaculate and chic, and our children to be star athletes and scholarship students. Usually, our standards for our physical appearances are excruciatingly high, too. There's almost no way to do it all without going slightly nuts; we multitask our way through the demands as best we can, dividing our energy and our attention into fragments that inevitably add up to be less than the whole.

Our growing concerns about how to live better and be healthier are related to threats we can't quite name or see. Environmental and social hazards in the world are undeniably affecting our health, but sometimes we get just enough information to scare us but not enough to help us make good choices. We hear so much about toxic foods, disease-causing foods, and fattening foods that it's hard to know what we can and can't eat. Almost everyone knows somebody who's living with cancer. How much of this epidemic, we wonder, is caused by pollutants that we knowingly consume through food and stimulants or unknowingly consume from our atmosphere? Meanwhile, natural things such as the sun have suddenly become controversial. Some say sun exposure will kill you, while others say we need regular stints of it to create vitamin D. (As you'll read later, I think moderate exposure to sunlight is critical to good health.)

Modern life delivers a steady stream of small stresses that affect the way we feel every day. Some come from our individual lifestyle choices and some from the world at large—and it's a lot of work to process them all. A stress is any kind of strain on our system. It includes those toxins we consume through eating, breathing the air, and drinking the water because our organs have to work hard to eliminate them. It includes the screwy sleep patterns we fall into by working or hanging out until 1:00 a.m. because falling asleep too late can throw our hormones, and subsequently our appetite and moods, way out of kilter. Stress can even come from too much sedentary activity, including spending too much time in the car, because our bodies need to move to function at their best.

Factor in the array of mental and emotional challenges that most everyone has to deal with—from finances and family issues to the fears and insecurities we have about our talents, looks, and futures— and doesn't it make sense that these days our stress loads are reaching maximum capacity?

The sheer amount of stress we face, combined with the speedy pace of our lifestyles, makes it hard to start and end each day with optimism and calm. Stress drives us to use certain foods and stimulants as crutches instead of figuring out a diet that creates a condition of optimal health. (Many of us use caffeine to get energized, but—hands up—who also relies on a strong cup of coffee to help them go to the bathroom? That's using food/drink the wrong way.) Stress contributes to mild anxiety issues and attention problems and even to negative thought patterns and behavior. The fact is that we've strayed too far from simple principles of looking after ourselves well. We're consuming things that cloud our minds, we're holding stress in our bodies, and more often than not we're too rushed to reflect on our lives. The result is that we often feel like our lifestyles are controlling us and not vice versa.

If I've learned anything over my years of practicing healthy habits, it's that we can transform any of these situations, and ultimately transform our lives, through some simple choices. We already have everything we need to counter modernity's stresses and create a life in which, day to day, we feel great. We can remedy that maxed-out state and get more energy by day and better rest by night. We can build a core of joy and peace at our center that keeps us balanced no matter what craziness is going on outside us. We can take control of our moods, boost our sex drive, and even shed a lot of the ghosts that keep us stuck in old habits. Now more than ever, the onus is on each one of us to empower ourselves. And it's not hard to do if we just start bringing a little more awareness to the things we do each day.

You might be saying, "What? I can't control the quality of the air outside my home. I can't choose to commute to work by foot or bike. I can't cut my stressful boss/parent/kids out of my life." But that's not the point. When it comes to your health and wellness, there are indeed many things you can't control. The trick is to ask, "What *can* I control?" The answers are fairly simple: The food I eat. The way I exercise. My response to emotional stresses. My home environment. Making even small modifications in these four areas can be extraordinarily powerful—and, should you need it, deeply healing.

If you make just a few changes in these four areas, you will notice physical and mental payoffs right away. Eating one or two different foods can make a huge difference in your digestion and detoxification, boosting your energy, immune system, and spirits. Taking a short time-out to sit in total quiet helps you shed the stress that accumulates in your mind and body, and even in your face. (Try it; you'll be surprised how quickly furrowed brows start to smooth.) Bringing a few touches of warmth and sacredness into your home soothes your soul and makes you feel more grounded. We're not talking extreme makeovers or overnight transformations; those quick-fix approaches can rarely be sustained. Instead, try making one small change here, another small change there, and slowly you will discover what works for you. With time, you can change the look and feel of your whole life for the better. Remember, giant leaps are made of inches.

Another, subtler effect will quietly take place at the same time. By focusing on the day-to-day choices that you can control, you anchor yourself squarely into your life as it unfolds right now. You bring your attention again and again to the present moment, and you stop worrying about what happened in the past or what might happen in the future. In doing so, you slow down the rush and enjoy your time. And I've found that when you approach your life from this starting point, in place of frustration you more often touch fulfillment.

We all have our different reasons for seeking a balanced life. When I started on my journey, I wasn't reacting to the environmental hazards of today or to the sheer pressure of work and life. I was just trying to survive.

My childhood was far from peaceful. In our house, outside the town of Ketchum, Idaho, life was lived at pendulum extremes—either chilly silence or flaming arguments, often back-to-back. As the son of Ernest Hemingway, my father had inherited a complicated burden: the genetic tendencies toward addiction and overconsumption; the pain of abandonment caused by the way his father lived and, most tragically, the way he died; and the guilt and self-doubt that come with being the child of a legend, fearing that nothing you can do will ever match what your parent achieved. My mother, by contrast, was very beautiful yet painfully bitter. Her first husband had died in World War II, and after she married my father, she resented him sorely for not being the man to whom she'd truly lost her heart. The two of them fought pretty much every day of my childhood. (I didn't find out that my mom had been married before until I was sixteen and stumbled across the fact by accident; that's what happens in the happy home of noncommunicators.)

I was the youngest of three daughters, and by the time I was old enough to be conscious of adult relationships, my parents had more or less given up trying to be great role models. My dad would depart to spend hours fishing in the nearby wilderness areas, and my mom eventually retreated more and more to her room. She got sick with cancer at the age of fifty-one, and as my two older sisters were entering their own phases of teenage trouble and rebellion, I became her young caretaker, quietly shuttling between her and my father, trying to stay out of the line of fire when they clashed. None of it was made easier by the fact that my family was always somewhat in the limelight. The enormity of my grandfather's myth meant everyone in town always knew our business. And when my middle sister, Margaux, became one of the first true "supermodels" in the late seventies, the drama increased exponentially. She jumped into the limelight at an early age, and she had to do battle with her demons in public, negotiating the ups and downs of celebrity and the temptations of drugs, food, and alcohol.

According to all I saw around me as a child, being an adult meant a roller-coaster ride of major highs and devastating lows that inevitably led to sickness, craziness, or self-destructive behavior. I didn't want any of that in my own future, so, beginning in my early teens, I sought ways to achieve calm and control in my own body and mind through diets, workouts, and what might be called inner work. I was using super-clean food and tough daily exercise regimens as preventive measures even before the word "preventive" was in vogue. I wanted to insure myself against ever becoming sick, fat, or insane, and I set about undoing the extremism I'd inherited from my family—the running-with-the-bulls approach to life encoded deeply in the Hemingway DNA.

Ironically, but not surprisingly, I took a pretty extreme approach to finding peace. I'd grown up pleasing people because it was the only way to get attention in my house, so I turned that talent to health and well-being. For a good portion of my youth I was the perfect student of any challenging diet and the perfect patient to any nutritionist, doctor, or healer who said they knew what was best for my body and, to some extent, my mind and spirit, too. Of course, I was also motivated by ego and fear about my appearance. I had entered the movie business at a young age, and throughout my late teens and twenties, I worked my butt off to stay skinny, svelte, and as sensational as a girl subsisting on celery and burned popcorn could be.

Even after I married my husband, Stephen, at the age of twenty-three, and we had our two beautiful daughters, I struggled to allow myself to relax and enjoy life. If anything, having children intensified my commitment to keeping "clean and balanced" in body and mind. My biggest fear was that I would pass on to my children the Hemingway clan's compulsive overindulgence. I ate less and exercised more, tightening the reins on all my health and beauty regimens. To put it bluntly, all my so-called healthy choices were motivated by panic. I kidded myself that I had the purest body on the block, but, in reality, I had built a lifestyle of deprivation, and my energy levels and immune function began to dip below par. Yet it was the only way I knew how to stay physically and emotionally consistent: withhold food from the emotional demons, or slay them with a tough workout. Of course, the messy emotions didn't go away; I was just too tired to deal with them.

What turned the tide for me were the practices of yoga and meditation, which I began to explore in my mid-twenties and then got serious about in my late twenties. In yoga, I found a challenge that couldn't be conquered with sheer discipline and sweat. Yoga practice didn't allow me to burn mindlessly through inner pain; instead, it gently turned me around to look at my pain and taught me to treat myself kindly enough to unravel some of my problems. I began to accept my body rather than constantly trying to dominate it. I became aware that it had its own systems of checks and balances: sophisticated biological systems that were able to keep my weight and moods in check if I let them. Yoga did its work on me—slowly. It forced me to peel back some of the armor in which I'd sheathed myself and examine the person inside. Eventually, I began to surrender to its way. I began to observe myself not only during yoga class, but also when I was cooking dinner or getting irritated when there were crumbs left on the counter. It slowed my reaction time and allowed me to become more conscious of who I was and how I was.

There was no sudden transformation or instant new start. But that yogic attitude I acquired led me to seek more peace in my life, and I learned some simple meditation. When I began carving out time to sit in silence on a daily basis, I got much better at observing and reflecting on all the events in my world. It was almost as if I were a concerned friend watching from the sidelines, asking, "Why the heck are you doing all that harsh stuff to your body?" In fact, I was becoming a kinder friend to myself in everything I did. This style of conscious living had major benefits. It allowed me to achieve things more calmly and easily and to be motivated by what was actually good for me rather than being driven by my emotions, which more often than not led to screwed-up and destructive behavior. It led me to start making healthy choices throughout my life—in my diet, in my relationships, and at home with the family.

Over time, living my life with more awareness and kindness powerfully transformed me as a woman, wife, mom, actor, and friend.

But it took until my late thirties before I truly mellowed out and learned to trust my own instincts rather than rely on a squadron of experts. I realized with something of a shock that I could be the expert on me. I'd certainly spent enough time in study and had accumulated tons of experience—so why wouldn't I know what was best for me?

I began to listen to what my body needed in terms of food, movement, rest, and emotional release, and I learned that if I made sure to structure my life so that every day included a few reasonably easy routines, I could create a consistency that allowed me to feel good every day, without highs and lows, without the scary pendulum swings I'd come to believe were a deeply embedded part of my personality.

Most important, I learned something huge: how to do things in moderation. A sustainable, lifelong healthy path didn't have to be bereft of treats and fun, nor did it have to come with a dose of shame. I no longer feared that I'd lose all my good work if I ate too much one day, or did a gentle workout instead of going for the burn, because I knew that now my choices were in tune with what I needed. I'd gradually developed the sensitivity to understand how my nutritional, physiological, and emotional needs changed from day to day, week to week, and year to year.

The result of finding my own way? My physical health has gotten better and better, to the point that I rarely get a cold or flu today and feel fantastic for my age because I've found ways to let my body function at a high level of efficiency. I've also lightened up enormously in my expectations of myself and those around me because I discovered that I could enjoy life, not just police it. (I also stopped trying to police my kids and husband, which has infinitely improved our relationships.)

Today, the simple but reliable protocols I follow in four important areas—diet, yoga and exercise, meditation, and caring for my home environment—are the cornerstones of my life. I know that when I do my work in all of them—for example, by eating in a way that makes me feel great and shedding any stress with some silent contemplation—I know that I've done the best I can to ensure I start and end the day feeling grounded and peaceful. Whatever happens in between, I can't necessarily control: bills pile up, work gets hectic, teenage daughters have teary meltdowns, PMS strikes, my husband gets cranky (occasionally). But by cultivating calm and balance at my core, I can observe, listen, and take a breath before I respond.

Even if you already know something about diet, about yoga, or about shifting the feel of your home, simply commit to learning a new way for a month, and be open to seeing the results.

The Quickstart 30-Day Program

Becoming a better you is achieved through the discipline of caring for these four avenues: food, exercise, silence, and home. These areas connect into a single whole. The choices you make in one area support the choices you make in another, without you even having to think about it.

Food (Nourish): Food affects you physically, mentally, and emotionally, and everyone has slightly different food needs. When you learn what works for your unique body, and know how to make tasty natural foods part of your diet, you can use food in a positive way to boost your body and mind and correct imbalances of weight, mood, and energy.

Exercise (Move): Exercise is pivotal to feeling and looking your best. Not only can you use it to strengthen and condition your body, you can also use it to heighten your awareness of how you feel in body, mind, and spirit. For this program, use yoga and simple hiking to transform not just your physique, but your mental and emotional state as well.

Silence (Observe): The ultimate benefits of life come from being quiet and taking the time to recognize how you feel inside. When you bring silent reflection into your life, you slow down the rush, observing your actions, and then you can make powerful changes with calmness and clarity.

Home (Restore): It's important to create the conditions for success. No matter where you live or how much you've got, you can make your home a haven that supports your quest for a balanced life—a place where you can rest and recharge, a sacred space to reflect and heal. Doing this not only brings harmony to your own existence, it also promotes harmonious interactions with your family and friends.

PART TWO

Flowing with Your Emotions

Deepak Chopra

Healing Our Hearts

CHAPTER
7

We have the deepest aspirations. We want to create a new mythology that says that peace and harmony and laughter and love are possible. That says that social justice and economic parity and ecological balance and a sense for the sacred and a universal spirituality irrespective of our origins are all part of the tangled hierarchy, the inter-dependency chorus.

Human beings have only existed for 200,000 years. For most of this time, we have been surrounded by predators. In order to survive, we have had a biological response, the flight/fight response. Because we have become so good at this flight/fight response, we have become the predator on this planet. We are the most dangerous animal.

That is not our whole history, however. Something very interesting happened to us about 4,000 years ago, when a few luminaries across the world appeared at once. They were the prophets of the Pentateuch, the great Greek philosophers, the sages of the Upanishads, the Eastern seers like Lao Tsu, Confucius and Buddha, and many others. They developed the ability to get in touch with the domain of awareness that is non-local, that transcends the space-time energy and everything that we can perceive with our senses.

The great English poet William Blake once wrote,

Deepak Chopra, MD, has written twenty-five books, which have been translated into thirty-five languages. He is also the author of more than one hundred audio- and videotape series, including five critically acclaimed programs on public television. In 1999 *Time* magazine selected Dr. Chopra as one of the Top 100 Icons and Heroes of the Century, describing him as "the poet-prophet of alternative medicine." Dr. Chopra currently serves as CEO and founder of The Chopra Center for Well Being in Carlsbad, California. For more information you can visit his web site atwww.chopra.com. This chapter first appeared in *Tikkun* magazine.

We are led to believe a lie
when we see with and not through the eye
that was born in the night, to perish in the night,
while the souls slept in beams of light.

When we see beyond the physical we see into our souls.

We can go a whole lifetime without getting in touch with our souls. But once we get in touch with this presence, there is no going back. This soul place is one of knowingness, of light, of love, compassion, and under-standing. Intention, imagination, insight, intuition, creativity, meaning, purpose, and decision-making are the attributes of this presence. When we get in touch with it, we have recourse to what is called the intuitive response, which is a form of intelligence that is contextual, relational, holistic, and nurturing. When I'm in this presence, and you are, we are in the same place.

We see that we are part of a great chain of being where we interdependently co-create each other. There is more that we share than what separates us. We all seek love, we all seek self-esteem, we all seek creative expression, we all seek self-actualization—these are the birthright of every human being.

There is no more important task at this moment in our history than to get in touch with the sacred core of our being that is common to all of us. Our practical proposals will be effective only when we get in touch with our souls, and feel this fundamental shift in our hearts. If we can feel that shift in our hearts, if we can join together and be living examples of this shift, then the world will transform, because the world is as we are. The world is nothing other than the projection of our souls.

Just because we are part of a collective insanity, we must not assume it is normal. It is the psychopathology of the average. We can emancipate ourselves from this psychopathology through the realm of spirit. Even though we have interesting scientific insights, the religious traditions of the world have access to universal truths.

A friend of mine sent me an English translation of an Egyptian papyrus discovered in the 1940s. The language is pre-Babylonian. We don't know who the author is, but he or she lived in the time of Solomon. The author is talking to God and he or she says:

You split me and you tore my heart open and you
filled me with love.

You poured your spirit into mine. I knew you as I
knew myself.

My eyes are radiant with your light. My ears delight
in your music.

My nostrils are filled with your fragrance. My face is
covered with your dew.

You have made me see all things shining. You have
made me see all things new.

You have granted me perfect ease. And I have
become like Paradise.

And having become like Paradise, my soul is healed.

At this moment, there is a rift in our collective soul. But there is
one part of our evolution that says this rift can be healed. And if we
heal it, we will all move into that ecstasy which is nothing other than
the exaltation of spirit.

Dean Ornish

CHAPTER 8

Love as Though Your Very Survival Depended on It

I am not aware of any other factor in medicine—not diet, smoking, exercise, stress, genetics, drugs or surgery—that has a greater impact on our quality of life, incidence of illness, or possibility of premature death than love and intimacy. Scientific studies show that people who feel lonely, depressed, and isolated are five times more likely to get sick and to die prematurely compared to those who have a sense of love, connection and community. The need for love and intimacy is a basic human need that's as fundamental as eating, drinking, and sleeping. And we ignore it at our own peril.

For example, one study at Duke University found that five years after an angiogram, half of those who were unmarried and had no confidant had died, compared to only 20% of those who either were married, or were unmarried but had a confidant. If they were married, but not particularly happily married, they still lived longer than people who weren't married. Again, I think it comes down to feeling known. Even in an unhappy marriage, at least the person knows you.

An extended family, a long-term neighborhood, or a church or synagogue used to provide a place where you were seen—and not just the parts of you that were the most likable, but also your darker parts. Those people were there for you, regardless.

Part of the value of a group is the re-creation of that lost sense of community where people feel safe enough to talk about their experiences without fear of abandonment or rejection. At a feeling level, we

Dean Ornish, MD, is one of America's best-known medical authorities. His ground-breaking experiments led to the development of diet- and exercise-based therapies that reversed heart disease without drugs or surgery, and earned him international renown, including the covers of news magazines and appearances on many national television shows. He is the author of *Eat More, Weigh Less* (HarperCollins, 1997), *Love and Survival* (HarperCollins, 1998), and several other books. He is the founder and president of the Preventive Medicine Research Institute in Sausalito, (www.pmri.org) and Clinical Professor of Medicine at the UCSF.

all want to be happy. We all want to avoid suffering. We struggle with similar life issues. When we talk about our issues it gives other people the courage to open up as well.

Healing is linked to how you react to suffering—be it betrayal, loss or any other aspect of being human. It's not that we should be without emotional defenses—they serve a function to protect us from pain. But if you have nowhere that feels safe enough to let down those defenses, and you have no one that you trust enough to open up to, then in effect, your walls are always up. If you've been hurt or betrayed, there's a natural fear of opening your heart. Ironically, the same defenses that we think protect us are actually killing us, or making us more likely to get sick and die prematurely. Hopefully, knowing this will give people the courage to begin the process of opening their hearts again.

The heart is a pump that needs to be addressed on a physical level, but our hearts are more than just pumps. A true physician is more than just a plumber, technician, or mechanic. We also have an emotional heart, a psychological heart, and a spiritual heart. Our language reflects that understanding. We yearn for our sweethearts, not our sweetpumps. Poets and musicians and artists and writers and mystics throughout the ages have described those who have an open heart or a closed heart, a warm heart or a closed heart, a compassionate heart or an uncaring heart. Love heals. These are metaphors, a reflection of our deeper wisdom, not just figures of speech.

The real epidemic in our culture is not only physical heart disease, but also what I call emotional and spiritual heart disease—that is, the profound feelings of loneliness, isolation, alienation, and depression that are so prevalent in our culture with the breakdown of the social structures that used to provide us with a sense of connection and community. It is, to me, a root of the illness, cynicism, and violence in our society.

The healing power of love and relationships has been documented in an increasing number of well-designed scientific studies involving hundreds of thousands of people throughout the world. When you feel loved, nurtured, cared for, supported, and intimate, you are much more likely to be happier and healthier. You have much lower risk of getting sick and, if you do, a much greater chance of surviving.

You can only be intimate to the degree that you're willing to open your heart and make yourself emotionally vulnerable to someone else. In my own case, I am in a committed, monogamous relationship with my wife. Our commitment to each other creates a sacred space—sacred meaning the "most special," a place where we feel increasing trust and safety with each other. We have that intentionality, that commitment to open our hearts wider and wider as we begin to trust each other more and more. As we do, the level of joy and intimacy and ecstasy is like nothing we ever could have dreamed.

Love promotes survival. Both nurturing and being nurtured are life-affirming. Anything that takes you outside of yourself promotes healing—in profound ways that can be measured—independent of other factors such as diet and exercise. There is a strong scientific basis documenting that these ideas matter—across all ages from infants to the most elderly, in all parts of the world, in all strata of life.

I've had patients say to me, "Having a heart attack was the best thing that ever happened to me." I would say, "That sounds crazy. What do you mean?" They'd respond, "Because that's what it took to get my attention—to begin making these changes I probably never would have done otherwise—that have made my life so much more rich, peaceful, joyful and meaningful."

Part of the value of science is to help raise the level of awareness for people so that they don't have to suffer as much to gain insight. Awareness is the first step in healing. They don't have to wait until they get a heart attack to begin taking these ideas seriously and making them part of their lives.

Intimacy is anything that takes you out of the experience of feeling separate and only separate. It can come in many forms. Most people think in terms of romantic intimacy, but intimacy can be between friends or family members, or even with pets. In fact, in one study, people with heart disease who had a dog had four times less sudden cardiac death than those who didn't have one. Intimacy can also be on a spiritual level, where prayer, meditation, or other spiritual practices can give us the direct experience of feeling like we're part of something larger that connects us all. In that timeless moment, wherever we go, we find only our own kith and kin in a thousand and one disguises; the Sufi poet Rumi wrote:

There is a community of the spirit.

Join it, and feel the delight

of walking in the noisy street...

Why do you stay in prison

when the door is so wide open?

Move outside the tangle of fear-thinking...

Flow down and down in always

widening rings of being.

BERNICE NELSON

Energy in Motion

The way you use your energy directly impacts your spirit, your emotional vibration, your drive, your creative instinct, your success, and your pleasure. What if you were taught how to utilize your energy system to influence these areas in positive directions?

Your emotional vibration is a clue to how you are utilizing your energy, whether you are stuck in place (at a Stop sign) or moving forward (at a Go sign). Emotional states that signal a Go sign—a moving, higher, lighter energy—include zeal, joy, lovingness, happiness, enthusiasm, optimism, hopefulness, positivism, and openness. Signals of a Stop sign—stalled or idling-in-neutral energy—include boredom, fear, worry, pessimism, negativity, frustration, feeling overwhelmed, disappointment, insecurity, doubt, jealousy, anger, and hate. The toxic energy of the stalled emotional states closes down your resources and keeps you at the Stop sign.

Where do *you* spend most of your time—at Go signs or Stop signs?

It is easy to feel the difference between the Stop and Go states. When stuck, you feel pressed upon and as though you are running in place. When moving forward, you feel free and elated.

The first step in learning how to direct your energy is to pay attention to what impacts it and how. Consider the following questions:

> Bernice Nelson is passionate about collaboration as a vehicle of shared power that enhances change and growth for optimal results. With undergraduate and doctoral studies in clinical and organizational psychology, she has brought collaborative methods into the public and private sectors for more than thirty years as a psychologist, therapist, consultant, and teacher. Her interest in building cultural understanding between peoples has involved study and travel abroad. She is a coach and energy psychology teacher, writing her pragmatic Growth and Developmental Concepts for a mass audience.

- Do you aim to create and shape your life experience or do you wait and react to whatever comes up? In other words, are you proactive or reactive? Is your action prompted by your choice or by default?

- Do you rely mainly on your thoughts or on your feelings to drive your responses? Put another way, is your behavior more shaped by your ideas or your emotions?

- Does your level of energy determine the quality of your thoughts and actions, or vice versa?

Conscious Energy Management

Give me a few hours and I can show you how conscious management of your energy system (which consists of the energy within your body and in your energy field, the "envelope" surrounding your body) can remarkably improve your relationships, clarity, communications, problem-solving skills, business effectiveness, ability to protect yourself, and connection with the Higher Power with which you relate, plus increase your sense of love, joy, and purpose.

Know that you already have a mechanism in place that shows you where you are heading: toward or away from your desires and wishes. This mechanism is the vibration of your bodily system that we call "feelings." Feelings are your energy that reports what is going on internally with your thoughts and externally with your actions. You have access to this useful information twenty-four hours a day. Noting the variation in your feelings—the drop or rise in their vibration—is vital for guiding and enhancing your success in life. It is no accident that feelings are called "*emotions*." They are what moves you, one way or another.

Early in my psychological training, I took a workshop whose title, "Anger Is a Hot Potato," intrigued me. An exercise we did in the workshop left an indelible impression on me and changed the way I conduct my life. The teacher had us visualize holding an apple in one hand. I was having fun up to the point where he said he had made a mistake and asked us to erase the apple and make it an orange instead. We could not do it; our apples insisted on remaining apples. Feigning perplexity at this result, he asked us to try something else. Perhaps, he suggested, we should replace the apple with a peach, which we also tried to no avail. How frustrated I was! My reaction was to try again and again in disbelief; I was on a treadmill of trying what was not working. Then he proposed that maybe it would work if we changed the apple into an orange or peach instead of trying to replace it. It did! Aha, the Master was teaching us a very important principle: It is easier to convert energy than to get rid of it.

That night, I told some friends about the exercise. They were intrigued, though skeptical. As if on cue, their preschool son awoke crying from a nightmare. His parents decided to try the conversion exercise in helping their son transform the chronic occurrence in his nightmares of being chased, falling, or drowning. For this dream, we helped him deal with the big bear chasing him by telling him he could turn into anything he wanted to be in his dream to deal with the threat. He loved that! And voilà, his fear disappeared. We could also have tried changing the bear into something more friendly, but my choice was to empower my little friend in handling this reoccurrence in his life.

Converting Energy

In dealing with a stressor in your life, it is more effective to alter the energy flow rather than match it. The challenge is to find a way to convert your perception of the stressor into a form that allows you to be more in control of it. Ideally, you seek the calm center in the midst of the personal storm you are experiencing and choose how you want to be. When controlled by the stressor, you become "in reaction" to it and the storm it creates in you.

So what do you do when you hit a Stop sign, come up against a stressor that has the potential to stop you in your emotional tracks? You find a way to transform the source, the stressor, instead of going into a reaction that ties up your energy. Raising your energetic, or emotional, vibration is the goal.

Stuck energy can be converted by utilizing the following "in power" tools:

1. Hang in with the situation in a different way than you have before. You can change how you look at the situation and what you choose to focus on.

2. Change the conditions. You can alter the direction you go by modulating your tone, attitude, posture, insight, or lens, or switching your primary "sensory overload" reaction to something more supportive (that is, eating fruit instead of turning to comfort food like sweets, or walking in nature rather than staying in the house).

3. Shift your viewpoint from "lack" toward "plenty," that is, move from "what you do not want" to "what you do want."

4. Acknowledge the presence of conflict. Note the behavior of

"being stuck" and the purpose it has served. Thank it for how it has helped you in the past, tell it you no longer need it, and ask it to be on its way.

Energy Is Pliable

Energy can be added to, transformed, improved on, combined, enhanced—all ways of moving forward rather than being stuck. There are many tools available to help you shift and raise your energy, to manifest what you want and to feel better. Among these are:

- Affirmations of intent
- Meditations
- Tapping exercises (i.e., Emotional Freedom Technique)
- Exercise
- Music
- Toning and vibrational sound healing DVDs
- Uplifting books
- Massage
- Acupressure or acupuncture
- Chiropractic alignment
- Time spent in nature, as in a walk on the beach
- Engaging in or observing art
- Lighting candles
- Writing
- Time spent with your pet
- Connecting with a friend who adds joy and fun to your life
- Whatever else helps you recover from your stressors

Each person is the authority on what he or she wants. But since there are many different ways for each of us to achieve what we want, we can encourage each other to try other, healthy avenues that we may not have considered to accomplish what we're after. We can do this for ourselves and others by simply posing the question "Can you find another way to do that?" Asking for a more acceptable way converts conflictual behavior into behavior that is helpful to self and other. This type of shared power expands the possibilities by tapping into the resources of all involved, rather than limiting who owns the conflicting behavior and who has the power to change it. Shared power is the act of cocreation.

Sometimes it is necessary to move sideways, move diagonally, leapfrog over, or back up in order to move forward! When geared toward reaching the goal, all movement can be seen as a step toward ultimate success.

Story: The Boy Under the Desk

I smile when I think about a young boy who, to the chagrin of his teacher, would not do his work. No matter what she tried, he persisted in his failure, though it added to his sense of defeat and ineptitude. I had been called into this classroom to conduct a general observation, in the course of which I talked separately with each child. When I came to this boy, he was doing nothing. I asked what he was supposed to be doing and his answer revealed that he was clear on the task at hand. I then asked how he could do it. He looked at me blankly. I reframed my question, asking, "Can you find a way to do it?" At that, he nodded his head. After hearing how he felt he could do it and after checking his sincerity, I requested his permission to ask the teacher about doing it this way. Surprised, the boy gave his permission. I whispered our request to the teacher, who responded with an incredulous look, then shrugged, as if to say, "Why not? Nothing else has worked." She consented to our trying it.

The boy was delighted. After looking in my eyes to be sure I meant it, he gathered what he needed to complete the assignment, went to the teacher's desk, pulled the chair out, crawled into the cubbyhole under the desk, and went to work. He lived up to his word and did what he said he would, without any prompting.

Later, the teacher and I entertained all the ways this helped him to achieve something he seemingly could not do at his desk. Perhaps sensitivity to motion, noise, or distraction or seating discomfort made it necessary for him to work somewhere else. The teacher subsequently learned that this student did not need to crawl into a cave to work. A study carrel or an alternate desk away from the windows and the noise of a reading group provided what he needed.

We learned from this to pay attention to how each student learns best and to make accommodations where necessary to help them achieve. From then on, I expected students to be in charge of their brains and *how* they learned, while their teacher(s) and staff were in charge of *what* had to be learned as well as finding ways to teach each child effectively.

Story: Excited by Thinking

One day in class, a star athlete who happened to be a slow reader answered a question about the differences between Greek and Roman life. His astute and detailed answer stunned his classmates and teacher.

I was there and asked, "How in the world did you learn that?"

He said proudly, "I got smart." Pointing to two fellow male students who were eager learners, he added, "I sat behind you when you were studying the other day. I listened to what you said."

"How many days ago was that?" I asked.

When I heard that it had been three days, I said to him, "That says to me that you have a good three-day memory." Noting his elation, I added that this was an asset to hold on to.

A month later, the same boy now considered himself a learner, despite reading and writing skills that were still subaverage for his age. On a test day, he told his teacher before the test, "Today, I take the test. I talk it." She gave him a tape recorder to do so. He cared enough about finishing that he showed up after school to add more onto his recording.

By the end of the school year, this student's slower reading and writing skills had advanced by two years.

It seemed that his excitement at being able to think well drove his desire to learn to read and write, not the other way around as often happens with children. In other words, the mental practice paved the way for him to learn the skills.

Utilizing Your Energy

If you are given a hypothetical amount of energy each day, let's say a hundred units, what do you do with it? Author, medical intuitive, and inspirational speaker Caroline Myss posed a question along these lines in a workshop in Oakland several years ago. The question goes to the heart of the issue of putting energy into motion. What and how do I regard the gift of energy daily available to me? Do I use it constructively or abuse it? Do I unconsciously use it the way I learned from my parents, who learned from theirs, and so on? Does this way serve me or block me?

Using your energy consciously is the basis of energy management. There are three basic tools that are invaluable in managing energy: grounding yourself, protecting yourself, and holding your space. In my experience, these tools lift and sustain energy, and bring a sense of ease to the manifestation of intentions. When you don't use these tools, you are more "at effect" rather than "at cause" of how events transpire, prone to react rather than act. You also waste effort and invite chaos. When you use these tools, you exercise choice and are more in charge of how your life unfolds. You are better able to tap into your inner wisdom and you experience greater clarity of thought. Here are the basic tools I learned that have become so much a part of me that now I can't imagine living without them.

Grounding

The aim is to connect your body with Earth. The most common practice is to drop a grounding "cord" or "column" from your body (e.g., from your head down through your torso and out your feet), down into Earth, perhaps all the way to its center. Or you can imagine a "harness" around a section of your body and anchor it beneath Earth's surface in any secure way you wish. Design your grounding cord any way you want—color, material, strength, width—and even "landscape" or "decorate" where you anchor it. If so inclined, you can seek your intuition, ask your Higher Guidance, for input on what and how it should be. Your grounding cord may vary for different events or tasks. Also, your preference may change over time. What is important is to find the way to sustain your connection and eventually be able to stay grounded throughout your day. Paying attention to what causes you to lose or shorten your grounding cord can assist you in deciding where to utilize your energy.

The benefit of grounding yourself is that it allows you to disconnect from your emotional baggage or intrusion into the pureness of the present moment. It offers a clean slate for what is before you right now! It anchors you into the current moment, which is the only time in which you can take action and accomplish something.

Protecting

In your mind's eye, surround yourself entirely with a sealed bubble, creating a boundary that distinguishes, defines, and declares your personal space. Visualize wrapping it entirely and securely around your body, including front, back, above, and below. Create your bubble with the intent that nothing can penetrate it to harm you or unsettle you as a cocreator of the outcome of your life. The size and thickness of the bubble's membrane will vary with your individual needs. Some people need more room or more shielding than others do to feel safe and protected. When people say they need more space, they often do in order to think clearly, modulate their feelings, and maintain a sense of self. When you encounter stressors and/or conflict, you may need to strengthen your bubble boundary. The color you give the bubble may change over time. Yellow-gold is often a comfortable choice when you first begin using this tool. Later, you will learn to tune in to your various senses to know what color to use.

Protecting yourself in this way allows you to sort out and define yourself from all the energies nearby. It permits you to secure your space so that you can govern your own growth and conduct your life purposefully and with the meaning you choose.

Holding Your Space

In doing this, you are "owning" and personalizing your space — the one you have already protected — so that it serves you well. How well you manage and hold it will help keep your vibration at a level where things move more smoothly for you. You personalize your space by choosing the color(s) within your bubble of protection as well as any symbols or signs that express your intentions. You put these up in your protected space and use them to empower you for any task or event. This is an act of creation available within you, so whatever comes from your inner guidance are the right colors or symbols for you; these change, too, from day to day, even hour to hour, or more frequently. As examples of personalizing your space, you might choose the color violet to respond in a healthy or loving way, magenta for converting any anger, an owl to help make a wise choice, a fence for "no entry," or a brook to help you cool down or relax.

Holding your space empowers your life by allowing you to consciously design your experience(s) the way you desire. Your symbols and colors serve as a message board for declaring what you want and activating your intentions.

The Three Basic Tools That Support Energy in Motion

1. Grounding. Connect to Earth; get into present time.
2. Protecting. Create boundaries; surround and shelter yourself.
3. Holding your space. Stabilize your space by personalizing it; create symbols and signs to signal your intentions.

The three tools of energy management are as powerful as they are simple to use. A fond memory comes to mind of when I was seated in a corner of a restaurant and trying to catch the attention of a waiter. I decided to try one of my energy tools, so I put in my space a pair of eyeglasses facing toward me. All of a sudden, three waiters emerged from different areas of the room having seen me.

Try these tools and see what happens. Keep what brings a desired effect. Notice what works and for which circumstances. Have fun with it!

When you purposefully manage your energy, the effects are remarkable. You can enhance and sustain your focus, steer your direction, empower wise choices, and manifest your intentions, all while becoming more centered and less stressed out! Also, by taking the road of ethical behavior, which is responsible use of energy, you move to a higher vibration and your inner self will flourish even more. The process of learning to manage your energy brings you face to face with your conditioning—your erroneous notions of yourself and how those notions limit you—and shows you what you need to let go of in order to move. Energy management helps you actualize who and what you are, and moves you toward your peak performance and vitality.

What would your personal vitality look like with this increased consciousness? How would it impact others and raise the spirit of being? Taking it further, how would our world be if we all utilized the gift we have at our disposal to raise our presence and our meaningfulness?

MARY ELLEN EDWARDS

CHAPTER
10

In Relation:
The Dance of Connection

To dance is a creation in movement. It is intentionality to commune, connect, and conspire in the expression of essence and being in relation. It is awareness and movement of the self within the fluid, living, interconnected life-context. To dance is to fling open a door of communication and a portal of interplay between the inner self, the moving moment, and the outer world.

We are "in relation" even if our attention is not called to that connection. A constant fluid "in relation" to ourselves, each other, and Mother Earth. We are both a part of and a part within the world, and the universe. That is inescapable, but it is also what it means to be alive.

To dance is a measure of intentionality and consciousness in the ebb and flow of the interconnectedness of life. To dance is creating within co-creation.

As a child, I would take long walks in the woods and meadows on my family's country property in Ohio. As the second youngest in my large family, at times I felt lost. But out there in the woods and meadows there was connection. I felt that I belonged. It was so inviting that it beckoned me to join.

It was magical and mystical. I would look up long, thick tree trunks to the branches high above, where sunlight played on leaves dancing in the breath of wind. I'd run up a hill in the meadow and lie

Mary Ellen "SpiritDancer" Edwards, LCSW, is a mind-body-spirit clinical social worker in private practice and a degreed, published professional writer. Mary Ellen has worked for over 22 years in mental health, hospice, and domestic violence, from development of services to mentoring, teaching, including continuing education courses working with death and dying, grief and loss. Mary Ellen is a shamanic apprentice and writes allegorical stories, essays about life's lessons and teaches workshops on creating stories as part of the healing and empowerment process. She is a Rhythm, Movement, Sound facilitator living near Los Angeles. See more at www.MaryEllenEdwards.com.

in its uncut grass and gaze at the clouds in awe and wonder. Mother Earth was holding me gently in the grass, soothing me, while inviting me to get up and run down the hill.

I would listen to the sweet songs of the birds, sometimes singing along; the song then danced and moved in a different direction. The birds, the leaves, and the stream talked, as they flowed over the rocks and down, disappearing beyond. They were all my playmates. Though I didn't know it at that age, the dirt path of Mother Earth was calling me to join an interconnected dance.

There, I felt a sense of aliveness, and that I was a part of that whole, while drawing me forward to the next moment. I was in relation to all. I was in the dance of connection.

As we dance in life, it is not the movement itself that creates the journey. Our journey is our growth, our lessons, our joy, our transformational phoenix rising. It rises in connection, in relation, unfolding at the moment with each other and ourselves.

It comes from letting go and experiencing the dance as it is happening, the surroundings in relation to ourselves, and the energy of the whole. It comes from the expression of self that we allow. It comes from the exploration of connection, in relation, adventuring into new waters, into territory not previously explored. Even in the connection with ourselves, we are exploring our sadness and experiencing it, grieving so that we may heal and begin anew; growing — instead of holding in, or running away, exploding, or becoming sick.

We are constant co-creators and collaborators in this world and as such, we have the choice and power to pull in and constrict. We can even stay in the same space. That is also a choice. Or we can experience, express, and explore, to create magic and expansion into something otherwise unimaginable, through the art and dance of allowing and Synergy.

My early experiences in nature helped me see and connect into more of how we are the same. Seeing our differences is really about seeing how we are the same, though uniquely expressed. Our essence. Our story. We affect each other with our story, the web of interconnectedness. We see how we affect each other in a young woman who was abused as a child, struggling to believe in herself and make a better life for her kids and make a difference in the world. Her story. We experience it when we reach out to help the victims of Hurricane Katrina. The universal story. Every day we dance it in our own lives and in our relationships. Our stories.

We dance both out of our sameness and our uniqueness, as a bird sitting on a branch on a warm sunny day, sings a song of its heart.

Let's dance together, not in spite of who we are, but because of who we are. Celebration.

The Dance of Sense of Self and Other

At the age of forty, loving water and wind, I started sailing. I had never sailed before, but I was hungry for adventure. I wanted to know more about myself, and so I adopted an explorer's heart, which gave me room to just be in connection and learn. I started first crewing on boats during races, and then went on to sailing a nineteen-foot sailboat solo. By just letting go of any preconceived beliefs about myself and my skills as a woman sailing a large boat by myself (which I got a lot of comments on), I could just be in connection with—melding, merging, gliding in a dance, as one with the water and the wind. I was exploring. Sometimes I celebrated the dance by heading into the wind, lowering the sails, and watching the setting of the same sun seen all over the world. At the close of the day, I saw the same moon rise that all others can see. The boat's name was, appropriately, "Windancer."

To learn about connection and being in relation to our larger world, we need to learn about connection and being in relation to ourselves. We need to understand what it means to be human; that universal sameness that is by design. We were designed, by whatever grand design you believe in, to be connected to, and part of, a whole. We were designed to grow and learn, in a process of synergistic and interactive development. We realize that to be human is to have feelings and to learn what these feelings are teaching us, instead of pushing them aside. We were never supposed to know how to do this as children. No one comes out of the proverbial birth canal that way. Otherwise our judgments, expectations, and baggage—patterns of thinking and relating—interfere with the connection between right and wrong, between good and bad thinking. The "I am less than" becomes our dance.

When we have an undeveloped, invalidated, or even wounded sense of self, we tend to stop time, point to an accomplishment, disappointment, moment, and say, "This is me." It is a legitimate attempt to make sense of who we are in the bigger world, and acknowledge important, wonderful aspects of the human journey. If we use those as the yardstick of self-definition, however, we must constantly seek new goals to affirm our identity—or stay stuck in the old accomplishment or disappointment. We then live and dance reactively, passively, never stepping fully into exploration; we remain hesitant to change careers, or co-create our dreams.

As a psychotherapist, I see many people who seek to free themselves of these patterns. In reality, you may be a loving, caring, and nurturing father, but may feel empty inside, defining your self as a success or failure by how many touchdowns your son makes, while telling him that he did his best. I once worked with a very successful physician who told me that if his patients knew he really felt as a person he was a fraud inside, they would never come to him. All his daily acts of saving lives didn't fill the emptiness he felt inside. His dance was angry, withdrawn, linear, escaping, and reactive, until he learned that he was unfolding, exploring, and whole.

We are not made less than. We are whole, and always have been. We are divinely in relation, growing, learning, and dancing in connection. We are made up of the same universal matter, and we matter in this universe. When we begin to embrace the universalism of sameness, we begin to heal ourselves and those things and people we feel separate from.

We are each beautiful gifts to this world to open and unfold into growth—a seeming paradox—as well as to share our innateness, presence with ourselves, and with the world. It is sometimes easier to hold others in significance, reverence, and value than is it to hold ourselves up in the same manner.

The Dance of Co-Creating

Letting go of our fears, self-doubts, and worries allows us to be more present for the unfolding. Our natural awe, wonder, and innocence of exploration comes out to play. Work sessions become brainstorming sessions, a pirate ship that takes you into new territories, new sights, new wonders; the world expands. A road trip includes stops along the way, just as a hike is an adventure down a new path. A career is heart-storming, life-storming co-creation.

When we dance, the connection is not about the past, but it embraces the past and propels us into explorations of the present. We learn about ourselves, and we empower ourselves to create in the magic of synergy. And we learn about the other, our world, to which we are connecting: "Teach me how to dance with you." In my sailing, I let the wind, water, and boat teach me how to sail. Once I learned how to dance with their dances, off we went, into new adventures and places.

We teach people who we are by our dance—passive or expansive; wounded or self-confident—and as such, we teach them how to dance with us. As you dance, you teach me about how to be in relation with you. Your presence and dance in this world teaches me about you, it teaches me about life, and it teaches me about me and how to be in relation with you. Dancing in relation, therefore, is a dance of expressing and experiencing each other in nonlinear flow within the art of allowing. We become playmates exploring oceans and mountains. We continue to grow and uncover, discover about our self in relation, and we do so until the day we die.

The seemingly oppositional dualities we find in life—black and white, accomplishment and disappointment—exist not so that we might live in extremes, but to teach us how to live balance in the fluid moments of ever-changing flow of life. We can see the dance of leaves as wind blowing against an object, the leaves, and the leaves reacting. Sometimes we conduct our lives in that same way: reactively.

The more I move in conscious mindfulness, in relation, the more I allow the exploration of give and take. Smiling and mischievous, establishing a heart connection in silent knowing through the eyes of another dancer, allowing and surrendering in the flow of the moment, I am open to both leading and following. This oneness takes me further, deeper.

Even in the spaces of silence within our selves, we dance. The ebb and flow within our heartbeat, our pulse, our breath, our thoughts of current and past events, are all movement. These are all in the moment, which itself is moving time, always leading us into the next moment. To be in stillness is to be moving in fluid relationship.

Since life and the self are inescapably entwined in constant relational movement, it is not *that* we dance, but *how* we dance. It is not the what of connection, it is the dance of how. It is the experience, the expression, the exploration. It is to recognize that the goal is not to get to the end of the dance, but to deepen and enjoy the ride, in a spiraling synergistic co-creation of the ebb and flow of interconnectedness.

The Dance of Significance of Self and Others

We are multidimensional beings, with history, beliefs, and context. We carry our perceptions of our relative significance and worth, our abilities, and place in life, with us. How strongly we are aware and mindful of our sense of self, and how we view our self within the context of the larger world, collaborates with the art of allowing in defining our daily life-dance. That dance may be with our self in work or play; with our partners, our career, children, and even how we drive our vehicles. The dance is we go about our day as a presence, present and participating in this world.

The concept of "in relation" is not necessarily about mutuality or reciprocity. It is "with respect to" but not "defined by" the other. "In relation" is defined by all; the participants, and the spaces in between. It is the varying degrees of awareness, attitude, and attention of one's sense of self within the space and place of the interconnectedness of the larger world. Interconnectedness exists; what is fluid is our awareness, attention, and attitude. This is why when there is a national tragedy, like 9/11, we suddenly feel closer to each other.

Whether we slow our car to yield to someone signaling their intent to move in front of us, or disregard the request and keep moving forward, depends upon our degree of awareness, attitude, and attention. It has to do with our perception of the degree of significance. If we shift our definition of significance, from subjective importance of self, to objective reverence for all, we change our dance.

This shift involves not so much attention as it involves an attitudinal awareness. The driver signaling to move in may not be important to you. But his or her journey, space, and place, are as important. The moment of interchange may be so brief as to require little of your attention, but the value of their journey on the road is unaffected; it is not seen as more or less important than yours. Significance lies outside subjective assessment. It just is.

When we dance through our lives in a state of awe and wonder, understanding the grand design of sameness, we dance with reverence. We connect out of an innocence of exploration, eager to discover what lies ahead. We take back steering our ship, one with essence of connection, in a spiraling synergistic, deepening exploration. We go places in our dance we could not have gone before. We are not stopped by preconceived history, by the importance of our dance. Instead, we want to learn what the "in relation" is teaching us as we merge and meld, gliding as one, in a reverent awe and wonder at the dance of connection.

If we allow ourselves to surrender into the exploration, then we see, feel, know, and recognize with our "soul vine's" eye, the third charka, gut, or, as I call it "wisdom pouch." We connect into essence, the reverent, unfolding story of each other. The soul vine's eye connects us to the all and everything. It is our umbilical cord. It is the site of intuition, our gut feelings. It is here that we "know" our interconnectedness, our connection to that which created us, and to our divine reverent humanness.

We have all probably had the experience of meeting someone for a mere instant, yet finding that they profoundly affected us. When you hold yourself and others in significance, in the dance of in relation, then you practice the art of allowing, and you fling open a door of possibilities. We can all, even in an instant, make a difference. Opening a door, letting the person in the next car weave in front of us, recognizes reverent significance. Neither person is diminished. Both are uplifted.

The Synergistic Dance of the Fluid Moment

The paradox of being in the moment is that in that place, we experience both active presence, and movement to the next moment. It is fluid movement, and thus is always developing, in process, as the "in relation" dance. To be a choreographer in your life dance is not to structure an outcome, but to be an actor, a co-collaborator, in the fluid moving design of the dance. To be in the moment is fluid activity in relation, moving forward to the next moment. O. Fred Donaldson, PhD, in his book *Playing By Heart, the Vision and Practice of Belonging,* writes:

"Playmates catch the moment rather than the expectation. There is a give and take as we learn the points of resistance, connection and flow between us...

To play is to be irrationally crazy, to engage in a metapattern of belonging that connects life forms across species and cultural barriers... When we truly play ourselves, we are authenticated by all things."

Play is our innate nonjudgmental sharing in the fluid moment. Play is not childish; it is childlike. It arises from a sense of innocence, a sense of wonder, awe, and anticipation.

It is experience, expression, and exploration.

A child of age six or seven doesn't care if there are no longer pirate ships, or that there is no real tea in the cups around the small table. Our instinctual nature as children is to explore, to see beyond what is there, to put invisible sugar in the cups, and to share. A child does not think about who he or she is; a child just *does.* A child supported has no judgments or preconceived beliefs. Pirate ships can grow wings and fly.

If we live out of a reactive state, we are still in relation, though we may remain asleep, blowing hapless in the wind. Nor can we choreograph a result. But we can choreograph the design of our dance, in the fluid moment, open to the sense of self and possibilities in the ebb and flow that might just allow us to grow wings and fly.

To dance we must be present. We must be the being in the fluid moment. We must show up. Motivational speaker Les Brown once said, "If you are not excited about your dance, how can you expect anyone else to be?" Showing up, being present in the fullness and wholeness, is what transforms the experience and expression and exploration into a spiraling synergistic, nondirectional expansion. And when we show up and dance with reverent significance, learning, the dance deepens into a soul celebration, and the journey of exploration itself is the destination. It is what enables us to fly over land in a pirate ship with wings.

The unfolding dance, and the presence of the present of each one us, in relation—to commune, connect, collaborate with each other—creates magic and expansion. To recognize that we are each a gift is to recognize the inherent significance, reverence, and value of every person. It is a reverence that lies outside of human assessment and is just a birthright for each one of us. When we dance in recognition of that gift, we conspire to dance in the magic and synergistic exploration of the essence of each.

BEVERLY DAVIES-MES

Body Earth Energies

A s a young child, I cherished time spent with my father. Many an afternoon or evening found me cradled in his lap, wrapped in his fatherly arms and familiar scent as he shared the precious stories and songs of his childhood. Reflecting on those early days of my life, I realize that I was quite conscious of the balance between the strong masculine and the divine feminine in my father's being (though I didn't have words for it then). I resonated with it, and loved it dearly. He sang to me the cheerful song of the "little brown bears with wings," flying into the garden to savor the flowers' sweet nectars, then gently carrying it away to make honey. There were exciting stories about his father as a young lad from Wales whose adventurous spirit led him to stow away on a ship headed for the wild frontiers of Australia, then journey to England, and eventually find a home in California's San Francisco Bay Area.

Often at night, after my mother had tucked her five children safely into bed, our father would visit each of us before we drifted off to sleep. I was thrilled and amazed as he would look deeply into my eyes and tell me what he could see. Somehow, mysteriously, he could see *everything*—good or otherwise—that I had done that day! He knew who had come to play, what I had for lunch, and even when I had taken my nap. He could see what kind of day I had in school, what my mood was like, and if I had been kind to others. In my innocence, I downloaded the truth that one truly *can* see into another

Beverly Davies-Mes and her husband, Servaas Mes, are the directors of the Somatic Health Center in St. Helena, California. They are involved on an international level in expanding the frontiers of rehabilitation, health, fitness, and overall human potential. Beverly has studied with Donna Eden, completing her inaugural two-year Energy Medicine certification program. She is also a Reiki Master, a certified massage therapist, and a Hanna Somatic Educator. Her warm intuitive healing abilities and her sense of humor are the foundation of her busy practice, creating a wonderful environment for health, healing, and relaxation. www.somatichealthcenter.com

being by looking deeply into them. I know now that my young psychic abilities were being awakened and nourished.

This ability to see is a powerful truth that I abide by and intuitively use personally as well as professionally to this very day. I know it as the gift of being able to look at the "essence" of another person. This gift allows me to bypass the variety of external illusions that so often block us from authentically experiencing each other. It keeps me neutral, yet strongly present with the other. Often, for the individual who receives the experience of really being seen, perhaps for the first time, surprise, wonder, joy, relief, peace, and gratitude flood through them. I watch the predictable smile emerge. It is an honor for me to observe this lovely phenomenon.

As I grew older, my father began to share stories of a different kind. These were the foundation of teachings that led to my understanding and use of metaphysical laws, consciousness, and spirituality. I can clearly recall him telling me: "Honey, everything is Energy! Everything! Even the most dense and solid objects around you. Consider your body, which appears to be strong and unchanging; it, too, is simply vibration. You will understand all of these things as you mature and experience life's mysteries."

As usual, he was right. I did not fully comprehend all that he was saying, nor could I explain it, but I believed him. It felt right. In the years that followed my initial childhood introductions to energy, I had an insatiable hunger for universal truths and continue to this day to be overjoyed by my discoveries in this realm. I find that the more I learn, the more there is to learn.

One of the most precious pieces of the puzzle for me personally was the discovery of the ability to work (or play!) with the human energy field. It is what I love to do, it is what I am good at, and it serves those around me in many ways. It is my right livelihood, allowing me the privilege of touching those in need in a unique way. Although I have always been organically sensitive to my physical and spiritual environment, my sensitivity increased dramatically in my early thirties. I began to see auras, or colors, around and within people. This was often accompanied by strong intuitive knowledge that fascinated me and those with whom I shared it. In 1993, I began a formal study and development of the art of meditation to facilitate energetic growth and healing within me, and then for others. I learned the valuable skill of maintaining neutrality in reading energy and in observing flows of energetic information.

Tapping into the vitality of the natural energies around us requires not only *awareness*, but *attention* as well. Just this morning I eagerly harvested the first offering of organic table grapes, still cool from the northern California evening, from the modest vineyard in our backyard. The juicy and much anticipated glorious moment of harvest was well worth the wait. Harvest requires *patience* and *timing*. Sure, I could have brought the grapes in the weekend before, but their extra time on the vine ripened them to perfection. If I had waited for another two weeks, the moment of perfection would have passed.

My husband and I had been carefully monitoring the maturation of these tiny orbs of goodness. We were mindful to keep them from touching the ground, keep them out of excessive shade, and were generous with their daily drink of water. In the spirit of generosity, we watched the vines meander over neighbors' fences and begin to cascade into their yards, providing the promise of riches for all. As the harvest approached, I was curious and happy to notice irregular empty places in the lowest grape clusters, which had been full.

"There is easily enough here for everyone. Joyfully give to the Earth's wild creatures, even as the Earth provides for you" became part of my daily spiritual (as well as pragmatic!) reminders. Thus *gratitude* and *generosity* are two more elements of living in synch with the vital energies around us, inclusive of the smallest of events such as the humble harvesting of grapes!

Our precious planet Earth has countless flows of natural energies, seen and unseen, which surround her as well as move deeply within her. We, too, have energetic flows that also influence, propel, surround, and move deeply within us. In both cases, these energies might reveal themselves as rhythms, pulses, vibrations, or currents. The pure joy of discovering these rhythms awaits those who use their multidimensional senses to become aware. Consider how wonderful it is to invite in the moment of awareness in order to listen to the invisible energy of the wind as it dances and plays in the canopy of the treetops. To feel its gentle caress or its relentless force against our skin or clothing, or through our hair. To experience delight in the unique mix of fragrances that it carries to us and the play of temperature it brings upon us.

This is an opportunity to be bathed in the fullness of authentic power. Imagine for a moment the force that is required by moving water to smooth even the roughest and jagged edges of great rocks lying in its path. This energy source is incredibly powerful yet still requires a great amount of time to achieve its natural result. Allow yourself to hold a rounded and smooth stone in your hand, grounded in present time, and appreciate or even feel the many years of effortless influence that it took for the water to achieve the end result. Then place the stone back into the riverbed. Can you imagine the rock's transformation in twenty years from now?

A powerful visual for tapping into Mother Nature's organic energy is the phenomenon of jet streams. The main jet streams are fast, narrow air currents that flow west to east and are found mainly in the stratosphere. These swift air currents circulate at 36,000 feet above the planet in both the Northern and Southern Hemispheres.

Another exciting natural flow of energy to identify with is the ocean currents of the Gulf Stream and its counterpart, the North Atlantic Drift. Benjamin Franklin first charted these warm currents in 1786. They originate in the Gulf of Mexico and are wind-driven northward along the eastern United States coastline and on to Newfoundland, Canada. From there, these warm, powerful, and swift currents travel eastward until they eventually split. The southern flow is directed toward West Africa and the northern flow moves toward Europe to influence the climate, resulting in warmer European winters.

These are but a few of the mighty forces of energy and nature to consider when exploring our personal relationship to the power of our planet. Studying these external examples of energetic cause and effect can help us to understand the energy system within us, for they are based on the same principles and function in the same way. With practice, we can navigate and control the flow of our own personal energies to achieve not only health, but also true well-being.

I love to be aware of, explore, and ride the energetic or unseen "jet streams" in life. Tapping into these ever-evolving streams of consciousness has resulted in a communion with my being that facilitates my journey of fulfilling the original blueprint of my soul. As my experience with consciousness practices has developed, *focused intention and nonattachment to outcome,* or *surrendering to the intelligence of the universe,* has allowed me to experience a "wonder-full" journey. This journey includes only mindfully inviting others into my world, which means being highly conscious of the energetic "fingerprints" I allow to influence my projects, ideas, and fields of potential. The following story is an exciting and typical example of this in action.

In 1999, my landlords raised my rent by 30 percent as property values and the rental market in my community skyrocketed. I had a choice to commit to another three-year lease or to relocate. As I meditated on my situation, I was surprised to find myself flooded with a strong awareness that I should...I would...purchase my own home. Now this might not seem like such a profound concept, but consider that I had no savings to spare for a down payment and the mortgage companies virtually laughed me out of their offices when I inquired about becoming preapproved!

On one occasion, I shared my quest with a close family member who stated that buying a home was an impossible and foolish goal. Still, I continued to listen to that firm inner voice and chose to follow my intuition regardless of the external judgments of others. I learned from this not to share my quest with everyone, but to choose wisely, for only positive support would propel me forward. From then on, I did not mention a word of my adventure to that family member, whose comment was a projection of personal fear of such a step. I realized how crucial it was to connect with those whose conscious development could hold the strength of the reality I was manifesting, and, at the same time, not to take personally the opinions of those who could not.

I began to search for my house, the one that the universe had set aside just for me, as though it were a done deal. I created a statement of manifestation: "The right and perfect home, with the right and perfect price, is available to me now. Thank you!" I never asked for the house again. I simply lived in the essence of gratitude that it was waiting for me. I reinforced that statement countless times each day!

A trusted friend who is a local real estate agent offered to help. Together we found a place that had been on the market for months without a single offer made on it due to its poor condition. Where most people saw a disaster, I walked in and saw nothing but potential. My radar sounded! My heart skipped a beat! Bingo! Now the magic really needed to happen. How was I going to pull this off financially? No worries, I thought. The solution has already been created for me. I just needed to continue to be mindful and keep my ears and eyes open.

On the day I was to sign the documents to open escrow, I walked by the house and asked the universe for a sign that this was the right decision for me. As I stood on the small bridge nearby, I saw two snow-white egrets, my personal totem for spiritual confirmation, standing motionless at the distant water's edge. I glowed with an enormous inner smile.

I thought of another wise, creative, and intuitive friend, who had been an inspiration as well as a mentor, from whom I could seek counsel. He is a successful semiretired developer in the San Francisco Bay Area. I knew that I could trust his advice without hesitation. He drove by the house for sale and also saw its potential, *and* the solution to my dilemma. In his kindness, he provided me with almost $100,000 for a down payment, which enabled me to easily qualify for a mortgage. One year later, I refinanced the property and paid him back with interest, per our agreement.

I hired my son to repair and remodel my newly acquired home, with funds negotiated from the sellers during settlement. Helpers appeared out of nowhere to lend a hand in painting, yard work, and more. Only when the project was completed did I introduce the home to my skeptical family member who smiled with delight and exclaimed, "This was the smartest thing you have ever done!"

I will never forget the incredible leap of faith that my financier took when he enabled me to purchase my first home. Several years later, I financed the "green" remodeling of our Somatic Health Center with the equity from that investment. As I began offering sessions in my beautiful new office space, I felt that there was something yet unfinished about the project. Then, in my mind's eye, I saw my financier's face and knew what was missing. I invited his wife and him to the office and thanked him for cocreating this space. The ripple effect of his generosity years before was still in motion and had allowed this unique healing center to come into being.

From these experiences, I learned that riding the jet stream takes courage, determination, and trust. I also realized that for me it is the only way to go! Paying attention to the minute signals of support and direction from the universe, listening to the powerful gut-level responses of intuition, and employing the practice of kindness is how to ride the jet stream.

Living in a conscious state of gratitude and doing no harm to ourselves, to any sentient being, or to the planet is fundamental to learning to move in synch with natural forces. These are the forces that allow us to live at our peak vitality. These forces long to communicate with us. They are there to guide and assist each soul's journey. As we learn to surf these forces — to ride the jet stream — they powerfully assist us and take us on thrilling adventures that we will wish to repeat and share with others. These adventures result from our focused attention on our intention. My beloved husband, Servaas, and I refer to this phenomenon as "holding hands with the universe, buckling our seat belts, and going for the ride!" We have learned that these power streams can be navigated, entered, and exited at will. We must prepare carefully, even cautiously, for this exhilarating adventure, however.

A visit to any of the beaches well known around the world to receive the fury of the ocean's largest rhythmic waves will reveal an array of brave souls who are masters of the art of surfing. They have devoted a lifetime of commitment to countless hours out on those menacing waves, learning to be as one with the energy and flows beneath them. Only through perfecting *strength, endurance, patience, intuition, awareness, courage, and balance* can they rise to the skill level needed to ride those waves. Be assured that many times a terrified surfer has found herself in the "washing machine," pulled quickly underwater, spinning head over heels without any warning, and hoping not to run out of breath before resurfacing. When she does, she returns to the challenge of riding the waves, but now with greater respect and knowledge.

Entering the jet stream of consciousness requires the same set of skills! Without them, we, too, might find ourselves tumbling head over heels in flows of energy that seem too strong to manage. By developing the universal skills found in many spiritual practices, we can choose to bump up against the jet stream to increase our ability to ride it. By paying close attention to life's journey and the lessons it holds for us in each moment, we can learn to feel our way around the course of the stream before diving in. These precious lessons are everywhere. Look for them and then consciously acknowledge them. From experience, I know that the jet stream will deny us access or spit us right back out if our own energy fields are not properly prepared!

The following guidelines can help you formulate a strategy for strengthening yourself, while identifying and having fun with the energetic flows in your life.

Keep your physical body healthy by eating and moving consciously. Choose naturally healthy foods that hold nutritional life force while avoiding the many processed foods available today. Before ingesting foods, ask yourself: Does my body want it or does my mouth want it? Learn to listen to the answer to this body-centered question and then to respect the answer—to respect yourself. It does not take much to listen for the response. The body must work incredibly hard to find nutrition in processed foods and even harder to metabolize them. Keep it simple! Learn about Integral Somatology (see Chapter 4, Servaas Mes), using conscious movement to balance the communication between the muscles and the central nervous system. A healthy body invites the being to be comfortable and at home in it.

Keep your energetic body balanced and vital. Meditation, prayer, stillness, mindfulness practice—try them all and learn which works best for you. Use them to connect with the powers that flow into your energy body from both the heavens and the earth. Find a copy of Donna Eden's *Energy Medicine* book and incorporate her powerful Daily Routine throughout the day to keep your energies humming. It works!

Live your life in present time. Many of us spend our days worrying about the future or focusing on the past. This keeps us from truly being, and from truly receiving the miracle of healing and creating healthy realities.

Follow your intuitive attractions regardless of mental judgments. Pay attention! Begin to look for clues, leads, prompts, and information on a gut level to inform your forward movement. This may appear as an insatiable hunger for education in fields that are new to you, for travel to and exploration of new places, or the appearance of unique opportunities or individuals in your life. Realize that everyone is your teacher!

Learn to focus on your intention. Become clear about what you would like to manifest or what you would like to learn. Allow the universe to guide you through the process, rather than becoming fixed on the route yourself. We can only guide another down the path as far as we have been ourselves. The universe, however, has been — is — everywhere, everyone, and everything! This truth allows us to let go of our attachments and surrender the ego to the adventure. Let yourself be supported and surprised beyond your wildest dreams! Own your clear intention as if it were a "done deal." Remember, the universe will match wanting with wanting. Move your attention from wanting to having, but always for the highest good of everyone involved.

Embrace gratitude as a lifestyle. Every breath, each heartbeat, the intricate perfection of our cellular functions are but a few aspects of life to be grateful for. They are often taken for granted, however, until they cease to serve us fully! Let the essence of gratitude become a beautiful force that intrigues, heals, and nourishes your body through all of your multidimensional senses. Extend this deep gratitude to the world. Step outside of your comfort zone to practice compassion with those who inhabit this world with you. Ask yourself how you can help. Even the simple gift of making eye contact with others is immeasurable in our society today.

Have fun with your journey in the universal jet stream! A sense of playfulness goes a very long way toward making the trip in this lifetime a bit better! Laughter illuminates the spirit and, in turn, illuminates the body. Some people have a glow that emanates from the inside out. It is unmistakable. These are the beings that we all benefit from being with! Be aware that energy — whether negative or positive — transfers from person to person. Keep it positive. Surround yourself with people who respect you and treat you well. Then do the same for others. It will help you to find your inner smile. Pass that smile on! It truly is contagious.

You have an inner compass. Use it! Use this chapter and the aforementioned tips to begin to tune in to the subtle guidance that is always available to you. You will soon be able to fine-tune your personal navigational skills to access your inner compass, leading you to the peak experience of riding the flow of the tides that naturally lead to an ever-deepening sense of your divine purpose on this planet.

LARRY DOSSEY

Optimism

It troubles me to recall him even now, many years later — the fifty-year-old attorney who gave me my most painful lesson in the value of optimism and what happens when it fades away. He was at the peak of his career, father of three, athletic, a picture of health. His only concern was a minor stomachache that had come and gone for a couple of weeks. Even though his physical examination was normal, he insisted on an abdominal scan just to be sure nothing was wrong. Although I thought this was overkill, I went along. To my surprise, the scan showed a mass in the pancreas the radiologist said was probably cancer. I discussed the situation with him and proposed a diagnostic workup, including the possibility of eventual abdominal surgery. "No surgery!" he declared emphatically. "It's worthless. Nobody survives cancer of the pancreas." I pointed out that he was mistaken. Although the statistics are not favorable, people do survive this disease. In any case, we weren't sure of the diagnosis and further tests were needed to confirm it.

He consented to be hospitalized that very day, but a light went out in him. He seemed terrified, and nothing I could say would comfort him. He began to stare straight ahead, refusing to speak to me or the nurses. When I made rounds that evening, he lay silent and rigid in bed with clenched jaws and furrowed brow. Even when I informed him that his preliminary blood tests were normal, he didn't seem to care. In his mind he was a condemned man going to the gallows. I

Larry Dossey, MD, is a physician of internal medicine. He was a battalion surgeon in Vietnam, and chief of staff at Medical City Dallas Hospital. He has lectured all over the world, including the Mayo Clinic, Harvard, Johns Hopkins, and Cornell. Among his many books are *Prayer Is Good Medicine* (HarperOne, 1997) and *The Extraordinary Healing Power of Ordinary Things* (Three Rivers, 2007). The first respected writer to make a serious scientific case for nonlocal consciousness, Larry Dossey is the editor of *Explore* journal and former editor of *Alternative Therapies in Health and Medicine*. Photo by Athi Mara Magadi.

resolved that if his behavior did not change by morning, I would ask a psychiatrist to consult on his case. I didn't get the chance. That night the nurse found him dead in bed.

His was a "hex death," widely recognized in premodern cultures, in which a previously healthy individual dies shortly after being cursed. The curse—in this case, his certainty that he had a fatal illness— removes all optimism and hope, and substitutes the inevitability of death.[1]

Optimism is the tendency to believe, expect, or hope that things will turn out well. Debates have raged over the past few years about whether it affects our health and the course of specific diseases. I find these arguments tedious, because I believe evidence of the healing power of optimism is in plain sight. These effects are most obvious when they vary from day to day, like shifting winds. In the 1950s, Dr. Bruno Klopfer reported such an example that involved a patient he was treating for advanced lymphoma. The man had large tumors throughout his body and fluid in his chest, and was terminal. Klopfer was so convinced that he would die within two weeks that all medical therapy except oxygen had been discontinued. In a last-ditch effort he gave the man a single injection of Krebiozen, an experimental drug later said to be worthless. Klopfer describes the results:

> What a surprise was in store for me! I had left him febrile, gasping for air, completely bedridden. Now, here he was, walking around the ward, chatting happily with the nurses, and spreading his message of good cheer to anyone who would listen.... The tumor masses had melted like snow balls on a hot stove, and in only these few days they were half their original size! This is, of course, far more rapid regression than the most radiosensitive tumor could display under heavy x-ray given every day.... And he had no other treatment outside of the single useless "shot."

Within ten days the man was practically free of disease. He began to fly his private airplane again. His improvement lasted for two months, until reports cropped up denouncing Krebiozen. When he read them, the man appeared cursed, and his attitude and medical condition quickly returned to a terminal state. At this point Klopfer urged the man to ignore the negative news reports because a "new super-refined, double-strength product" was now available—a complete fabrication—and injected him with sterile water. The man's response this time was even more dramatic than initially, and he resumed his normal activities for another two months. But his improvement ended when the American Medical Association released a report stating that nationwide tests had proved Krebiozen useless in the treatment of cancer. A few days after reading this statement, he was admitted to the hospital, and two days following admission he died.[2]

If optimism can make such dramatic differences, you'd think we physicians would do everything in our power to increase it in our patients, but sometimes we seem hell-bent on depriving them of it. Some of these instances are so outrageous they are almost funny.

Andrew Weil, MD, who is director of the program in integrative medicine at the University of Arizona in Tucson, often sees patients for a second opinion.[3] "You wouldn't believe what those doctors did to me," one woman related. "The head neurologist took me into his office and told me I had multiple sclerosis. He let that sink in; then he went out of the room and returned with a wheelchair. Then he told me to sit in it. I said, 'Why should I sit in your wheelchair?' He said I was to buy a wheelchair and sit in it for an hour a day to 'practice' for when I would be totally disabled. Can you imagine?"

In his book *The Lost Art of Healing*, Harvard cardiologist Bernard Lown gives examples of "words that maim" by depriving patients of optimism and hope. They include, "You are living on borrowed time," "You are going downhill fast," "The next heartbeat may be your last," "You can have a heart attack or worse any minute," "The... angel of death...is shadowing you," "You are a walking time bomb," "I'm frightened just thinking about your [coronary] anatomy," and "Surgery should be done immediately, preferably yesterday."[4] To these medical hexes, Weil adds a few more: "They said there was nothing more they could do for me," "They told me it would only get worse," "They told me I would just have to live with it," and "They said I'd be dead in six months."[5]

Why do we physicians find it so difficult to accord optimism a role in health? Why is it so hard for us to be optimistic? You might think we'd be positively euphoric, because we have more potent tools in our black bags than ever before, and the human lifespan is at an all-time high. Why aren't we joyful? The fact is, physicians are trained to be realists, not optimists, and our realism often shades into pessimism. The specter of death hangs over every clinical encounter, a shadow that never goes away no matter how powerful our therapies become. We know that all our treatments will eventually fail and the patient will die; never has there been an exception. Thus the beginning assumption of medicine is tragedy. No other profession rests on such a morbid foundational belief. This is why it is so natural for a physician to be a pessimist, and why optimism is the hard thing.

Pessimism dominates some physicians and colors everything they do. I've known physicians who actually cultivate cynicism and take pride in a morose, gloomy personal style. Some wear their pessimism as a badge of honor. This often involves what's called "hanging crepe" — black crepe, as at a funeral — in which the physician emphasizes the worst possible outcome of any situation. If the prophecy comes true, the physician is wise; if not, he is a hero, having rescued his patient from his dire predictions.

It is unethical, we are taught, to paint a rosy future for a patient who is facing a grave health challenge when we know the outcome is likely to be the opposite. The problem, however, is that the physicians realism can trigger disastrous results. Consider medical prognosis. When a physician tells a patient she has a fifty percent chance of *living* twelve months, the patient is likely to interpret this as a fifty percent chance of *dying* by the end of a year. The patient, failing to understand that the doctor is simply making a calculated guess, often converts the statistical prediction into a death sentence by dying on schedule.

But it is never only a matter of the words that a physician uses to deliver bad news, it's also how they are conveyed. Some physicians are able to express bad news with such compassion that the sense of impending tragedy is annulled. How do they do it? The way physicians always have — through deep empathy and caring for those they serve. They convey a sense of love and oneness with their patient, as if to say, "Together we will do our best. No matter what happens, I am with you every step of the way; you will never be alone."

If profound pessimism can kill, why is it so widespread? Why would evolution have permitted it to persist? What purpose would pessimism have served? "The benefits of pessimism," suggests psychologist Martin E. P. Seligman, former president of the American Psychological Association and author of *Learned Optimism,* "may have arisen during our recent evolutionary history. We are animals of the Pleistocene, the epoch of the ice ages. Our emotional makeup has most recently been shaped by one hundred thousand years of climatic catastrophe: waves of cold and heat; drought and flood; plenty and sudden famine. Those of our ancestors who survived the Pleistocene may have done so because they had the capacity to worry incessantly about the future, to see sunny days as mere prelude to a harsh winter, to brood. We have inherited these ancestors' brains and therefore their capacity to see the cloud rather than the silver lining."[6]

The survival value of pessimism may date from the era when humans descended from treetops onto the savannas of Africa. These open grasslands were the home of the great stalking cats and were dangerous places. Pessimism would have lent an edge in the struggle to survive — not pessimism that overwhelmed and drove our ancestors back into the safety of the forests, but enough to guarantee wariness and survival.

But perhaps we should not concede too much to pessimism. It is difficult to imagine how *Homo sapiens* could have advanced from savage to barbarian to civilization without a sense that things might be better. How could we have journeyed from caves to castles, from skins to silks, from dominance to democracy, without optimism? Without the beckoning light of a brighter future, it would have been easy to quit in the early days and settle for the status quo. Something kept us going toward a dawn not fully glimpsed, and optimism is as good a name as any for this indwelling itch.

Ultimate Optimism

It's easy to be optimistic about optimism these days. Research shows that optimists on average get sick less often and live longer than pessimists. The immune system seems to be stronger in optimists, and the cardiovascular system more stable. Optimists are the go-getters, achievers, and leaders who are held high in public esteem. Optimists are generally likable; they pump others up, and people enjoy their company more than that of pessimists. There is a new field, positive psychology, that stresses the value of optimism. Optimism is so hot it recently made the cover of *Time* magazine.[7]

A sense of control is largely a belief one can either reject or adopt and cultivate. As Blair Justice, professor of psychology at the School of Public Health, University of Texas-Houston, says in his admirable survey of the mind-body field, *Who Gets Sick: How Beliefs, Moods, and Thoughts Affect Your Health*, "Cognitive control stems from the belief that we can affect the hurtful impact...of a situation by how we look at the problem. It means that by choosing to regard losses, hurts, frustrations and stressful life changes with less gloom and doom and not as the end of the world, we control their power to damage us."[8]

In study after study, people who were most resistant to physical and mental illness used a style of coping in which they viewed their situation with less pessimism. This led to taking action, where possible, to change the external problem. Then the individuals usually palliated the physical and mental effects of the stress through exercise, relaxation training, or some other healthy behavior.[9]

"Optimistic appraisal" is simply a good attitude or upbeat approach to a given situation. Lawrence Hinkle and his colleagues at New York Hospital-Cornell Medical Center followed several populations over twenty years, looking for evidence that optimistic appraisal makes a difference in health.[10] One group was a hundred Chinese immigrants who were marooned in the United States because of political unrest in their homeland. Their lives were in upheaval — uncertain about their fate and that of their families back home, and how they would survive economically. Those who remained healthy — and many did — were distinguished by how they viewed their difficulties. They saw their past and present as difficult but also interesting, challenging, and relatively satisfying. Those who got sick more often took a different view, seeing their situation as threatening, frustrating, and demanding.[11]

Hinkle and his coworkers also found that in trying circumstances there is another way to promote good health that does not involve optimism. If one insulates oneself emotionally, invests little in life, and builds walls to keep others out, the incidence of illness is also reduced.[12] But there is a downside to this approach. As Justice says in an understatement, "[O]ur social health will suffer and our relations with others will have no depth."[13]

Cardiologist Daniel B. Mark, of Duke University School of Medicine, followed the progress of 1,719 men and women after cardiac catheterization. After one year, 12 percent of people who were initially pessimistic about their health had died, compared to only 5 percent of the optimists. Dr. Nancy Frasure-Smith, of the Montreal Heart Institute, found that heart patients who scored high on pessimism were eight times more likely than optimists to die over the course of eighteen months. Dr. Geoffrey Reed, of the University of California-Los Angeles, showed that fatalism, optimism's polar opposite, and the loss of friends predicted negative outcomes in patients with HIV disease.[14]

How does optimism actually foster longer and healthier lives? Seligman suggests four ways.[15] First, the brain registers the experience of optimism and reaches down via humoral, chemical, and nerve pathways to affect cellular function throughout the body, including the cardiac, immune, and other systems. Second, because optimism is correlated with motivation and taking action, optimistic people are more likely to *want* to be healthy and to believe they *can* be healthy. This makes it more likely that they will follow healthy regimens and medical advice. Third, optimists experience fewer noxious events in their lives than pessimists, including fewer threats to their health, because their sense of control assures them that they can make a difference in what happens. In contrast, pessimists often seem to roll out a red carpet for chaos, convinced that what they do doesn't matter. Finally, optimists enjoy greater social support than pessimists. And evidence shows that even mild social interaction is a buffer against illness.[16]

Cultivating Optimism

Optimism is not a given. It can fluctuate, like our body weight, and can be learned. In his book *Learned Optimism,* psychologist Seligman shows how.[17]

It's a matter of ABC, Seligman explains. When we encounter Adversity, we begin to think about it. Over time, these thoughts ossify into Beliefs, which can become so habitual they are unconscious. Our beliefs about adverse situations have Consequences, causing us to respond either optimistically or pessimistically.

Seligman teaches people to become aware of their habitual, automatic behaviors and to substitute more adaptive, optimistic responses. Here's a typical exercise. Allow yourself to vividly imagine an everyday adversity, "A"—someone has squeezed into the parking space you were eyeing. Next, you identify the thoughts and beliefs, "B," that you have about this situation. You then imagine the consequences, "C," of these beliefs, such as honking your horn, shaking your fist, or yelling. Seligman adds a "D" and "E": Disputation, in which you engage in self-dialogue or analysis of the situation (I don't own the parking spot; others are available); and Energization, in which you seek an optimistic perspective (the driver of the other car was elderly; she needed the parking spot more than I do; giving it up is an act of kindness; I feel better having done it). Seligman advocates keeping a journal of ABCDE exercises to help jostle the mind out of habitual, pessimistic responses.

These methods have been used in children, college students, and adults. They appear capable of generating not only optimism, but positive physical changes as well. In patients with cancer, for example, sharp increases in immune function have been observed in participants using these techniques.[18, 19]

Pessimists often resist methods like these because they sound gimmicky, and because they disdain efforts by optimists to convert them. Pessimists are often convinced that they "see the world aright," as the cantankerous pessimist Ambrose Bierce put it; why should they trade in their perspective for rose-colored glasses? Perhaps the most concrete reason is that optimists, research shows, get sick less often and live longer than pessimists, and that optimists are happier.

1. Halifax-Grof, J. "Hex death," in *Parapsychology and Anthropology: Proceedings of an International Conference Held in London, August 29 – 31, 1973.* Allan Angoff and Diana Barth, eds. (New York: Parapsychology Foundation, 1974), 59 – 79.

2. Klopfer, B. Psychological variables in human cancer. *Journal of Projective Techniques.* 1957; 21: 331-340.

3. Weil, A. *Spontaneous Healing* (New York: Alfred A. Knopf, 1995), 63-64.

4. Lown, B. *The Lost Art of Healing* (New York: Houghton-Mifflin, 1996), 65.

5. Weil, A. op. cit., 61.

6. Seligman, M.E.P. *Learned Optimism* (New York: Alfred A. Knopf, 1991),

III.

7. The science of happiness: why optimists live longer. *Time,* January 17, 2005. Front cover

8. Justice, B. *Who Gets Sick: How Beliefs, Moods, and Thoughts Affect Your Health* (Houston: Peak Press, 2000), 63.

9. Ibid., 64.

10. Hinkle, L.E., Wolff, H.G. Health and the social environment: Experimental investigations, in Leighton, A.H., Clausen, J.A., and Wilson, R.N., eds. *Explorations in Social Psychiatry* (New York: Basic Books, 1957) 105-132. See also Hinkle, L.E., Christenson, W.N., Kane, F.D., et al. An investigation of the relation between life experience, personality characteristics, and general susceptibility to illness. *Psychosomatic Medicine.* 1958; 20(4): 278-295.

11. Hinkle, L.E., Wolff, H.G. Ecological investigations of the relationship between illness, life experience and the social environment. *Annals of Internal Medicine.* 1958; 29: 1373-1388.

12. Hinkle, L.E. Studies of human ecology in relation to health and behavior. *BioScience.* August 1965; 517-520.

13. Justice, B., op. cit., 67.

14. These studies are reviewed in Dreher, H. *Mind-Body Unity: A New Vision for Mind-Body Science and Medicine* (Baltimore: The Johns Hopkins University Press, 2003), 59-60.

15. Seligman, M.E.P., op. cit., 172-174.

16. Seligman, M.E.P., op. cit., 174.

17. Seligman, M.E.P., op. cit., 205-234.

18. Ibid, 182-184.

19. Ibid, ix.

PART THREE

Shifting Your Energy Field

DONNA EDEN

Dancing With the Five Rhythms of Nature

We are, Dianne Connelly observes, "a replica of the universe passing from season to season in a natural unending season of life." By carefully observing the Earth's seasons, the Chinese sages gained penetrating insights into the way nature conducts her business. In the seasons of nature they found analogies for understanding the growth and cycles of all things under heaven. In addition to the four seasons of winter, spring, summer, and autumn, the transition times between seasons were collectively treated as a separate season. These periods of transition were originally thought of as occurring for about two weeks four times each year, with one of the solstices or equinoxes at their midpoints. In recent centuries, however, the four transition periods have been abbreviated into a single season, placed between summer and autumn, and compared with Indian summer. Indian summer prolongs the summer, as if trying to hold off the death that inevitably accompanies autumn.

The name of the Chinese system is often translated in the West as "the five elements" because the early pictograms depicted the familiar, concrete, and observable — the five elements of water, wood, fire, earth, and metal. But the system has always concentrated on processes within nature, not her static forms (the literal translation is "the five walks" or "the five moves") — and this dynamic emphasis will be ours as well. Thus, the element of water corresponds with the season of winter, wood with spring, fire with summer, earth with the time of the solstice or equinox, and metal with autumn.

Donna Eden is widely recognized for her inborn ability to literally see the body's energies, to accurately determine the causes of physical and psychological problems based on the state of those energies, and to devise highly effective treatments. She has treated over 10,000 clients individually and has taught hundreds of classes, speaking to packed houses throughout the United States, Europe, Australia, New Zealand, and South America. She offers a certification course in Eden Energy Medicine, and is the author of *Energy Medicine* (Tarcher, 1999) and the forthcoming *Energy Medicine for Women* (Tarcher, 2008).

Each person is characterized by one of these elements or seasons, or a specific combination of them. In the human life cycle, we also travel through periods or phases that are analogous to the seasons of nature in tempo, intensity, and function, each potentially lasting for years. I find the language of the seasons to be wonderfully descriptive of the distinct rhythm that vibrates throughout the entire energy body at any moment in time. Each season has its own rhythm. I think of people in terms of the energy of the seasons, and I speak in terms of the rhythm of summer or the rhythm of autumn when describing a person's "element."

While each of us contains all five seasons, one season or a particular combination of two or three will blend themselves into your personal rhythm. You will vibrate more naturally to people, environments, and activities whose rhythm corresponds with your own. Those that do not will be more challenging for you, but potentially more enriching as their influence expands you.

Understanding the Rhythms that Affect You

Of the many systems that sort people into one category or another, the five-rhythms approach has the advantage of being grounded in the person's core bioenergies. At the same time, it tells you a great deal about that individual's health challenges, personality, and spiritual journey. When I look at a person's energy field, it is characterized by a distinct vibration that corresponds precisely with at least one of the elements described by the ancient Chinese physicians. I believe I am seeing what they saw. For instance, when I look at someone whom the Chinese would call a winter or water element person (the derivation of the word "winter" is "to make wet,") the energy literally has a watery, languid, rolling quality, and this manifests in the way the person walks and talks. If the person is well balanced, the rhythm is smooth and flowing, and it runs deep.

You will see that each rhythm has certain strengths and certain vulnerabilities. Many factors determine whether you will manifest the best or the worst qualities of your basic rhythm. For instance, your way of living is related to the way your family and early social environment supported or failed to support that rhythm. Children whose primary rhythm is appropriately recognized and supported grow into adults who express that rhythm in its more positive form. The qualities of a child's primary rhythm may, however, be so prized and reinforced that the child not only learns that rhythm but overdevelops it to the point that little is learned of the other rhythms and there is no balance. If, on the other hand, the qualities inherent in the primary rhythm are punished or bring disapproval, the child may grow up alienated from his or her core rhythm.

While most people embody a combination of two or three rhythms, I will describe each of the types in its unmixed form in order to get you thinking about your own personal rhythm.

The Rhythm of Winter: Embryonic Possibility. Winter's rhythm embodies the seed, the embryo, potential. The time of long nights and little light, winter embodies the promise of the future. While life appears to have ceased, it is growing decisively under the ground, waiting to burst forth.

Winter people, when in their strength, embody a fresh spirit that is infused with childlike enthusiasm because their season is about beginnings. They know how to envision a project and joyfully get it under way. When they feel safe, they utterly trust their surroundings, and they laugh and play with the spontaneity of a baby. Their energies may be limited, since their season has little sun, but like a hibernating polar bear, they are able to retreat into themselves and regenerate. They are deeply reflective about the meaning of life and the direction it should take.

As with each of the rhythms, the winter person's potential weaknesses are the polarity of these strengths. The playful energy of good beginnings is not so well suited for going the full distance of completion. They may have little sense of direction or motivation for the long haul. Just as special care and protection are required to survive in winter, people moved by winter's rhythm often need and demand special attention, so they are particularly vulnerable to narcissism. Rooted in nature's embryonic time, there is a babylike quality to this rhythm. Winter people may be unable to recognize how they are affecting others, focusing only on what others are doing to them. They can have difficulty feeling loved unless love is showered upon them. Needing the mother's succor like the seed needs the unfailing sustenance of the earth, winters who feel unloved tend to retreat within, becoming cold, isolated, and paranoid. Your first cycle of winter's rhythm extends from conception through about eighteen months. But if stress or trauma prevented you from sufficiently garnering its lessons, its issues can become fixated into a lifelong pattern where you behave as if you are the center of the world, for it is possible to become arrested while moving through any of the rhythms.

The talk of a winter person is a slow, flowing kind of groan from deep within. The walk is unhurried and elegant, like a rolling wave, almost a swagger, knees slightly bent so the body seems more aligned with the ground. The sustaining mental state is courage. Under stress, courage may become fear, which is the stress emotion of a winter person. Because the future is hard to see from winter's embryonic shadows, winter people are afraid to move forth, afraid to make a commitment. They reflect deeply, motivated by their fear of what is to come. In the wild, a newborn animal is utterly vulnerable and must quickly learn to distinguish between what is dangerous and what is safe. During your first eighteen months, your first cycle of winter's rhythm, fear alerted you to that which was dangerous. Through fear you learned to establish boundaries. You defined a zone of safety. Dangers, both real and imagined, can tend to paralyze a winter's rhythm, making it even more immobile, more hidden, more pulled toward hibernation. With maturity, however, a winter's fear becomes a wise and discerning caution.

The Rhythm of Spring: New Growth. The energy of a spring or wood element person is reminiscent of the seedling you might see bursting forth through a rock in the springtime. It is solid within its space. The rhythm is staccato yet insistent, like a marching soldier.

Spring's rhythm embodies the power and insistence of new life. Earth becomes warm, and the hours of light begin to outnumber the hours of darkness. Life bursts forth as the landscape explodes with color and exuberance. Spring is assertive—life pushes onward.

Spring people take a strong stand. They unabashedly claim their space, as if proudly announcing, like a budding rose, "I am a force to be reckoned with." Their strength is that their vision is potent, seeing inequities and assembling forces for justice and truth. Their vision of truth and wholeness inspires others. They see the truth. They see the way. They can marshall their intellect and their energies into a plan. They are sure of themselves and shine in a crisis. Their sense of timing cuts to the quick. Their ability to assert themselves and organize efforts is characterized by sound goals, good judgment, and wise decisions.

The spring person's self-confidence is at risk of becoming arrogance; assertiveness can become inflexible, self-indulgent, and opinionated. They may hold a narrow and rigid vision that causes them to harshly judge those who do not subscribe to their truth or follow their direction. They may righteously hold to this position and become easily and vocally frustrated about the beliefs and actions of others. Or they may lose their vision and be left disorganized, hopeless, and despairing.

The talk of a spring person is choppy and syncopated, almost a shout. The walk is also choppy, hitting the ground decisively, with clear concise movements, like percussion. The sustaining mental state is assertiveness. The stress emotion is anger. In nature, the energy that has been accumulating beneath the ground in winter explodes forth above the earth in spring. Ideas or opinions may take root within a person, growing and expanding until they ferociously burst forth. During the "terrible twos," your first cycle of spring's rhythm, you are exploring, expanding, moving outward, and whoever or whatever blocks this energy will know your fury. If spring is your primary rhythm, your disposition is to push forth. Your roots are firm, your territory is well marked, your purpose is strong. You meet obstacles decisively. If they do not give way, your anger is quick and forceful. With maturity, however, a spring's anger becomes a wise and healthy determination.

The Rhythm of Summer: Fulfillment. The energy of a summer or fire element person blazes up and out, creating the impression that the person is everywhere at once. Like wildfire, which jumps ravines and spreads in every direction, its rhythm is rapid, random, and rising.

Summer's rhythm embodies fruition. Earth becomes warm and the days long. New light bursts forth in the early morning. The fruit on the tree has matured, ripe and luscious. Summer holds the radiance and joy of youth in all its glory. It gives delight in the richness of the moment.

Summer people move from their heart, open and vulnerable. Their strength is that they are warm, empathic, joyful, and exuberant. With passion and radiance, they are able to draw out the positive and the hopeful in others, co mmunicate with them in their uniqueness, and elicit cooperation. With charisma and a grasp of the whole picture, they ignite the actions of others with insight, compassion, and clarity. In recognizing what is possible, they are the magicians and catalysts who help others believe in themselves, free themselves of self-imposed limitations, and move with confidence to a better future.

Summer people may become junkies for love, for the "high" — whether through parties, drugs, sex, or spirituality. They may go into a panic of frenzied activity, trying to make everyone happy. They often have difficulty with discernment and setting priorities. They may give from their hearts until they have no more to give. Summer people often burn themselves out, overcommitted and exhausted. They are so drawn to the bright side of life that they may not register the dark, the negative, or the dangerous. To those who look to them for leadership, their optimism and enthusiasm may set up expectations that were never meant and are rarely met.

You can hear laughter in the talk of a summer person. The walk is like a skip, with an up and down movement, arms rising and falling like flames. The sustaining mental state is infused with joy and passion, which under stress can escalate into panic or deteriorate into hysteria. In summer, the light is dazzling, the fruit abundant, and the fish are hopping. Excess is all around. During adolescence, your first cycle of summer's rhythm, you lived for thrill and exhilaration.

Joys and sorrows were laced with passion, taken to excess. If you are a summer person, you want to enjoy, not strive. The present is all that matters, and as you bask in its warmth, you radiate your excitement. Others may find your Pollyanna optimism either contagious or irritating. With maturity, a summer's nondiscerning enthusiasm, passion, or infatuation become discerning love and involvement.

The Rhythm of Solstice/Equinox or Indian Summer: Transition. The energy of a solstice/equinox or earth element person, who is oriented toward the transitions from one season to the next, has a centering, side-to-side roll. The rhythm sways, as if the person is moving to the rhythm of Earth herself.

The solstices and equinoxes embody the rhythm of transition. As the midpoint between two seasons, the time of transition is governed by a balance between opposing forces, holding both the past and the future in the present moment. Most familiar as Indian summer, its colors are bright and glorious, a last burst of the waning season. This rhythm creates stability amid transition, assimilates change, and coordinates between the season that is ending and the season that is arriving.

Solstice/equinox people know about holding steady. Like the balance scales that are the symbol for justice, they embody fairness. At the center of the cyclone, their strength is to stay stable while nurturing the changes happening around them. Like a midwife or Earth Mother, they bring support, compassion, and confidence to times of transition. They hold the center, staying in the present moment as they add their tranquil touch to life's changes. Keeping a fresh perspective as the old order passes, they pave the way for stable change, rarely seeming rushed or stressed. Because they exude compassion, people feel safe with them. They bring equilibrium to chaos, peace to the threatened, and shelter to the displaced.

With a compulsion to help others stay in a comfort zone, solstice/equinox people may hinder another's transitions. This aversion to rocking the boat, combined with their characteristic desire to support the other, may also lead to obsessive worry. Or they may involve themselves in a manner that stunts the other's growth, babying and overprotecting. "The helping hand strikes again" is the epitaph of a solstice/equinox person whose life has lost its balance. In their joy at helping others flourish, they may neglect to give enough attention to their own growth. Skilled at helping others integrate lessons and experiences, they may have a harder time integrating their own. Knowing bone-deep that loss is an inevitable part of transition, they may anticipate it and try to prevent it, staying with a bad marriage or an unfulfilling job. And so they may turn their strongest suit into a losing hand by interfering with the cycle of necessary change. Also, because they do not have a designated season of their own, solstice/equinox people may live with heartrending questions always in the background, such as: "Where is time for me? When will my season come?"

The talk of a solstice/equinox person has a singing quality, as when you are talking to a baby. The walk has a relaxed, lyrical manner, a slow, rhythmic side-to-side sway, lightfooted as a deer. The sustaining mental state is compassion. The stress emotion is a codependent sympathy. In moving from one season to the next, the two seasons come into a resonance, a sympathy, as one transforms into the other. In times of transition, the ability to provide nurturing is no less than a survival tool, and no one does this better than the solstice/equinox person, whose archetype is the Earth Mother. In your own transitions, you must activate that archetype within yourself, supporting yourself through endings and new beginnings. The harvest of the season that is passing must be incorporated into the season that is coming. Solstice/equinox people instinctually help others in transition to transform past mistakes into lessons for the future. A transition person's generosity may be martyrish; with maturity, however, exaggerated sympathy ripens into a wise and balanced compassion.

The Rhythm of Autumn: Ending. The energy of an autumn or metal element person seems to be stretched between the heavens and Earth. Like a tall tree that has lost its leaves, the energies seem restrained yet serene, barren yet dignified. The rhythm glides like a ballet dancer—elongated, still, and graceful.

Autumn's rhythm embodies completion. Each day turns to night earlier than the last. The warmth fades. Yet autumn embodies the peace of completion, the meaning found in attainment, and faith that dying to the old makes way for the new. The leaves fall to earth, fertilizing the next cycle. This rhythm garners the meaning of the cycle that is coming to an end, evaluates what has been useful and what has not, and eliminates all that is not valuable so as to bring about a worthy completion.

Autumn people have the ability to mine truths out of their experiences and apply those truths. Living in the last cycle, there is an urge toward perfection, high achievements, and model results. Autumn people can see what needs to happen and are highly motivated to make it happen. Out of this vision of perfection grow standards of excellence that are true and pure, concerned with a higher good, and inspiring to others. That which is impure—whether ideas, behavior, or systems—is eliminated. As the last season of the cycle, autumn carries a sadness, and those whose rhythm vibrates with autumn carry a simpatico with the world's grief. From this affinity with sadness grows kindness, honesty, and integrity. They have a capacity to express themselves clearly, and they receive well the ideas and inspiration of others, for they have a gift for discerning the pure from the impure. They have an urgency to find meaning and serenity in what has been, for theirs is the final cycle. Forgive them their persistence. It is their rhythm.

Autumn people are vulnerable to becoming overly serious or sinking into depression. Shunning fun and lacking pleasure, they may find their energies becoming restrained and dry, like a tree without leaves. They may appear dreary and aloof. Living always in the energy of the final cycle, they may have difficulty with time, trying to cram more into each day than it can contain. Oriented toward the future, they see life through the lens of death, and they may become trapped in depression or in the pressure to reach perfection before the last grains of sand have emptied from the hourglass. Their ability to make pure judgments may be clouded by this despair or perfectionism, and their standards may be tarnished by hopelessness or inflated through unrealistic assessments. Either may paralyze them so that they become unable to let go into change, obsessively evaluating and reevaluating to the point of exhaustion, lacking the capacity to complete a cycle of their lives, again failing to reap the benefits of their strongest suit.

Elisabeth Kübler-Ross observed that the best way to prepare for your eventual dying is to meet with consciousness the "little deaths" life continually provides. When you are actually in the process of dying, you will be in autumn's rhythm. Each cycle of completion, each "little death," each autumn in your own life's flow is an opportunity to glean the lessons of the cycle that is ending, to create a meaningful completion, and to open the way for whatever is next to come. Each cycle trains you for all the autumns yet to be. So it was when you had to die to adolescence to be reborn into adulthood. So it is when your own children leave the nest. So it will be when your body comes to its final season.

The talk of an autumn person has a weeping sound. The walk is tall, straight, and subdued, gliding with head high and gaze forward. The sustaining mental state is reflectiveness. The stress emotion is grief. As the leaves fall and the wildflowers die, loss is in the air. The cycle draws to its close. When you come to the close of a cycle in your own life, there may be sadness for opportunities missed and for what must be left behind. If autumn is your primary rhythm, you are oriented toward completions, toward discerning what has been worthy and meaningful. There is a heaviness in these tasks, and you know the grief of what might have been but was not to be. With maturity, however, an autumn's grief transforms into an identification with the whole cycle, at peace with life, at peace with death.

From these descriptions, you may recognize within yourself one, two, or three of these clusters of traits. Fully understanding your rhythm and all its implications is a lifelong process. The system is that basic and that profound. If you understand your own primary rhythm and its dynamics, you will know a great deal about your needs and your blind spots in all areas of your life, from your choice of a mate to your vulnerabilities for illness. Your primary rhythm manifests itself in the way you look, walk, sound, feel, act, and react. If you know the primary rhythms of a colleague, client, friend, or family member, you will be able to understand that person's behavior with greater insight and empathy.

If you do just ONE energy practice every day it would be the 5-Minute Energy Routine.

To order more Eden Energy Medicine Charts and Energy Medicine tools see www.TitanyaSpirit.com.

DAVID FEINSTEIN

Mobilizing Your Body's Energies

Energy is not just the force that causes your heart to beat, your lungs to breathe, and your cells to metabolize nutrients. It is the intelligence that orchestrates millions of such biological actions every second. Though the body's energy intelligence generally operates beneath the mind's radar, it dwarfs the capacities of the mind in its ability to keep you breathing and alive. Your body is, in fact, an exquisitely engineered energy-driven, energy-managed machine.[1]

Our energy systems evolved in resonance with our anatomy and our environment over millions of years, but the environment has changed radically since industrialization. We evolved for a world that hasn't existed for centuries. A matter of centuries is but a blink in the evolutionary eye, far too short a period for natural selection to have updated the arrangement, so we adapt to the industrial and postindustrial world with energy software that was designed for living in the wild.

Nonetheless, your energy system strides on as the intelligence that animates millions of processes in your body every second. Each cell emits and responds to electrochemical signals in an unimaginably complex and coordinated dance that keeps you breathing, keeps your heart pumping, your food digesting, your eyes blinking, and your tissue safe when microorganisms invade. Your mind is not required to assist the intelligence of your energy system in accomplishing these feats.

David Feinstein, PhD, a clinical psychologist, is an international leader in the field of Energy Psychology. Author of six books and more than fifty professional papers, he has served on the faculties of the Johns Hopkins University School of Medicine and Antioch College. Among his major works are *The Promise of Energy Psychology* (Tarcher, 2005), coauthored with his wife, Donna Eden, and Gary Craig; and *The Mythic Path* (Energy Psychology Press, 2006). Three of his six books have won national awards, including the *USA Book News'* 2007 Book of the Year award in the Psychology/Mental Health category. More at www.InnerSource.net.

Evolved for a World That No Longer Exists

But the costs of attempting to adapt to an environment for which our bodies did not evolve are seen everywhere. Our immune systems keep us safe by attacking what they do not recognize. Unfortunately, they evolved over millions of years with a finite number of foods and few foreign particles in the air. Now with tens of thousands of artificial chemicals in our food and high concentrations of pollutants in our air, the immune system is on continual alert, a "code orange" emergency response that drains our energy and depletes our life force.

Meanwhile, the unyielding stress of daily life triggers another type of emergency response. We are regularly on the edge of the fight-or-flight response. While this heightened state is one of nature's most brilliant achievements, it is now being called to manage all forms of stress for which it was never designed, from an argument with your spouse or child to a malfunction of your computer. In attempting to adapt to an environment that is biologically unfamiliar, your body's energy intelligence is operating outside its scope of competence. It is required to make unprecedented compromises in applying its time-tested strategies to novel circumstances, and such compromises often have their costs. Energy runs in established patterns, like water cutting a riverbed, so such compromises become habitual.

Keeping you alive is the first priority of your body's energy intelligence, and caution trumps inconvenience in the strategies it uses. Left to is own devices in the modern world, your energy system relies on patterns that are simply not the best possible adaptations to the environment. Chronically marshalling extra amounts of energy for the immune or fight-or-flight response, for instance, because the body treats whatever is unfamiliar as a potential invader, tends to undermine your overall health and vitality. If you are to thrive, your energy habits need your help.

Strengthening the Partnership between the Mind's and Body's Intelligence

We are increasingly required, with our lifestyles so alienated from the natural order, to live in conscious partnership with our body's energy systems if we are to live fully. We need to update our body's energy software so that it is compatible with the world in which we live.

Is it reasonable to hope that we can update biological patterns inherited from our ancestors and "evolve our bodies"? According to the work of Bruce Lipton and other epigenetic biologists, the answer is yes. Epigenetic biology shows that we are not prisoners of our genes. Our genes do not determine our fate in the ways once thought. Epigenetics shows that the environment, including our internal environment, determines which genes are given expression. This, in turn, determines which proteins develop in our cells and how those proteins come together. And that determines not only how our body functions, but our mind as well. Even the brain, once thought to be genetically fixed, is continually changing its own structure and function, even into old age.[2]

More good news is that it is at the level of the body's *energy fields* that these processes originate. Not only is gene expression partially within our control, it can be influenced by working with the body's malleable energy fields. By keeping our energies positive, flowing, and healthy, we establish an environment for optimal gene expression. We bring out the best of our internal resources, mobilizing inner forces that enhance our health, empower our minds, and literally brighten our spirits.

Updating the Body's Energy Software with Energy Medicine and Energy Psychology

The developing field of practice that focuses on updating the body's energy software is called *energy medicine*.[3] Energy medicine is based on the supposition that a person's physical and emotional health reflects the health of the body's energies and energy fields and can be enhanced via interventions into those energies and energy fields.[4] While a fledgling but growing field, the roots of which lie in ancient healing and spiritual traditions, energy medicine is now recognized by the National Institutes of Health (NIH) as one of five established approaches within the area of "complementary and alternative medicine."[5] Psychologists have been applying the principles of energy medicine to psychological issues to overcome emotional problems and further a person's highest potential.

I am a clinical psychologist. My training included the major conventional approaches to psychotherapy, and my internships were in relatively traditional institutions (a county mental health clinic and a department of psychiatry at a major university). The application of the principles of energy medicine to psychological issues is the most exciting and promising innovation I have seen in my thirty-plus years of practice. Called *energy psychology*,[6] its implications for fostering peak vitality are just beginning to be appreciated.

Practitioners of energy medicine and energy psychology witness the power of epigenetics in action every day. By establishing greater vitality and health in the energy fields of their clients, shifts occur at the biological and psychological levels that are believed to be no less than changes in gene expression. This extraordinary claim has yet to be proven, but early evidence is compelling.

Epigenetics in Action

A dramatic illustration of the of dynamics of epigenetics is seen in a study of the long-term effects on health of adverse childhood experiences, conducted by Kaiser Permanente's Department of Preventive Medicine, in collaboration with the U.S. Centers for Disease Control and Prevention (CDC). The researchers collected information about detrimental formative events in the histories of 17,421 adults and scored them from 0 to 8 in terms of the presence or absence of eight categories of "adverse childhood experiences" (ACE Score). These categories of abuse or household dysfunction included:

1. Experienced recurrent physical abuse
2. experienced recurrent emotional abuse
3. experienced sexual abuse
4. lost one or both biological parents
5. grew up in a household where someone was in prison
6. grew up in a household where the mother was treated violently
7. grew up with a drug user or an alcoholic
8. Grew up in a household where someone was chronically depressed, mentally ill, or suicidal

People who reported having had none of these experiences received a score of 0. People who reported having had five of them received a score of 5. The average age of the subjects at the time of the study was fifty-seven, so the reported experiences might have occurred fifty years earlier or more. The two most important findings from the ACE study are:

1. Adverse childhood experiences are vastly more common than generally recognized or acknowledged.
2. Adverse childhood experiences have a powerful relation to adult health a half-century later.

Many health measures correlated strongly with the ACE Scores. A person with an ACE Score of 4 is, for instance, 390% more likely to have chronic obstructive pulmonary disease than a person with an ACE Score of 0. Of course, many factors are involved, so it is not just a simple cause-effect relationship impacting the person's health. For instance, the higher the ACE Score, the more likely that the person smokes cigarettes or abuses alcohol or other drugs, which unfavorably impacts health. Bottom line for Kaiser, however, is that the relationship between adverse childhood experiences and adult utilization of their medical services was surprisingly strong. ACE Scores correlated with higher incidences of cancer, heart disease, and diabetes, as well as behaviorally induced health disorders such as obesity, fractures, unintended pregnancy, and sexually transmitted diseases. Occupational health and job performance also worsened progressively as the ACE Score increased.

Energy Psychology from an Epigenetic Perspective

Back to epigenetics. Why would early childhood experiences make a person more susceptible to cancer? They don't change the person's genes. The person is still living in the same society and physical environment. While the mechanisms have not yet been scientifically established, they perfectly fit the core premise of epigenetics: Our internal environment determines which genes are given expression, and adverse childhood experiences have a strong and damaging impact on a person's energy field. They tailor the internal environment in a manner that appears to negatively affect gene expression and thus overall health.

The practical implications of these relationships for physical and mental health are enormous. Three predictions about the potential value of energy psychology, which take an epigenetic perspective in building upon the ACE study, include:

1. If physiological and emotional arousal relating to traumatic memories is reduced in people with high ACE scores, these individuals will be less susceptible to future physical illness. It is not the fact of having been exposed to trauma, but the way that trauma has been processed that sets the internal environment and determines susceptibility. Trauma can lead to emotional wounds that are readily reactivated, causing the person to avoid challenging situations and live in anxiety and fear, or it can be processed so the wounds are healed, with the person becoming more robust and more capable of adapting to new challenges.

2. Psychotherapeutic interventions derived from energy psychology can significantly and permanently reduce this

arousal, and do so more rapidly and effectively than other available therapies, even established approaches such as cognitive behavior therapy.

3. These interventions will improve the patient's health as measured by reduced medical system utilization.

These predictions can be tested, and investigators are already conducting studies to determine if energy psychology treatments produce measurable medical improvements.[7] In time, they will demonstrate: 1) that it is not the *fact* of having been exposed to trauma, but the *way* that trauma has been processed that determines susceptibility to illness, and 2) that practical and relatively inexpensive interventions are available for reducing that susceptibility. The economic impact of this recognition, not to mention the reduction of human suffering and increase in personal well-being, could lead to far-reaching changes in our approach to health care.

Energy Psychology and PTSD: Healing from War

These predictions hinge, of course, on the premise that energy psychology can significantly and permanently reduce an individual's arousal response to traumatic memories, and can do so faster and more effectively than other available therapies. At the time of this writing, eleven randomized controlled studies lend support to the efficacy of energy psychology, seven of which were relatively tightly designed, and two of which meet the criteria set by the American Psychological Association's Clinical Psychology Division that would establish energy psychology as an "evidence-based therapy."[8]

But it is in the strong results being observed and reported following natural and human-made disasters that energy psychology has been cutting its teeth. At least three international humanitarian relief organizations have adapted energy psychology as a treatment in their post-disaster missions, and field observations of its effectiveness have come in from the Congo, Guatemala, Indonesia, Kenya, Kosovo, Kuwait, Mexico, Moldavia, Nairobi, Rwanda, South Africa, Tanzania, Thailand, and the United States.[9] Energy psychology may be proving itself to be among the most effective approaches available for reducing hyperactivity in the parts of our brain that govern fight-or-flight, for stress management, and for overcoming a wide range of affect-related disorders.

Thousands of accounts of such results with everyday emotional challenges, as well as more serious ones, are described on one of the major energy psychology websites (www.emofree.com), but few are more dramatic than the reports coming after disaster relief efforts.

For instance, Carl Johnson, a clinical psychologist retired from a career as a posttraumatic stress disorder (PTSD) specialist with the Veteran's Administration (VA) has, for nearly two decades, been traveling to the sites of some of the world's most terrible atrocities and disasters to provide psychological support using energy psychology methods. About a year after NATO put an end to the ethnic cleansing in Kosovo, Johnson found himself in a trailer in a small village where the brutalities had been particularly severe. A local physician who had offered to refer people in his village had posted a sign that treatments for war-related trauma (including nightmares, insomnia, intrusive memories, inability to concentrate) were being offered. Johnson described how, as a line of people formed outside of the trailer, the referring physician told him, with some concern, that everyone in the village was afraid of one of the men waiting outside for treatment. The others in the line had actually positioned themselves as far away from this man as possible.

Johnson asked the physician to invite the man into the trailer. Johnson, whose VA career had seasoned him in working with war veterans, recalled that the man "had a vicious look; he felt dangerous." But he had come for help, so with the physician translating, Johnson asked the man to bring to mind his most difficult memory from the war. Everyone in the village was haunted by traumas of unspeakable proportion: torture, rape, witnessing the massacre of loved ones. As the man brought the trauma to mind, his face tensed and reddened and his breathing quickened. Though he never put his memory into words, the treatment began. Johnson tapped on specific acupoints that he determined to be relevant to the trauma. He then instructed the man, through the interpreter, to do a number of eye movements and other simple physical activities designed to accelerate the process. Then more tapping. Within fifteen minutes, according to Johnson, the man's demeanor had changed completely. His face had relaxed and his breathing normalized. He no longer looked vicious. In fact, he was openly expressing joy and relief. He initiated hugs with both Johnson and the physician. Then, still grinning, he abruptly walked outside, jumped into his car, and roared away, as everyone watched perplexed.

The man's wife was also in the group waiting for treatment. In addition to the suffering she had faced during the war, she had become a victim of her husband's rage. The traumas she identified also responded rapidly to the tapping treatment. About the time her treatment was completed, her husband's car roared back to the waiting area. He came in with a bag of nuts and a bag of peaches, both from his home, as unsolicited payment for his treatment. He was profuse and appeared gleeful in his thanks, indicating that he felt something deep and toxic had been healed. He hugged his wife.

Then, extraordinarily, he offered to escort Johnson into the hills to find trauma victims who were still in hiding, too damaged to return to life in their villages, both his own people (ethnic Albanians) and the enemy Serbs. In Johnson's words, "That afternoon, before our very eyes, we saw this vicious man, filled with hate, become a loving man of peace and mercy." Johnson further reflected how often this would occur, that when these traumatized survivors were able to gain emotional resolution on experiences that had been haunting them, they became markedly more loving and creative. While survivors, even after a breakthrough session like this, are still left with the formidable task of rebuilding their lives, the treatment disengaged the intense limbic response from cues and memories tied to the disaster, freeing them to move forward more adaptively.

The 105 people treated during Johnson's first five visits to Kosovo, all in 2000, had each been suffering for longer than a year from the posttraumatic emotional effects of 249 discrete, horrific self-identified incidents. For 247 of those 249 memories, the treatments successfully reduced the reported degree of emotional distress not just to a manageable level, but to a "no distress" level ("0" on a 0-to-10 Subjective Units of Distress, or SUD, scale). Although these figures strain credibility, they are consistent with reports by practitioners in numerous countries. Approximately three-fourths of the 105 individuals were followed for eighteen months after their treatments and showed no relapses—the original memory no longer activated self-reported or observable signs of traumatic stress.

Johnson made a total of nine trips to Kosovo between February 2000 and June 2002. His later visits were as much to train local health care providers as to treat additional patients. The follow-up information on approximately 75 percent of the people he worked with during his first five visits came primarily from two physicians who participated as translators in the initial treatments and who continued to care medically for the individuals who received them. Their reports consistently suggested that once a memory had been cleared of its emotional charge, it remained clear. The initial treatment appeared to have provided a potent and durable healing in each case that was followed. Reports of these outcomes came to the attention of the chief medical officer of Kosovo (the equivalent of the U.S. Surgeon General), Dr. Skkelzen Syla (himself a psychiatrist), who investigated them and subsequently stated in a letter of appreciation on January 21, 2001:

"Many well-funded relief organizations have treated the posttraumatic

stress here in Kosova. Some of our people had limited improvement, but Kosova had no major change or real hope until ... we referred our most difficult trauma patients to [Dr. Johnson and his team]. The success ... was 100 percent for every patient, and they are still smiling until this day."

From Overcoming Trauma to Peak Vitality

Beyond its potential for reducing susceptibility to illness and preventing and treating PTSD in severely traumatized individuals, energy psychology has a great deal to offer in promoting peak vitality. While it is beyond the scope of this chapter to teach the simple energy psychology protocols that put its basic methods into people's hands for use on a self-directed basis, that instruction is readily available.[10]

One area where energy psychology has been demonstrating its power for enhancing positive functioning is in helping athletes, artists, and actors attain peak performances. Pat Ahearne, who pitched in the Australian League, has publicly credited energy psychology for his having won the Pitcher of the Year Award for the 1998–99 baseball season. Energy psychology is now being introduced to entire teams, and while the results are only anecdotal, and many factors influence a team's performance, they are very encouraging. But at the level of the individual athlete, the results are often dramatic.

Jane, nine years old, had been studying gymnastics since she was three. She was a local star, but she suddenly became fearful and simply refused to return to practice. Brought to a counselor who does energy therapy,[11] she revealed that she was learning to do a backward handstand on the balance beam and was afraid that her hands did not know what to do. Beyond this, she didn't know how to fall if she had to while doing this particular routine.

In a single session, she was taught how to tap on acupuncture points that reduce fear while focusing on the fear of falling, on not knowing how to fall, on the fear of being hurt, the fear of having people watch her fall, and the fear of letting her team down. When she reported that one of those fears had been completely eliminated, the next fear was addressed. Once they were all resolved, she mentally practiced each part of the routine (both seeing herself and feeling herself on the balance beam) as well as how to fall, while continuing to tap selected acupuncture points. She saw herself moving backward on the beam, her hands knowing where to go, and her feet landing on the sweet spot of the beam. She saw herself knowing how to fall, how to use her hands, how her knees could bend, and how she could land and remount. Jane's fear of returning to practice was no longer there by the end of the session. The therapist asked the mother to have Jane review with her coach how to fall safely and to walk it through on the grounded balance beam. Jane returned to the gym and moved up to the next level. At a chance encounter several months later, Jane's mother reported that they had needed to use tapping only one other time and were able to do it successfully.

Jane's story encapsulates the basic principles of applying energy psychology to peak vitality. While peak vitality is a much more global goal than enhancing an athletic performance, they share two basic strategies: *overcoming obstacles* and *enhancing potentials*. Once Jane had overcome the fears that were interfering with her ability to even get to the gym, mental rehearsals of ideal executions of each aspect of the routine were combined with energy interventions.

Of course mental rehearsals are not unique to energy psychology. Many of the well-established procedures psychology already has to offer for enhancing performance and vitality are still applicable and can, in fact, be turbocharged by introducing energy interventions. For instance, uses of hypnosis, guided imagery, cognitive restructuring, and related procedures have demonstrated that suggestion and self-suggestion are powerful interventions for changing feelings, beliefs, and behavior. Combining words and images with the stimulation of energy points appears to send signals to the brain (see http://www.innersource.net/energy_psych/epi_neuro_foundations.htm) that further boost the potency of these methods.

Such ways of enhancing one's potential, however, can be undermined if inner obstacles to succeeding have not been addressed. Jane's mental rehearsals were not going to be effective if her fear was the dominant part of her experience. If you want to improve your relationships, increase your success, or embrace your joie de vivre, positive thinking and other ways of "trying harder" will remain merely noble intentions unless you overcome the internal obstacles to your goal. With or without energy interventions, the use of positive images and affirmations are simply not as effective if there is a contradiction between the intended change and your self-image, core beliefs, or emotional landscape. Until self-limiting core beliefs or emotional patterns are transformed, all other efforts will be like so many unkept New Year's resolutions.

Energy psychology can be used to transform internalized images or beliefs that are holding you back from a more vital life, instilling core beliefs and emotional responses that support your natural capacities for joy, love, and success. Activating energy points while mentally rehearsing a goal, after internal obstacles to reaching that goal have been eliminated, may be a giant step toward attaining that goal. Focusing on your hopes or on images of achievement, while stimulating energy points, can release a flood of chemicals in your brain. Energy psychology can be combined with other methods for enhancing human potential to activate the brain chemicals that bring out your best.

1   William Collinge, *Subtle Energy: Awakening to the Unseen Forces in Our Lives* (New York: Warner Books, 1998).

2   Norman Doidge, *The Brain that Changes Itself* (New York: Viking, 2007).

3   See Donna Eden's *Energy Medicine* (New York: Tarcher/Penguin, 1999).

4   National Center for Complementary and Alternative Medicine. (2005). Energy medicine: Overview (Bethesda, MD: NCCAM, 2005). Posted at http://nccam.nih.gov/health/backgrounds/energymed.htm

5   National Center for Complementary and Alternative Medicine. What is complementary and alternative medicine? (Bethesda, MD: NCCAM, 2002). Posted at http://nccam.nih.gov/health/whatiscam

6   See David Feinstein, Donna Eden, and Gary Craig's *The Promise of Energy Psychology* (New York: Tarcher/Penguin, 2005)

7   http://www.soulmedicineinstitute.org/research.html, accessed 12/18/07.

8   David Feinstein, *Energy Psychology: A Review of the Preliminary Evidence. Psychotherapy: Theory, Research, Practice, Training* (provisionally accepted, December 17, 2007).

9   David Feinstein, Energy Psychology in Disaster Relief. *Traumatology*, 14(1), 2008.

10   See *The Promise of Energy Psychology.*

11   Denise Wall was the therapist.

EOIN FINN

Yoga for Happiness

Yoga has become synonymous with Hatha (physical) yoga, the calisthenic practice of yoga postures or asanas. Should we despair that our body-obsessed, material culture has taken a classical Indian tradition of dissolving the ego through meditation (Raja yoga), knowledge and study (Jnana yoga), service (Karma yoga), and devotion (Bhakti yoga) and reduced it to a base level? Not necessarily.

As someone involved deeply in the yoga "industry," I see armies of people who flock to yoga classes in search of fitness, strength, or flexibility and I watch the competitive side of human nature emerge when people push themselves to be better than others in the class. In plenty of yoga classes, a subtle "rat race" dynamic holds sway.

Despite this emphasis on the physical, Hatha yoga can be a powerful way to cultivate what we all ultimately seek: happiness. It can be a practice that not only reshapes the look of your body, but transforms your mind as well. The bending, twisting, physical practice of yoga as a means of cultivating happiness is, unfortunately, seldom discussed in the yoga industry.

When presented properly, Hatha yoga can have a profound effect on your attitude, which is the seed from which happiness grows. Through yoga, virtually every quality that leads to lasting happiness—contentment, interconnection, awe, being present, living from the heart, setting realistic goals, and compassion—are all, day by

Eoin Finn is a writer, yogi, surfer, blissologist, and ocean worshipper. He has studied yoga, meditation, and martial arts since 1987 and has a degree in philosophy and comparative religions. He has trained Olympic skiers and NHL hockey players in customized sports performance yoga routines. His vision of energy- and consciousness-based yoga, using yoga as "fluid therapy," has been featured in several yoga DVDs. He has also brought many yogis together to catalyze social change. In between leading YES (Yoga Ecology Surf) retreats all over the world, he resides in Vancouver and Ucluelet, Canada. www.EoinFinnYoga.com.

day, pose by pose, ingrained into your perspective. I call this "Yoga for Happiness."

Hatha yoga is action and every action is preceded by an attitude. For example, when you feel loving toward someone, you behave differently than when you feel spiteful. What Yoga for Happiness recognizes is that the perspective from which you do the practice eventually becomes much more important than the physical prowess you exhibit in the yoga poses. *How* you are doing things becomes more important than *what* you are doing. Yoga for Happiness is a deep and powerful training ground for your attitude toward life. I often tell my students that yoga is really an acronym for You've Only Got Attitude.

Most of the time in daily life, your attitudes and actions are not at the forefront of your consciousness. Most of the decisions you make in a day are unconscious: "Should I wear the red shirt or the blue one?" "Paper or plastic?" Ideally during Hatha yoga practice, you are free enough of distractions to begin to feel how your attitudes and actions manifest in the world. In yoga, you are the recipient of your own actions. You become both the trainer and trainee, the painter as well as the canvas, exploring the cycle of attitude, thought, and action.

Let's look at how you can create an attitude of happiness with qualities like contentment, interconnection, and living from the heart.

Contentment and Competition

One essential attitude that should preclude a yoga pose is contentment: that relaxed and clear state of body and mind in which you recognize how things really are. In yoga, you learn quickly that you had better be content with what you have. There is now and has always been pressure in society to compare yourself to others, to compete, and to rise to the top. There is a time and place for competition—after all, if humans hadn't had that drive, we might still be one-celled beings—but when the competitive drive takes you over, you ignore the potential harm you could be doing to yourself, to others, and to the world around you.

One of the first recorded interactions of Europeans and yogis was in the time of Alexander the Great in the fourth century BC. In the spirit of conquest and expansion, Alexander entered what is now modern Pakistan and was amazed to find long-bearded, white-haired men sitting in the forests in quiet meditation. One account of their interaction is the Romans (who had learned the local dialect) asking the yogis to tell them about their philosophy.

"Who can talk about philosophy dressed like that?" the content yogis replied. "Get naked and sit by a river for thirty years and then we will talk."

Nearly two thousand years later, when the Spaniards left Spain in search of treasures in new lands, they found peoples in the Caribbean that spent time relaxing in hammocks and enjoying the splendors of nature.

In a world of fifty- to sixty-hour workweeks, where the dominant business ethic is expansion at any cost, whether it be to our bodies, our relationships, or the environment, the question these examples pose is one of the most pressing of our times: Could the ability to relax and enjoy simple pleasures be a greater treasure than any of the resources or power that our expansionist cultures were seeking?

The whole concept of working fifty to sixty hours a weeks is based on competition — the drive to keep up. We override the body's signals to rest and make it through our weeks on adrenaline and caffeine. In the process, we end up working more and enjoying less.

"Retail therapy" is another example of losing touch with the feeling of contentment that surrounds us during and after a yoga practice. Because we lack inner contentment, we are pulled to find satisfaction in the purchase of the mountain of material goods that are marketed to us at a rate our ancestors could never have imagined. Some of us even, insanely, try to make ourselves feel better about debt by shopping.

How does this relate to the Hatha yoga practice? The answer is that, in yoga, you have to find the perfect balance of contentment and the competitive ego drive. Too little drive and you sit like a blob; too much leads to exhausting your resources. Almost everyone who has been to a yoga class has had the experience of trying to keep up with the people around them. Too much of a competitive attitude makes you jam yourself into an expression of the posture for which you are not ready. You need to learn to quickly temper competition with contentment as there are only two possible outcomes to letting actions motivated by a competitive attitude override those of contentment: Either you get hurt or you get frustrated and quit.

For some people, this inability to stop comparing themselves to others prevents them from going to a yoga class in the first place and underlies comments such as the commonplace "I suck at yoga" or "I'm too inflexible to do yoga." The interesting thing is that saying you are too inflexible to do yoga is the perfect reason to do it. Saying you are too inflexible to do yoga is like saying you are too dirty to have a shower!

A Sense of Interconnection

When yoga is used as a means of cultivating happiness, you also develop a strong sense of interconnection. You learn this first of all somatically in your body-mind. As your mind becomes more at ease, the tightness and tugging in your lower back subsides. When your breath is harmonious with your movement, there is a whole-body release. You feel that the cells are really billions of independently operating, intelligent units that work together for common purposes.

These are all things that you can grasp with the purely rational aspect of your mind, but in yoga practice, the feeling expands beyond the rational. Bathing in this sea of interconnection, you feel the connection in your heart, in your viscera.

The lesson that has been passed down to us from numerous wisdom traditions is that what obscures this feeling of interconnection is the ego, or differentiating principle. The traditional prescription for laying aside the ego is quiet meditation. But Hatha yoga can also bring you back to this attitude of interconnection. It requires the mind to observe itself, to check in constantly and get off the autopilot mindset that can easily pit you against the world. During the practice, every time you feel your ego assert itself in its competitive drive, ask yourself if it is serving you or hurting you.

One of the best yoga moments I have ever experienced occurred a long time ago when I practiced yoga with other people early each morning. The person beside me on this particular morning was an acquaintance of mine who I knew suffered from a bad knee. We were doing a pose that I could do and he couldn't because of his injury. In spite of all my training, I heard in my inner dialogue, "Ha! I can do this pose and he can't. Look at me! I am so good at this stuff." Realizing that my mind was unconsciously reverting back to base human nature, I stopped doing the yoga poses. I stopped moving, closed my eyes, and did nothing but send love and healing energy to this person's knee.

Following these feelings took me on a journey of the most intense joy I have ever experienced. Recognizing the ridiculousness of my ego-driven quest to attain something better than the person beside me led me to explore our interconnection. What emerged was a powerful exploration of the realm of the heart.

Living from the Heart

And that brings us to the next aspect of Yoga for Happiness, which is living from the heart. What does it mean to live from the heart? It means getting in touch with the feeling of love and letting it guide you. "Love" is a word that only poets can come even close to defining, but one way of thinking about love is that when you experience it, you feel that the needs of the recipient of your love matter as much or more than those of your own ego-self. It is almost like a scale with ego-desires on one end and altruistic goals on the other.

In the practice of Yoga for Happiness, you get in touch with the vibration of love and direct it toward yourself. This involves the quality of listening. You have to listen to the needs of your own body and then, like a mother guiding her child, move your body in and out of the poses. By contrast, yoga to feed the ego involves not listening but getting into the poses by pure force of will. The body is the barometer for what side of the equation you are on. When you are forcing, your body is rigid, your lips are pursed, your breath is more irregular, and you ignore any signals that the body is sending that it has had enough. When the force of love is guiding you, however, your breath is smooth and deep, your face is soft, and you are receptive to body feedback loops.

Whether you are conscious of it or not, this type of self-love experienced through the yoga practice strengthens your ability to generate the same feelings toward others out in the world. You become more receptive to the needs of others and less apt to blindly impose your will without first considering how your actions could negatively affect another.

The other major way that Hatha Yoga strengthens your love-force is through the subtle yet powerful process of continually making you feel as good as possible. The bottom line is that the yoga practice makes you feel so damn amazing that you want more of it. You want to feel better and better—cure your little aches and pains; clear old, stale emotions; allow vital energy to flow. You can practice yoga from the realm of the ego and ignore the feedback your body is giving you, but that ultimately never feels as good as listening and giving your body what it needs.

Some get the lesson faster than others, but in order to feel as good as you possibly can, you need to develop the attitude of healer. How do you become a good healer? Knowledge is key, no doubt, but the foundation is love. There is no substitute for powerful human connection from the heart in the healing process.

Recently, I was in a class with Body-Mind Centering founder Bonnie Bainbridge Cohen. Someone asked her what, in her decades of therapeutic research, she had found to be the most powerful healing technique. Her answer was one word: Love.

Hatha yoga can feed the mind and you become like a scientist in a lab coat, exploring muscles like levers on the bones. It can feed your pride when you practice like a gymnast pushing past the pain threshold to master some routine on contest day. But you will never feel as good as when you treat yourself with love and kindness. When you listen to your body right down to each individual cell, you hear a message that sounds like "I want to heal" or "I want to cooperate so we all experience the vibration of joy and rapture." Once you hear that inner voice, you become your own doctor and your own patient and explore ways of healing. It becomes obvious that the poses done with an attitude of love are the ones make you feel the best. Once you allow this love into your life, it leads to that radiant state we all want more of, called Happiness.

Something unique starts to happen in the process of discovering what provides lasting happiness for you. You start rejoicing in and contributing to the success of others; you observe the impact that your life has on others and minimize some of the harm; you feel awe and gratitude for the simplest things. Ultimately, you tune into a level of consciousness at which you experience how deeply all things are connected and you live from that place. Then you go into the world with the fuel you need to spread good and your life becomes an upward spiral. You can start this process now: Before this day ends, do something kind for your body.

Stephen Lewis

Energetic Balancing

I n the "unbroken wholeness" of everything, as it was called by visionary physicist David Bohm, there is no dimension, time or space, or other defining characteristics. Eternal and everywhere, this flowing matrix is formless and invisible. When something — you, for instance — does appear to be separate and solid, it is energy that has been slowed down and shaped into material form by consciousness, but it is still only energy. We think we are separate entities, walled off within our physical bodies from everything else, because our limited perception doesn't allow us to see the truth of universal interconnection. And we also falsely believe in division within ourselves, as though we're more like stacks of separate blocks labeled Spirit, Mind, Emotion, and Body, rather than the seamless, indivisible whole we really are. As part of this very convincing illusion, we believe that both illness and healing come from outside ourselves.

In fact, both illness (or any sort of poor well-being) and healing happen within. At the spiritual-energetic level of each of us is an innate, self-organizing principle designed to maintain perfect health at all levels of our being. Though we might believe that invading germs or renegade cells make us sick, illness originates with an imbalance in our energetic organization, which then manifests at the physical level. Restoring our energetic harmony returns us to a state of well-being.

In hearing the centuries-old adage "Physician, heal thyself," most

Stephen Lewis, founder of EMC² and co-author of the novel *Sanctuary: The Path to Consciousness* (Hay House, 2002), has been exploring energetic balancing for more than twenty-five years. His extensive studies and research led him directly to the insights upon which the spiritual energetic balancing technology of EMC² is based. Lewis's technology, called AIM, has been used by tens of thousands of individuals worldwide and has earned the endorsements of Dr. Wayne Dyer, *The Secret* teachers Dr. Michael Beckwith and James Ray, author Kevin Trudeau, and many others. For more information please visit www.StephenLewis.org.

of us think that it only applies to actual doctors. But we are, each one of us, our own physician.

There are two things to know about self-healing. First, it requires an empowering shift in our consciousness that allows us to take back our power to heal ourselves. This power may come from prayer, from meditation, or more recently from exciting new applications of technology designed to alter our own energy and create a new reality. Second, we must accept responsibility for the circumstances that caused our need for healing. Once we do that, we can ignite our own unique self-healing capabilities and alter our material world.

Kabbalah, Bohm, and Sanctuary

When I was growing up in Philadelphia, I liked to hang around my highly intelligent grandfather and his card-playing buddies, many of whom were mathematicians and scientists and all were students of the Kabbalah. They doted on me, and as long as I was willing to listen, they were willing to teach. Although it wasn't clear at the time, they were laying the foundations for my life's work. There were other motivations, too. My parents would often say to me when I was a child, "Stephen, whatever you are going to do, you better do it fast, because the people in our family don't live very long." I wondered why that was and how it could be different.

Now I know the answer lies in healing. As I grew older, I was guided to quantum physics, to energy, and, ultimately, to ways to shift and alter energy in consciousness to create wellness. On this path, I felt compelled to earn many degrees, including in acupuncture and homeopathy, which are forms of energetic healing. I saw that quantum physics is not just a complex theory to be used only by scientists exploring the origins of everything, for instance. It is also a pragmatic endeavor with practical applications that, if true, will guide our entire lives. Among my early heroes were Nils Bohr, David Bohm, and Wilhelm Reich; they still are.

I have come to believe the message of the millennium is that consciousness is the dominant force in our lives, and we are empowered to use it to create ourselves, just as we are responsible for the manifestations of our consciousness, for better and for worse, in acceptance and in denial.

Above all, I have realized that we must be grateful for our empowerment. Gratitude is the lubricant that allows us to perceive easily our connection to everything and everyone. It is the nutrient that feeds our holographic "oneness." Early in my life, I began to wonder why people thrived or failed and, indeed, why they died prematurely. These early questions evolved into my soul truth as an adult, which is my primary message to humanity: *Anything can be healed.*

It is imperative that we distinguish between healing and curing. Curing is in the realm of medicine. Healers teach you to access your own healing power. Curing is what is done to you. Healing, on the other hand, is an "inside job." Only you can heal yourself, but many can help.

Healing and healers have existed since the beginning of time. In fact, you can read about healing in reputable medical journals in discussion of the many instances of utterly inexplicable, spontaneous remissions of many kinds of serious medical conditions. Over and over again, these stories indicate that we create these things with our consciousness—which means we can also un-create them.

My vision became a search for a technique that would facilitate people healing themselves. My vision was rewarded with a revelation that has defined my life: I am the custodian of a miracle. This miracle has helped more than 45,000 people heal themselves. In an effort to communicate my revelation in an understandable form, in 1998, I cowrote (with Evan Slawson) my story as a novel. In *Sanctuary: The Path to Consciousness*, we had only one purpose—to communicate in simple terms what I had discovered mathematically: We can shape energy with consciousness to heal ourselves.

Energetic Balancing

My work with quantum mechanics had also led me to investigate spiritual teachings ranging from Jesus and Buddha to New Thought leaders such as Ernest Holmes and the Fillmores. I now describe my work as a "Spiritual Technology," the link between science and spirituality. Both spring from the same two foundations: consciousness gives energy material form, and the universe is composed of holograms within holograms (a hologram is a three-dimensional picture, any piece of which contains the entire hologram, much like any cell from your body contains your entire DNA). The holographic principle is applicable in both physics and spirituality. To speak of "being in Oneness" is a holographic statement, as is, "What you do to the least of them, you do to me."

This is an era in which it is clear that legitimate science, when practiced with intellectual honesty, is a form of religious striving in humankind. The esoteric work of physicists, psychologists, and philosophers explores the same terrain as mystics have throughout time. Healing, spirituality, and consciousness cannot be separated, which makes the process of self-healing a spiritual one. So, out of my revelation, I created a computer technology called the All-Inclusive Method (AIM), which uses energy to help people bring their own energetic field back into balance. In 1998, I founded EMC^2 along with Evan Slawson and Roberta Hladek as a way of offering AIM to the general public, rather than to a select few.

In *Sanctuary*, through the words of the character Max, I explain the basis of this method: "The human body is the most sensitive radio receiver ever made. It receives and processes both quantum and analog energies across the entire electromagnetic spectrum, from the lowest possible frequency to the highest—beyond microwave, beyond light, into realms of energy as yet undiscovered or unrecognized by most human beings." The entire universe is composed of holograms. Anything unique to you, a piece of your hair or a drop of your blood is a hologram of you, as is your photograph. The presence or absence of DNA is irrelevant. Consciousness is the power that both creates and changes DNA.

Here is how AIM works: A huge bank of computers sends about 500,000 subtle energy-balancing frequencies to metal trays that hold the photographs of AIM program participants, which act as holographic stand-ins for their bodily presence, and the energy is transmitted directly to the participants, no matter where they are at the time. Each person's "higher self"—sometimes called the Buddha nature or Christ consciousness—selects the several dozen frequencies appropriate to correct his or her energetic imbalances and focuses on them until the imbalance is removed from the selector's consciousness. When an imbalance is removed from consciousness, it cannot continue to manifest on the physical plane. That is the essence of healing. As a person's energy comes back into balance and self-healing occurs, the life force (also called *chi* or *prana*) and consciousness increase. This allows the body to use its innate wisdom and resources to create well-being not only on the physical level, but also on the mental, emotional, and spiritual planes. No one can heal you but you, and no one should say, "I'm going to heal you." There is no technical basis for the latter. While the world teaches us that everything is out of our control, in reality, we create it all.

Personal Responsibility for Healing

Since we do create it all, self-healing demands only one thing from participants: accepting responsibility for the events, actions, and circumstances that caused the need for healing. In *Sanctuary*, Max says, "What responsibility means is being your own guru. We can only help you find the way. Any healing, any progress, any hope, and any despair are going to come from you. It is *your* energy that matters. I can't give you *my* energy, and I wouldn't dream of it."

As energetic beings, we all choose our imbalances (often unconsciously by suppressing painful emotions), and until we accept responsibility for that, we cannot transcend them. Much like an alcoholic cannot quit drinking until she admits she is, in fact, an alcoholic or an overweight person cannot slim down until he understands he has been eating without awareness, we cannot resolve any negative circumstance until we take responsibility for our role in its creation. And—here's the good news—once we do that, we can change the situation: We can alter our material world. In fact, accepting this responsibility is the first step to empowering ourselves and elevating our consciousness. When we can no longer blame outside forces for the negativity in our lives, we can take control.

Perhaps taking control of your energy entails being assisted by acupuncture, Reiki, meditation, prayer, the AIM program, or some other modality. What matters is not which modality you choose, but rather that you shift to accept that your own unconscious energies have created an imbalance. With this knowledge, you now have the opportunity to heal it. I created the AIM program because I wanted to heal 24/7. I saw tremendous value in a system that could deliver balancing energies around the clock to help participants face everything that's caused them pain and fear. It forces them to focus on healing themselves and allowing them to release their imbalances on all levels.

Some energetic imbalances are hereditary, even generations old, passed down unconsciously through a family. For instance, I have found that the energetic imbalance for some frequencies associated with cancer comes from unresolved, unconscious bitterness "handed down" from earlier generations. (AIM can reveal the origins of hereditary imbalances.)

Imbalances can also be acquired from natural or man-made sources, such as viruses or pollutants. We're all exposed to thousands of these energetic frequencies all the time, but not everyone so exposed manifests the imbalance. For example, if someone is exposed to the frequency imbalance associated with HIV but has enough life force to ward it off, it may not manifest.

This is not a revolutionary statement. Louis Pasteur, the father of germ theory, said at the end of his life, "It's not the seed, it's the soil." Even he understood that the most powerful germs have no power against a system healthy enough to withstand the onslaught. That is the goal of all healing. It is why physicians advise those who are frail, elderly, or immune-deficient to have a "flu shot." In other words, we must strengthen our energetic "soil" so that only the most positive, beautiful "seeds" can grow there.

Beyond Simple Health

Since energy creates the material world, and anything and everything is energy, what applications do balancing frequencies have outside the physical body? I had never considered the impact the AIM program could have beyond self-healing a particular physical problem until we started receiving letters of gratitude from people across the world. A woman had not dated for nearly twenty years and then she self-healed her avoidant personality while on AIM and reported a full social calendar. A man reported he had financially struggled for years, and after improving his confidence and altering his self-defeating energy, he secured multiple business deals. A woman wrote to us that not only had her diabetic father reduced his insulin level from one hundred units down to zero after two years on AIM, but also, for the first time since her childhood, he opened up and told her he loved her. Each healing is unique and each person used his or her own energy for that specific healing.

When you no longer have to use your precious life force to keep imbalances at bay to survive physically, you have access to your life force to create your higher, more etheric life. There are frequencies that replace fear with courage, anger with patience, denial with acceptance. There are frequencies to help you appreciate the miraculous, to attract abundance, and to reduce procrastination. Whatever frequency you need, you will select it via your higher self.

Einstein discovered $E=mc^2$, which tells us that everything is energy. Functionally, that information is useless because energy has no properties, nor does it have time or space; it simply "is." Every discernable, measurable aspect of life is energy that has been shaped by consciousness. In response to that knowledge, I've spent my life cataloguing energetic imbalances in units of consciousness, which I believe is the universal language. These frequencies correspond to various illnesses and conditions, and provide other frequencies to balance them. One of our greatest outreach activities has been to offer AIM free to children and adults with the frequency of autism or Down syndrome. (One of our champions who often dares to think far outside the box, Dr. Wayne W. Dyer, suggested this scholarship program and facilitated its beginning.)

Some skeptics have said that energetic balancing is nothing more than a placebo effect, but I find that their disbelief does not hold up.

Hundreds of autistic children knew nothing about the AIM program, and yet they've made remarkable recoveries. Even more obviously, we have never discussed the AIM program with any pets, yet they respond. Consciousness is universal.

Each and every AIM program success story has one central theme: You create your life using your life force energy, and thus YOU must be the one to heal it. I have said many times that AIM is just a tool. It assists you to heal any and all areas of your life. There is nothing you cannot heal. That is a given. The only question is, will you?

LING CHEN

Seeing Your Life Rhythms

I lived an ordinary life. I believed in myself, in playing by the rules, and in creating my future through hard work. For fifteen years, I put my doctorate in analytical chemistry to work, moving steadily up the career ladder in the biotechnology instrumentation industry. During this time, my loving and equally diligent husband and I were busy raising two children and acquiring the financial stability and career status for which we longed. I enjoyed my predictable life, which reflected the weather of our San Francisco Bay Area home: sunny and warm all year round.

The first sign of "winter" came when my mother became ill with an unknown disease. For months, various doctors and specialists ran test after test, but none provided any hint as to the cause of her mysterious loss of weight and vitality. During this same period, my son was struggling in middle school. He saw no value in his assignments and lost motivation to learn. Anything we did to help him seemed to push him closer to the edge. To complicate matters, my husband took an extended overseas work assignment. I was in a quandary. I contemplated quitting my job to look after my family, but simply could not imagine the company without me, or myself without a "profession," especially one that so clearly defined my life. In an effort to compromise, I requested a three-month family leave.

To my dismay, difficulties and obstacles continued to materialize.

Ling Chen, PhD, has dedicated her energy in joyful service to humanity. Her passion in life is exploring and sharing the secrets of natural healing. She is a partner of Lifescape Services (www.lifescapeservices.com), providing services and tools for healing, well-being, and self-exploration. Born and educated in Taiwan, she moved to the United States to pursue her scientific career; she obtained her doctorate in analytical chemistry from Ohio State University, and did postgraduate research at Johns Hopkins University School of Medicine. She worked on instrumentation for biotechnology research for fifteen years before discovering her passion for natural healing.

The final blow came on the second day of my family leave, when I was let go in a company restructuring. For the first time in my life, I felt helpless and confused. The values and skills I had relied on in maneuvering through and managing my life no longer seemed valid, 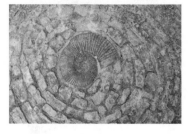 nor were they able to remedy what was apparently out of balance.

Throughout our lives, we are taught to trust our health to the doctors, our children to the schools, and our livelihood and self-worth to our jobs. So what happens when the systems no longer serve our needs?

Winter—Awakening: Physical Challenges, the Blessings in Disguise

When the old ways stop working, what can we do? Push forward in the same direction with stronger force? Turn away and hope for the best? Blame the world? Accept our fate? These are all options, of course, but they often lead us away from the true potential of any difficult experience. It is only when we stop and honestly assess what isn't working, when we shift perspective and begin to trust the rhythm of life's ebb and flow, that the meaning of our circumstances may be revealed to us.

Unable to find an answer through logic and reasoning (my normal mode of problem solving), I looked up into the blue sky, searching for the possible meaning of this seemingly chaotic turn of events. I needed to make sense of it all. But more important, I needed answers.

As questions swirled around in my mind and in my heavy heart, they seemed to swell into one gigantic, impassable iceberg. There seemed to be no way around it, yet a tiny spark in my heart ignited some part of my consciousness that began melting away the hard ice, creating droplets of possibilities, yet unknown. Another question came to mind: Could the challenges be, in fact, the wake-up call for change?

I came to realize that the obstacles in health, family, and work were, indeed, wake-up calls to pursue a new direction, to find a new balance in life. My ego and the self-imposed responsibilities I felt toward my job had stopped me from making the right moves. Now, suddenly free from the job and old labels, I was starting anew!

As Albert Einstein stated it, problems aren't solved by using the same kind of thinking that created them. I decided to start a new path where the old one left off. This decision opened the way to flowing with nature's rhythms, striving for balance in all areas of life and evolving with the lessons learned.

We have the power and ability to create our own futures. Instead of focusing on the "incurable" disease, we can choose to focus on ways to achieve physical wellness and quality of life. Instead of letting the job run our lives, we can choose a job that is part of our life's purpose. Instead of carving the child to fit the system, we can choose a system that more closely fits the needs of the child, to partner with the child in finding his or her own place in the world. A change of lifestyle, a change of priorities, or a change of focus to more closely embody a natural flow may be the key to experiencing renewed and prolonged health, joy, love, peace, and abundance. From this perspective, life's challenges are, in fact, blessings in disguise.

Spring—Self-Growth: Exploration of the Unknown

With a newfound sense of possibility, and determined to restore my mother to comfort and health, I delved into the world of complementary natural remedies and self-help practices.

Conventionally, we depend on medicine for quick fixes and absolute answers and often forget nature's healing power, which is within every one of us. When we have a wound, doctors may cut away the heavily damaged parts, sew the sections together, use antibiotics to rid or prevent infection, and prescribe medicine to numb the pain. But it is always the body that ultimately heals itself. The magical self-healing power is always at work — in you and me, in all life forms — by regenerating the cells, forming new connections of the skin, blood vessels, nerves, muscles, and bones. Natural healing methods enhance the *self-healing power within the body*.

My search for complementary methods opened the door to a wealth of ancient practices, remedies, and healing systems. At first, I was overwhelmed by the wide array of possibilities, and by what seemed like unbelievable claims of efficacy. There were too many choices, and each appeared too simple, too good, or too mystical to believe.

I applied research skills to selecting the most natural, safest, and least expensive methods to start my personal "experiment." It was evident that proper oxygenation, hydration, diet as well as emotion, and environment are important to our general health. My new healthy-living program started with something as simple as drinking enough pure water in a new way (in small sips while envisioning the drops hydrating every cell) and breathing in a natural way (focused and relaxed abdominal breathing). I was encouraged by the ease and benefits of these ancient health tips.

Before long, the curiosity, careful observation, and creativity of the scientist came into play in my exploration of nature's wisdom teachings and practical methodologies. To accelerate the selection process, I relaxed the rules of experimentation by allowing for several variables at the same time in a small sample size (me first, then my mom). Coincidentally, this suited the natural healing principle of multiple components working together synergistically.

-§-
Create Your Own Reality with "Mind Power"
The energy of intention, thoughts, and feelings. Write down a positive affirmation in the present tense. Raise your head slightly, hold your breath, and hold the thought or image of the affirmation for as long as you can. Take action toward the goal in small, achievable steps. Repeat daily. -§-

Another universal principle that I came to understand in a new way is that everything is energy. Scientists understand energy in the forms of heat, light, sound, electricity, magnetic force, gravity, and the deep connection between energy and masses in the equation $E=mc^2$. Ancient Chinese doctors, however, have long understood energy in its relationship to the body. Energy has been given different names in different cultures: *ch'i* in China, *prana* in India, and *reiki* in Japan. It is widely understood and accepted that energy flows through the body in channels and concentrates in specific centers, all of which are mapped out in meridians, acupuncture points, chakras, and so forth. It has been demonstrated that an energy system can be optimized via exercises, meditation, and energy healings. The body's energy system can be influenced by external energies in various forms: electromagnetic force, sounds, lights, thoughts, emotions, and the energy of nature.

This top-level understanding of energy triggered my curiosity to probe deeper. I started practicing qigong meditation, during which I learned to discern subtle body sensations, indicating energy flow. I also experienced the benefits of improved vitality, physical wellness, and a sense of calmness.

Having experimented successfully on myself, it was time to apply the techniques to my mother. She has been the best "client" I could have hoped for: willing to try these new approaches to wellness, sensitive to her own body's feedback, and persistent in doing her homework. In her case, her homework was a daily regimen of proper hydration, twenty minutes of gentle qigong meditation, and laughter to restore joy to her life. I also used energy testing to identify the proper diet and natural supplements for her. Within three months, she returned to normal weight, regained her vitality, and was once again radiant and joyful. I became increasingly convinced that healing is not only possible, but probable when we work with the body's own healing energy.

Summer—Transformation: Opening the Heart to Connect to the Soul

As I experienced positive gains, I ventured to learn other energy techniques. To my dismay, my mind started to struggle when I tried to make logical sense, to compile, and to integrate the new tools. During

one workshop, this became a major problem. One moment, my mind was as clear as the blue sky, happily taking in the teachings, when in the next moment, it was overshadowed by thick dark clouds, unable to remember or relate to anything being taught.

I became deeply troubled, and my friend Nancy, who I met at the workshop, sensed my confusion. "Your left brain is feeling threatened by this new awakening, so it went on strike," she said. This intriguing insight shone the light into the scary darkness. Having been a logical, analytical, linear thinker all my life, I had relied primarily on my left brain (the linear, logical, and rational side) to learn, memorize, analyze, make decisions, and lead the way. The abrupt activation of the right brain (the feeling, sensing, and organic learning side) had seemingly frightened my logical mind, causing what amounted to short circuits. The left and the right brain were fighting for dominance, refusing to work together. I could no longer process information—not in my old way nor in the new. My shutdown was the result of the fear of losing control.

This turned out to be another great opportunity to experiment with energy solutions. During meditation that night, I set the intention to bring balance and clarity to my mind. I offered gratitude and thanksgiving to my left brain, thanking its hard work in helping me maneuver through this plane, getting me to where I am today, and providing the freedom and resources for my next step. I felt the gradual calming of my mind, as if the ocean was embracing me; the chattering, fear, and doubt washed away with every wave. In a deeply relaxed state, my hands waved spontaneously in many small and big circles, making the infinity symbol, connecting the right and the left, the logical and the intuitive, the Yin and the Yang. I felt gentle energy

flowing in the many loops of circles as the boundaries dissolved. The energy danced within me, and I became like a vibrant tree, trying to achieve balance of its many branches in all directions, while attuning to and making a strong connection to the trunk and the roots, to enable it to grow taller and taller. When I opened my eyes again, everything around me looked clear; the room seemed especially quiet, and the moon outside the window was pulsating with bright light.

After the workshop, I wandered into a bookstore and decided to experiment with my new skill of following my intuition. Instead of logical thinking. I picked a book randomly from a shelf. It was Gary Zukav's *Soul Stories*. I flipped it open to a page somewhere in the middle, and read. The words rang loudly in my ears, answering directly the challenges I had been facing for the past few weeks: "Sharing and clarity are twins. When you share, you give something special to a special person. When you see clearly, everyone and everything is special.... When you order, you share with the universe. When the order is filled, the universe shares with you."

I placed my order of to the Universe for achieving clarity to serve my highest purpose. I felt my heart pounding with joy. The long-lost feeling of "I know I can" returned with an explosive force, releasing all worry, self-doubt, and sense of limitation.

The first day back home from the workshop, I had a nice chat with a lady, the owner of a coffee shop I had been drawn to since the previous autumn. The owner was friendly, and I was friendly to her, but the boundary of customer and owner prevented us from saying anything more. That day, I felt the urge to mention the workshop to her. One thing led to another: I shared some energy tips to help with her back pain and stress, and we brainstormed ideas about connecting this lovely coffee shop with people of the same mind. We connected so wonderfully, as though we knew each other from a long time ago. It was as if the intention of sharing opened the door for souls to connect, not just the owner and the customer chatting. Ironically, the name of the coffee shop is "Sufi."

-§-

Connecting and Crossing Your Energy with Body Movement

Weave a web of big and small figure eights (the infinity symbol), interconnecting your whole energy system, by swaying your arms in figure eights in front of you, to your sides, and up and down the body, and imagine tracing the same pattern behind you where you cannot reach.

-§-

Empowered and encouraged by recent events, I experimented with the power of setting an intention, and connecting on unseen levels. The next morning, as I was gently awakening my son, I silently said to him from my heart that I love him. He mumbled, half asleep, "I know, me too." I was speechless. This is what we usually do with words, but I was able to communicate with him from a place without words. With more practice, perhaps I would be able to speak to his soul. And what healing would be able to occur from that sacred place!

My life was rapidly changing. As if the Universe was answering my order, teachers started showing up in my life, whenever the time was right. The teachers were actual teachers, challenging tasks, and even setbacks. I was seeing things differently. The lesson plan was evolving as I grew, and I was being led to understand the multiple levels of healing, from the body and the mind to the soul and beyond.

Throughout any learning, it is critical to discern whether a teaching embraces and upholds deeper truth. We must keep an open mind, but not blindly believe in everything we are told. There is always an element of choice, an element of discernment. When we validate what we learn through experience and inner dialogue, we often find that the answer truly comes from within. The teachings or techniques are merely the catalysts, resonating with us to bring out and awaken our inner knowing. I learned to consult with my mind, listen to my intuition, and follow my heart, always weighing my options.

Solstice/Equinox—Assimilation: Connection with Mother Earth

For my mother's eightieth birthday, I took her on a journey back "home." We flew from the United States to her birthplace in Wu-Han, China, a northern city from which she had fled during the war, separated from her family forever at the age of only six. With only her fragmented childhood memories to guide us and not knowing a single person there, our expectations were low that we would be able to find her family home in a city flattened in the war and rebuilt many times over. Miraculously, the strangers we met—the taxi driver, the busy street-stand owner, the stern-faced police officer, the old man carrying his grandson to the market—went out of their way to offer help and each encounter provided clues that took us closer to our hoped-for destination.

-§-
Energy Exercise for Opening the Heart
Gently tap your heart center (center of chest). Take a few deep breaths, relax, and smile at your heart center.
-§-

The morning after we had arrived, we found the place where my mother's family mansion had once stood. Standing on the busy street, over the little creek in which my mother bathed as a child, I felt the mystical connection to the land and to the people I had never met.

For the next twelve days, my mother, my ninety-three-year-old father, and I traveled in the footsteps of their life journeys: from my dad's village in the countryside to the nearby cities in which he studied, to the cities my mother had migrated to during the war, and finally to Taiwan, where my parents had been married and where I was born and raised. Along the way, I used simple energy medicine and pranic healing techniques to minimize their jet lag, optimize their immune systems, and keep their energies balanced. They were healthy and energetic beyond their wildest dreams, and the trip brought us full-circle home. I felt a familiar sense of knowing, a connection to something old, even ancient. It was as if the old had melded with the new, the East merged with the West; I was the child of the two worlds. This realization mirrored my recent personal journey, the melding disparate methods of healing and ways of thinking. Perhaps there were never boundaries in this seemingly ailing world. We are all connected through our very existence on this precious planet Earth, home to everyone. We are all children of Mother Earth. Could we truly achieve wellness for our own bodies, without caring for others, without caring for the world, without taking care of the Earth? I contemplate whether the energy approach to healing the physical body might be applied to global healing. After all, energy is universal; energy has no boundary.

Autumn—Implementation:

The Joy of Service, the Fruit of Labor

As I continued on this path that began in the winter, energy healing became my passion. I started to wonder, "What am I to do with the wonderful knowing? What is the purpose of my life?" The questions intensified after each "accidental" encounter with people. Bumping into long-lost friends, connecting with total strangers, the simple casual greeting of "how are you?" often turned into deep exchanges. Without effort, or logical knowledge, I might happen to share the one thing that met an urgent need. They might begin to question and explore on their own. Perhaps the true magic of healing is to help people become who they really are.

-§-

Connecting to Earth
Be aware of the beautiful gifts from nature and the connection to your body. In nature, all the elements exist in harmony. While your energy flows with nature, you regain the balance and harmony. Float in the ocean; hug a tree; enjoy the sunlight; walk barefoot on the grass, the sandy beach, or a gravel path. Take in the fresh, clean energy from the air, the sun, the moon, and the earth.

-§-

There are so many little wonders, each so special, each leading to the next like fire passed from one person to another in ancient rituals. The joy of service has become my new life force, propelling me forward. As I grow, the next stepping-stone reveals itself and the next service project comes my way. All I have to do is to prepare myself, act when asked, and act from my heart—always from the heart.

At times, the tasks seem daunting. Self-doubt and fear bubble up, only to teach me to go deeper, embracing new faith and trust. Ego creeps up, only to remind me to let go. So many of us hold onto the old and familiar like branches that are hesitant to shed old leaves in the autumn. When suffering and loss become too heavy to bear, pondering the true meaning of life, the natural cycles, can ease the burden.

-§-
Giving and Receiving: Oneness with the World
Open your arms with palms facing outward, imagining golden light coming into your heart center and radiating out from your hands into the world. Bless the world with love, joy, and peace, and offer a prayer of gratitude.
-§-

Providing service to others leads us to our teachers and teammates, the many holding the radiant light in their hearts, lighting the path for others. They may bear the label of prophet, healer, teacher, engineer, parent, spouse, or child, but they touch us in the same way, with the kindness of their hearts. They allow us to experience and share life with them in ways both big and small. And for that I am grateful.

We are all here to learn, to assist, to love, and to evolve. Through each experience, our awareness deepens. Through each act of giving and receiving, connection strengthens. We are no longer separate; we become One.

Acknowledgments

I wish to thank my spiritual teachers for their guidance; Master Shen-Chu Wu, Dr. Lai Chiu-Nan, Donna Eden, Dr. David Feinstein, Sandy Wand, Rayman Grace, Grandmaster Choa Kok Sui, and Master Stephen Co for their teachings; my personal photographer—my thirteen-year-old daughter Kelley; and Nancy Auspelmyer for her encouragement.

CANDACE PERT

Hardwired for Bliss

The latest and most comprehensive research I know of on the endorphins {natural pleasure-inducing hormones} has been done by Jaak Panksepp, a scientist whose work has been published in the scientific literature, and whose *Textbook of Biological Psychiatry* has been well received. I've always had a lot of respect for him, so I was excited to attend his lecture, "Affective Neuroscience and the Social Brain," at the spring 2005 conference of the Bowen Center for the Study of the Family held nearby in Washington, D.C.

I recall how I raced across the Potomac River to the hotel where the conference was being held and slipped into the back row of the lecture hall just as Dr. Panksepp was beginning his talk. Thank God that he—not I, for a change!—had to find meaning in all the tiny, tediously proven factoids that he and other scientists had meticulously managed to collect, and then present them in an accessible and entertaining way. His job was to arrange and present the data to an overflowing roomful of family therapists gathered from all over the world, to give them something useful to take back with them to help their clients heal.

Bowen Family Therapy, as it's often called, is a very advanced form of psychotherapy. It's based on the idea that members of a family are so closely linked by invisible but powerful emotional forces that only one person needs to be regularly treated for the whole family to benefit. As that individual changes, the whole system then rearranges

Candace Pert, PhD, is an internationally recognized psychopharmacologist. She is a former research professor at Georgetown University School of Medicine, and former Section Chief at the National Institute of Mental Health (NIMH). Dr. Pert's appearance in the movie *What the Bleep Do We Know!?* and her book *Molecules of Emotion* (Simon & Schuster, 1999) have popularized her groundbreaking theories on consciousness, neuropeptides, and reality. She has published more than 250 scientific articles. Her most recent book is *Everything You Need to Know to Feel Go(o)d* (Hay House, 2007). www.CandacePert.com.

and corrects itself. Panksepp's research has shed much light on the strength of our human bonding, connecting it to endorphins and the opiate receptor, which is why he was speaking to this group.

Years before, {my husband}Mike and I had sent {our son} Brandon into Bowen treatment, hoping to help his serious adolescent "acting out," not realizing that (as the Bowen therapists joke among themselves) it's usually the healthiest person in the family who gets sent in by the others! While my husband and I were having trouble dealing with our own issues, we alighted on Brandon's temporarily slipping grades as a distraction, sending him off for help when we were the ones who needed it.

Later, it became clear to me how interdependent the whole family is, how the most effective way to help your children or the family members you're concerned about is to begin solving *your own* personal issues, one by one. When you grow, the people around you do, too—once more, we're all connected.

Panksepp's work has shown that endorphins are the peptide not only for bliss, the "high" of the heroin addict, but also for bonding and attachment, scientific words for *love*. He studied maternal bonding in rats and chicks and noticed that when the babies were removed from their mothers, they made distress vocalizations, sounds of loss and grieving. When given a shot of morphine, or exogenous endorphin, these young animals ceased to grieve and instead became pacified, even blissful in their separated state.

But if given naltrexone, an antagonist drug that blocks opiate receptors, the babies were even more upset, showing that the endorphin was carrying the message of attachment and bonding. Naltrexone is the drug given to comatose, overdosed heroin addicts when they arrive at the emergency room, effectively bumping opiates from their cellular receptors and instantly awakening them, thus saving their lives.

Similar studies have been done with dogs, animals whose behavior is more familiar to us than rats. Tail wagging is shown to be associated with low endorphin levels, indicating an eagerness for social interaction, such as petting and touching. Give Fido some morphine, and the wagging stops; block the dog's receptors with naltrexone, and it increases.

So, should we worry about Fido becoming a junkie? Maybe! But that's another study. The point is that Panksepp showed endorphins are the balm, the antidote, the soother provided by nature to deal with the distress of separation, a condition we all suffer from in our alienating, modern world. His findings should give us pause to consider — is addiction to heroin caused by a profound sense of non-belonging, a painful disconnection from close relationships or even from community?

Does *feeling good* — slang used by heroin addicts to describe the act of shooting up — point to a more basic human need, such as the blissful bond of mother and child, or a close, loving adult relationship? Are people drawn to take the drug who lack either of these? If so, we have a new direction to look in for healing addiction closer to the source. Rather than focusing on a chemical cure, we could apply what we know about the healing power of *mind, emotions, and spirit — not* just the body alone — to help people feel their very real, but often unacknowledged, connection to each other, their community, and their planet.

Religious or spiritual mystics have reported experiences of blissful ecstasy when united with the divine through prayer, meditation, trance, and even dance. It makes sense that the 12-step program Alcoholics Anonymous, with its strong spiritual component of seeking help from a Higher Power, has been the single most effective method for recovery from addiction. Could that success perhaps be due to this connection between the experience of spiritual oneness and the body's own bliss juice, endorphin?

For his talk to the family therapists, Panksepp included some fascinating studies on laughter, joy, and depression in connection to endorphins. Guided by the concept of epistemics, which predicts that animal brain research can tell us about the internal experiences of humans, he discovered that laboratory rats were making high-pitched, supersonic chirping sounds, a behavior he called "rat laughter."

How did he know that the rats were laughing and not just making random noises? Easy — he and his research assistants tickled the animals, an action that elicited the supersonic chirping! Also, the amount of time the rodents spent chirping peaked as young adults and declined in age, which is a similar pattern for humans, who typically laugh less as they grow older.

It turned out that rat laughter was moderated by endorphins, which Panksepp proved by using naltrexone to block them from binding to their receptors. The chirping sounds were then stopped. Panksepp concluded that laughter is a psychological birthright of the human brain, the evolutionary antecedent of human joy, and perhaps the basis for a new approach to curing depression, if we can find ways to reliably augment it.

Panksepp's findings also shed light on how children learn through play. Tickling and touching, often a part of rough-and-tumble play, are normal activities that children engage in as they grow. During these activities, children are biochemically bonding, belonging, and connecting to each other—all a part of their healthy, natural development.

Children who don't laugh and play with other kids are vulnerable, Panksepp proposes, to attention-deficit/hyperactivity disorders (ADHD), pointing to well-documented findings that social isolation is associated with learning deficits. He questions our school culture's prohibition on rough-and-tumble play, and the related use of drugs like Ritalin to control children's classroom behavior. His findings suggest that these measures might be suppressive and detrimental to a child's development. The simple matter is that when laughter and play are curbed because they don't fit school agendas, endorphins stop flowing, children don't bond, and learning suffers.

Are We Having Fun Yet?

Play and laughter are vital to feeling good. Recreation isn't merely a frivolous addition to life or a hard-earned reward for work, two beliefs stemming from early Puritanical times. I believe that in a society driven by a strong work ethic, with so many individuals burdened with workaholism, people aren't getting enough endorphinergic surges throughout their bodymind on a daily basis.

For you to not be laughing and playing during some part of every day is unnatural and goes against your fundamental biochemistry. I recommend that you consciously seek out opportunities to cut loose every day, scheduling them into your calendar, if necessary. Here are a few of my favorite ways to get those daily chuckles:

- Rent a stupid, funny movie and let yourself enjoy it.

- Dance for ten minutes to your favorite rock music.

- Play with small children and let them tickle you.

- Call someone up and tell them a joke. Make sure the person knows why you're doing it, so he or she can call someone and do the same thing.

- Most of all, don't wait until you're depressed or in a low mood to do something playful. Be spontaneous! Include play every day as part of what you do naturally, like brushing your teeth or going to the gym to work out.

- Finally, don't worry about looking foolish. The only time you really look silly is when you're popping pills from a bottle while your natural pharmaceuticals are just waiting to be released from every cell of your bodymind!

Dr. George Stefano, an innovative researcher whose Old Westbury, Long Island laboratory I'd visited recently, reported that he could isolate biological morphine from animals. Not peptide endorphins, but *morphine*—the active ingredient of opium that's extracted from the poppy plant! In spite of much initial resistance from skeptical scientists, Stefano reported that he'd also found a primitive opiate receptor for this morphine: a tiny, truncated version existing in lobsters, mussels, and other primitive creatures. Most astounding was his discovery that we have the same enzymes in the human brain that are found in the poppy plant, providing a pathway for our bodies to make morphine using the same exact biochemical route as the botanical.

As I've said before, receptors for the bliss chemicals—morphine and endorphins—are located in the greatest abundance in the human frontal cortex, the most recently evolved and the highest command post of the brain. We have thus been hardwired to experience the pleasure of bliss, a bodymind state of unity and resonance with a loved one or the divine.

Rollin McCraty

Emotions Drive Your Body

"It's just stress." How many times have you uttered those words to yourself to dismiss an emotional outburst, forgetfulness, headache, pain, or illness? "Stress" has become one of the most widely used words in everyday vernacular. People describe themselves as "stressed" when stuck in traffic or when experiencing the dissolution of a long-term relationship. Preparing for an examination, having difficulty communicating with a coworker, dealing with serious illness in the family, and adjusting to new living or working conditions can all be "stressful."

Stress is not "just" some benign complaint. Rather, it's a powerful risk factor for disease and an important predictor of health. According to a recent article in the *Journal of the American Medical Association* (Cohen, Janicki-Deverts, and Miller, 2007), there is a documented link between stress and an increased risk for heart attacks, depression, cancer, and the progression of HIV and AIDS. Another article in the same issue shows that workplace stress may be as bad for your heart as smoking and high cholesterol (Aboa-Eboule et al., 2007). The research literature is also clear in pointing to a negative relationship between stress and vitality. But what defines the experience of stress?

Stress and the Emotions

In essence, stress can be thought of as *emotional unease*. From a

Rollin McCraty, PhD, is director of research at the Institute of Heart-Math. He is also an adjunct professor at Claremont Graduate University and a visiting professor in the Department of Family and Community Medicine at the University of Alabama at Birmingham. A psychophysiologist, Dr. McCraty's research focuses on the physiology of emotion, especially the mechanisms by which emotions influence cognitive processes, behavior, and health. He has published numerous influential scientific papers, and applied these findings to the development of tools and technology to optimize health. More at www.HeartMath.org.

psychophysiological perspective, emotions are the main ingredient in our experience of stress; indeed, it is the *emotions—feelings* such as anxiety, irritation, frustration, lack of control, or hopelessness—we are referring to when we describe ourselves as "stressed."

Though mental processes clearly play a role in emotional experience and stress, it is well recognized that thoughts carrying an emotional charge tend to be perpetuated in consciousness. It is also emotions—more than thoughts alone—that activate and drive the physiological changes that correlate with the stress response. The key to optimal vitality is directly related to our ability to self-regulate our emotional experience. Simply said, the emotions we tend to call negative do indeed disrupt optimal physiological and mental functions. Even short periods of these disruptive emotions lead to depletion of the various physiological systems. In other words, they drain our energy. On the other hand, the emotions we tend to call positive facilitate a wide range of physiological functions, renew our energy, and optimize the body's natural regenerative processes.

Many individuals believe that if they could just learn to relax, they would be healthier and happier. Relaxation and breathing techniques are beneficial in that they calm the system, temporarily draw attention away from distressing feelings, and reduce physiological arousal. In fact, breathing at the appropriate rhythm facilitates both a physiological and an emotional shift, and for this reason, heart-focused breathing is the first step in a number of the emotional refocusing and restructuring techniques developed at HeartMath. While the breathing step is helpful for calming, sustaining shifts in engrained attitudes and strong emotions takes much more than that.

From our perspective, this is done by learning to engage the *power of the heart's intent*. The important part of the process is learning how to shift attention to the heart and activate a positive feeling or attitude replacement. Once the *feelings* shift, then the thoughts automatically become more positive. In most cases, the mind alone doesn't have the power to shift emotional stress or change negative attitudes. The key to sustained attitude and behavioral change is transformation of the deeper, recurring physiological and emotional patterns that give rise to stress-producing feelings. Without these more fundamental changes, any relief from stress and the resulting system depletion and reduced well-being is likely to be short-lived.

Our research has identified a specific mode that the body naturally shifts into when we experience positive emotions. We call this the "psychophysiological coherence state," which is characterized by increased synchronization, harmony, and efficiency in the interactions within and among the physiological, cognitive, and emotional systems. Numerous studies show that this state reflects a global state of optimal function. Coherence can be naturally activated with intentional shifts to a positive emotional state, such as appreciation, compassion, and love. This shift reflects increased synchronization in higher-level brain systems and in the activity occurring in the two branches of the autonomic nervous system. These observed linkages might provide an important aspect of the mechanism that explains the growing number of documented correlations between positive emotions and increased cognitive flexibility and creativity, broadened thought action repertoires and increased personal resources, and improved health and increased longevity—in other words, vitality.

Taking Energetic Self-Responsibility

If we want to grow in vitality, then we must learn to take energetic self-responsibility. This means recognizing that certain emotions we habitually choose to run through our system—our *emotional diet*—deplete our resources, and ultimately lead to increased cortisol (the "stress" hormone) and decreased DHEA (a prohormone important to immunity and the stress response). It is not about denying the depleting emotions, or stuffing them away. It is about being honest with ourselves, recognizing our own experiences, and starting to look beneath the surface, then learning how to shift and replace those depleting attitudes and emotions with those that renew and regenerate our system.

Back in 1969, Karl Pirbram introduced a theory of emotions postulating that the brain is essentially a pattern-analysis system. This idea is gaining wider acceptance today. Scientists are finding that the brain is designed to become familiar with patterns and rhythms on an ongoing basis, internally and behaviorally. Physiological processes—hormonal rhythms, patterns of muscle tension, facial expressions, digestive rhythms, breathing rhythms—take place simultaneously and without our conscious awareness. The heart, the primary source of rhythms in the body, is a key player in these patterns and processes. From all of these patterns, the brain creates a familiar frame of reference or set point—a stable baseline against which it compares all other energetic states at any given moment. The brain looks for a match or a mismatch between the current rhythms and the set point, and the degree of match/ mismatch creates the feeling, or the texture of an emotion.

Fortunately, these set points can be modified. We are changing them to a greater or lesser extent all the time through our emotional experiences and attitudes. Emotions have a profound and ongoing effect on our physiological set points as well; think of the connection between anger and blood pressure, for instance, or stress and elevated cortisol levels. If we are in a stressed state long enough, the increased blood pressure level becomes the new set point or normal level.

Emotions drive physiology. One can be the purest vegetarian health-food enthusiast, but if following such a diet leads to anger and judgment toward non-vegetarians, the effect is worse than it is for the person who eats junk food but who is kind to others. To heal ourselves, we need to be willing to stop playing the same old patterns and listen to our deeper, intuitive wisdom.

Right now is a great time to be alive on Earth, because the planet is going through a dimensional shift. This shift can be described in many ways, but a simple way to say it is that we are learning to operate more from the heart than the head. We are integrating more of the intelligence of what people commonly refer to as the spirit or higher self into the three-dimensional mind-body. At the Institute of HeartMath, we call this "heart intelligence." As we learn to access more of our intuition via the heart and integrate more of the intelligence from our energetic spirit level, this leads to increased hormonal balance and realignment of the physiological systems. For example, these shifts can actually be measured in dramatic changes in our heart rhythms and various hormones such as cortisol.

Essentially, we have been working from an incomplete paradigm of emotions. Psychologists have tended to see the brain as the primary source and influence on emotions. We believe that the emotional system is much more complex than this. We have found that it is through the emotional system that the language of intuition filters, and that as we learn how to increase our coherence, we increase access to our heart intelligence. This brings us into greater alignment with the intelligence of our spirit. The mind also benefits, with improved memory, faster reactions, and increased ability to make discriminations.

The heart rhythm pattern shown in the top graph, characterized by its erratic, irregular pattern (incoherence), is typical of disruptive emotions such as anger or frustration. The bottom graph shows an example of the coherent heart rhythm pattern typically observed when an individual is experiencing sustained, modulated positive emotions. This graphic demonstrates that, with respect to our physiological response, some emotions drive our physiology into chaos, and others drive it into coherence. Those emotions, such as anger and anxiety, that drive our system into chaos deplete our physiological and energetic resources, just as those that drive it into coherence rejuvenate and regenerate those resources.

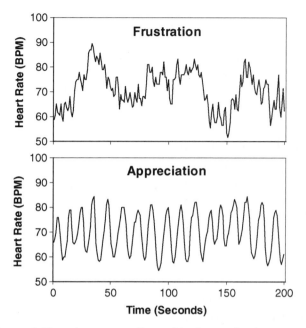

Figure 1. Emotions are reflected in heart rhythm patterns.

Most people get into trouble by either trying to achieve the consciousness shift mentally or giving up and letting their emotions lead them. The way to achieve the shift is to access our intuitive intelligence to bring the cognitive system and the emotional system into coherence, or the state of heart alignment. Attempting to keep things under control by quieting the mind doesn't work because the emotional system is energetic. Without making these shifts at the energetic level, we can only effect temporary change.

Think about emotions in terms of a radio in an old car. As the car moves out of the reception area, the signal starts to crackle and fade. Relying solely on conscious will or cognitive process to quiet the static of the mind is like tuning the dial in hopes of getting a clearer signal. But what if one could just double the transmitter's power? Shifting to the heart has exactly this effect. Increasing heart coherence is equivalent to increasing the signal strength. It's really that simple, and yet it isn't easy to make the change because our ingrained patterns and neurocircuits keep us reacting in our habitual ways.

Shifting to a higher dimensional experience means that we begin to manage our emotions through the intuitive intelligence of the heart. By intuition, we do not mean being able to see through a deck of cards or picking the winning lotto numbers. Real intuition is the inner guidance that comes from the spirit or higher self. To use our intuitive intelligence in the discriminations we make and in our relationships is to learn to stop ourselves in the midst of overemotionality and drama and *choose a more balanced way of responding*—not out of some sense of duty or guilt, but because we are looking out for our own well-being. And by doing that, we are also looking out for the well-being of the entire planet.

The Heart's Role in Intuition

There is a secret hidden out in the open. It is everywhere you look. All the great leaders and religions have been pointing directly to it since the beginning of recorded history. The secret is: We have a spirit! We really do have an energetic system. And at the energetic level, the heart is the central conduit of that nonphysical part of the self—the spirit. To demystify things even further, intuition is nothing more or less than the flow of information from our spirit via the heart to the mind, and then to the body.

The heart is at the center of all religious traditions. The ancient Hebrews, Greeks, Egyptians, Sumerians, Hindus, Muslims, Christians, and Buddhists all saw the heart as a major force in spiritual birth and rebirth. To ancients, the heart was not merely a metaphor for the home of the spirit, it was literally that home. In fact, many traditional cultures saw the heart as the locus of the intellect, memory, spirit, and regenerative power. In many early texts, we find the idea of offering one's heart to deity. The Bible uses such language as God creating a new heart for those who seek to change their lives, purifying one's heart, and having God's word written on one's heart. Similar ideas are found in Muslim, Buddhist, and other sacred texts.

One of the strongest common threads uniting the views of diverse cultures and religious and spiritual traditions throughout human history has been a universal regard for the heart as a point of spiritual influx and as a source of wisdom and positive emotions. The Buddha referred to this center of consciousness as the "reflective current of the heart." (It is striking how close this phrase comes to capturing the essence of our scientific model of emotion, in which the rhythms and patterns of heart activity are interpreted by the brain and mind as feelings and emotions.)

Such ideas about the heart flourished in Western society until the seventeenth century. Since then, however, the heart has been reduced to a simple pump or a sentimental valentine. We contend that much of the alienation of the spirit in the West is related to the loss of understanding of the heart as a central organ in spiritual transformation. In "The Rehumanization of the Heart" (*Harpers,*

February 1980), Charles Siebert argues that we may "be suffering a kind of collective heart attack, a modern metaphysical one—pained by the weakening of long-held notions of the heart as the home of the soul and the seat of deep emotions."

One of these notions is that intuitive insight is related to the connection between the heart and spirit. In this context, a number of studies have shown that the body often responds to a future unknown emotionally arousing event *four to seven seconds* before experiencing the actual event. In addition, depending on whether the future event is positive or negative, the heart sends a different pattern of information to the brain before the brain itself responds. This ability of the heart to respond to emotionally relevant information indicates that the heart seems to be tuned to or accesses a field of information that is not limited by the boundaries of time and space. Research demonstrating this phenomenon suggests that the heart may indeed be linked to what might be called the higher self or spirit, as all the great religions and ancient civilizations have maintained.

This gift of intuition, this day-to-day inner guidance, increases our natural vitality and affects the quality of energy we radiate.

We Affect Each Other Energetically

The interaction between two human beings is a sophisticated dance that involves many subtle factors. Just as there is energetic coherence in personal vitality, so too is there an energetic entity present in the interaction of individuals within a family or community. It is possible, in fact, to measure the energetic states of communication between people. With the proper technology, scientists can now see the connections between one person's heartbeat and another person's brain waves. This demonstrates that our personal vitality and coherence can be intrinsically linked to those of the collective. Our sensitivity to detecting and perceiving the information communicated energetically appears to be directly related to the degree of emotional and physiological coherence we have. When in a coherent state, individuals not only operate more efficiently, but they also become more receptive to and aware of the information encoded in the electromagnetic fields radiated by other humans and living things. Likewise, it is possible to measure resonance at the global level by looking at correlations between human energetic patterns and patterns in the ionosphere, which is like the planet's cell membrane.

Global Stress

People worldwide are experiencing mounting concern about such things as climate change, terrorism, fossil fuel dependency, food and product safety, and financial insecurity. The accelerating pace of change, along with increasing levels of stress, is contributing to a momentum of global incoherence and instability. Research at HeartMath laboratories has shown that stressful feelings not only affect personal health and vitality, but they also radiate outward from the heart like radio waves and are detected by the nervous systems of others in our environment.

Stressful events all over the world are repeatedly broadcast globally via television and the Internet, creating and amplifying stress waves. Detection of these stress waves by our nervous systems can create a background feeling of unease in us. When we don't know how to manage the unease, our mental, emotional, and physical systems can become overloaded and drained. Unresolved stress accumulates in people's systems and creates incoherence in their personal lives, workplaces, and families, and in society in general.

A positive side of this increased stress is that more people are naturally turning to their hearts to take a deeper look at their inner resources and to seek deeper connections with others. An increasing number of people are looking to their hearts for guidance to adjust to the pace of change, manage the stress, and make more peaceful adjustments with stressors they can't yet change. They are becoming more aware that there is a planetary shift taking place, which is about the opening of the heart in the individual and the collective consciousness. As a result, many people are feeling a desire to put out more genuine heartfelt care to each other and to a planet in need.

Evidence of a global effect when a large number of people create similar outgoing emotional stress waves has been provided by research from the Global Consciousness Project, which utilizes a worldwide network of random number generators. There is compelling evidence that human consciousness and emotionality create a global field effect that can change the randomness of these electronic devices. The greatest change in the random-number generators occurred during the September 11, 2001, terrorist attacks.

More intriguing was the fact that the random number generators were significantly affected four to five hours before the attacks, suggesting an unconscious worldwide collective intuition of the impending events. Furthermore, two space weather satellites monitoring Earth's geomagnetic field also displayed a significant spike at the time of the attack and for a period thereafter, indicating the stress wave was detected in the geomagnetic field.

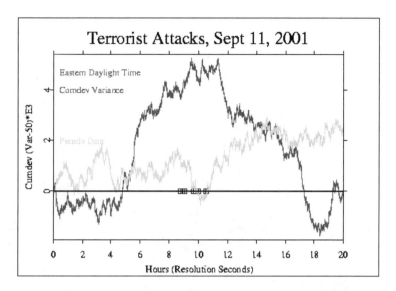

As individuals grow in emotional self-regulation and connection to their heart intuition, it will result in greater connectedness to others, which will, in turn, contribute to social harmony as self-centered behaviors are replaced by greater attention to humanistic ideals. As more individuals make the effort required to maintain true wellness in their lives, the resiliency and overall quality of life of the community at large will benefit as well.

GARY CRAIG

Emotional Freedom Techniques

A s babies and children we have no emotional defenses and very little experiences of our own. We are like little sponges unable to resist absorbing beliefs held by the people around us. While we certainly absorb positive ideas, we absorb negative ones too, and they disrupt the natural balance of our body's energy system.

Beliefs such as "You'll never learn," or "Without hard work, you're nothing," or "Our family never has any money," plus all the fears and guilt they pile on can hold us in their power long into adulthood. Even after we're grown, we can acquire negative beliefs about ourselves and behave in not so beneficial ways. Over time, all these harmful beliefs and behaviors become like heavy rocks that bury our once-free emotional selves and pin us down. But if we can release them, we can regain our emotional freedom, which I believe is everyone's birthright.

The Emotional Freedom Techniques, or EFT, is one easy and effective way of restoring our emotional freedom. It has provided thousands of people with relief from emotional issues as well as pain and illness. It's an emotional version of acupuncture—no needles necessary! Instead, using your fingertips, you tap on points along certain energy meridians that run through your body, which resolves the energy disruption. EFT is easy to memorize since you always tap on the same points, no matter what the problem or condition. And you can use it anywhere.

Gary Craig has been deeply interested in personal improvement through psychology since the age of thirteen, when he recognized that the quality of his life mirrored the quality of his thoughts. He created Emotional Freedom Techniques (EFT), a needle-free, emotional version of acupuncture that has provided thousands with relief from pain, diseases, and emotional issues. He is a Stanford engineering graduate, an ordained minister in the nondenominational Universal Church of God and an avid student of *A Course in Miracles*. He is also a Certified Master Practitioner of Neuro Linguistic Programming. www.emofree.com.

The EFT Discovery Statement says, "The cause of all negative emotions is a disruption in the body's energy system." Those disruptions create a short circuit in the subtle energy system of the body. I like to imagine it being the Bzzzzt! you hear when the power on your television or radio goes out. Yet this disruption goes beyond our emotional selves. Since our physical pains and diseases are so obviously connected with our emotions, this statement has also proven true: "Our unresolved negative emotions are major contributors to most physical pains and diseases." Resolve the emotional issues and you resolve the physical ones as well.

EFT is a common sense approach that draws its power from two sources. The first is tested and time-honored Eastern discoveries, such as acupuncture, that have been around for five thousand years. The second is Albert Einstein, who told us that everything, including our bodies, is composed of energy. Even though these ideas have been largely ignored by Western healing practices, they are the reasons why EFT often works when nothing else will.

Thanks to its nature being so different from any other healing technique, EFT applies to everything, and I mean that quite literally. It applies to even the most severe emotional issues like schizophrenia and PTSD, as well as garden-variety phobias and fears. It also assists beautifully with physical health issues, from headaches and allergies all the way to serious diseases like multiple sclerosis. And it is even successfully applied to performance issues, such as improving a golf score, singing a higher note, and speaking in public.

Comfort Zones and Beyond

We're all familiar with the term "comfort zone." But if you think about it, a comfort zone is just another way of describing those personal limits we get used to and don't question. Beyond our comfort zone, though, is what I call a Palace of Possibilities. In truth, we all live in this palace. We know about all the other rooms and know that we could go there, even though some of them are much more expensive or luxurious than we're used to. Yet since these rooms are outside our comfort zone, we don't enter them. We're comfortable down in the kitchen or the basement, but not in the penthouse or the corner suite overlooking the beach. That's for richer people, bigger people, smarter people, for men or for women—for anyone but us. Fortunately, EFT can expand our comfort zones and provide us entry into the Palace of Possibilities in ways that many other techniques don't or can't.

Let's say you would like to increase your financial abundance. If you were to look at your ideas about money and wealth, you would likely discover all kinds of beliefs that are holding you back from having more. Logically, there is probably little truth to your beliefs; what limits you is your emotional response to them.

In my own case, when I was thirty, I was making $18,000 a year, and working hard for that much. One day a man showed me how my beliefs about money were holding me back. He asked me to describe a wealthy man. In my mind, this rich man was portly, smoked stinky cigars, rode in a big, black, polluting limousine, was dishonest, and stepped on people to get his wealth. No wonder I didn't want to be wealthy! I didn't want other people to judge me this same way. Additionally, even though I was a life insurance salesman, in the back of my mind I believed that salespeople were pests. That certainly kept me from being very effective in sales. And the icing on this cake was a belief I inherited from my father: profits are bad because they come from high prices that he couldn't afford.

At the same time, I also believed that providing for my family was a good thing. I believed that America was the land of opportunity where anyone could be a success, and having lots of money was a badge of that success.

Unfortunately, the conflict between my limiting and my empowering thoughts kept me at a rather low balance point within my comfort zone.

I learned how to create more empowering beliefs about money by slowly and purposefully conditioning my thoughts. My first affirmation was, "I earn, easily and consistently, $40,000 per year." That amount was still within my comfort zone, so I could imagine myself earning at that level. The words "easily and consistently" took out the element of gritting my teeth or suffering. I said that affirmation many times during the day. I wrote it down often, and I also began writing in a journal how good it would feel to have this money and what I could do with it. I even daydreamed about it. But at no time did I try to decide "how" I was going to bring this amount of money into my life. That would have stopped me cold because I would have made the "how" much too difficult. I wanted to have fun with my new beliefs, and I did.

Within a year, I was making that $40,000. So I upped my belief to $60,000, and gradually moved up from there, until I was earning $400,000. What happened? By changing my beliefs and transforming my emotional response to having financial abundance, I was able to collapse the barriers to entering wonderful new rooms in my Palace of Possibilities.

Understand that this happened many years before I developed EFT, and it took longer than EFT usually takes. But this was the situation that put me on the path to not only changing my own life but also developing EFT so I could help others improve their situations.

The Writing on Our Walls

Just like those thoughts I had about rich people, all the beliefs and experiences we have are embedded in our subconscious mind. Without even realizing it, we consult them all the time and then let them control us. I call these beliefs and experiences "the writing on our walls." Many of them are comedies, they are logically absurd, but we rarely question them. With EFT, however, we can uncover and transform them.

Take the word "dog," for instance. It's a simple, common word, but we all have writing on our walls about dogs. The writing on your walls might say that dogs are friendly and lovable, so it's safe to be around them. But your neighbor was once badly bitten by a dog, and the writing on her walls says that dogs hurt people, so is terrified every time she sees one.

Here's another example. A young basketball player has the ability to jump even higher than he already does and become a professional. But perhaps the writing on his walls tells him, "If I jump higher and the pros want me, I don't think I could stand that kind of pressure." Or, "If I jump higher than my big brother, I'll lose his love." He may not even realize these beliefs on a conscious level, but they hold him back nonetheless.

What we want to do is find out what's written on our walls, and start collapsing those beliefs until they become very tiny and can be easily replaced with more positive ideas. It's my view that our true nature underneath all these limiting beliefs and thoughts and emotions is joyous and spiritual. If we just take away all the limits, the good stuff comes bubbling to the top, as it should. Once you get all the limiting beliefs out of the way, then the more prolific and expanding beliefs that are available to you will appear. They won't have the competition; they won't have the yes-buts that come from old writing on our walls. That's what we can do with EFT: We tune into these problems, tap on them, and then resolve the disruption in our energy system.

Tailenders

Affirmations have become a popular way of attempting to change the writing on our walls. They always work, but only if we first discern the true affirmation behind the one that we use. When they don't appear to work well, it's because of what I call "tailenders," or those unspoken and unconscious beliefs lurking underneath the stated affirmation. Here's an example.

A woman who weighs 200 pounds wants to lose weight, so she creates an affirmation: "My normal weight is 130 pounds and that's what I weigh." It sounds good—it's in the present tense, it's clear and concise. But she has many tailenders hanging around in her subconscious that will sabotage her. Here's a short list: But if you lose the weight, others will expect you to keep it off... you'll have to spend lots of money on new clothes...men will hit on you and expect sex... men won't hit on you and then you'll know you aren't lovable.

We human beings are extremely inventive and can create endless lists of subtle, powerful, hidden reflections of obstacles to our goals. We might eventually be able to override them with persistent use of our affirmation, but many people give up when they don't see any immediate results. Additionally, they feel uncomfortable with the emotional discord that goes on between the stated affirmation and the competing tailenders. They often conclude that they are lying to themselves and just give up. As you can see, the affirmation process usually needs help. It needs EFT to erase those existing tailenders. Once they are gone, the affirmation will take root and become the new reality.

EFT and Illness

Recall this statement above: "Our unresolved negative emotions are major contributors to most physical pains and diseases." EFT works very well with physical issues too, by resolving the underlying emotional beliefs that cause them. With EFT, we maintain our right to heal ourselves rather than rely on some outside force.

Typically, when we have an illness we go to a doctor who prescribes a treatment, which could be anything from drugs to surgery. While these can be useful tools, they are often used without the understanding that, for most diseases, the real cause isn't something like a virus, although that can be a contributor. The real cause is unresolved emotional issues—the anger, the guilt, the traumas we carry around—that compromise our immune systems because they disrupt our energy systems so badly. If we don't recognize that in the vast majority of cases we are contributing to the cause—if not completely causing it ourselves—then we are asking the doctor to do a job he or she can't really do. The medical profession may disagree with me on that, but then they don't truly cure very many diseases. By and large, they are dealing with symptoms but not with the real causes.

EFT, on the other hand, resolves the true causes of illness and pain. Some dramatic success stories of healing have resulted from its use. Ask Hank.

When he was a boy, Hank fell twenty-five feet and landed in a sitting position on concrete. He underwent six back surgeries to correct the spinal compression that resulted from his fall, but each operation increased his pain. Severely traumatized physically and emotionally, his only relief came from popping pain pills "like candy." After developing MS and becoming wheelchair-bound, Hank fell into despair, wondering what he had done to deserve such a fate. But then he discovered EFT. After five years in a wheelchair, he was able to progress to using arm crutches, and then, as he says, "I'm fifty-four and doing jumping jacks." He was also able to give up Social Security disability payments and return to work.

EFT works very well with so-called "hereditary" conditions, which some researchers believe MS to be. In my experience, however, I see less and less validity to the argument that many physical conditions are hereditary. Bruce Lipton's *Biology of Belief* is a big breakthrough in this area. In this book, he effectively presents the science behind how our genetic makeup actually has little to do with our health. Instead, the root cause is our emotions, which affect our genes in certain ways that cause them to be healthy or not healthy.

It's very well known in medicine that in someone who's undergoing joyous emotions produces chemicals that are positive, healing chemicals in the body. It's also proven that when somebody is angry and full of rage, the body produces harmful chemicals. After the body is subjected to these harmful substances for a period of time, the result is disease. It may have different names, like cancer or MS, allergies or migraines, but it all comes from the same source: disrupted energy. I believe that if physicians skillfully applied EFT *first* to all of their patients, the number of required surgeries, medications, and radiations would dramatically fall.

Pursuing our Possibilities

What more exciting adventure could there be than to pursue our possibilities? What greater insight could we have than to realize that the walls that seem to limit us are made of cellophane? For the most part, our "limits" are mental fictions. We are, indeed, only a few mental shifts away from truly enjoying the Palace of Possibilities in which we live. But then, you already know that, don't you?

There is a freedom involved in fully recognizing what we do with the writing on our walls. Recognizing that everyone (including ourselves) constantly consults that writing for their version of the "truth" leads to more peaceful understandings and forgiving attitudes. It helps us to stand back from disagreements and de-personalize other people's actions. After all, they're just spouting off what other people have written on their walls as though it was somehow the "truth." It allows us to smile at our own comedies and recognize our personal "limits" as being mental fictions that are little more than hand-me-down beliefs from previous generations of parents, teachers, peers, and many others. The peace that comes with this understanding serves us well. It can eliminate disease, enhance relationships, and enrich life. We can regain our inherent vitality and love ourselves without judgment or condition: All that from a simple mental perception. Not bad, eh?

There is a dimension to our existence that we tend to overlook because it is not contained within the familiar three dimensions of space. It is the dimension of thought. Thoughts are things. They have no limits unless we choose to limit them ourselves. We can imagine anything. We can dream things and make missions out of them. No telling how far they will take us. How exciting! How awesome! Thoughts move and shape our individual worlds as well as the world around us. Thoughts make things happen, and our consistent thoughts become our reality. We can use EFT to make our reality the best it can possibly be.

PART FOUR

Creating Vibrant Relationships

STEPHEN POST

Doing Unto Others: The Benefits of Giving

H ere's the recipe for a good and joyous life: Enjoy being a generous, giving person and be generous and giving often.

In case you think that idea is naïve or too simple, I'd like to give this gift to you: A growing body of rigorous research shows that generous people who frequently give of themselves to others live healthier, happier, longer lives than people who don't. More than fifty studies at major universities have demonstrated that giving, particularly if begun in childhood, will protect you for your whole life. From the individual all the way to entire societies, giving is the most potent force in the world.

This kind of unselfish giving behavior directed toward others is called altruism. It helps us discover in a deep way that the happiness and the security of others means as much to us as our own. This doesn't mean we aren't allowed to feel good when giving—because we are—but only that when we're "doing unto others," we're moving beyond our own egoism or narcissism and expanding our concern outside of ourselves.

Just as being selfish is part of our human nature, being altruistic is also part of our emotional repertoire. And I would venture to say that altruism is the more crucial and essential element. Think about it for a minute: How could we humans survive without cooperating at least some of the time and taking the welfare of at least some others as seriously as we take our own? We require the love and care of others,

Stephen Post has been making headlines by funding studies at the nation's top universities to prove the life-enhancing benefits of caring, kindness, and compassion. They show that when we give of ourselves, especially if we start young, everything from self-realization to physical health is significantly affected. In his life-changing new book, *Why Good Things Happen to Good People* (Random House, 2007), Dr. Post, along with coauthor Jill Neimark, weaves the growing new science of love and giving with profoundly moving real-life stories to show exactly how to unlock the door to health. www.brightsightgroup.com.

and we seem to have a profound, deeply evolved need for close, giving relationships. Parents, for example, are generous and giving to their children, sometimes to the point of sacrificing their deepest desires and even their lives for them. Friends are also frequently generous with their friends, and strangers are often compassionate towards one another. Some people even have a love for their enemies.

Being concerned with the welfare of others simply has every kind of evolutionary advantage. Children do not thrive unless they feel cared for and experience empathy and loyalty. People in a particular group will prosper to the extent that altruistic emotions and behaviors like compassion and cooperation operate effectively. However we look at it, there are big advantages to altruistic emotions and behaviors. At the same time, it can be difficult to move from concern for our own group to concern for humans as a whole, for the "we" in the sense of a shared humanity. But that's where spirituality and religion and also the power of the mind can be used to move us away from the very shaky ground of thinking of ourselves as superior and others as inferior.

Even Charles Darwin, whose concept of survival of the fittest is often misinterpreted to mean every man for himself, believed that groups whose members regularly provide compassion and altruism to one another survived far better and far longer than those groups that did not. Even though we have the propensity to dehumanize outsiders and those different from us, he said reason alone is enough to tell us that we are fundamentally equal and that whatever differences we have between us have no moral significance. Understanding the dire consequences of what happens to us if we don't give attention to our better natures, Darwin very much appreciated our capacities for giving and for positive emotion.

The Science of Altruism

Being giving and altruistic—and in that, I include qualities such as compassion, empathy, love, forgiveness, listening, and generosity—offers concrete benefits to the giving person. Without any question, people who are generous and giving are happier than those who are not. That is very well defined in the literature, whether it's from Victor Frankl, concentration camp survivor, psychotherapist, and author of *Man's Search for Meaning*, or a Time/CNN poll where 75 percent of Americans say what makes them happiest is contributing to the lives of others. People who are selfish tend to be unhappy. Ebenezer Scrooge is a perfect example of this; he's a fictional character, but Dickens got it right. There are some people who are isolated for reasons of creativity and perhaps spiritual discipline who can be happy. But by all the measures we have, those who live isolated, selfish lives, or even selfish lives where they're reasonably social, are not as happy as givers are. You can be surrounded by a thousand people who love, worship, and adore you, but until you yourself become a source of generosity and giving and love, you just won't be happy.

Altruistic behavior also helps you to live longer, and to live a healthier life. Many studies continue to demonstrate this. Here are some examples.

- Adolescents who are giving, particularly boys, have a reduced risk of depression and suicide. The way to be a happier, more active, involved, and challenged teen, regardless of gender, is to be giving, hopeful, and socially effective.

- Giving in high school predicts good physical and mental health more than fifty years later, based on an ongoing study that began in the 1920s and continues today.

- Volunteering significantly reduces mortality in later life. One study of people over age 55 shows that those who volunteer for two or more organizations are 44 percent less likely to die than those who don't volunteer, once health and other variables are taken into account. This is a higher percentage than even with mobility (39 percent), exercising four times weekly (30), or attending religious services (29).

- Giving is more powerful than receiving in the ability to reduce mortality. One study of churchgoing adults found that offering social support to others reduces people's anxiety over their own economic situation when they face economic stress.

- We can more easily forgive ourselves for our own mistakes when we provide emotional support to others, particularly among older adults who are African American.

Researchers have also found that there's even more of a boost in mortality reduction for those who find meaning in what they're doing. People who, for instance, volunteer through their church often find a great deal of meaning in volunteering because they are following a higher example. We have a human tendency to quest, to raise big picture questions about the nature of the universe. Despite some of the most ugly, deadly realities of the world, people want to have a sense that by living a good, benevolent life, things will turn out positively. They believe that there's a deeper meaning in the whole scheme of history and in the whole scheme of the universe than meets the eye. So they like to think about a God of love, for example, a compassionate, loving God, because that gives them the sense that even though a particular scene in the play may be very dark and despairing, it's still love that wrote the whole play. This is one of the reasons why in so many traditions, even when those traditions fall short, people still believe ultimately in the victory of love.

As humans, we construct world views and their meanings, and those meanings really matter. One of the most important ways we seek meaning is with other people. We recognize that the most noble purpose of life is actually pretty simple: be generous, be kind, be compassionate. In *A Course in Miracles*, for instance, the miracles are just random acts of kindness—that's interpersonal and meaningful. But I also think people often want meaning that goes beyond the worldly level to the fabric of the universe and asks whether, in fact, the universe is friendly to love or not. Einstein asked whether we live in a friendly universe, and this can be the most important question people have to answer. Is there some higher presence in this universe that somehow amplifies or resonates with a generous and loving life? That is what helps people keep going in tough times.

Something about moving beyond preoccupation with the self and looking toward others brings happiness. John F. Kennedy was right to say, "Ask not what your country can do for you but what you can do for your country." When people stop demanding everything from everyone and stumble on the happiness of doing things for other people, it's a wonderful transformation. That's what a lot of spiritual transformation is about. Look at the Dalai Lama, Mother Teresa, Helen Keller, and so many others: These are all people who described a sense of joy and even mirth in living as much for others as for self. That's happiness.

One very interesting study demonstrated how the brain reacts to merely thinking about giving. People were given a list of charities and asked to which one they might like to contribute. As soon as they chose one, an ancient part of the brain dealing with emotions, called the mesolimbic pathway, lit up. This meant that chemicals were being produced just by their thoughts about giving, and those were feel-good chemicals, including serotonin. So you give to help others, but you also help yourself at the same time. You'll feel better, you'll probably have better emotional and physical health. So doing unto others is great for others, but it's also good for us. We get meaning, we get a role, we get purpose. With altruistic behavior, our main motive is not to seek happiness mostly for ourselves, but it's fine to recognize that part of the human essence is that we flourish more when we do unto others than when we don't.

Four Domains and Ten Ways

Giving can take many forms beyond volunteering and making charitable donations, and we can give in four major domains. The four domains begin with our most intimate circle and expand outward: family, friends, community, and humanity. The Love and Longevity Scale, developed through the Institute for Research on Unlimited Love at Case Western Reserve University, captures ten of the numerous ways of giving in these domains:

- Celebration: Pure fun that wells up from gratitude and appreciation.
- Generativity: Nurturing others so their lives develop in unexpected and beautiful ways.
- Forgiveness: One of the most studied ways of giving, this frees us from inner pain and bitterness.
- Courage: Confronting harmful behaviors while remaining caring.
- Humor: Can change pain to joy in an instant.
- Respect: Offers tolerance, civility, acceptance, and even reverence as it allows us to look beyond our biases and judgments.
- Compassion: The emotional core of morality, compassion is love's response to suffering.
- Loyalty: Love through time and difficulties.
- Listening: A quiet yet powerful form of attention that allows us to be present in a reassuring way.
- Creativity: The most spontaneous, joyful expression of life itself.

We all do better in some of these ways than in others, depending on our personalities and life experiences. For instance, Sir John Templeton, age 94 and one of the most famous mutual fund managers of all time, is an excellent giver in terms of funding research on spirituality, science, and human potential (including the Institute for Research on Unlimited Love), as well as investing in emerging markets so struggling economies can improve. However, he grew up in rural Tennessee and went to Yale University, largely on his own efforts, so he is not as interested in giving to individuals. One teenaged boy, only moderately interested in becoming more of a giver, volunteered as a math tutor to students struggling in that subject. He found that he enlarged his ability to give as well as his connection with others, so he continued to tutor a few hours a week. I do best with humor and courage, while I'm often impatient with people in my community, especially when I feel too busy to show kindness to others. We're all only human, so we do the best we can when we can.

To Become More of a Giver

We know that what we think becomes our reality. If you want to become more of a giver (and improve your life at the same time), focus on some giving behavior and strive to do it more often. If you want to be more compassionate, or a better listener, or more loyal, start by thinking about those qualities and how you might offer them to others. When you focus your mind on something, it becomes important to you, and it's more likely to be reflected in your actions. So just be conscious of this as you go through the day. Try this: early in the morning, think about the people you'll be interacting with that day and simply ask yourself, how can I interact with them in loving ways? You can also visualize yourself in a situation and imagine yourself being more loving. If you know you have a difficult encounter coming up, envision yourself acting with warmth and hope and optimism. The likelihood is that by keeping that behavior in mind, it will be more likely to happen.

In the end, this kind of behavior is transmitted. The best thing you can do is get yourself around people who are generous and giving in these various ways. In the end, modeling is extremely important. We had one rare medical student here at Case Western Reserve who lacked compassion and actually scared patients a bit. We asked him to spend a half-day every day for six months with the most compassionate doctors we could identify. The student did change his behavior by observing and interacting with professionals of profound love and care.

If you feel that you're not a giver, throw yourself into a social context where giving is the norm, whatever that might be. It could be a volunteer organization of some kind, a particular faith community that you're inspired by. Get yourself some new friends if you need to, but look to be around givers because that's really important. We need to create more networking situations where people can thrive as givers because a generous life is one that is encouraged, accepted, and rewarded.

But be kind to yourself, too. Nobody I know has ever reached a life of perfect giving, of perfect love. We also have to be concerned with our own health and keep a balance as much as possible. Love is more of a direction than a destination that we ever, ever arrive at. There are some people, though, who amaze us. Like a fastball pitcher who can throw a ball at a hundred miles an hour, there are some people who are incredibly generous and loving, and they're like that all the time, and they're happy in the process.

If people can start being a giver when they're young, that's a great start. It's important that parents try to raise caring children and involve them in giving opportunities. And then in everyday life, wherever you are and however old you are, remember that positive emotions are supported by positive actions. When we're doing unto others, we're typically going to be in a mood of care and compassion. When we think about others more than ourselves, we're going to be celebrating their lives, we're going to have a kind of freedom from self, so we'll probably be more mirthful and more positive. When we involve ourselves in social kinds of behaviors instead of antisocial ones, we elevate a side of ourselves that is more joyful and healthier, more likely to prosper, and less stressed out.

You can be a giver right where you are, at any time. You don't have to be a Mother Teresa to be a giving person. Even she said, "We can do no great things; only small things with great love."

MELODY BEATTIE

Brilliant Choices

When you learn your lessons, the pain goes away. That's what she wrote in *The Wheel of Life.*

The famous *Death and Dying* lady lay on the hospital bed in her living room. She couldn't get up. A series of strokes—nineteen or more—had left her severely handicapped. Paralyzed on one side. It was morning. She was thirsty. Elisabeth Kübler-Ross said a quick prayer. "God, please send someone. A cup of tea would be so nice."

I got lost on the back roads in Arizona. Even with a navigation system in my car, I couldn't find the address. I bumped around on the roads in my four-wheel drive. The woman with me, Lori, frowned.

"Haven't you ever been four-wheeling before?" I asked.

"No," she said.

"Then it's time." She had quit her job as a reporter at the *Miami Herald.* Now she was freelancing and writing a book. Together we were on our way to interview Elisabeth Kübler-Ross. I don't have a lot of female heroes in this world. Elisabeth is definitely one. She had done so much groundbreaking work on the subject of grief, death, dying, and life after death. And I wanted to meet her before she died.

Finally we found the address. Rang the doorbell. "Come in," Elisabeth yelled. We pushed open the door.

Melody Beattie is a best-selling author and journalist. She has written fourteen books and published hundreds of newspaper and magazine articles during the course of her writing career, including the iconic *Code-pendent No More* (Hazelden, 1986). Born in St. Paul, Minnesota she now lives in Southern California. Her hobbies include skydiving, Yoga, travel and hiking. Beattie has been a frequent guest on many national television shows, including Oprah. She and her books have been featured in national publications including *Time and People*, and most major newspapers in the United States and Canada.

CHAPTER TWENTY-TWO

"Hi, Elisabeth," I said. "Would you like me to make you a cup of tea?"

We helped fix her some food. She asked me to help her put her shorts on. Carefully I did as she asked.

"It's about receiving," she said. "I never learned to receive. Now God has put me in a position where I have no choice but to ask for and accept help."

I helped her get in the wheelchair, pushed her into the bathroom. I looked away, trying to give her some privacy while she washed her face and brushed her teeth.

I pushed her back to the living room. Lori and I sat down in front of her.

"Go ahead," she said. "Ask away."

Lori cleared her throat. "I've been researching a book. I'm trying to find out what it means to own my power."

"That's easy, my dear," Elisabeth said. "All you have to do is be who you are."

Elisabeth looked at me. "And you," she said. "What do you want to ask?"

Now it was my turn to clear my throat.

"Do you really believe in life, after death? Aren't you afraid of death, at least a little bit?" I asked.

Elisabeth laughed. "Didn't you read my book, dear?" she said. "It's not about believing. I know there's life after death. Dying is the easy part. It's life that's hard."

We said our good-byes. Elisabeth did what she called an ET touch—gently extending her finger, as any more touch than that caused her pain.

I leaned over and whispered in her ear, "Thank you. And have a safe trip home."

Lessons. Lessons. And more lessons. Every step of the way there's something to learn. Just when you think you've got them all under your belt, another lesson comes blowing your way.

Some of them come disguised as problems or issues to solve. Others are normal effects caused by life and by getting older each day. Within each category of lessons, there are many little mini-lessons, too.

Fear can be a fun lesson to learn. I started jumping out of airplanes as part of learning about that. Play is an enjoyable lesson too—although some of us are stiff and forced at first. Some people's lesson is to stop playing and learn to work. Some of the other lessons aren't as pleasurable. They hurt when they're happening to us. Grief, a broken heart, hurts physically and emotionally, and can go on for a long, long time. The pain from loss and grief can take two to eight years—sometimes more.

Guilt is the worst. Absolutely the worst. The feeling is paralyzing, and we often push it down so deep inside of us we're not even aware it's there. But the thoughts keep floating through our mind.

It's like being in a relationship with the most tormentive person on the planet. Constantly our guilt is telling us: you don't deserve, people might find out, you can't be who you are. Sometimes it can take us to the edge: you don't deserve to be happy; you don't deserve to live. It's subtle and insidious. Even if we tell it to shut up, it still stares at us with condemning eyes.

Some of us not only have guilt as a lesson, we have guilt about the lessons we find ourselves going through. Guilt permeates our lives.

I thought the concept of lessons was interesting as a general idea—until these lessons kept happening to *me.* I kept waiting for the lessons to stop. And I would have moments of rest, play, respite. Until the winds blew another lesson my way.

Well, this is fine, I'd think. *Let's just get it over so I can get my piece of the pie, get my share of the dream.* In the *Big Book of Alcoholics Anonymous,* Bill Wilson talks about happy, joyous, and free. I wanted to get to that part. And each time I'd get another lesson under my belt, I'd think, *now I'm finally there.* Until the next lesson began.

At a seminar in Pasadena in 2001, the Dalai Lama said that all people want the same thing—they just want to be happy.

That's what the big grinding Wheel of Life is trying to do—get us to that place of being happy and free. We do get the big brass ring—but it's often not what we thought it would be. Sometimes slowly, sometimes in a flash of transformation, we get it—whatever the lesson we're going through is. After years of waiting, we finally become so patient we forget that we're waiting and what we're waiting for. After years of trying to control everything around us, we wear ourselves out and finally surrender. After years of keeping our hearts hardened and afraid, we become flooded with forgiveness, tolerance, and compassion. After years of grasping at other people, we finally feel content and complete taking care of ourselves.

After years of being selfish and not considering anyone but ourselves, we learn to give. Or the opposite may be true. After years of giving everything away, we allow ourselves to become vulnerable and receive, too.

Experience. It's both a noun and a verb. Things happen to us, and we immerse ourselves in those scenarios. We dive in. Go through it. Submerge. Then come out changed—or not. We may go around and around the lesson wheel again and again, sometimes at different levels, until we *get* the lesson being taught.

The lesson may be over, but don't forget what you learned.

You're going to need it while you climb mountain number two.

SHILOH SOPHIA McCLOUD

The Awakened Heart

B e patient toward all that is unsolved in your heart and to try to love the questions themselves as if they were locked rooms or books written in a very foreign language. Don't search for the answers, which could not be given to you now, because you would not be able to live them. And the point is, to live everything. Live the questions now. Perhaps then, someday far in the future, you will gradually, without even noticing it, live your way into the answer.

—Rainer Maria Rilke, *Letters to a Young Poet*

Peak vitality in my life is a result of creative expression. How I access creative expression has to do with my relationship to the Divine, my relationship to others, and my relationship to myself. The way I specifically relate to each of these is through a process of questions and answers, which I celebrate here in the form of a letter written to an old friend.

Dear One,

I want to write you a letter as if we are old friends. So this would be a good time to make yourself a cup of tea. If we were together right now, as I wish, I would make you a cup like the one I am having, with cream and honey, and cinnamon sprinkled on top. Candles are lit on my kitchen table, and we have red velvet pillows behind our backs. We suck slices of summer's last watermelon from glistening pink layers on crystal plates. On the table before us is a vase of blue

Shiloh Sophia McCloud, Minister of Sacred Arts, is a gifted teacher, visionary artist, author, and independent publisher. She painted the image on the cover of this book, and lives on the Mendocino Coast with her husband, Isaiah McCloud, with whom she co-owns Wisdom House Gallery. For more than a decade, the gallery has been featuring Shiloh's artwork, books, and workshops. Shiloh's life work is to invite people to experience art and creativity as spiritual practice and a path of transformation, as well as to discover their own life path as a vehicle of awakening. For prints see www. WisdomHouseCatalog.com. Photo: Beth Baugher.

hydrangeas. I tell you that they are the last from the bush you can see through my kitchen window.

We are blessed with the first rain of autumn. When my husband opened the window this morning, there it was. Like an old and welcome friend after a long dry spell, its quiet arrival woke me to this need to speak to you.

We are here together because we want to ask the burning questions. Why do the questions burn? Because if they don't get asked, they will burn us in some way, and not necessarily in the way we hope. But when they are asked, whether or not they are answered, they set our hearts on fire — with life, with love, with possibilities.

Tell me, what is on your mind the first thing in the morning, right before your eyes are open, when your thoughts have just begun to shake off the night? If regrets are what you find, then cast them into the morning fire and let them crackle and die there in the red embers of yesterday. If there is joy at the dawning of this new day, tell me of all the deliciousness of your joy. Tell me what you have never told anyone before.

I want to know what dream keeps coming back that is yet to be fulfilled. I remind you of your wild ways, and you remind me of mine. I remind you of who you were before everything else happened. You remind me of who I was. Do you remember what was important to you when you were a child? Before everything got so very busy. Did you grow up to be who you wanted to be? Are you doing your life work — not just a work life? Did you give up too much of yourself to others? Have you let go of too many dreams? Is there a dream you are nursing in quiet?

If you confess to having let go of too much of who you are, I will challenge you. Maybe you do not want this conversation and would rather speak of everyday things. Maybe you will challenge me back. I hope you will. Maybe you won't let me forget what is possible, if I believe in myself. And I will tell you boldly, I believe in me and I believe in you!

You might laugh nervously because you do not want to answer me. I know this makes us feel vulnerable, uncomfortable. And I am sorry, and I am not. Where else but here? When else but now? Who else but us? The burning questions will never go away. They insist on being courted like an eternally new lover. They must be sought and sung to, nurtured and adorned.

Ani Di Franco says, "If you don't ask the right question, every answer sounds wrong." We must do as Clarissa Pinkola Estés suggests in *Women Who Run with Wolves* and seek the river beneath the river. We must call aloud upon the name of the door that opens it. "O tocar alla puerta!" We can do as Jesus invited, "Knock and the door shall be opened, seek and ye shall find." Let's build an altar for our questions and pray to the Holy One to help us see the path more clearly. To hear the call!

I am not just trying to get you to answer these questions. I am trying to get you to ask them with me and of me. If I am not living my questions, living my way into the answers, how can I ask you if you are living yours? And I want to ask, must ask, cannot help but ask. One of my most burning questions is how to ask the questions. And, of course: What is the most expedient way to live into the answers?

I want to know, if you could do *anything,* what would it be? What does your perfect day look and feel like? From beginning to end. As you speak, I will bring a listening that creates safe space for you to speak into, a listening that searches for clues to what is needed. If your day includes two naps, I will know you need to rest more. If your day does not include any art, I will know you have forgotten how much you liked to draw and color when you were little, and it was late, and you did not want to put your crayons down. If your day does not include a lover, I will ask you about your heart's desire. If you love being alone, I will congratulate you on this great victory in a place where many struggle.

I want to know, have you been truly loved? Do your loved ones get who you are in all the poetry that is you? Do your loved ones ask you any of the questions we are asking today?

We cannot expect people to figure out what is important and sacred to us. Let's learn to gently show them before the resentment of unfulfillment begins to tear away at the sweetness. We need to tell them what is important to us. And we must make ourselves seen, experienced, and honored. Yes, and we must try as hard as we can, to really see, experience, and honor others. If they feel seen, they might even see us. Sometimes it works this way, and sometimes not.

If we don't feel we have a powerful circle of friends we can trust right now, then we should try to make one. We need to be able to speak our minds and not be afraid to be ourselves with people who think they know us. We want friends with whom we can share our secrets. I will tell you my secrets and visions, because the secrets long to be shared and enjoyed.

We all have a vision of some kind, and some of us have a vision so big that we are embarrassed to speak aloud because it sounds too grand. Like wanting to end world hunger, or start an orphanage, or plant an organic garden for our town. Although the big visions are about blessing others, we often feel alone in them. That is because we need to talk about them. We must have the courage to share and act on our grand desires. Alice Walker says that one of the things we can do for the world is to be in conversation about what is going on personally, collectively, cosmically. Our big visions give us clues as to what we truly care about. If we do not know what we truly care about, how can we know our purpose here on Earth? How can we know what to manifest? To attract?

Alice also says, "No one can end suffering except through dance." What does this mean, really? For me, it means to dance no matter what! It means that my dancing, my painting, my joy, and my love for others are contributing to the great goodness of the world. It says that art is medicine. That our dancing, like our prayers, lift one another up. It says that our dancing does not fall on empty streets, nor our prayers on empty ears. We don't have to do *everything* to participate in a big vision, just our own part, however small it may be. We do not have to become whole first, or suffer more, or do a better job before we contribute, we just have to choose a way to participate, and then act on it. We have to commit art with intention, says my art teacher.

I am not afraid to tell you of my unreasonable desire: I want to do what I can to end suffering in the world. I cannot help it; it is something that just came alive in me one day. And it is this vision, this desire, that leads me to create: to write, to paint, to teach, to dance, to be in conversations like this one!

It is my experience, and I cannot share from any place but my own experience, that through our spiritual creative practice, and seeking the face of the Divine, we are naturally led to our own unique purpose. My work with people and with myself has shown me that purpose and passion are found on the journey itself. Not at some remote destination in the distance, but along the way.

I cannot be true to myself, or to you, without sharing that it is through my relationship with Ma and Pa Divine that I have made art my life, and life my art, and that has made everything possible. They cause me to love beyond any love I could conjure on my own. To care beyond reason about people I do not even know. I cannot understand how I can feel so much pain for my brothers and sisters that I slump and cry and scream. And then I go to the canvas or to the classroom and my pain is transformed into more prayer, peace, sharing of insights and wisdom, and, even, bliss. The suffering, my own and that of others, informs me, opens me, awakens me to my love for the Divine, for you, and for myself. I attempt to touch and soothe the suffering, and express the love by creating what beauty I can in response to the tragedies of life. I can respond with more sadness and anger, and sometimes I do, or I can respond with a healing remedy, whenever I am able.

I don't have the words to express the mystery and ecstasy of being an artist who makes what I call sacred art. Especially since we all believe different things about how it all happens.

I know that what religion has made of God does not work for a lot of us, including me. But we can go on seeking and find other ways to be in relationship with Source. Each of us needs to extract whatever Source is for us, which may mean busting it free from the halls of religion and academia and making a whole different place to experience what it is, to get closer and go deeper.

Maybe that means meeting the Divine in a cabin on an expanse of countryside overlooking the sea. Maybe it means exploring the heart of the Divine while you practice creative expression. You could write, draw, garden, meditate, or pray—or, like Alice Walker, dance. My mom, who thinks that it is in wrestling with God like Jacob did that her purpose is revealed to her, says that maybe sometimes we just need to go someplace where we can scream at God for a while, and that sometimes prayer can look a lot like screaming.

It just so happens that I met Jesus at a Holy Roller church. All the women were dancing with their Bibles, and singing and laughing. I completely loved them. I had never seen women behaving in such an ecstatic way. One woman with smiling eyes came up to me while the tears were rolling down my cheeks and said, "That feeling you have right now is called Jesus! Do you want to have him for yourself?" Of course, I wanted what they had, and I said *yes* and Yahoo! Well, one way or another, I have never left him and he has never left me. Eventually, I met his mother too, but she came in a quiet way, when I was alone, to make herself known to me. I cried out to Jesus, "Where is my mother?" And indeed she came. Mama Mary, Our Lady of Everything. And honestly, my art, my paintings, really didn't come until after that. That is why when I am talking with people, I cannot help but ask about their spirituality, because I know firsthand how it can inform our art, our passion. I feel that it is the Divine that gave me the tools to live here on Earth and thrive instead of only survive. The Divine gave me art. Sure, I did art before, but after what I call my second awakening, that is when the real me came up for air and got hold of a big paintbrush!

My experience of the Divine may be different from the experiences you have heard about from others. It is so easy to offend people when speaking of the Divine, but if we do not share our hearts, truly, responsibly, how are we to grow our relationships? If you were really here at my table with me, we could talk about all this, talk it on out, and you would share with me your story of the Divine and of your spiritual path. If we all did this, maybe war could end, and justice and compassion could reign.

About spirit, some say we must surrender. Others say the universe is a series of chain reactions based on our actions. I say that if we seek the Divine, and pray and create, we can find a path to peace.

CHAPTER TWENTY-THREE

What Jesus called the "peace that passes understanding."

I also say, as I often do: The work of a visionary is to know the past, dream the future, and take powerful action in the present. I say that we must celebrate, create art, make love, share in beauty, and spread joy and hope and information however, wherever, and whenever we are able.

And isn't it amazing how hard it is to practice self-care? Some of us serve and serve, but never serve ourselves or allow ourselves to be served by others. Some of us just serve our own interests and don't serve others. But if we are to find peace, we must honor both serving and being served. To know the suffering in the world and to be sick from it, to be overburdened and overwhelmed by it, to be too sensitive, to become hopeless or let suffering make us mean does not do anyone any good. Well, maybe it helps at first. We have a right to be mad; there are a lot of terrible things happening. But at the same time, there are so many good things! We have to find a way to hold it all in context.

The next burning question is: How do we find and practice self-love? If we could do just that, transformation would become our rhythm, instead of being a goal we keep trying to reach.

My grandmother told me that when she was a young woman, she decided she was going to love herself no matter what. I was amazed, as that seemed so progressive for her generation. She said she discovered that the more she loved herself, the more others seemed to love her. She made a decision, and then backed it up with consistent action all her life. I wish you could have met her. She often wore a leopard-patterned silk shirt, rhinestone-crusted cat glasses, and hot pink lipstick and her hair was as white as dove feathers.

But if, unlike this extraordinary woman, we can't just decide to love ourselves right now, then how are we ever to get there?

We know there is more to experience than what is perceived on the surface of things. We are vaguely aware of an ever-widening landscape of bounty somewhere in the distance. Oh, how we long for it! We buy books and tapes and go to workshops that promise to give it to us. But it stays in the distance.

It's time we rid ourselves of the wounds that poke us in the eye when we gaze at the horizon. We have to let go of those harmful stories about ourselves. We have spent enough time tending them and licking our wounds. We must do whatever we can do to get them out of our immediate sphere. *right now*! We can store them for later if we're so damned attached to them, but for now, we release them, we send them out to be dissolved, we compost them, bury them, throw them into that fire where we threw our regrets this morning. We do it *immediately*!

We fill the space we created with choices that delight us. Let's begin with things that are so inspiring that our old wounds haven't the room to surface. Only through creating our lives as powerfully as we are able, so help us God, will we be able to move beyond the wounding. Let's pray right now that wounds no longer keep us from our highest good. Clear the path! We are breaking on through! A tribe of folks who love themselves enough to create miracles is moving in.

I will close this long letter to you with a few more of the burning questions I ask myself, the ones that seem to provide me with—if not always answers—the vitality that comes with the awakened heart.

What stories no longer serve me? What guilt can I surrender? What project can I begin that inspires me? How can I deepen my spiritual practice? What am I excited about, I mean, thrilled about? How do I self-medicate and is it working? What is healing for me? What infuriates me? What do I find the most beautiful? What scares me? What question would I ask God/Goddess if I could ask any question? What good message can I tell myself when I start to think harmful thoughts?

Needless to say, this can go on and on. Through exploration, information and inspiration break forth like a hummingbird flying out of a fuchsia shaft drunk with flower honey but ready for the next hit.

First thing this morning, I stood in the dark, in the rain. Enclosed in this letter to you is a maple leaf that was on the wet grass. And a seagull feather I found at the beach a few blocks from my house.

I close this letter with bright blessings to you, and love burning in hot-pink flames.
Your Friend,
Shiloh

JOHN BRADSHAW

The Four Degrees of Family Secrets

I was born in 1933 during the time of the Great Depression, when Hitler was just beginning to rumble in Europe. My dad and mom had to live with my grandparents, and my dad, at eighteen years old, was selling apples on the street. Although most of my father's life was about survival, he had a great deal of ambition. When he retired, he had cards made up that read: *Jack Bradshaw, Inc.* He always wanted to be more and do more than he was able to be and do. While I was working on my book *Family Secrets*, I had a very profound sense that I was acting out my father's frozen dreams.

In family systems therapy we use a family mapping system to understand the cross-generational context in which someone's issues or symptoms occur. Developed by Murray Bowen, the Genogram is a useful tool that gives a quick picture of family dynamics that may have influenced an individual's development. Bowen felt that most failures in families were due to developmental deficits and immaturities in a parent, who might function perfectly well as an adult in some areas, but behave more like a child in others. Bowen discovered that people often carry projections of their parents' immaturity into their own lives. This can affect our development and behavior in myriad ways. By tracing problems back to the previous generation, Bowen found that he could identify similar deficits in parents whose own parents may have been extremely immature.

John Bradshaw has been called "America's leading personal growth expert." The author of five *New York Times* bestsellers, his books have sold over four million copies. He created and hosted four nationally broadcast PBS television series' based on his best-selling books, which are in turn based on living through all the challenges he writes about. John Bradshaw pioneered the concept of the "Inner Child" and brought the term "dysfunctional family" into the mainstream. He has touched and changed millions of lives through his books, television series, and his lectures and workshops. Find out more at www.JohnBradshaw.com.

The Genogram provides a visual map that places individual and family dynamics in a larger context. In a concrete and graphic way, a person can see that his father and his father's father struggled with the very problem he is working to overcome. This can help reduce self-blame. For example, I had an alcohol addiction and a propensity to be a hypochondriac, always worrying and fretting about bodily illness. When I did a family map, I saw that my mother had similar patterns and my grandmother was agoraphobic and spent periods of her life bedridden. In addition, I saw the history of alcoholism in my family.

Once I saw my problems in a larger context I was able to stop blaming myself. Also, I was able to tell my son about the family history of alcoholism before he reached drinking age. Although he did his own experimenting, he certainly didn't do what I did with respect to drinking. I believe it helped him a great deal to understand the genetic and emotional history of alcoholism in our family.

The family map is not about blame-shifting, however. It is about seeing the history of the problem. You can freeze-frame your family map to the moment you were born and see what was going on with mom and dad in their marriage, or what was going on in the family the day you were born. You can even look at what was going on historically that may have influenced you and your family. The value comes with seeing clearly that the problems you struggle with are not all about you — your individual "badness" or "goodness." Knowing that you are part of something larger, you can let go of pathologizing yourself or your family. Having let go of blame, you can simply acknowledge the cross-generational vulnerability — see it, name it, and tell the truth about what happened. Then you can work toward change. That is the power of family mapping.

Doing a Genogram gave me rich knowledge about the context of my life. By using the family map, we can break old patterns in order to make the family stronger, and to make our own lives stronger. This is especially important and challenging for people who have experienced some type of abuse within their family.

Most people who have survived abuse have tremendous strength. They have often found ways to survive that are quite heroic. They have developed strategies to take care of themselves when no one else would. Like the phoenix rising out of the ashes, they have tremendous resilience and courage. Once they do some of the grieving and completion work around abuse issues, the strength they have developed just to survive can be used in other areas. I don't believe there is any "right way" to do the work of grieving or finishing — but it is important to do it — and then go on and apply the strengths to other goals and life tasks.

There are certain areas where I will always be wounded, but I can learn to develop other strengths. I saw a man with one leg on an ice-skating rink, for example. He was out there doing figure eights, skating better than anybody else! He had adapted to his wound and was functioning better than the able bodied people on the ice. Now, he may never be an Olympic champion, but he can certainly enjoy himself in the rink, draw a great deal of pleasure out of ice-skating, and inspire folks like me who stand and watch.

The same is true for those of us who have wounded families. I think that the more wounded a family is, the more resources a person possesses to bring to their healing process. When the violation was chronic or severely abusive, it takes longer for a person to get through that and start focusing on strengths, but it can be done. I caution people who have experienced heavy abuse not to rush into healing and uncovering family secrets. In the initial excitement that comes with discovery and coming out of denial, there is a tendency to go too fast. Even therapists can be a bit overeager or zealous. Take the healing and recovery process at a very easy pace. Be gentle. Avoid extremes. When people spill everything out on television, for instance, the experience can be quite traumatic. I think the talk shows re-victimize people by having them expose family secrets in a very public way.

In my work, I have discovered and identified four distinct types of secrets. Secrets that involve criminal activity are what I term *first degree lethal secrets*. These are the kind of secrets that violate life, liberty, or pursuit of happiness. All secrets of this type need to be dealt with under specific guidelines. Theft, arson, sexual crimes, crimes that involve emotional or spiritual abuse—these are all examples of first degree secrets.

Second degree secrets are addictions that may not be against the law but nonetheless can destroy a person. They not only diminish the individual's life, they affect other people around that person. These secrets need to be confronted. Substance abuse, eating disorders, gambling, or work addictions are all second degree secrets. I believe that people have a right to know about their birth, their identity and their origins, so I put those kinds of issues—including adoption—in the category of second degree secrets as well.

Third degree secrets must be looked at in the context of the family. These are dynamics that are best understood systemically, such as enmeshment issues where one person is singled out as the scapegoat or the "problem" in the family. Marital secrets, including infidelity and suffering-related secrets, such as mental illness, are also in this category.

Let me give an example of why context is important. Two different men were both involved with women who decided to have an abortion. When the mother of the first man found out, she moralized and raged against him. As a result, this man became very defensive and began to promote abortion. Then he married a woman who held an anti-abortion point of view and didn't tell her this secret. Their marriage got increasingly dysfunctional because of their argument over abortion. In this case, I would recommend he tell the secret and talk about what actually happened.

In the case of the second man, however, after his girlfriend had an abortion, he felt horrible. He became anti-abortion and married a woman who was also anti-abortion. Did he need to tell his new wife his secret? I don't think so. What happened in the past need not affect his marriage in any way. The abortion experience was formative in that it contributed to who he became. Exposing that information is not necessary. With third degree secrets, the very same content can be treated quite differently depending on the circumstances. Some secrets need to be dealt with, while others may be best left unsaid.

Fourth degree secrets are individual secrets that do not hurt anyone else, but may diminish a person's freedom, nonetheless. Toxic shame issues, fear, guilt, anxiety, depression, cultural shame—including issues around one's ethnic background or socioeconomic status—fall into this category. Fourth degree secrets do not cause anyone other than the person with the secret pain. The distinction between secrecy and privacy is helpful in such cases.

At some point in my investigation into family secrets and their effects, I realized that we have a natural covering called modesty. I think of it as natural shame. Natural shame guards privacy. When someone violates our privacy, we blush. That is, when we are suddenly uncovered and we want and need to be covered, we feel embarrassed. That is an innate signal from the organism that says, "Hey! You're exposing me and I'm not ready to be exposed." This is what we feel when someone walks in on us in the bathroom, or we're the only one eating and everybody is watching us. It is a natural reaction that signals a need for privacy. This is not the same as secrecy.

Looking at our family secrets in terms of the four degrees discussed above can help people understand themselves and their family as something much larger and maybe more mysterious than most of us tend to think. Suddenly, all of the problems you think are yours and yours alone can be seen in a larger light. Blame no longer has much weight when you see that your mother had the problem, and your grandmother, and God knows how many generations before her. That makes you realize that you are up against something very profound. On the positive side, we realize that our strengths are the fruit of many other people, too. We pick up the good vibes in the family, as well as the secrets. The family is my fate. And yet the family is also my grace.

Auriela McCarthy

CHAPTER 25

The Power of the Possible

To forgive is to set the prisoner free. And then to discover that the prisoner — was you.

You may call God love, you may call God goodness, but *the name for God is compassion.*
— Meister Eckhart

Forgive me for starting this chapter with an old joke, but it is simply too appropriate to pass over. "How many psychiatrists does it take to change a light bulb?" "Just one. But the light bulb must *want* to change."

What is it going to take to finally learn the simple and obvious truth that has been staring us in the face all our conscious lives? Trying to change another person is a hopeless and pointless task. It doesn't work. It can't. And it never will.

Yet even with the evidence stacked up against us, we don't give up easily. So sure that we know *what's best,* we make our displeasure known one way or another. Sometimes we don't say anything at all. Just wish silently and desperately for the person to change, unaware that an energy field forms between us with each wishful thought and each hopeful feeling. An energy field that lets the other one know we disapprove. An energy field against which he or she will now bounce.

It is an energy field of resistance — to us and to our desire to change them.

Auriela McCarthy, MA, born in the former Soviet Union in Riga, Latvia, came to the United States in 1980. After only five years in the country, she opened her own art gallery, which became a San Francisco Landmark. But behind the bright façade lay conflict at home and health problems. After a spiritual awakening, Auriela ended her marriage, became a private art dealer and immersed herself in reflection and metaphysics. She emerged twenty years later, a spiritual teacher with a clear message of hope, compassion. This chapter is from *The Power of the Possible* (Beaufort, 2008). www.AurielaMcCarthy.com.

Whichever way we go about trying to control their behavior — from verbal confrontations to silent sighs of unhappiness, to quiet expectation, to obvious disapproval, whether we talk about it constantly or never say a word — it really makes no difference.

The field is there. They know it. And they resist.

In fact, the more you push them, the harder they will push back. At some point it won't even be about change any longer. *It will be about fighting you.*

The field of resistance between the two of you will become *the barrier* to the very change you want to happen, keeping you both stuck on either side of it until you won't even see each other any more. The colored prisms of your control will be distorting your view and blocking out everything that is real.

As long as one of you insists, the other one will resist it. Some can go on like this forever. Sometimes — they actually do.

Insisting that someone changes, and resisting making that change, are the opposite sides of the same coin. Is it any surprise that nothing changes at all?

If you remove your need for other people to change, the field of resistance between you collapses. The barrier is replaced by a mirror, leaving them face to face with themselves. With nothing to fight against, they are forced to make a choice.

They can choose to change or *they can choose not to.*

It is their right. Not yours, not mine, not anyone's.

Whether they are your lover or your spouse, your parent or your child, your friend, your colleague or anyone else — this right is not negotiable.

Freedom can mean different things to different people. But among the many things freedom is, and among the many choices it brings us, one choice stands out.

This choice is *our right to choose for ourselves whether to improve or to diminish our lives.*

This choice is our inalienable right as human beings. It means that at any given time every one of us is free to make a choice that to anyone else may look bad, wrong, ridiculous and crazy. And yet it is still ours to make it. Ours and ours alone.

* * *

When we accept the fact that a person is the way he or she is, and there is nothing *we* can do to change this, when we stop imposing our choices for them upon them — the energy field of resistance between us disappears.

It does not mean we have to suddenly agree with the way they are.

It simply means *we let go of trying to have them be different.* We stop fighting it, hating it and resisting it, even though we may not know what will happen next.

In this new state of emptiness, with no expectation and without the interference of our control *we have surrendered to the Power of the Possible,* and with it to limitless outcomes and endless options.

We have been blocking this door for so long. . . . Leaning on it with all the weight we could muster, insisting on getting our way, thus holding off all other possibilities.

Now we have swung this door open.

We've made space for magic to enter our reality.

Don't plan for it, don't expect it and don't try to figure out what it might look like. Let go of trying to control anything. *Free all this energy* and *turn it towards living your own life.* By setting free the one you have been trying to change, you successfully free yourself.

Robert's Story

A young man I once knew talked to me about the hatred he felt for his father. He likened it to a rubber band that held the two of them together. No matter how far he moved to get away from his father, the rubber band of his hate would always pull him back. It was a magnet. An energy field he could never escape. He would leave home, move to a different town, but he would always come back, return to the "battle field," drawn to his father by the hate he felt, a force from which he could not break free.

It was palpable, alive—as alive as he was, maybe more. And it consumed him. It fueled his every action, fed his every thought. He lived it with each breath he took. "It was visceral," he told me. "I could feel it on my skin."

He had reasons—real reasons—for hating his father. His father had beaten him severely all through his childhood getting more and more inventive with his punishments. But the emotional abuse had been even worse. His father had a genius for it, and he had used it expertly, aiming to take away the last shreds of his son's dignity.

Had he done it consciously? Probably not. He had been too drunk for that. In fact, he was always drunk, often too drunk to stand on his own two feet. Robert's mother drank as well, and so did his older sister.

If you can't beat them—join them. Robert became an alcoholic by the time he was twelve. Many people expected him to kill his father one day. No one would be surprised if he did. But he knew he never would. Just as he knew his hatred was killing *him,* turning him into someone dangerous and destructive, someone people stayed away from, sensing the secrets in the darkness, not wishing to know.

He did not expect to live long. Could not remember a day he wasn't drunk. And since everyone in the family was an alcoholic, it was okay. No one cared, no one paid much attention. He would throw away the articles a friend would bring him from time to time. Articles about sons who killed their fathers. If he were to kill anybody, it would be himself. He tried that when he was little, but like his father told him, he "couldn't even do that right."

There were car crashes, many of them, but he always came out unscathed as if protected by an invisible hand that would pull him out of danger each time.

He had very few friends. He was a loner, living behind the glass wall of pain, looking at the world with the eyes of an outsider.

"I would have died young, had I not stopped drinking," he told me. "I was absolutely sure of that." But he stopped. At twenty-six, he woke up one day and just knew he would never drink again.

It was the turning point in his life. He dragged himself to AA and began the slow process of recovery. He never touched another drink.

* * *

Our lives are rich with examples of triumph of the human spirit. Alcoholics and drug addicts finding the strength to end their addiction, often dedicating their lives to service, inspiring others with their own example. And while all this is actually true of Robert's life as well, there is much more to his story.

One morning when he was twenty-eight years old, he woke up with a distinct feeling that he needed to forgive his father. The urgency he felt grew and intensified as he was trying to go about his day, a persistent pull dominating everything else. *Go home, forgive him. Forgive him today.*

It was an instant, out of the blue obsession. It was all he could think about.

There was no time to lose. He was sure of it without knowing how he knew this to be true. Over time, he had learned to trust his feelings and his intuitive sense. He never questioned this.

His father was fifty-one at the time, though, looking at him, he might as well have been eighty. Haggard, unkempt, grey stubble covering his unshaved face, his eyes pale and lifeless. His stoop had gotten worse over the years. He had difficulty walking and had to hold on to the walls to keep himself from falling. His liver was as good as gone. He did not have long to live. No one ever dared mention his drinking in his presence. He ridiculed his son for being sober. "So you think you are too 'clean' now for this family, don't you?" he used to say.

"I must forgive him," his son thought that morning.

It was an especially cold winter in Minnesota. The roads were icy and dangerous, and it was snowing hard. The son lived three hours away from his father, but nothing was a problem that day. He got into his car and started driving.

What happened to the hate he had been living with for so long? It seemed to have been suspended, lifted into some place he could not access. That morning—it didn't matter. It was a moment of grace, the only thing he could feel as he was driving home breaking every speed limit was his intense need to forgive and, with it, a wave of absolute compassion for his father.

"I would have never survived the childhood *he* had," he told me. "Mine was nothing compared to his."

* * *

He arrived at his family home in the early afternoon.

"What are you doing here, Mr. Saintly?" was his father's greeting. But it was like water off a duck's back. The more his father tried to taunt him, the less it mattered. He was immune to his insults. There was no hook inside him to which his father's darkness could attach itself. And so it slid off him without having any impact.

Imagine a situation where someone suddenly accuses you of something that is so out of the realm of the possible things you could ever do, that even getting angry at the accusation would be ridiculous. Wouldn't your first reaction to that accusation be to laugh at it? Would you even bother to argue? Would you bother to defend yourself? Wouldn't you just shrug it off? Walk away? Dismiss it because whoever was saying it must be crazy?

Now imagine someone accuses you of doing something that is, in fact, quite possible for you to have done, but you didn't do it. Now—you will fight. You will argue. You will try to prove your innocence. You will get very angry. You will get indignant. "How dare you?! How dare you accuse me of this?! I would never! I would hate to think!!!"

Why such different reactions? It is quite simple actually. In the first call—you do not feel vulnerable to the accusation, and so it doesn't stick. There is no hook for it inside you.

It is a very different story in the second case. You have been accused of something you could have easily done, but didn't this time. Now, the vulnerability, the weakness is there, and it trips you up. You can't stay calm, can't just laugh off the accusation. You lose your temper, you start acting as if indeed you are guilty. Crazy, but true, the more you defend yourself, the less believable you sound.

Similarly, as long as Robert was consumed by his hatred of his father, any ridicule or insult from him would bring out a violent, angry response. But on the afternoon of that day and for the first time in his conscious life, he was able to see his father through the eyes of compassion only. He saw a frail, very sick man desperately trying to hold on to his last bits of dignity. He saw a man who was scared and lost, too weak to walk on his own, doling out insults more out of habit and fear of dying than out of any real malice. He could not get angry with this man, no matter what he was saying. In fact, he barely heard him. He was detached in the truest sense of the word. He also knew he could be seeing his father for the last time.

The old man grumbled on for a while and then stopped and looked at his son.

"I must stop drinking," he said suddenly, then quickly looked away.

If lightning were to strike in the middle of a bright sunny day, it would have been less unexpected and less unimaginable. Yet there it was, a taboo subject, never to be mentioned for fear of death itself, and he was bringing it up himself.

"Sounds good," his son said calmly. He had spent years in AA and knew better than to try to force anything. Any overt interest on his part would guarantee an opposite reaction from his father.

He got up to make himself a cup of coffee, reached for the coffee maker, poured the water into the pot. The old man shifted in his chair, coughed loudly and spat the phlegm into the ashtray by his side. He lit a cigarette, inhaled and then put it down. Something was making him uncomfortable, and he couldn't put his finger on it. He got up, walked to the window, and leaned against the windowsill.

"You making coffee?" he asked his son without turning his head. "I'll have a cup."

It was snowing hard all day, and Robert was glad to be inside, in the old kitchen once again. He poured the coffee into the cups placing one in front of his father.

"I'll start the fire," he said and leaned by the fireplace to arrange the logs.

If one didn't know better, the scene in the kitchen was a picture of quiet domesticity. The crackling of fire in the fireplace on a cold winter day, father and son having coffee in the afternoon with the son resting his feet on top of the coffee table looking through the newspaper.

"Still sober?" his father chuckled, knowing the answer in advance. He wanted to add something else, something mean and sarcastic, but found himself at a loss for words. It wasn't entertaining anymore to be his old nasty self, and it bothered him. He finished his coffee in one gulp and pushed the cup away. Something was different about his son, too different, and it was throwing him off guard, making it difficult to relate to him in the old way. He prodded some more, looking for the familiar resistance, but the wall was gone and his barbs just flew through the air and landed on the floor.

"What are you up to these days anyway?" he asked. They talked for a bit about nothing in particular, a simple conversation, something they hadn't done in years. They ate some pie, then Robert fixed the broken drain in the sink.

Several hours had passed since Robert had arrived, and he was deciding whether to spend the night. It was still snowing, the days were short, and it would get dark soon. He had never felt so peaceful in his parents' home. There was hardly a time in the past when he wouldn't be seething at the very thought of his father, anticipating his attacks, ready to fight in an instant. Now it was as if he had simply dreamt his horrible past, as if the man in front of him coughing noisily into his big folded palms was someone else, someone he was just beginning to know.

"It will be dark soon," his father said.

"Yes, it will," said Robert.

"I am sick and tired of this cough."

"I know," said Robert.

He looked at his father. Bending over the sink, the old man was splashing water onto his face. He reached for the kitchen towel, put it to his cheeks.

"Perhaps I should go and check myself into a rehab center," he suddenly said.

"It would be good," responded his son.

There was a pause. A long pause. No one spoke again for a while. Robert got up and added some logs to the dying fire. It was soon ablaze again.

"I can't do it today," the father spoke again. "I promised Mother to take the books back to the library. They are past due."

"I'll take them for you, if you want," his son said, not turning his head. The sound of a siren broke the afternoon's quiet as a fire engine sped by the window and disappeared.

"Linda!" the father yelled. "Linda, come here this minute."

"What is it?" Robert's mother entered the room. "Why are you yelling? I am watching a show. Where do you think you are going in this weather?"

Reaching for his hat and gloves, her husband turned and looked at her without blinking.

"I am checking into a rehab right now, Linda. Put your coat on. You will drive."

And that was it. That was how it happened.

* * *

Staying in the rehabilitation clinic had begun the process, which led to AA and to many months of painful but steady recovery. As it turned out, the haggard, beaten down man still had some fire, and his will was stronger than his addiction. Once he had made his choice, he stuck with it. He stopped drinking on the day his son came home to forgive him, and he did not drink again.

I met Robert at a friends' Christmas party in New York. By then he was thirty-eight years old, married and had twin sons. While in New York on business, he had been buying Christmas gifts for his family. He showed me a wonderful thick woolen sweater he had just bought.

"Who is it for?" I asked. "Is it for you?"

"It's for my Dad," he said smiling. "He rides his bike in pretty much any weather. I thought he could use something like this."

I sensed the warmth in his voice when he spoke about his father, and it touched me. "You must be very close," I said.

"Yes, we are," was all he answered. Robert told me his story years after we met and gave me permission to share it. It is a magical story—a story of kindness and love—a story of the incredible force of forgiveness and of one's courage in the face of pain.

Not once in the many years after he had stopped drinking did the father acknowledge how abusive he had been to his family. It was something he couldn't do. But he lived his love for them with every breath he took. His dedication was total. And so was his loyalty. Without the alcohol in his blood, he was a new man.

"I never had a better friend in my life," Robert told me. "He is my best friend, and I trust him with everything."

The Gift of Forgiveness

To forgive is to set the prisoner free. And then to discover that the prisoner — was you.

At the depth of forgiveness lies the magic of healing. Its workings are not ours to understand. The miracle of forgiveness heals our very Souls, steeped as it is in the purest, cleanest waters of love.

When you have an impulse to simply forgive someone, do not ignore it. Do not dismiss it, and do not postpone it.

A friend once quoted me something I found to be very powerful.

"If you suddenly learned that you have one hour left to live, who would you call? What would you say? *And why are you waiting?*"

Most people would call the ones they love, and the only regret they have is that they haven't told them more often that they love them. Some recognize they have to make amends. There are still things left in their past for which they need to seek forgiveness. Yet others realize it is time *to forgive,* to let go of the past and *to set themselves free.* They have been carrying the sword for too long, and it has become too heavy.

It's time to set it down and to let their wounds be healed.

The impulse to forgive comes from a sacred place. It is presented to us at exactly the right time, placed in front of us by our Souls and, if followed, has the power to change not just our lives, but also the lives of others.

Trust that call. Trust the knowing you have. Call it intuition. Call it instinct. Call it a hunch. The label is not important. What is important is *the more we trust it, the stronger it gets*. The stronger it gets, the safer we feel relying upon this knowing, so it can finally lead us to where we need to go.

I once asked a friend of mine, an enormously successful New York lawyer, how he chose the cases he represented. What was the final criterion in his decision? He answered quickly and without a hesitation: "Intuition."

Trusting his intuition, Robert got into the car and drove for hours in the snow to forgive his father. He did not postpone it till the weekend. He did not tell himself he was busy and had to go to work and that the weather was unsafe and that he should wait until the storm passed. He got into the car and started driving. And when three hours later he had arrived to find his father drunk and mean and barely walking—the way he had been for so long—he had already forgiven him. Forgiven him without any conscious knowing that he had done it.

There is a mystical quality to choice. *When it is made unequivocally and with absolute clarity of will, it will override all our conditioning, all our previous choices and all the beliefs we hold.* At that level the choice we make can transform and change anything.

Propelled by his strong need to forgive his father, the son made a powerful choice. "I will forgive him" was his choice, followed by "I will forgive him now."

The intensity of his choice had urgency and momentum. It seemed his entire being was being rearranged in that instant, as if a tightly held lock had just been unhinged, letting in the light for the first time ever. He felt a movement inside his chest, but did not pause to analyze what it was. He simply knew he had to go, knew that it was important, and he followed what he knew.

The process of change had begun and nothing could stand in its way.

When I imagine that day, I see the events lining up in a beautiful curve, or better yet—I see them moving in a wavelike motion— an undulating wave of change comprised of several smaller waves, all parts of the whole, all flowing powerfully and decisively towards the shore of healing.

CHAPTER TWENTY-FIVE

The Mystery of Change

With the choice to forgive came forgiveness itself. And with forgiveness came change. And nothing in the life of that family was ever the same.

Did it happen in the early hours of the morning, when the thought of forgiving his father first came to Robert and he did not dismiss it? Did it happen as he was getting ready to leave, hastily throwing a change of clothes into his backpack? Or during the hours he was driving, trying hard to stay on the road, fighting the blinding wind-driven snow? Somehow, somewhere in-between the thoughts and feelings he had about his father, his hatred lifted, suspended just long enough for forgiveness to slip in.

We can never pinpoint the exact moment when we have changed. We just know we have, because we feel it. We act differently, we feel different feelings, we think different thoughts. "You are different," people tell us. "You have changed." And we know they are right. It is true. We are no longer who we used to be.

Change is a mystery, and so is forgiveness. And mysteries they will always remain — not to be solved and thus stripped of their magic, but received, like treasured and precious gifts, healing us in an instant.

By the time Robert arrived at his parents' door, he had already forgiven his father. *The moment it happened — his father knew.* It wasn't conscious knowing — and yet he knew. And when his son opened the front door and entered the house, this knowing was confirmed. It wasn't something the father could articulate or explain, but it was unmistakable, and it threw him off guard.

He looked for the hatred he had always felt from his son, but found kindness instead. There was something peaceful about the way Robert was which made him feel uneasy. He tried to resist it, looking for the familiar tension between the two of them but could not find it. And he had no idea how to be without it. He tried to pick a fight, used a few of the old tricks that had never failed to make his son angry in the past, but got no reaction. He tried again, half-heartedly this time, but had to give up. He was lost. Irritated, annoyed, thrown off balance, he felt like a grumpy old fool. There was simply no way to have a fight with Robert, try as he might. His son had not come home for that. He had simply come to pay a visit.

He looked at Robert again, stealthily. Saw how handsome he was. His eyes clear, his face bright and clean shaven, the very skin radiating good health. No longer the pale shadow of a youngster who wouldn't look him in the eye. He could tell Robert hadn't been drinking in a long, long time.

He actually felt a twinge of pride for his son, something he could not remember having felt before. "Good for him," he thought. "He beat it, didn't he? But it's too late for me." He looked at his son again. A quick glance. Turning away at once. *Maybe it isn't,* the thought came. *Maybe I still could.*

When he was in the car three hours later, his wife at the wheel, taking him to the hospital for detoxification, he had no idea how it had happened to him. But he was going, and that was all there was to it. He had given up. He was not fighting any more. He felt his son's forgiveness — offered freely and without condition — and it had brought down the elaborate bastion of the old man's resistance. That fortress had taken decades to erect and fortify, and yet it crumbled with the slightest touch. With no one to resist him, the fighting became meaningless. The walls came down, and with them the roof, the ceiling and the locks on the doors. And into the place where darkness, self loathing and hate had lived side by side for so long, light could penetrate again. And with it — a flicker of hope, a touch of love. A new possibility.

Until that moment — beyond the imagination. Now suddenly — a reality. Approaching faster and faster as he was being taken away, down the freeway to the rehabilitation center.

* * *

At the root of all destructive behavior lies pain and our inability to deal with it.

Whether someone is hurting us, or themselves, it is important to understand that *pain* is the *primary reason* behind their actions. It doesn't make their behavior okay. We don't have to stick around and continue to suffer the consequences of their pain. Understanding why they act the way they do *does not excuse* it, but it makes accepting the facts and forgiving them more attainable.

If you are sincere in your desire to help the ones you love, stop talking to them about it. Stop saving them. Stop trying to convince them that they really need to change. They already know it. *They cannot hear you.* Not under these conditions. Not as long as you are on the other side.

Try seeing it through their eyes. What are you seeing? It's a life of me against them, isn't it? And the "them" is simply everyone. *Including yourself.* Because "you don't understand." That's why insisting that someone changes does not work. You simply become one more person to rebel against.

Remove your need to have the person be different. Remove your resistance to the way they are. Remove that barrier. Stop trying to have them *get it.* Accept that they are exactly where they need to be, however detrimental it may look on the outside. Have the humility to trust that you don't know or understand everything.

It doesn't mean you have to stay with them. But if you want them to have a flicker of a chance — *accept them.* It doesn't have to be perfect. It doesn't have to be a hundred percent. Do the best you can. Accept them the way they are. Hold the hope, hold the light of your love for them, but *do it from a neutral place.* Honor them in this way. *Respect their freedom of choice.* Allow them to just "be."

* * *

The path of one's Soul is a mystery. Its plan is often invisible and not for others to comprehend. The Soul will stop at nothing to bring us the healing we need. *The Soul has just one goal* and one goal only. *And it is that we grow.* Grow spiritually. Grow as human beings. And if we don't yet know how to grow through love — then we will grow through pain. But grow we *shall.* That is the ultimate purpose of our being here, whether we know it or not. That is the absolute, highest truth; that is our only reason.

It is not for us to judge the way others choose to grow. Nor for us to decide what one should or should not do. Ours is to be understanding. Ours is to carry compassion in our hearts. Ours is to forgive.

Tonja Demoff

From Giving Up to Living Up

I've always had an enormous respect for money. From as far back as I can remember, money has represented freedom to me. My family taught me this lesson, though they didn't realize it, and I feel blessed by that.

When I was young and being raised by my grandparents, one of my uncles who also lived in the house would come home in the middle of the night with bags of White Castle hamburgers and wake everyone to pass out twenty-dollar bills. I loved my uncle and hated seeing him drunk and acting so foolishly. His behavior was humiliating to everyone in the house. Instead of giving his money freely and joyfully, my uncle insisted that we get out of bed to take the money from him. He was both trying to control us and feel superior to us. My brother took the cash, but I would not, and my uncle mocked me for it. But I did not feel right taking his money in this way; I knew the cost to my spirit of accepting those twenty-dollar bills was too high a price to pay. I resolved to make my own money in a healthier, more pleasant way.

At some point, I also realized that my grandparents' unsound financial choices throughout their lives meant they would face an impoverished retirement. Since they had not learned how to take good financial care of themselves when they were younger, they would be dependent on someone else to take care of them in their old age. This strengthened my resolve to make my own money and

Tonja Demoff is one of the world's most respected real estate agents and wealth strategists, recently winning RE/Max's Diamond Club Award for $1 million in commissions in a year. She is the founder of ten companies and has inspired thousands to improve their lives and boost their incomes through real estate. Tonja is author of *Bubble Proof: Real Estate Strategies That Work in Any Market*, (Kaplan, 2007), *The Casual Millionaire*, (Arbor, 2006), and *Commission Checks!* (Kaplan, 2008). Her Tonja Demoff Foundation helps families buy homes and build businesses while enhancing their lives and incomes. www.tonjademoffcompanies.com.

secure my own financial future. The way I saw it, giving up the idea of being "taken care of" was the only way to create a personal financial path that was not only reliable, but would also give me a sense of pride and fulfillment. I still walk that path today and, through my workshops and books, share with other people how to create and stay on that path.

I let go of the idea that money was going to be given to me and instead embraced the idea that I would create money. This was my first step to what I later called "creative wealth building." Even at a young age, I saw that there were lots of ways to build my wealth. Delivering newspapers, mowing lawns, shoveling snow, lifeguarding, and cutting up chickens at a local restaurant—I did them all. People paid me many compliments for my good work, and I could feel a strong, positive energy inside that fueled my desire to succeed. I also chose carefully and consciously the things or activities I spent my money on, since I was the one paying for them. This was freedom! My early jobs taught me I could do anything I wanted. All I had to do was see the possibility in my mind and take the steps to design what my mind had already imagined.

One day when I was in high school, I went to a parade where clowns were wearing big buttons printed with funny sayings attached to their suspenders. The sayings made me laugh, and I wanted a button of my own. So I went to a novelty shop in a nearby mall and asked them to make one for me with the message "I want to be rich. I want to be dirty, rotten, filthy, stinking rich." I was trying to be funny, but when my grandmother read my button that afternoon, she said, "Oh, Tonja, that's just awful. Why do you want that?" I said I didn't want to be broke and poor like the rest of our family, and the button was going to remind me. She responded, "If that's the case, take out the words 'dirty, rotten, filthy,' and 'stinking,' and just say, 'I want to be rich.'" Her insight was powerful: Pick what you really want, and get rid of negative thoughts that stand in the way.

My early financial lessons were invaluable. Today, I have founded more than ten successful companies, and I'm a respected realtor, workshop leader, and author. My mission is to inspire others to achieve greater wealth with greater purpose, and my deepest desire is to create more millionaires than any other person on the planet creates. The process of becoming a millionaire is all about "giving up to living up"—giving up old limitations, which we unconsciously agreed to accept after someone else imposed them on us, and replacing them with consciously chosen new beliefs that will allow us to live up to our truly magnificent potential.

Creating Wealth Energy

As an adult, I learned another important lesson about wealth creation, one that sprang directly from my own actions. Early in my career, I started a business that became very successful and then failed, so I filed bankruptcy. At first, I believed I must be not only a terrible businesswoman, but also a bad person. I soon came to see, however, that even though I had grown the company to be very profitable in a short time, I hated doing it. With that came the amazing insight that changed my life: I had in some way created the failure of that company so I could have the freedom to create a new opportunity more in alignment with who I am and what I want to share with the world. How perfect was that? I believe that the deepest part of my soul and spirit were saying that this particular company was not the one for me, and since I wouldn't pay attention to all the signs they sent, they had to wake me up.

With the grace of Spirit, I suddenly saw my bankruptcy as a choice that did not define who I was but rather what I was experiencing. In a time that could have been the darkest of my life, I found the strongest light and passion. I found myself, my truth, and my core character, and I found more love than fear. I found wisdom, respect, and clarity. A vibrant energy filled my body, mind, and spirit. The darkest moment changed my entire direction. I felt so alive! The risk was the reward!

This experience taught me that creating wealth requires a lot more than just managing your finances. I had learned earlier that everything in the universe is energy, including money, and everything is connected. So now I saw in my own life that the creation of "wealth energy" is manifested through love, joy, happiness, excitement, laughter, friendship, and passion. A love for life, a zest and passion for experience, and an overall excitement that permeates our very being are energetically stimulating. This is the energy that draws wealth into your personal orbit, so creating an environment where you can have this zest is crucial to wealth.

Creating the "wealth environment" isn't always easy, but it is worth it to your spirit and to your bank account. If you are in the presence of people who do not uplift your spirit, then remove yourself from their presence. Consciously decide to remain only in an environment that uplifts you and pays you with a stronger energy return than what you've invested.

Many people don't want to hear that they have to do inner work to manifest a better financial life. That became clear to me years ago when I created a CD program called *Developing Your Character*. It showed how to enhance your financial prosperity by working from the inside out, and I did my darnedest to sell it at my seminars. But people would not pick up that program for anything. Nobody wanted to hear upfront they had to go inside and do any personal work to build their inner wealth before they grew their financial wealth. When I retitled the CD, however, calling it *Prosperity Consciousness*, it sold like hotcakes. It was the very same program, but the new title attracted people instead of scaring them off.

As I tell people on that CD, if you're going to increase your bank account, the first thing you have to do is get comfortable with the fact that growing wealth is a deeply personal process. To grow your wealth, you have to develop your character and do the inside work. When you do, you begin to see how your world and everything in it is your creation. *It is all your creation!* The outcome of what you create is your manifested reality, and your reality is the only one you can see.

Here's a way to understand this concept more clearly. When you find yourself getting upset with people or circumstances, that's a great opportunity to stand back and see your part in creating the situation, to see how the situation is mirroring something in you. Once you see this, you can make a more serious commitment to owning your responsibility for creating the situations that bother you. The beautiful thing is, since you created it, you get to change it. Keep your eyes wide open for situations like this, and you will discover many opportunities for self-improvement and self-awareness. You create it, you see it, and you can change it.

Goals vs. Intentions

When I used to do training in corporate America, there was always a curriculum that would instruct people to make their goals "real and achievable." I don't subscribe to this way of thinking. I don't believe in *goal* setting; I believe in *intention* setting. Take goals out of the equation, and then set your intention for your wildest dreams, your greatest fantasy. Visualize: If you could have every single thing you want and you could be the person you choose to be, what would that look like? Then work backward. Create the entire visualization—write out your life, including your every desire. Then keep that as your focal point, seeing the intention clear and strong. This will release your limitations and replace them with everything you want or desire. In this way, as the intention becomes the baseline, you typically begin to experience even more than you intended. Opportunities open up, and then all you have to do is decide whether to be in the flow with them or to resist them.

I've used this process many times in my life. It works.

Here's an example. About four years ago, I had an idea to create an educational lead-generation vehicle for realtors that would enable them to list and sell more properties. At the time, I had no idea how to do this; I just believed I could. So I went to Re/Max, where I am a realtor, and explained my idea. Of course, they asked what my plan was, and I had to say I didn't have one yet but would definitely create one. They must have realized my confidence because they gave me the go-ahead. On a daily basis, I focused on this intention in meditation: How could I serve real estate professionals and consumers with this new program? Slowly, it all came together, and I created a franchise called the Financial Freedom Seminar System. It became successful and, as the icing on the cake, led to me becoming the #1 Re/Max agent worldwide.

In the process, I learned that when doors open easily, you should walk through them, but if you have to push against them, don't try to batter your way through—those doors are closed for a reason. Just stay focused on your intention, and you won't have to fight. The perfect doors will open at the right time.

Many times when I ask people what limits they place on themselves, they often reply, "None," or "I don't put any limits on myself. I do everything I want to do." With a little more prodding, they might say, "Well, I don't have any limits. I just haven't gotten around to doing that yet." So I'll ask them what they're waiting for. That opens a whole different conversation.

The real question is always: Will you do the inner work? It takes a lot of faith to believe a process can help you accumulate wealth if only you'll take the time to do the process. The commitment level is always a question, but everybody can do it. To create more of this wealth energy, you must be aware and conscious of what you're creating with your thoughts. If you are aware and conscious of your thoughts and how they're actually playing out in your life, then you can redirect those thoughts and focus them into positive energy. Focusing very positive energy on what you want leads you toward everything you want—and away from the things you don't want.

This type of energy needs to be created in the company of people who share a similar desire and belief that will support you. Stay away from the dream busters, those people who, after you've told them your dream, will give you fifty reasons why it won't happen. Suddenly, you're drained and exhausted, and all the zest has dribbled out of your dream. And don't ask yourself how you will accomplish your dream. When you start asking how, your mind will invent all kinds of reasons why your dream will never come true, and you'll feel defeated. Instead, just hold on to your intention, and when it's time for you to achieve it, you'll be given all the resources you need. You'll be amazed that you have the necessary strength, wisdom, and skill, or the ability to attract the right skill. The most important element is not that you're going to reach the dream your way, but that your dream is going to happen in the highest and best way.

Risk

The number-one question people ask in my wealth-creation workshops concerns risk. They are comfortable with what they know, and risk means stepping out of that comfort zone. Even if their situation is somehow bad or harmful, they understand it and prefer to remain there and tell themselves they can control it. To change their situation, they have to understand risk.

For me, the greatest risk is taking no risks because if I took no risks, my life would not have changed much from when I was young. My life would be exceptionally different from what it has become. In my opinion, risk is a must. When you take a risk, an energy rises up. It's a kind of fear, but it's also a vitality that awakens your spirit and nudges you to take the risk. Feeling the fear and taking the risk anyway will help you to learn trust. This tingly bit of fear wants you to understand that you're not in control of every single thing, and if you open up to that, you can learn to have faith in your ability to cocreate your dream with Spirit, God, the Universe, or whatever you choose to call it. At that point, the energy can settle down as you determine what's risky in a hurtful way and what's risky in a way that will push you and help you grow toward a good ending.

Sometimes it's only the word "risk" that frightens people. If they think of it as "opportunity," that can encourage them to move forward. For instance, if I'm talking about financial risk but call it "investing," people are fine with the risk. But if I call it a "cost," as in it's going to cost this amount to take this opportunity, they may associate it with a loss and not take the risk. For myself, I carry the intention that there's more than enough, that I can always have the resources at my disposal whenever I need them and whenever I want them. There's never any lack or limitation.

Fired Up with Vitality

Living an intention or a dream that fires us up builds our vitality like nothing else. It excites us on an energetic level and opens us up to resources, people, and situations we might never have attracted into our lives before. When you allow that intentional energy to resonate throughout your entire body, when you *embody* your intention, you're walking in the belief that it's already happening, it's meant to be, and so there's no struggle, no willpower, no effort involved. Inside you, a light begins to shine, and it radiates an incredible vitality from the inside out. It's not a chaotic energy. It's peaceful, and it moves you in such an eloquent way, you feel like you're floating. You're in the flow. When a door opens, you simply go through it. And when you come to a door that once upon a time you would have pushed and pushed against, you just patiently wait until it opens or you go to other doors. You begin to use the vital energy inside you in service of the law of attraction, which brings things to you so you no longer have to chase after them. That's vitality and the wisdom of growth.

I remember when I didn't have this peaceful energy. Instead, my energy was an aggressive one: I was going to be somebody! I was going to make a name for myself! I was going to push through all the doors, and fight, and make *this* happen and *that* happen. I did make things happen, but then I realized I didn't want them and wondered how I got there. In the case of my company that eventually failed, I had forced my way through to making it successful. I recall thinking that I didn't want this company, but I wouldn't acknowledge it. People would say, "This doesn't seem like something you love," and I would insist, "Oh, yes it is."

After I declared bankruptcy and realized that I truly did not want to own that company, I understood about the two forms of energy. If you use willpower to push your way through something, you can get it, but that doesn't mean it's in your highest and best good. And when it's not, that saps your vitality. But when you set your intention and simply allow it to happen, you are filled with energy that is both peaceful and euphoric. When you give up to live up, it's a wow!

Topher Morrison

Get Lost!

For most of my adult life, I've loved to travel, to adventure, really. Mountain? Canyon? Ancient temple? I love them all. Give me a map, a backpack, and a bottle of water and that's all I need to keep myself entertained. At age nineteen, I had my first epic adventure and it didn't even involve a treasure map, ancient ruin, or snow-covered mountain. It involved a rental car and a freeway.

I was on my first business trip for the company where I worked. It was my first taste of absolute freedom. A fake I.D. that said I was twenty-one years of age and no family in the city to keep me in line meant I had access to all the nightlife of a "real" adult. On my first night out, armed with my Avis car rental map, I got on a freeway in Dallas and just started driving. Not knowing which way to go, combined with my blossoming sense of adventure, I flipped a mental coin and thought, "Wherever the road takes me, it will be an adventure!"

My adventure lasted slightly longer than I had anticipated. As a result of my "wherever" approach and my reluctance to ask for directions, the drive turned out to be a painful and frustrating four-and-a-half-hour trip of U-turns, map-staring, and bladder control exercises. After the first forty minutes, the landmarks I had memorized stopped appearing and I realized I had no idea how to get back to my hotel. After trying unsuccessfully to find my way back on my own, I finally forced my male ego to give way and asked for directions from

Topher Morrison has trained tens of thousands of people worldwide, and is acclaimed as a dynamic presenter on the topic of "Effortless Winning." He is internationally recognized for his columns on personal development, keynotes, and leadership training. Innovative and prolific, Topher is the author of the bestselling book *Stop Chasing Perfection and Settle for Excellence* (2006). In contrast to most personal development experts, Topher's shockingly honest and irresistibly down-to-earth approach is surprisingly infectious. His personality and straightforward manner is endearing to audiences who are tired of fleeting success in self-help sinkholes. www.TopherMorrison.com.

a gas station attendant who told me to go east on the freeway. I was still lost because I was ashamed to admit that I didn't know which way east was on the map (the map only had an N at the top). In fact, throughout the evening, I had no idea where I was on the map. And a map, no matter how detailed or accurate, is useless if you don't know where your starting point is.

One of the oldest clichés that many of the leaders in the field of personal development use is the metaphor that our goals become the treasures on the maps to our success. As with all clichés, there is some truth in it. Goals do keep us focused and heading in the right direction on our map. But the one shining element that seems to be missing from many personal achievement programs is stressing the importance of knowing where you are on that map before you even begin. You may know the direction you want to head in, or even where your destination is, but if you don't know where you are on the map—your point of origin—chasing those goals can lead to endless frustration and going in circles.

I see this all the time in the personal development world. I see well-intentioned people who are inspired by the works of great minds. They congregate regularly with their other positive-minded friends. If you ask any of them how they are doing, they most commonly respond with an enthusiastic, "I'm doing great!" and the smile on their face is even brighter than their words. And yet, in reality, their lives are still a mess. They say they're doing great, but they are still in financial debt or in a bad relationship, hating their job, resenting where they live, wishing they were healthier and more at peace, or even wishing they were truly proud of who they see in the mirror. The slogan "Fake it till you make it" has polluted the world of personal development by encouraging people to claim that their lives are fantastic when they are actually in ruin. It's created a level of inauthenticity matched only by Hollywood.

Perhaps even more shocking, this phenomenon also exists in the lives of so-called personal development experts. In a recent poll of more than eight hundred UK life coaches, the average annual income was less than £15,000! Many well-known authors and speakers who talk a great talk in the field still have major issues in their own lives, to which their sage words of advice have offered no cure. How do I know this? Because I've been there myself. Correction—because I am one of them!

The only difference may be that I have no problem admitting where I am on the map. If something isn't working in my life, I'm quick to tell people this, so they don't turn me into a false idol. This wasn't always the case, however. In my early twenties, I purchased a personal development franchise, and within nine months I had run up nearly $85,000 in debt and was eating every third day. But whenever anyone asked me how I was doing, I painted the smile on my face and said, "I'm doing great!" I can see the inauthenticity that is running rampant in the personal development world because I've been there. Similar to the way a reformed drug addict can spot a user or deal going down on the street, I recognize all the symptoms of an individual living an inauthentic life.

So what are the symptoms? There are many. How lost you are determines how many of them you are currently experiencing. The symptoms are:

- You tell everyone how great your life is, but you still don't feel that it is.

- You're always needing to fill up your emotional gas tank by attending the next seminar or reading the next book because you just emptied your emotional gas tank from the last program or book by going around in circles.

- You try fooling yourself into thinking that you are making progress, but when you check back to your goals sheet, you are still just as far away from them as you were when you started.

- When you are alone, and it's quiet, you feel like a fraud.

- You look around at everyone else and see them achieving their goals much faster than you are. (This is an illusion; just because a car is traveling faster than you are, or in your direction, doesn't mean that driver isn't lost, too.)

- You try to hide the reality of your situation in life from others.

- You financed a car with a loan spread out over more than three years to get the payments low enough that you could afford them and, even at that, you barely can.

- You don't contact people to whom you owe money because you know they'll ask when you are going to pay and you'll have to make up a lie.

- You have a hard time keeping track of all the lies you are telling people about successes that haven't happened.

- You budget your life on the hope of things working out rather than the reality of how it is right now.

- You distract yourself by watching endless hours of TV.

- You're exhausted no matter how much you sleep.

People come up to me in my seminars all the time to tell me that they have read all the books, been to all the seminars, and really applied the tools they learned from them, but they still haven't achieved the same level of result that the people giving the advice have, and they want to know why. The answer is simple: They keep traveling on life using great maps, but they don't know where they are right now on the map.

If life isn't working and you say, "I'm doing great!" not only are you being inauthentic, but also your unconscious mind can't determine where you are on the map. And if you keep traveling, you'll never get to where you ultimately want to go, and it is exhausting.

Let's address that symptom: exhaustion. When people are living a lie, they waste an incredible amount of energy keeping their "facts" straight. Very rarely does one lie support itself. Often, we have to create other lies to support or validate the original lie.

Someone asks us how we are doing and we say, "Great! Things couldn't be better at home!" We then have to take the family on a vacation, when we should be going to counseling. We say, "Great! Business is better than ever before!" We then have to buy an expensive car that we can't really afford in order to reinforce that lie. We say, "Oh, I'll just cheat this once and have dessert," knowing darn well we have dessert every chance we get. We then buy a membership to a health club that we never use to support the lie that we are committed to health, or we buy a bike that collects dust in the garage.

And all of these small lies lead to greater lies, and on and on. Keeping track of what lies we've told who is frustrating and exhausting. But when we start telling the truth, when we are willing to pull over and say, "I'm lost, and I'm embarrassed to admit it, but I don't even know how to read my map," is when we actually first accelerate ourselves toward our destination— exponentially.

By the time I returned to my hotel in Dallas, I had driven more than five hundred miles that night. Dawn was just beginning to break and I was exhausted, but I couldn't sleep because I had wired myself on so much caffeine to stay awake. The next day, with bloodshot eyes and frequent yawns, I told of my adventure to the locals at the company. One of the workers gave me a mnemonic to memorize north, east, south, and west on a map. He said, "Going clockwise starting at the top, just say, 'Never Eat Soggy Waffles.'" And it's stuck with me ever since. Now when I'm looking at a cost-cutting map that only has N pointing to the top, I repeat that phrase. I learned from this experience that the simplest words can have profound effects.

So where are you on your map to success? In what areas of your life are you being inauthentic? And if you find there are some areas in which you are lost, follow these two simple steps.

1. Pull over.

2. Ask for help.

Not complicated. Not profound. But the results from these two little steps can be awesome, to say the least. You might feel embarrassed, but you'll gain new energy to deal with the roadblocks in your life. You might think it will waste valuable time in your pursuit of excellence, but in the long run, you'll get there much quicker and far less the worse for wear. Sometimes you might even have to turn around and go back from where you just came, but isn't that better than continuing to follow a path that pulls you further from your goals and dreams?

Until your next journey, take care, dare to dream, and make each day an epic adventure!

JOHN GRAY

CHAPTER 28

Breaking the Blame Box

My wife and I were on our honeymoon in Canada when I got a call telling us that my father had died. We had just seen him a few weeks before and he was in really good health. He and I had a wonderful relationship. He had just been found dead in the trunk of his car.

My father was a retired Texas oilman. He was a very generous person, always helping the poor. When we last saw him, he was really proud to share what he was doing with his life. He took us on a drive over to the poor side of town and showed us all the places where he had coached young kids and started basketball and football teams. He was proud of making those things happen.

I had said to him, "Well, Dad, now I'm grown up and I need to give you some advice. We hear the stories of all the people you help, particularly the hitchhikers you're always picking up. But it's not safe these days to pick up hitchhikers."

He said to me, "John, some men, when they retire, go on safari. Me, I pick up hitchhikers." That was his adventure; that was his joy. And that was how he died.

My mother had a premonition the night before he left on his last journey, and asked him not to go. But he reassured her and went anyway. When he didn't arrive at his destination, she called the police.

John Gray, Ph.D., is the author of fifteen best selling books, including *Men Are from Mars, Women Are from Venus* (HarperCollins, 1992), the number one best selling book of the last decade. In the past ten years, over thirty million Mars and Venus books have been sold in over forty languages throughout the world. He has appeared on *Oprah, The Today Show, CBS Morning Show, Good Morning America, Larry King,* and many other shows. He has been profiled in *Newsweek, Time, Forbes, USA Today, TV Guide,* and *People.* John Gray is a certified family therapist, and is the premier Better Life relationship coach on AOL. More at www.MarsVenus.com.

His death was a tragedy for many reasons. The hitchhiker had robbed him and forced him to climb into the trunk of his car. Then the hitchhiker called the police and said, "There's an abandoned car here, check it out."

But the police didn't respond. Somebody else called to report an abandoned grey Mercedes, and another person again later. Three times the police got calls reporting an abandoned car. When my mother called, the police finally sent a patrol car to investigate. They found the car—with my father dead in the trunk. He wasn't beaten up, or hurt in any way. He had died from the heat of the Texas sun.

I was deeply shocked and upset at my father's death. How could one person do that to another? My soul was crying out for information, so that I could ultimately let go and forgive. It wasn't just an emotional process, although that's a big part of it. It was not just my intention to be a good and loving person. It was not just the knowledge that lack of forgiveness is killing us. I had to understand how somebody could do what had been done to my father in order to let go.

My family and I visited the car. It was still parked where my father had died. We stood outside the car. Suddenly, I felt as though I simply had to get into the trunk, to experience what my father had experienced. I had to descend into the coffin and feel its reality.

I climbed into the trunk, squeezed my body in, and the others closed the lid. Inside, I saw a screwdriver. My father had found it, and used it to hit the roof, while calling for help. I noticed that he had bent the lock, trying to open it, but he couldn't make that lock open. I noticed a place where he had broken the back of the taillight in the trunk.

I pulled the shattered lens a little bit further back toward me. I put my hand out through the opening. As I was pulling my arm back, my brother—on the outside, said, "John, see if you can reach around and push the trunk release button." So I reached around and pushed the button. The lid opened.

If only my father had thought of getting in when he was trying to get out.

I wanted something significant and meaningful to come out of my experience. As I healed emotionally, I kept thinking about the metaphor of trying to get out, when really the answer is very simple: try to get in.

We all live in boxes. People are in their own boxes. They're outside of somebody else's box. I have made it my goal to stand outside of people's boxes and help them find the buttons, and let themselves out. Men and women live in different boxes. We're always trying to change and fix each other, yet that tangle doesn't have to persist. We can strive to simply understand what it's like in the other box. So I started revising my approach to relationships. When a woman would come in for counseling, I'd allow that maybe my ideas about possible solutions might not necessarily be good for her. Maybe I needed to just listen to her, to understand her, and to help her reach her own solution. That was often a solution opposite to the one that would have worked for a man. I began seeing things from another point of view.

Many of us are boxed in by our feelings of powerlessness to affect the world around us. When we feel powerless, we feel afraid and anticipate loss. Some people will just fall into despair; others buy into fear. Fear frees us from feeling powerless. Some people get caught in grief, a feeling that something has been taken away. People who dwell in their sense of loss, their personal inadequacy, or their insufficiency in life, suffer depression. But once we consciously feel our pain and identify the thoughts that are linked to it, a self-correction mechanism that is an automatic part of the mind-body-heart connection comes into play. It can often be activated in the presence of a therapist or someone who loves us, because love is the ointment of inner healing.

In this process, forgiveness is vital. People mistakenly think that to forgive is to release someone else from blame, and that means that the only blame remaining lies with the forgiver. We can't bear that, so we stay in the blaming box. Yet true forgiveness occurs when there is a justification of blame: somebody did something to me, and I need to forgive him or her. This is the recognition that there is real pain, there is real abuse, there is real injustice, there is a real problem—and letting go of making the other person responsible for how we feel. To get out of the blame box and emerge into forgiveness, we need the confidence that we have the power to create everything we need in our lives. Then we are able to let others off the hook, to forgive the debt. At that point we can go back and try to improve the situation.

So the way out of the box is the way in. Instead of struggling against the walls, reach out your hand, feel how you got in, then invite love to open your box and free you. All you have to lose is the limits that constrict you life. All you have to gain is everything outside your box.

PART FIVE

Living on a Small Planet

PRINCE CHARLES

The Indigenous Roots of Healing

In many ways, and over rather too long a period, we have maintained a dangerously fragmented and abstracted view of our world, which has led to the abandonment of a great deal of valuable traditional knowledge and wisdom. As a result, we are beginning to reap the harvest we have sown through living off Nature's capital rather than her income. I believe that there is now a desperately urgent need to redress the fragile, but vital balance between man and Nature through a more integrated approach where the best of the ancient is blended with the best of the modern.

I am convinced that this is of increasingly crucial importance when it comes to the collective health of people in our countries. None of what I say should detract in any way from the extraordinary success that modern medicine has achieved, particularly over the course of the Twentieth Century, in preventing and treating such terrible diseases as smallpox and polio. The biophysical model has served us well, and continues to do so, for diseases from TB to HIV. But at the start of the Twenty-first Century we are still challenged by frightening new pathogens threatening to cross the species divide, by the tragedy of natural disasters, and the health implications of military conflicts and population migrations.

In preventing and controlling such suffering, we must think beyond the practice of reducing everything to component parts, and this is where, I believe, modern medicine needs to accommodate a

His Royal Highness, Prince Charles is heir to the British throne. His wide range of interests are reflected in 'The Prince's Charities' a group of not-for-profit organizations of which the Prince of Wales is president. The organizations are active across a broad range of areas including opportunity and enterprise, education, health, the built environment, responsible business, the natural environment and the arts. He served as a pilot and commander in the Royal Navy from 1971 to 1976. He has two sons, William and Henry. He and his wife Camilla travel widely, and are actively involved in Britain's evolving social dialog. Photo courtesy AP.

more integrated and holistic approach. To my mind, this is even more true in regard to long-term diseases. I have heard them referred to as the "silent epidemic," but the statistics speak as loudly as those of infectious diseases. According to the World Health Organization (WHO), of fifty-eight million annual deaths worldwide, a staggering thirty-five million are the result of chronic diseases. They are now the major cause of death among adults in almost every country of the world. In the United Kingdom, the Government's Department of Health has discovered that 80 percent of all consultations are taken up with chronic complaints, which range from heart disease, stroke, and diabetes to depression and addiction.

None of us is immune. And it is vital to be very clear that these conditions are not just diseases of affluence. They belong to rich and poor alike. I am told, for example, that in Nigeria 35 percent of women are obese. In China, one hundred and sixty million people are reported to be hypertensive; while in Asia, cases of diabetes will apparently rise by 90 percent over the next twenty years. In the UK, the number of obese children is predicted to double over the next ten years. Indeed, the Chief Executive of the UK's Audit Commission recently said that this alone will lead to a reduction in the overall life expectancy of the next generation of British adults.

Not only do these conditions drastically reduce life spans, but they seriously compromise the quality of many lives as well, causing people to become progressively ill and debilitated. This acceleration in long-term disease, it seems to me, can be seen as the result of fragmented approaches to health which, in turn, fail to produce that apparently most elusive quality, which is harmony.

I do believe most strongly that we should not view poor health as something that exists in isolation, but which forms as a direct consequence of our communities, our cultures, our lifestyles, and the way we interact with our environments. The state of our health reflects the food we eat, the exercise we take, the water we drink, the air we breathe and the quality of our housing and sanitation. I believe it also extends to our social needs and circumstances—the need to belong to a community, the need for meaningful work and daily purpose; the need in our lives for dignity and kindness, for self-respect, for hope and, above all, for harmony and beauty. It encompasses the power of art, the healing properties of loving human relationships, and the role of the human spirit. Human health is the sum of all these parts. If we reduce or belittle these fundamental elements of life, are we not neglecting what it is to be human?

Yet, too often, we appear to do just that, on a daily basis. The pollution of our environment (in almost every sense) is widespread.

As Sir Tom Blundell, the former Chairman of the United Kingdom's Royal Commission on Environmental Pollution, put it in a report entitled *Chemicals in Products:* "Given our understanding of the way chemicals react with the environment, you could say we are running a gigantic experiment with humans and all other living things as the subject." If we poison and pollute our earth, we poison and pollute ourselves. Food colorings and additives can cause a range of health problems in adults and children; hydrogenated fats and unhealthy diets are linked to heart disease and—frighteningly—the residue from pesticides used in conventional farming methods can remain in our bodies for years.

In tackling these issues, I feel we need to be prepared to think radically—and certainly beyond the range of conventional health approaches. I have long felt that we have somehow lost touch with our instinct and intuition for each other, and for our environment. The time has surely come to appreciate that the complexity of chronic diseases requires considered and multi-dimensional solutions. We must reconsider how we farm our land, how we produce our food, how we build our cities, and how we care for our precious natural heritage.

In future, for instance, it will not be enough to boast that a new development of houses is merely cost or fuel-efficient. We must ask: is it human-efficient? Does it encourage better physical and mental health, satisfaction with life, or help to foster a genuine community? Does it respond to the human need for beauty? As few long-term diseases are curable, we need also to think radically about our objectives in improving the lifestyles of those who suffer from chronic conditions. The need to prevent deterioration, to maximize the quality of life and the ability of a patient to function, calls for a more holistic approach—one which respects an individual's choices, culture, and expectations.

This is where orthodox practice can learn from complementary medicine, the West can learn from the East, and new from old traditions. For the past twenty-four years I have argued that patients should be able to gain the benefit of the "best of both worlds"—complementary and orthodox—as part of an integrated approach to healing. Many of today's complementary therapies are rooted in ancient traditions that intuitively understood the need to maintain balance and harmony with our minds, bodies, and the natural world. Much of this knowledge, often based on oral traditions, is sadly being lost. Yet orthodox medicine has so much to learn from it. It is tragic, it seems to me—and indeed to many people who have studied this whole area—that in the ceaseless rush to modernize, many beneficial approaches, which have been tried and tested and have shown themselves to be effective, have been cast aside because they are deemed to be "old-fashioned" or irrelevant to today's needs.

There are clear examples which come to mind, particularly in the fields of acupuncture and herbal medicines. While scientists try to learn more about how acupuncture works, increasingly robust evidence, drawn from a number of international studies, indicates that it does work, particularly for the treatment of conditions such as osteoarthritis of the knee. It can, according to the evidence, also alleviate the nausea and vomiting that can be so debilitating for those taking anti-cancer drugs. In the case of herbal applications such as St John's Wort *(Hypericum perforatum)*, which has been used since the time of the ancient Greeks, about thirty clinical trials have shown some positive effects in treating non-severe depression, with a remarkably low incidence of side-effects.

However, just at the moment the world has begun to realize the immense value of Nature's gifts in the management of our health, the ecological or traditional habitats from which they come are being rapidly destroyed. If we are not very careful, we shall lose a vital life-support system for future generations. We all have so much to learn from each other — whether we live in an affluent country or a developing one. Hippocrates said "First, do no harm." I believe that the proper mix of proven complementary, traditional, and modern remedies, one which emphasizes the active participation of the patient, can help to create a powerful healing force for our world.

In every treatment, the human attributes of compassion, empathy, touch, and rapport are as vital to the art of medicine and healing as they are to the essence of humanity. An integrated approach gives each individual the means and hope of contributing to his or her own healing. Integrated practitioners provide time, empathy, hope, and reassurance — the so-called "human effect" — which can produce major changes in the immune system. These changes can be demonstrated using brain scans, and provide scientific clues as to how beliefs and emotions can influence our physical health and sense of wellbeing. The "human effect" can, therefore, play a demonstrably significant role in the whole approach to healing…

In the UK, my Foundation for Integrated Health has been the leading champion of this integrated approach for the past eleven years. Another of my organizations, the International Business Leaders Forum, has been working with the WHO on a number of projects aimed at, amongst other things, finding ways of improving health through better diets and increasing physical activity, in a number of countries. My Foundation for Integrated Health (FIH) has, as part of its approach, encouraged better research and regulation of complementary medicine so that patients can be confident of its safety and effectiveness. I am delighted that FIH is now also working with the WHO and the King's Fund in London on a new project which has, as its main objective, the aim of examining and exploring different approaches to the regulation of complementary medicine worldwide.

The Foundation also has an awards scheme for integrated projects. I recently visited one clinic in a deprived inner city area which showed how an integrated approach, involving acupuncture and other complementary treatments, appears to have been particularly helpful for patients with mental health problems. Recently, my Foundation has also created an association of clinicians who are developing integrated approaches throughout the UK. What was once regarded as peripheral is increasingly now seen as mainstream.

The question, to my mind, should no longer be whether healthcare services should be integrated, but how and how soon it can be done. In the UK, research in recent years has shown that 50 percent of General Practitioners are referring their patients to complementary practitioners, and, according to BBC Television surveys, over 75 percent of patients would like to have the choice of a complementary as well as an orthodox approach to their problem. I very much hope that my Foundation will be able to work with and learn from similar organizations in other countries. We all have so much to learn from each other.

The humanitarian, theologian, and Nobel Peace Prize-winning doctor Albert Schweitzer said, "The first step in the evolution of ethics is a sense of solidarity with other human beings." The first steps in sharing our integrated solutions are, it seems to me, happening already. The WHO is compiling a Global Atlas on the use of traditional, alternative, and complementary medicine. This provides a useful start for planning integrated health approaches across the world.

The case of Artemesia is a classic example of where real progress can be made. A naturally growing plant, long used in China for treating Malaria, Artemesia is now a treatment of choice in many parts of the World. I have also heard that it is currently being grown in Africa and that the WHO is working to try to ensure that it will eventually become available to all who need it. I have similarly been made aware of a program called "Puente," an anti-poverty program aimed at the poorest families in Chile. By adopting an holistic approach that nurtures well-being through initiatives in health, employment, housing, and education, it appears that this initiative is strengthening the health of families who are struggling to escape from long-term poverty. In the UK, the Beacon Project in Falmouth has shown that if you support and empower a deprived community, this can help to bring about improvements, including a reduction in the incidence of asthma and post-natal depression as well as a decline in the number of teenage pregnancies.

Together, we must find creative new ways of developing an integrated approach to health that will encompass nutritional, medical, agricultural, environmental, and social policies. In our battle against the complex problems of chronic disease, which could all too easily overwhelm us in the years to come, and in our efforts to control the global environmental crisis, we need to re-discover and re-integrate some of the knowledge and well-tried practices that have been accumulated over thousands of years. I urge all health ministers, politicians, and Government representatives to abandon the conventional mindset that sees health as solely the remit of a health department.

In ancient China, the doctor was only paid when the patient was well. In modern health systems, perhaps your visible success should depend on health outcomes and the degree to which health has become the responsibility of every single department in a country's Government. Only through collaborative thinking can we paint a complete picture of world healing.

Only through collaborative approaches can we develop the best ideas and the best plans. Every country could develop an integrated plan for future health and care that reflected its disparate cultures and medical traditions, and recognized the importance of all aspects of the natural environment. It would integrate medical services with individual and community approaches to health and self-care, and build upon current examples of integrated health and care, which exist everywhere. Why not ask Finance ministers to quantify the savings from this new and emphatic focus on prevention as well as cure?

Last year I commissioned a report in order to encourage a better-informed debate about the effectiveness of different therapies and treatments which might eventually result in savings. The report, compiled by a British economist, Christopher Smallwood, was published last October and it found evidence that complementary approaches could help to fill gaps in some orthodox treatments, particularly in relation to many chronic conditions such as lower back pain, osteo-arthritis of the knee, stress, anxiety and depression, and post-operative nausea and pain.

Today's burden of long-term disease is, in part, the legacy of having treated our bodies and our world as a collection of unrelated components. But, of course, it is futile to rue the past. The British Prime Minister Winston Churchill once wrote, "Of this I am quite sure: If we open up a quarrel between the past and present, we shall find that we have lost the future." You are the guardians of that future. And the responsibility lies with us all to understand the complex relationship of human health to our diverse societies, to our modern lifestyles and to our fragile ecosystems. Centuries ago, Plato said, "The cure of the part should not be attempted without treatment of the whole." Centuries later, the World Health Organization recognized this principle in its 1948 constitution when it defined health as a "complete state of physical, mental, and social wellbeing."

Today is our chance to redefine our health systems so that they provide the balance and connectedness that the Twenty-first Century so desperately needs. If we nurture the humane, intuitive guiding principles of integrated health through combining the best of the ancient, well-tried methods with the rigors of science and the technological imperatives of our age, we will be taking the first bold step in a new vision for the future healthcare of the world.

JAMES ENDREDY

The Art of Counter Practice

"**D**o you understand what it is that we are doing here, son?" the old shaman asked sternly.

I had spent more than a decade living with various indigenous tribes throughout the world, learning from experience about their spiritual and secular connection to the Earth itself. On this particular day, several years ago, I found myself deep in the Western Sierra Madre of Mexico with the Wirrarika tribe, helping to clear an area for a new cornfield. For the previous two days the Shaman, his workers, and their wives and children had engaged in ceremonies asking permission from and making offerings to the land and all the beings both seen and unseen that inhabited the area. Now the men had felled a large tree and, excited to be allowed to join them in their work, I hacked violently with my machete at a thick limb. After several minutes of fierce determination, I noticed out of the corner of my eye that the shaman himself was eyeing me closely.

"This is not simply the mechanical clearing of the land," he said seriously in broken Spanish. "We are this land and this land is us. You must step through the nierika and join us in this sacred act."

Nierika is a Wirrarika word with many meanings, including spiral, portal, and mirror. The old shaman was asking me to leave my Western, American, industrial point of view behind and understand our work the way they perceived it. It must have been clear that I didn't completely understand what he was trying to tell me, because

James Endredy is a teacher, mentor, and guide to thousands of people through his books, workshops, and rites of passage. After a series of life tragedies and mystical experiences as a teenager, he changed direction from his Catholic upbringing and embarked on a lifelong spiritual journey to encounter the mysteries of life and death. He learned shamanic practices from all over the globe while studying with kawiteros, lamas, siddhas, roadmen, and leaders in the fields of ecopsychology, bioregionalism, and sustainable living. Visit him at www.JamesEndredy.com.

in the next moment the shaman gave me a truly incredible gift. He grabbed the machete from my hand and in one swipe took off the limb I had been struggling to remove. Then he placed the branch in my left hand so that the cut end was facing me, he positioned my right hand palm up next to it, and he very forcefully said, "Now you look!"

I stared at the branch and at my open hand, feeling very self-conscious. But after several excruciating moments I actually stepped through the nierika and my perception was changed forever. What the old shaman was showing me was that the outward spiraling rings on the flesh of the tree branch were the same as the spirals on every one of my fingertips!

He was trying to get it through my thick head that I wasn't so different from the tree after all, that everything is connected, that we come from the Earth and then we go back to it, just like all living things. I learned that day that my habitual way of perceiving is not the only way — or even the best or the healthiest way. I learned that what we normally perceive is only a small part of what is really going on around us.

Personal perception is based on many things, such as education, experience, and culture. And as a culture, most of us Western/modern folks have forgotten how to perceive the ways in which we are connected to the great powers and rhythms of nature, and to a large degree even the rhythms of our own bodies. It's not our fault really. For the most part we aren't taught these things in school or through our cultural experiences. But the good news is that we can learn to be different, healthier, and therefore more vital if we enlarge the scope of our awareness and perception. This can happen for us when we purposefully engage in thoughts and actions that are not part of our normal routines. I call this *counter-practice*.

As the name implies, counter-practice involves actions that move counter to a habitual pattern or practice. It turns our habitual way of doing things upside down and inside out so that we can see and feel from a place other than our accustomed point of view. Counter-practice is employed specifically to enlarge and expand one's consciousness by experiencing shifts in one's perception. Therefore, counter-practice is not at all the simple "opposite" of something we currently do. For example the counter-practice of working at a job just to "make a living" is not simply refusing to work, but rather working at something that fills an authentic calling from deep inside of you. It is a very delicate art form that requires sensible and sober judgment, but in a way that allows for creative and innovative practices to be employed.

To understand this better, let's start with the most personal thing we have: our physical body. At both the perceptual and physical levels our culture does a fantastic job of suppressing the ancient wisdom that our bodies hold. When we open ourselves to that wisdom, we not only gain in human potential but we also reconnect with the larger body that provides us with life: our Mother Earth.

The organic reality of Earth is found not only in mountain ranges and the depths of oceans, but inside the human body as well. Alienation from our bodies by over-intellectualizing and technologizing often causes us to feel like disembodied minds with disenchanted bodies. Our true identity becomes weak and vulnerable when divorced from our bodily feelings and from the Earth. To reconnect the sense of *self* with one's Earth-grounded body is also to reclaim a connection with the body of Earth and the dynamic interaction between body, mind, and environment.

Reconnecting with our physical body can affect us spiritually, as well. Non-incarnated spirituality, disconnected from our bodies and from nature, alienates us from the sacredness of Earth and from the profoundly spiritual reality of the natural world, of which our body is a part. When we discover that our body is not the dwelling place of spirit but, rather, the physical manifestation of spirit, we move to a place of honoring and cherishing not only our own flesh but also the flesh of the world and the whole universe.

One of the primary ways we have become alienated from the body is through our endless pursuit of control. To achieve "success," our ego attempts to control as many of our life circumstances as it can. But the body, on the other hand, functions as a highly complex system of mostly involuntary actions (blood circulation, digestion, metabolism, and so forth), over which we have little or no possibility of conscious control. It is precisely due to the inability to completely control our body that we develop the feeling of being trapped by it, by the pain it makes us feel when we are injured or sick, and by the perceived chain of flesh that promises only one final outcome. In response to this we struggle against the inherent wisdom of our body.

Since our bodies are inextricably connected to the Earth, the issue of control extends beyond just our personal physical body to the Earthbody as well. Yet the natural world surely doesn't need human beings to make order of and control it. Quite the contrary, the Earth has evolved quite nicely without us. In fact, the destructive force of humans in recent history strikes considerable resemblance to a parasitic attack—the host, in this case, being the Earth and all its living species.

The wilderness areas and wild animals of the world do not *need* to be controlled and exploited by us. They are self-regulating systems. That is what makes them wild. The same goes for the human body. It is a highly complex, self-regulating system that more properly belongs to the wilderness than to a sterile building, whether home or office. In terms of control we will be much better off when we allow our body to be wild. Our body is perfectly capable of telling us where it likes to be, what it prefers to eat, what level of activity it needs, and what relationships are healthy for it.

Counter-practice – Letting Your Body Drive

An effective form of counter-practice relating to the physical body is to periodically set aside time for intentionally listening to your body in a way that your body, not your mind, guides your actions. Our bodies send us clear signals all the time, but we often don't listen or attend to those signals and messages because they interfere with beliefs and priorities determined by our rational mind. For example, have you ever awoken in the morning still tired, your body pleading with you to stay in bed, but you got up anyway because you simply *had* to go to work? Or, after being indoors working in an office for extended periods of time, have you ever felt your body silently begging for fresh air, natural light, and physical activity? Did you listen to your body's wisdom, or did you tune it out and suppress your natural urges in order to keep being "productive?"

While we certainly need to fulfill responsibilities in our lives — which often means temporarily suppressing our physical, emotional, and mental urges until our tasks are complete — this type of suppression becomes unhealthy when it becomes a habitual way of relating to life. As we train ourselves year after year to endure excessive periods of time cocooned indoors, we come to completely disregard the spontaneity and the creative forces that come and go with the many seasons and phases of the natural world, and to neglect and suppress the natural urges and needs of our own organic being.

Our bodies have a unique way of communicating to our minds what we need to be healthy. By renewing that flow of information and then developing and deepening the dialog between body and mind, we place our entire human organism in a healthier, happier position. Setting aside specific times when you let your body "drive" your actions is the first step to developing this awareness. This can be easily done when you have time to yourself after work or on weekends, or at any time when the demands of life are not totally consuming your attention. Once you have consciously and intentionally experienced the positive effects of taking a nap when you need it, prying yourself away from the computer to take a walk outside, or eating a certain food that was not on the day's menu, you quickly learn that your human organism has its own rhythm and pattern of needs that may be very different than the schedule you are imposing on it. From these initial experiences, the simple exercise of letting your body drive can transform into an integral part of your life whereby your daily actions — as well as the habits, patterns, and cycles of yearly, monthly, and weekly activities — become more in tune to what your human organism is asking of you.

Counter-practice – Relating to the Elements

Another potent form of counter-practice relates to working with the five fundamental elements of life: earth (soil), water, air, fire, and spirit/space. The names that we give to these elements are purely symbolic; they simply describe the fundamental forces and energies of the world, both internal and external to the human organism. There is nothing in our world that is not formed and sustained by the interactions of these five elements.

The counter-practice of working with the elements is developing a form of awareness that begins not in the typical way of the ego looking out, but rather, from the perspective of what is seemingly outside of us looking in.

This perspective is the reverse of that to which we are accustomed. From here we realize that the world does not begin with our own mind and extend out, but rather, we learn to make what is "out there" a seamless part of our own perception. The world, and the reality of all life and spirit, was here far before us; it is we that are born *from* it. We are not unlike a flower that has sprung from the earth and receives its nourishment by taking in the sun and the rain, by circulating the sacred air through it's body and turning the nutrients of the soil into a creative expression of its true being. When we work with the elements at the level of counter-practice we need to proceed with this kind of feeling in mind or else all we are doing is projecting ourselves into the environment, which is what we ordinarily do.

The waters of the earth are fundamentally no different from the water of our bodies. The heat of the fire is the same as our metabolic fire within. Our flesh is the flesh of the world to which it is destined to return. The air in our lungs is communal to all aerobic life. The space that holds the world and all the elements is the universal continuum of matter and consciousness with which we are at one.

Therefore, the condition of our internal elements also affects the quality of our lives. When we are in balance our blood pressure, insulin, hormones, and so on, are within a certain optimal range, but when there is an imbalance we suffer or even die. Our emotional state naturally fluctuates in a healthy way, but severe imbalances are debilitating. When our internal elements are balanced we can more easily face environmental extremes such as cold temperatures or intense physical work, and internal pressures such as stressful relationships or frustrating tasks. But when we are out of balance not only is it more difficult to handle challenging situations, even moments and situations that should be happy and rewarding lose their flavor. Through working with the elements we can deepen our understanding of what it means to live in a healthy environment both inside and out.

In the descriptions that follow I have listed as "luminous" the human qualities that we readily identify with because they are usually seen as "positive" traits for a person to have. On the other hand, those qualities that we tend to not associate with who we are—even though they may be perfectly visible in us to some else that knows us—are listed as "shadow" qualities, as they are often seen as being less than positive traits to have but are equally tangible and valid.

Air

Luminous qualities – Communicative, spontaneous, flexible, refreshing, intellectual, open-minded, idealistic, objective.

Shadow qualities – Impractical, insensitive, tactless, inconsiderate.

Balanced qualities of the air element within us promote open and clear communication with other people, with ourselves, and with our environment. Air energy promotes the power of speech, the written word, poetry, and music. When air is balanced we acknowledge the interconnectedness of all life and the relationships between all things. We are inspired toward mental balance, freedom, and curiosity. We are open conduits for creativity, inventiveness, and intellectual discourse. Air also opens us to the magic of spiritual and mystical phenomena.

Air energy is stimulated by direct exposure to the wind at the top of mountains and in wide valleys, canyons, deserts, and plains. Breathing techniques that promote the opening of creative and meditative channels, as well as social activities that engage in spontaneous expression and creative writing in any form, all help in the movement and deployment of air energy.

Earth

Luminous qualities – Grounded, steady, focused, strong, stable, earthy, practical, dependable, conservative, sensual.

Shadow qualities – Dull, slow, possessive, overly materialistic, stubborn, bull-headed, self-centered.

When the earth element is balanced within us we feel stable, confident, and grounded. We are keenly aware, not easily swayed, deceived, or knocked off balance. Comfortable and secure in our actions and intentions, we are neither too rigid nor too flighty. We have determination to succeed in our goals without being obsessed by them. We have resiliency to accomplish tasks that can lead us to opportunities for success.

Activities steeped in earth energy include gardening and land reclamation projects, developing relationships with and reclaiming forests and populations of other rooted beings, intentional burial (which I explain in my book *Ecoshamanism*), and deep connection to caves and caverns.

Water

Luminous qualities – Fluid, sensuous, calm, relaxed, receptive, emotional, sensitive, compassionate, complex.

Shadow qualities – Moody, raging, easily influenced, self-pitying, wavering.

With a balance of water energy we experience contentment and joy in being alive in a way that is not reliant on joyous external circumstances. As we embody joy it tends to flow from us to the people we meet and the situations we encounter. We are able to *fluidly* move in and out of situations, knowing that sometimes we are required to be calm and gentle, and on other occasions forceful and dynamic. We are flexible and cooperative. Compassion is embodied as a calm, mirror-like wisdom. When water is in balance it makes the soil of earth fertile to the creativity and passion of air and fire.

The water element is stimulated inside of us when we simply let things flow, when we don't hold back our emotions, and when we intentionally place our body into the flowing water. Acts of giving and sharing also encourage this energy, as does the sharing of sweat and tears with others.

Fire

Luminous qualities – Passion, energy, inspiration, creativity, will, eagerness, spontaneity, independence, enthusiasm.

Shadow qualities – Forceful, consuming, domineering, and overbearing.

When fire energy is balanced within us we have a high degree of passion for life, but we don't let our fire rage uncontrollably. We have the drive to create, initiate, and complete the important undertakings in our life. Guiding our impetus is the intuition and insight that is the essence of the fire element. Balanced fire allows us access to our most primal awareness of the interconnectedness of all life. Fire connects us to our star, the sun, and the sun connects us with the universe. When we attend to this inter-connective awareness we may become more mindful not to waste our life force on self-centeredness and self-indulgence. Fire teaches us the true meaning of power and how every one of our actions reverberates through the universe. Mindful of our actions, we begin to understand and develop ways of using our energy in proactive ways and also in ways that can facilitate healing and purification. In this way the fire element inside of us becomes an agent of transformation, transcendence, and regeneration.

Fire energy is stimulated by bursts of physical and creative action. Activities that speed up the rhythm of our organism, metabolism, and cognitive functions raise the level of fire energy. Think of it this way: When you connect to a tree, your rhythm slows and you could touch or hug the tree indefinitely; but if you put your hand in a flame you will draw it back as quickly as possible. This applies to fire activities as well. Strong physical activities such as chopping wood for the fire will only last a short while, but during that time the fire level inside of you could be very high. This also goes for creativity. Those moments of flow, when creative expression just seems to pour out of you, don't tend to last continuously for days on end. But when you are inside those moments your organism is filled with fire energy.

Spirit

Luminous qualities – Being, clarity, animation, expansiveness, spaciousness.

Shadow qualities – Lack of presence, spaced out, lost, wandering.

When spirit is balanced we feel fully seated in our sense of being. We have time and space for everything. The other four elements of our being are brought into harmony and balance. We have clarity, focus, and purpose, but our actions are tempered with an awareness of expansive humility. A sense of our vast spinning galaxy is combined with the immediate presence of the moment.

Spiritual energy is stimulated when you touch the spirit of other beings and places of the world so that you feel the universe as a continuum of spirit-consciousness. The best ways to find the spirit inside of you is to become aware of the spirits surrounding you. Explore the world at the luminous level and see into the deeper meanings of the activities and circumstances around you. Look deeply into the hearts of animals, plants, and trees, and then stand back and feel the collective spirits that form the sacred places on earth. When you feel at one with those spirits, you also have found new strength and meaning in your own spirit.

Moment-to-moment Counter-practice

The art of counter-practice is a powerful form of personal growth with endless possibilities. One of the ways that we can begin to realize our true potentials is to engage in activities completely foreign to the habitual modes of being that are imposed on us by industrial society. While my space here does not allow for any more extensive examples of counter-practice, there are thousands of smaller forms of counter-practice that, when combined, can create significant momentum and radical shifts in consciousness. I refer to these as moment-to-moment counter-practices, as they can be performed during our daily lives. When taken all together and done on a daily basis, these types of actions can affect considerable changes in the way we perceive the world, lead to more healthy lifestyles, and foster a renewed relationship with our natural environment. Here are a few examples:

- Reclaim your mind and revolt against the brainwashing of commercial advertising. Cut down on or stop buying products advertised through psychological manipulation. Seek out local products and those from small businesses that aren't mass marketed.

- Every time you see or hear an advertisement, state out loud what button it is trying to push inside of you.

- Try to never buy another disposable battery. Buy rechargeable.

- Don't kill insects. Adopt a spider.

- In the summer time when people are watering the biotic desert they call a lawn, turn off their sprinklers that are running during the heat of the day, and adjust the ones that are watering more driveway and sidewalk than lawn.

- A sheet of paper has two sides. Use them both.

- Create something beautiful and then give it away to someone you don't know and will probably never see again. While you are giving it you may feel regret, but you will learn that you need not posses something to own it.

- Read *The Man Who Planted Trees*, and then see how it feels to be like him.

- With the help of a friend for safety, blindfold yourself for 24 hours while still performing many functions of your everyday life.

- Spend a whole day exploring various tasks in a wheelchair.

- Walk backwards for a half an hour each day for a week.

- Take a tape recorder with you and record yourself during various conversations and situations. Is that really you?

- Tell a total stranger a secret that you've never told anyone before.

- Tell yourself lies in front of a mirror. Tell yourself how great you are, how good looking, how intelligent, smart, funny, successful... after a while the lies and the truths are all the same. Do it now.

- Read out loud all the ingredients of the packaged food you eat each time before you eat it.

- Put the specialness back into simple items—only use one plate, glass, fork, pair of shoes, socks, or underwear.

- Color your world without petroleum-based paint products.

- Never buy or eat anything that comes in Styrofoam. Tell businesses you currently frequent that you will go elsewhere unless they provide alternatives.

- Use a cloth rag not a paper towel.

- Each time you flush 3-5 gallons of water down the toilet, become aware of how wasteful it is to defecate into water that is made pure for drinking.

- Say "thank you" to everything. If you stub your toe say thank you to the kid's toy that caused you pain. Before you start to eat, say thank you to your fork.

- We've all seen the "adopt a highway" signs. What about adopting something really important like a stream or an old growth forest?

- Revolt against helium party balloons; they always seem to end up where they don't belong.

- Make peaceful rebellion your church. Revolt against your own self-imposed limitations, and those put on you by society. If your rebellion feels uncomfortable then you're doing it right.

- Adopt an endangered species.

- Don't put your groceries into anything but a reusable cloth bag.

- Don't speak for at least two days. Spend your time listening instead. Write it out if it's really that important.

- Just like a child who knows the world is still a mystery, ask the question "why?" to everything and to everyone.

Daryl Hannah

Living Consistent with Your Values

C H A P T E R
31

My awakening to responsibility for our world began when I was about ten years old. My uncle, an Academy Award-winning cinematographer, sat me down and told me about nuclear power, something that I had never heard of before. I was horrified. I couldn't believe that we as a species were creating waste from nuclear power plants that had a half-life of hundreds of thousands of years. I also couldn't believe that our tax dollars were being put to such use. I was absolutely appalled. When I started working in the movies at the age of eleven, I got my first paycheck. I immediately went into my dad's office and told him that I refused to pay part of it in taxes because I didn't want the money going toward war or toward nuclear power. My dad responded that I would go to jail for that belief, and I said, "That's okay." That's where my awakening began, and it is still happening as my awareness grows.

It manifested even more personally the following year. Suddenly, I was not able to disassociate my food from the creatures that I was eating. So at a relatively early age, I became a vegetarian. After that, my idea of living my life harmlessly and well kept expanding. I realized that all my concerns—about the cleanliness of our air and water, about the health of our soil, about the preservation of our natural resources, and the protection of people who are being exploited—all have the same roots. Humanitarian and environmental concerns are one and the same. I've never been someone who can pick

> **Daryl Hannah is an accomplished actress and producer. After graduating from the University of Southern California School of Theatre, she studied drama at Chicago's Goodman Theater. Her breakout role was the gymnastic android in the movie "Blade Runner" (1982) starring opposite Harrison Ford. She portrayed a mermaid in "Splash" (1984) and went on to star in "Steel Magnolias" and many other movies. At the Berlin Film Festival in 1994, she won the Best Short award for a movie she directed and produced entitled "The Last Supper." She is currently involved in several new movie projects. Photo by Sandrine Weinstein.**

one specific cause, and make that the only thing I work for. They're all notes of the same song; it's all connected. I really love this quote from Francis Thompson:

Thou canst not stir a flower

Without troubling of a star.

As an actor, I've had a hard time figuring out the most effective things I can do personally, aside from giving money to organizations that I believe in. A musician can go out and play a concert and raise money and awareness in a big way. What comparable gift can an actor offer?

I have decided that the best thing I can do is to make sure that, in every area of my life, I am actually living by my own ideals and principles. My home was built with green materials. We salvaged a barn that was being torn down to make way for a post office. The barn was built from exquisitely beautiful old wood, giant lengths of good, solid board. You can't buy anything like it new because we don't have old growth forests anymore. I did a lot of research about different types of green insulation materials, about non-toxic paint, and about gray water system. I equipped the house with solar power; it has a backup generator that runs on biodiesel.

I also pick all-organic ingredients in my food, and use non-toxic products in my house. I am actually living within my belief system. And that's really important to me, because, in a sense, the strongest effect you can have is a personal one. When people come to my house, they witness that this lifestyle isn't just nice in the abstract. Everything actually works well, and it's beautiful. Even those who want lavish lifestyles can still employ green and harmless methods and materials. You can still have a refrigerator and have earth-friendly values. You can keep nearly all the amenities that people assume you have to give up in order to live in harmony with nature.

Another choice that many people can make is the vehicle they drive. I drive a 1983 diesel El Camino. I drove from Southern to Northern California on about twenty gallons of recycled french-fry grease. Our society is realizing that there's a limit to our reserves of fossil fuels, and that it's very wrong to go to war and incur the wrath of the world to steal oil. We have other options. Even Detroit is starting to realize this. Family-sized hybrid cars are starting to be sold. The demand for new, low-impact vehicles is going through the roof. In the foreseeable future, all the auto manufacturers will be making them because once consumers change the way they consume, big business is right behind them.

I'm moving into a new phase in which I'm focusing on getting the information that supports these choices out to a great many people. The world is open to it at last.

My manager is the kind of person who has never concerned himself with any cause like the environment. However, his dog began getting sick repeatedly, and developing tumors. He couldn't figure out why. Then he realized that he was using chlorine cleaners on his floors, and the fumes were affecting the dog. He began using a non-toxic cleaner, and his dog hasn't had a problem since. It made him think about what he could do for his own health, and the health of his wife and kids. Many families have a member who has cancer, or know a family that has been touched by cancer. This is causing us to consider the toxins that surround us and that we've been ingesting.

It may take a difficult experience to wake people up to the wonderful alternatives that are now available. My effort now is to make sure that the information we need is easily available, to assist us in making good choices. It's getting easier to find the best alternatives, to discover what really works. The formula is pretty simple: what's good for the planet is also what's healthiest for humans. So I recommend we choose organic everything, buy local produce, eat organic food, and eliminate toxic cleaning products from our homes. The harmless ones work just as well, smell better, and are good for you.

Americans are raised to be short-sighted, and to look just at what we need now—not the price of our needs in the long term. We are going to have to learn to be a different kind of consumer. Big business isn't going to take us there, but big business will follow once they see the huge market for natural products. It's already happening: suddenly, Heinz is marketing an organic ketchup. There are even organic versions of the silliest foods, like potato chips and Cheese Curls. People are coming around.

On this planet we have one, and only one, beautiful, magical, karmic set of circumstances. We have this unique atmosphere, water and soil, and all these wonderful fellow creatures. Let's keep it going, rather than turning downward in a drawn-out spiral. Do we really want fish genes in our tomatoes? Are square tomatoes a good idea? I don't think so. This direction doesn't make sense to anyone who understands the situation. We have a great struggle before us, but we're all in it together. We have excellent tools, and alternatives to our destructive path. I'm excited to be one of millions of people actively making a contribution to a green and growing future.

DAVID GRUDER

The Self-Care Paradox

Melissa was a connector and a giver. Her husband, children and church community all adored her dearly. She felt surrounded by love and like her life had meaning. Melissa was shocked when she learned she had cancer. It was difficult for her to understand why someone who valued connection with others and making a positive difference in her community could have become so betrayed by her body.

Melissa sought assistance from me in unraveling this mystery in the hope that this, along with her spiritual work, might help her respond more positively to her medical treatments. She began to consider the possibility that she had developed cancer because of having spent far too many years being there for others and so neglectful of herself. She came to appreciate that the severity with which she neglected her own self-care and personal needs had finally caught up with her in the form of cancer. She had not considered that her drive for personal "authenticity" was as important as her drive for connection with others and to have positive impact in her world. It had never occurred to Melissa that being out of integrity with herself could be just as damaging as being out of integrity with other people or with the collective.

Once Melissa embraced that her own authenticity was not only just as important as her love of connecting with others and her need to make a positive difference in her world, she began to overcome

David Gruder, PhD, D.CEP, is a psychologist and award-winning self-improvement author. He is the author of *The New IQ* (Elite, 2008), and coauthored *Sensible Self-Help*, Colliers' 1997 Mental Health Book of the Year. David is the Executive Director of Willingness Works and is dually licensed as a psychologist & marriage & family therapist. He was the Founding President of the Association for Comprehensive Energy Psychology (ACEP). He trains and consults worldwide on integrity, intentionality, boundaries, anger intelligence, and energy psychology. His award-winning website is www.willingness.com.

her cancer. As Melissa took charge of her self-care and tapped into her own forms of creative self-expression and authenticity, she began feeling more whole and complete in ways she had never before experienced.

Melissa's story is a perfect example of our three core drives and how interconnected they are.

Did you know that we human beings have three core drives that live at the heart of our existence? Virtually all of us want to be fully who we are. We yearn to experience some degree of connection with others. We want to make a positive difference in the world. These are our three core drives: the drive for authenticity, the drive for connection and the drive to have impact.

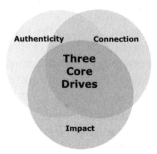

Awareness of our three core drives converts the notion of integrity from a vague, abstract, philosophical concept into a concrete, practical, actionable way of living. Our three core drives make it clear that there is not just one type of integrity. Integrity has three dimensions and they all need each other for full 3D Integrity to bloom. Authenticity is about personal integrity. Connection is about relationship integrity. Impact is about integrity with the collectives of which we are a part. Some people have a degree of integrity in one of these spheres but few of us seem to have developed 3D Integrity. Imagine a world populated by both leaders and citizens who embody 3D Integrity: people like Oprah Winfrey, Billy Graham, Sidney Poitier, Queen Noor of Jordan, Jimmy Carter, Dennis Prager, Barak Obama, Diane Sawyer, Jon Bon Jovi, LaDanian Tomlinson and Stephen Covey.

I believe we are on the cusp of being able to develop such a world. I propose a practical road map for accomplishing this in my latest book, *The New IQ: How Integrity Intelligence Serves You, Your Relationships and Our World.*

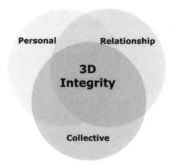

People travel one of three paths with their integrity. Some are Natural Developers. These are people who, like natural athletes, develop 3D integrity effortlessly. The second group are Deliberate Developers. These are like athletes who practice, practice, practice till they excel, even if their initial abilities don't put them in the first group. Finally, there are those who don't choose to continue to develop as adults.

Natural Developers intuitively know how to express their three core drives in a coordinated and integrated way. Their capacity for 3D Living enables them to experience levels of fulfillment that many of the rest of us only yearn for but don't attain. 3D Living is the fulfillment we experience when we attain high levels of personal authenticity, a deep capacity to co-create synergy with others and a joy over having positive impact in the world as stewards of collective highest good. This way of living in full integrity with our three core drives is the secret to Peak Vitality and true fulfillment.

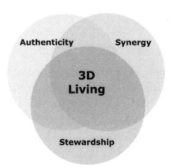

Studying Natural Developers for the past 25+ years has taught me that they achieve this because they seem to instinctively develop seven core life skills. I refer to these core live skills as WisePassions. In teaching Deliberate Developers how to develop on purpose these

WisePassions, I have found that they start to experience the same levels of 3D Integrity, 3D Living and 3D Fulfillment that Natural Developers experience.

The seven WisePassions are:

1. Teachability: I am consistently and authentically open to new ways of understanding and acting that may be useful for me, even if they are substantially different from my pre-existing beliefs and habits.

2. Self-Care: I consistently have the life energy and organization I need to support all three of my core drives (authenticity, connection, impact).

3. Discernment: I consistently blend keen insight, good judgment and strong intuition in order to recognize fact from spin and to discover what fits and doesn't fit for me, so that I have right relationship with input from others, from my own inside and from my intuition.

4. Harvesting: I consistently am able to get the most out of every situation I'm in and experience I have, especially the ones I didn't want to happen.

5. Power: I consistently embrace my strengths and the light I carry, honor my personal boundaries, and am effective in manifesting my intentions.

6. Synergy: I am consistently deepening my capacity for love and for co-creating with others.

7. Stewardship: I am consistently effective at co-discovering with others what serves collective highest good and I consistently do what serves highest good in small everyday ways and in larger ways as well, especially when no one is looking.

These seven WisePassions appear to be the basic building blocks for personal, relationship, leadership and integrity development. They appear to be the key elements need for 3D Living and fulfillment. Let's delve more deeply into the WisePassion of Self-Care.

How Selfish Must We Be In Order to Be Selfless?

Those of us who are passionate about making a positive difference in the world and serving collective highest good must contend with a particularly important paradox: how "selfish" must we be in order to be "selfless?" A surefire path to limiting your ability to be of service in the world is self-neglect. The more depleted you are, the more your ability to give to others will be impaired. True Self-Care is simply "enlightened self-interest in service of higher good." It is vitally important that those who value being of service in the world, from parents to educators to helping professionals to leaders, appreciate that *Self-Care is a prerequisite to sustainable selflessness*. If sustainable selflessness is one of the key purposes for developing Peak Vitality then impeccable Self-Care is mandatory rather than optional.

As a psychotherapist and leadership mentor, I am not only intrigued by how few people have come to grips with the Self-Care paradox. I am also fascinated by how few people have a clear and complete picture of what Self-Care includes. Self-Care is not a mix and match, one from column A and one from column B proposition. It is a package of non-interchangeable elements. All are needed and none substitute for the other. Simply put, *Self-Care provides you with the life energy you need to honor all three of your core drives* (authenticity, connection and impact).

There are three dimensions to Self-Care: internal, environmental and logistical. The more you neglect any of these aspects of Self-Care, the more you are giving yourself and others the message that you don't matter; that you are expendable. If you do this for long enough, your body will ultimately get the message and give up on you too. That is, you will become ill.

For all of us, well-rounded Self-Care is unavoidably a daily practice. It may be tempting to think that exercise and nutrition can compensate for chronic lack of sleep, or that a beautiful home and living within your means can compensate for ignoring your physical health. The human organism is a complex machine that is part physical, part spiritual, part psychological, and part energetic. No one part can ever be a substitute for the rest and no amount of passion about what you do as creative expression, in your career, or as acts of service, can be a substitute for Self-Care.

I am one of those people with a tendency to forget myself. It has taken me a very long time to truly accept that the less I take care of myself the more emotionally unavailable I am to others and the less centered I am when being of service in the world. For this reason, Self-Care is one of my least and most favorite topics. How about you?

Your Self-Care Self-Assessment

How good are you with your Self-Care? Take the following self-assessment and find out. Rate how much of the following you experience in your life right now on a scale of 0-10 (0 means not at all and 10 means an extreme amount):

- ❧ Exhaustion: 0-1-2-3-4-5-6-7-8-9-10
- ❧ Irritability: 0-1-2-3-4-5-6-7-8-9-10
- ❧ Weight problems (overweight or underweight): 0-1-2-3-4-5-6-7-8-9-10
- ❧ Chronic stress: 0-1-2-3-4-5-6-7-8-9-10
- ❧ Psychological or emotional distress: 0-1-2-3-4-5-6-7-8-9-10
- ❧ Physical imbalances, distress or illnesses: 0-1-2-3-4-5-6-7-8-9-10
- ❧ Self-indulgence or gluttony in general: 0-1-2-3-4-5-6-7-8-9-10
- ❧ Tolerating home or work ambiences that drain me rather than feed me: 0-1-2-3-4-5-6-7-8-9-10
- ❧ Tolerating being close to people who undermine my well-being, self esteem or growth: 0-1-2-3-4-5-6-7-8-9-10
- ❧ Tolerating being close to people for whom crisis and melodrama is a lifestyle: 0-1-2-3-4-5-6-7-8-9-10
- ❧ Making commitments to other people that I can't keep: 0-1-2-3-4-5-6-7-8-9-10
- ❧ Tolerating being chronically disorganized: 0-1-2-3-4-5-6-7-8-9-10
- ❧ Tolerating being chronically stretched too thin: 0-1-2-3-4-5-6-7-8-9-10
- ❧ Tolerating an improper balance between work and play: 0-1-2-3-4-5-6-7-8-9-10
- ❧ Tolerating an improper balance between spending and saving: 0-1-2-3-4-5-6-7-8-9-10
- ❧ Tolerating being chronically behind with home maintenance or errands: 0-1-2-3-4-5-6-7-8-9-10
- ❧ Not having enough time for the creative outlets I most love to do: 0-1-2-3-4-5-6-7-8-9-10
- ❧ Not having enough time to make a positive difference in the world in the ways I most love to do: 0-1-2-3-4-5-6-7-8-9-10

Now, add up your totals:

36 points or less = your Self-Care is better than most but you probably still have a couple of areas that could benefit from strengthening – put an asterisk (*) next to specific items that you scored 4 or higher because those are the ones on which to focus.

37-90 points = your Self-Care is suffering even though you're in a range where you've got a lot of company.

90 points or more = your Self-Care needs some serious focused attention sooner than later

Self-Indulgence and Self-Neglect

Joe just couldn't get enough exercise. Whether it was a run in the park, a workout at the gym, kayaking, skiing or whatever, Joe lived to move. Joe had a difficult time pinning down exactly why he came to see me. He viewed himself as a physically fit specimen who had a great job in the computer industry that paid him good money while leaving him with lots of free time as well. It bothered him that he didn't have many buddies outside the gym and that he couldn't keep a relationship for more than a couple of months at a time. In his mind, he was a pretty good catch and he didn't understand why it seemed that others didn't agree with him.

In time, Joe came to see that what he viewed as Self-Care was actually a form of self-indulgence. He gradually discovered he had been using exercise as an anesthesia and that there was far more to Self-Care than only exercise, nutrition and sleep.

Sue never got enough sleep; there was just too much to do and not enough hours in the day to do it all. Lack of sleep turned out to be the tip of the iceberg for Sue. In time she confessed that her home was so full of clutter she was embarrassed to invite friends or dates to visit. Virtually every available wall in her amply sized executive office suite had stacks of papers, files and books propped up against it, always on the verge of teetering over. Similarly her mind felt like it was bulging at the seams. Her internal chatter was incessant and this in part was why Sue never got enough sleep.

Sue's life revolved around on getting validation; her strategy involved busy-ness and productivity. It did not matter to her how many work hours she had to put in, whether in the office or at home, Sue was always drained, perpetually scattered and alone. Her social and love life were nearly nonexistent. She had no time for the jewelry and macramé she so dearly loved to create. Nor did she have time for the social causes that were close to her heart. She had resorted to making sizable donations, but instead as guilt offerings rather than love offerings. Speaking of money, her bank accounts were a mess and as a result she was regularly bouncing checks despite having enough money to cover her expenses.

Sue had an under-energized, self-neglectful relationship with Self-Care, while Joe had an over-energized, self-indulgent relationship with Self-Care. Both self-neglect and self-indulgence mean that too little life energy is left over for self-expression, relationships and service. The **Task** of Self-Care is to replace your survival strategies of self-neglect and self-indulgence with effective internal, environmental and logistical Self-Care 'climates.'

Self-Care is about:

- ❑ Keeping your energy strong and balanced
- ❑ Keeping your mind calm yet alert
- ❑ Keeping your body capable of supporting you in all areas of your life
- ❑ Keeping your environment nourishing
- ❑ Keeping your life logistics under control and in service of all three of your core drives

The Key Ingredients of 3D Self-Care

Inner Self-Care includes daily habits for keeping your energy field strong, developing a caring and nourishing relationship with your body, and learning to quiet your over-active mind.

Basic Physical Health Habits include enough good quality sleep for your body's needs, movement, high-quality nutrition and energy system balancing. (In the Glossary contained in *The New IQ* you will find a definition of "energy system" and you will find some basic energy balancing exercises in *The New IQ Workbook*.)

Soothing, Recharging and Play Habits: Soothing habits are anything that makes you purr, such as a massage or a bath. Recharging habits are anything that restores your inner juice, such as watching your favorite sitcom, gardening, or just about any truly creative endeavor that gives you energy rather than takes energy from you. Play habits are anything that brings out the kid in you. Anything that is not an anesthesia but calms you down is a Soothing habit. Anything that is not an anesthesia but gives you energy rather than takes energy from you is a Recharging habit. Anything that is not an anesthesia but brings out the kid in you is a Play habit. You may find that some of the things that soothe you are also recharging and/or feel playful to you and vice versa, but that some are only one or the other.

Internal Quieting Habits are practices that enable you to enter inner silence so you can take vacations from constant mind chatter. Some people use prayer to quiet their mind. Others use one meditation form or another. Yet others use physical disciplines such as Tai Chi, Qigong or Yoga, enabling them to simultaneously take care of both their daily need for physical movement and internal quieting. Some people find that their Internal Quieting habit is also soothing and recharging.

❧ **Insufficient Inner Self-Care** results in exhaustion, irritability, weight problems, chronic stress or psychological symptoms, physical imbalance or illness, and gluttony.

Environmental Self-Care includes arranging your surroundings so that they most deeply nurture you. This includes not only your physical environments but your people environments as well.

Physical Environments include home and work, as well as also regularly spending time in the natural settings that most nourish you.

People Environments include not only who you regularly spend time with but knowing what your optimal blend is of one-on-one time, small group time and large social setting time. It also includes knowing your optimal blend between "alone time" and "people time."

❧ **Insufficient Environmental Self-Care** results in tolerating home or work ambiences that drain you rather than feed you, and people who undermine your well-being, self esteem or growth, or for whom crisis and melodrama is a lifestyle.

Logistical Self-Care includes keeping your stress levels low through making sure that tasks (such as chores, errands and finances) are handled as efficiently as possible so that your life logistics support your Peak Vitality rather than keeping you from it. This includes:

Details Management: Mastering goal setting, implementation planning, time management, file management and money management.

Streamlining your chores and tasks, including home maintenance and errands.

Choices Management: Balancing work with play, spending with saving, and making sure that your job and financial choices support your needs for creative self-expression and your ability to spend quality time with those you love while still having energy left over to be of service in the world in ways that call to you.

❧ **Insufficient Logistical Self-Care** results in tolerating being disorganized or stretched too thin, being imbalanced between work and play or between spending and saving, and falling behind with home maintenance or errands.

WisePassion #2: *Self-Care*

Internal

Basic physical health and
soothing, recharging and
internal quieting habits

Environmental

Creating nourishing living
and work environments;
surrounding yourself
most closely with
people who support your
3D Development/Integrity

Logistical

Simplifying your
commitments and tasks, and
organizing your life logistics,
in ways that best support your
3D Development/Integrity

Assessing the Strength of Your Specific Self-Care Habits

Grab a piece of paper and go back and review the items listed in each of the sections and subsections in the 3D Self-Care description above. Rate your strength and weakness with each one. As you do this, please keep in mind that if you find you are weak in a number of Self-Care areas, this is not at all unusual. What is important is that you discover how much your capacity for 3D Integrity and Peak Vitality depends on the extent to which you utilize *all* of these Self-Care Habits. If you make the link strongly enough inside you, this will help motivate you to upgrade your Self-Care habits.

Inner Self-Care

My Basic Physical Health: 0-1-2-3-4-5-6-7-8-9-10

My Soothing, Recharging and Play Habits: 0-1-2-3-4-5-6-7-8-9-10

My Internal Quieting Habits: 0-1-2-3-4-5-6-7-8-9-10

Environmental Self-Care

My Physical Environments: 0-1-2-3-4-5-6-7-8-9-10

My People Environments: 0-1-2-3-4-5-6-7-8-9-10

Logistical Self-Care

My Details Management: 0-1-2-3-4-5-6-7-8-9-10

My Logistics Streamlining: 0-1-2-3-4-5-6-7-8-9-10

My Choices Management: 0-1-2-3-4-5-6-7-8-9-10

After you have completed this self-assessment, review where you are strongest and weakest, and which self-care dimensions are natural for you to do and which feel less natural. Select no more than one or two weak areas to upgrade at a time. You will find a much more extensive Self-Care self-assessment in *The New IQ Workbook*.

If you notice that you have a large number of areas that need upgrading, expanding your Self-Care habits may well be a top priority for you at this time. Should this be true for you but you find you have inner objections blocking you from doing this, I encourage you to learn self-help methods for overcoming objections to success. Energy Psychology methods provide some of the most promising new ways to achieve this. You will find Energy Psychology basic balancing exercises as well as brief self-help instructions in *The New IQ Workbook*. Should whatever self-help methods you select to overcome your success objections not work for you, I strongly encourage you to seek professional assistance.

How Self-Care Amplifies Our Integrity

Self-Care is the foundation of personal, relationship and leadership integrity. It is your most fundamental way of demonstrating to yourself and others that you truly do matter. Self-Care also provides the foundation that makes it possible for you to express all three of your core drives. You might be someone who, like me, is blessed with a strong stamina. I have learned the hard way that no matter how productive I am able to remain, even when I am neglecting my own Self-Care, in the end my self-neglect always ends up doing harm.

How does your relationship with yourself suffer when you are out of integrity with your Self-Care needs? How does your relationship with others suffer? How does your ability to lead or to serve collective highest good suffer? If you're not sure, get some help with this before your denial catches up with you. I offer this as someone who paid a high price for neglecting my own Self-Care simply because I thought I had enough stamina to get away with it.

Four Keys to Evaluating Your Self-Care System

How do you know when your Self-Care system is working for you? When:

❑ You score 36 or less on the Self-Care Self-Assessment

❑ You spend the bulk of your days feeling a vibrant sense of wellbeing and having the life energy you need for creative self-expression, connection with others and being of service in the ways that call to you (that is, to express and coordinate all three of your core drives and to live in 3D Integrity)

❑ Everything you need done logistically takes as little time and effort as you think it can, either because you're using great systems and/or because you have hired others to assist with some of your life logistics

❑ You feel like there are indeed enough hours in the day and there is enough money to pay your expenses

You can find a free list of key inexpensive resources for upgrading your Self-Care in the *Best Resources* section of my Willingness Works website: www.willingness.com. If, despite your best efforts, you find that you just can't get it together to care for yourself, you likely have some significant self-sabotage programs going. Consider doing the Energy Psychology Self-Help treatments that are described in **The New IQ Workbook**, focusing on removing whatever blocks are in the way. If that does not do the trick, or doesn't resonate with you, please get professional help to remove your blocks. Your Self-Care is simply too foundational to your capacity for Peak Vitality, and to 3D Integrity, for you to have the luxury of neglecting it. Make it a living breathing cornerstone of your daily life from now on!

Barry Sears

Simple Solutions for Global Wellness

CHAPTER 33

Ibelieve that we may be witnessing the de-evolution of the human species. That's the bad news. The good news is that we can correct our course, in as little as thirty days, if we choose. How do I reach this startling conclusion? The evidence is clear as we look back through the development of human beings, what made us what we are, and the options that will shape our future. Diet has an enormous effect on behavior, and it can change our collective future worldwide.

There are some thirty million species on earth. What gave *Homo Sapiens* the ability to become the dominant species? What made us so special? It certainly wasn't our physical skills.

If we go back 150,000 years, genetic modeling now allows us to trace every human being on the face of the earth today to a very small African tribe. This group probably numbered about 1,000 individuals, certainly no greater than 5,000. How did this one small tribe of Africans, and their descendants, come to dominate the world?

You have three options, and all of them are compatible with the genetic evidence saying that we all come from the same genetic stock. Option One: God put Adam and Eve in the East African Rift Valley. That theory is consistent with the genetic information.

Option Two: Aliens from outer space came and interbred with our pre-human ancestors. That too would be consistent with our genetic information.

Dr. Barry Sears is a leading authority on the control of hormonal responses through food. A former research scientist at the Boston University School of Medicine and the Massachusetts Institute of Technology, he continues his research today through biotechnology company Sears Labs. Dr. Sears has been a frequent guest on many national programs such as 20/20, Today, Good Morning America, CBS Morning News, CNN, and MSNBC. More than 4 million hardcover copies of books, including *The Zone, The Anti-Aging Zone* and *The Omega Rx Zone,* have been sold in the United States.

The third option, and the most plausible, is that our ancestors in that small group of Africans blundered onto brain food by pure luck. This has nothing to do with Darwinian evolution based on natural selection. This is Lamarckian evolution, based on the luck of the draw.

The geology of the East African Rift Valley in ancient times created large lakes that provided an environment ideal for the growth of algae. The people living on the shores of those lakes didn't eat the algae directly. The algae were the main food for shellfish, and the human beings ate the shellfish that washed ashore. Their powers extended to cracking the shells in order to get to the meat inside. That meat contained large amounts of Omega-3 fatty acids. This food gave this one small group of Africans a significant advantage over all the other tribes and species.

Over the next 50,000 years their numbers built up. Then, about 100,000 years ago, groups of this larger population left Africa and meandered throughout the world. Through all their wanderings, they always stayed close to the seashore, with its supplies of shellfish.

The breakthrough in human dominance in evolution occurred about 40,000 years ago, when out of nowhere our species developed new tool-making abilities. Religion appeared. We developed art. Where did these major accomplishments come from?

That time frame corresponds almost exactly with the point when humankind learned to fish. This allowed us to obtain even higher levels of Omega-3 fatty acids than we'd previously absorbed from shellfish. There's a very strong argument for saying that these higher intakes gave us sufficient brain power to dominate the world.

If that's true, then the converse is also true. What if you take Omega-3 fatty acids out of the human diet? Will you see a significant drop in brain power?

The answer is that you do. But not for the first generation. There's still enough reserve capacity present to maintain the same level of brain function for a while. By the second and third generations, however, severe neurological deficits manifest themselves.

Brain power made humans dominant in the world. Brain power is highly dependent on our diet. There are two things we need in order for our brains to work at peak efficiency. One: A stable supply of blood glucose. That's the only fuel the brain can use. Two: An ongoing supply of these long-chain Omega-3 fatty acids. That's why your grandmother called fish oil "brain food."

If we want to maximize our human potential, we have to make our diet compatible with our genetic makeup. That genetic makeup is dependent upon stabilizing blood sugar for optimum brain function, which means stabilizing insulin, and finding adequate levels of long-chain Omega-3 fatty acids for optimal brain output.

If either of those begin to slip, the things that make us human begin to erode. For example, one of the things that we like to think of as a hallmark of being human is acting with civility. But when somebody has low blood sugar, what's the last thing on their minds? Politeness. That's what happens when you don't stabilize blood sugar to the brain. Yet you can rectify that blood sugar deficiency rapidly.

On the other hand, this very subtle and insidious decrease of the supply of Omega-3 fatty acids to the brain begins to short-circuit all the key factors that gave us our evolutionary advantage.

We have two major problems facing the world. One, we have too many people. We're competing for resources. Thomas Malthus was correct, but 200 years ahead of his time. We're outstripping the capacity of our food supply to provide us with nutrients that are in concordance with our genes. Our population is exceeding our production of the nutrients consistent with optimal hormonal function.

There's no hard science to tell us precisely when this point might occur, but my sense is a time frame of ten to fifteen years. For example, if we in America in fifteen or twenty years have not changed the way we eat, our country, as rich as it is, will be bankrupt. The medical costs we incur will drive us under.

A more ominous aspect of our plight is that, if fish oil is the thing that makes us human, we're doing everything in our power to drive the agent, the ingredient, to extinction. There's enough fish oil right now for the next fifteen years. But from that time on, there'll be a bifurcation of society into two groups: Those who have adequate access to fish oil, and those who do not.

Can we use biotechnology to make fish oil? Possibly. We can make mutant algaes, but they're very expensive. And they're not very efficient at producing long-chain fatty acids.

Can we farm fish? It takes two pounds of natural fish to make one pound of farmed fish. And farmed fish are much worse for you than natural fish. All the contaminants we've thrown into the environment—things like mercury, dioxins, PCBs, and flame retardants—all wind up in the food chain, concentrated in fish oil. To grow farm-raised salmon, you have to feed them fish oil, otherwise they will not grow. When you feed them crude fish oil, you're feeding them high concentrations of these contaminants, which they further distill into even higher concentrations. Farm fish are much richer than wild fish in these contaminants, which are known carcinogens and neurotoxins. The government presents us with a Hobson's Choice. On the one hand, it says, "Eat fish, they're healthy." On the other hand it says, "Don't eat fish, they're contaminated." They're right on both counts.

Vegetarian fish like tilapia, which are being harvested increasingly as populations of carnivorous fish decrease, have less toxins. But they have low amounts of fat, and therefore low amounts of fatty acids. They're a good source of protein, but not a very good source of brain food. So supplements are the best source at this point.

Omega-3 fatty acids aren't just important to the brain. These nutrients are vitally important to the body's ability to control inflammation.

When you step back and view medicine as a whole, you see that much of its focus is on controlling inflammation. Every chronic disease we fear—heart disease, cancer, Alzheimer's—is an inflammatory disease. Even the aging process is inextricably tied to inflammation.

Can we get away from this problem by taking anti-inflammatory drugs for the rest of our lives? Unfortunately not. When taken long term, anti-inflammatory drugs cause immune suppression, osteoporosis, and death. What's the alternative? What's out there in nature that has powerful anti-inflammatory properties without side effects? It again turns out to be fish oil.

Malthus was right, but wrong. He was right to ask the question, "Are we outstripping our capacity?" but he was wrong about the cause. Our problem is not a lack of calories, but a lack of the nutrients that control our hormonal responses. Things we want out of life—better health, better physical performance, better mental acuity, longevity, better emotional stability—are all controlled by our hormones. We control our bodies' production of those hormones by the food we eat. But the availability of the nutrients crucial to controlling those hormonal responses is growing scarcer by the moment. For many centuries, the basic human problem was staving off outright starvation. But today, for the first time in history, we have more overweight people on the face of the earth than malnourished people.

This has not been caused by any genetic change. What has changed in a major way is the methods we use for processing food. Today, the cheapest forms of calories are refined vegetable oils and refined sugars. Twinkies are the cheapest source of calories. While we can feed our growing population, we can't feed them right.

These are now global dilemmas. They are far more frightening for the future of mankind than global warming, because the changes can take place very quickly, within one or two generations. Yet we have the technology and the power to reverse them if we choose to. The question is, do we have the political will?

Science allows us to discriminate between different possibilities. Science says, "Every human came from a small group of Africans." We have three possibilities that give rise to the same output: aliens, Adam and Eve, or brain food. The first two, we can't do anything to reverse. The third possibility gives us the option of reversing the process.

A recent study took kids who had Attention Deficit Disorder (ADD) and gave them fish oil instead of Ritalin (*EFA [Essential Fatty Acids] Supplementation in Children with Inattention, Hyperactivity and Other Disruptive Behaviors, Lipids* magazine, September 2003). Their behavior normalized. It took about 30 days. I'm conducting a study at Harvard Medical School using higher doses of fish oil, because we've seen that within about six weeks, children don't just become better; they become superkids. Kids with ADD have learned a variety of tricks to try to help themselves cope with the world. Once you solve their basic problem, their need for these behaviors diminishes.

Hormones are the key to our future, and food is the key to our hormones. If we make the right choices of food, we can see significant changes in our society at every level within a matter of months. To make the world a better place, we need to feed the world right.

We have too many people on the face of the earth to supply them all with sufficient quantities of animal protein. We need renewable sources of protein, and the best renewable source turns out to be soybeans. One of my books, *The Soy Zone*, says, "Here's the answer. If we want to have six billion people on the face of the earth, we can do it if we make good use of renewable vegetarian sources of protein." But you need adequate amounts, like any drug. If you give a placebo dose of the drug, it doesn't work. If you administer adequate amounts, it works every time.

The other dilemma is that soy doesn't provide fish oil. We may have enough basic fish stocks at the moment, if we use them sustainably. But right now we're hunting fish to extinction.

The fish oil used in clinical studies comes from "trash" fish. These are species like sardines and anchovies, not the varieties you find on the menu in a five-star restaurant. These species are not under intense cultivation. But the time will soon come when supplies of even these abundant varieties start to decrease. When we deplete one fish stock, we start overfishing another. Our technology is so sophisticated that fish can run but they can't hide. The nutrients that made us human may well be disappearing from the face of the planet. When they're gone, they're gone. And when they're gone, we're not far behind. It won't happen in my lifetime, but it will probably happen in my children's lifetime. That doesn't mean the human race will disappear, but we'll evolve into a new form, similar to Jaba the Hutt, both in demeanor and physical appearance.

With sustainable sources of protein, and sustainable sources of fish oil, you can take the most impoverished people in the world, and—in just six months—dramatically change their future. I know it can be done. The question is, "Will it be done?" The kinds of studies I've been doing, and referencing in my books, point the way for governments and policy-makers.

In Mexico, governments have embraced this technology much more than in the United States. Mexico has the benefit of not having lots of money to throw at the problem. Mexicans have to find ways of solving their health problems that are more innovative than buying yet more drugs.

A number of state governments in Mexico have endorsed the Zone diet and Zone supplements. They've witnessed significant improvements in health among people following this regimen. After seeing the data, two of the twenty-eight state governments in Mexico have endorsed the program for all their residents. Zone products are dispensed through physicians who have their own Zone Centers. They're making food the primary drug to improve the health of their people.

You have to set a hormonal baseline for your body. It's like building a house. You can either build it on a concrete foundation, or on sand. The one on concrete will have a longer life-span. The more you control the hormones in the body through the food you eat, the less drugs, if any, you need to maintain a state of wellness. This is my clarion call. Our society treats medicine as a discipline for treating disease. But the days of the magic pill are over. Penicillin was a magnificent exception: one bug, one pill, game over. But its success mislead us into taking the same approach for other diseases; what we now have instead is chronic, multi-factorial diseases. All that conventional medicine can do is treat the symptoms of these diseases.

The focus of our medical endeavors needs to shift, from treating the symptoms of chronic disease, to maintaining wellness as long as possible.

How do we define wellness? Medicine can provide standards for wellness; one very useful one is the degree of inflammation you have in your body, as measured by blood samples.

Inflammation as an indicator of wellness is a growing measure in the medical world, at least at the highest levels. Whatever technology controls inflammation will command the high ground of medicine in the twenty-first century. All the drug companies are looking for new, remarkable, powerful anti-inflammatory drugs. I believe we've already found them: one is fish oil, the other is the Zone diet.

How can the Zone diet be anti-inflammatory? Fish oils are anti-inflammatory by a direct interaction. There's a group of hormones called eicosanoids that control the inflammatory process. The more fish oil you consume, the less inflammation you have. If we ask questions like, "Who are the longest-lived people in the world today," or, "Who are the people with the longest health-span?" (health-span equals life-span minus years of disability), or "Who has the lowest rates of heart disease," or, "Who has the lowest rates of depression," or, "Which nation seems to have the most civil society," the answer in every case ought to be the Japanese.

By contrast, who are the most warlike people in the world today? Which nation is filled with factions that love to fight for the sake of fighting? This prize might go to the Afghanis. You don't see a whole lot of fish oil consumed in landlocked Afghanistan.

There are two fatty acids in the blood that serve as markers of inflammation. One is called arachidonic acid. It's the building block of all the pro-inflammatory eicosanoids. The other fatty acid is called eicopentaenoic acid. It is the building block of all the anti-inflammatory eicosanoids. The ratio of these two fatty acids gives us an anti-inflammatory goal to aim for. You don't want this ratio too high, you don't want it too low. If you keep it within a certain range, you control inflammation. And if you control inflammation, you take a giant step toward improving world health and world civility. All of a sudden, much of the complexity of medicine can be reduced to the balance between these two fatty acids in the blood.

Americans are not only the fattest people on the face of the earth, they're probably the most inflamed. The average ratio of these two fatty acids in the Japanese population is about 1.5. In Americans, it's about 12. In kids with attention deficit disorder, it's between 40 and 50. For kids in the ghetto, the ratio is closer to 100. They don't have a chance.

Yet within thirty days we can change their prospects. It takes up to thirty days to build up sufficient levels of fatty acids in a depleted body. There are sixty trillion cells in your body. Each of them can make eicosanoids. It takes some time to build fatty acids in all of those sixty trillion cells.

Sugary snack foods also provide a drug solution to low blood sugar. From that standpoint, they are very effective drugs. If you have low blood sugar, you are self-medicating when you eat a sugary snack. You say, "I feel better." You're going to pay a price an hour and a half later, but it solves your problem right now. It's a lot cheaper to eat a Krispy Kreme than inject some glucose into the bloodstream.

How do we compete with Krispy Kremes? We have to provide attractive yet healthy alternatives to convenience foods. They have to look like junk food, they have to taste like junk food, but they have to be hormonally correct. They have to allow us to control our hormonal responses, and supply adequate levels of fish oil.

Food technology is the modern battleground. It got us into this unhealthy mess. It can get us out. How can it solve the problem within thirty days? It can provide alternative products: ice cream, candy bars, milkshakes. Hormonally correct snack foods in these packages can be a training wheel. After eating them, consumers say, "I feel better." Once we've set up that stable hormonal baseline, we educate and train them into achieving the same feel-good results by adjusting the composition of their daily meals.

Our studies of kids with ADD have shown that they need very large amounts of fish oil to bring their blood ratios down to the single digits. How do we deliver large amounts of fish oil? We put it into milkshakes. My background is in drug delivery. Drug delivery works best when you make it easy for the patient to comply. You have to get their hormones stabilized first. If those hormones are unstabilized, all the admonitions, all the education, all the evidence, will go in one ear and out the other. It's a self-reinforcing problem.

Fish oil also raises levels of serotonin. Serotonin can be thought of as a morality hormone. The line between savage and compassionate behavior is a thin one. The less serotonin in the body, the thinner the line. Fish oil is one of the few drugs that can raise both serotonin and dopamine, the hormone in the brain that produces a sense of well-being, and of focus. Fish oil is so effective in these clinical studies because it treats not only ADD—lack of focus; it simultaneously treats depression with serotonin.

In *Zone Perfect Meals in Minutes,* I demonstrate that it's fast and easy to make Zone meals. Once people try it, they discover they like it. If you can keep your hormones in balance, life will be very good. Let them fall out of the Zone, and it becomes much tougher than it needs to be.

Once you try this method for as little as seven days, it becomes so self-evidently gratifying that no further argument is required. Human nature says, "Keep doing whatever feels good." That's why if you get a person into that Zone for a little while, they not only say, "I feel good," but they also say, "I feel so much worse when I'm out of the Zone." Human nature becomes your greatest ally, because we want to feel good all of the time.

The scientific data supporting this approach is clear. It's now a matter of marketing. It's like a political campaign; we're competing for the hearts and minds of human beings, saying, "Here's the way to a better life."

Philosophy and religion give you rules for living a civil life. When you stabilize your hormones, all those injunctions about doing good make sense. People who've learned to keep inflammation under control can live the longest, healthiest and most moral lives. They can lead civil lives, lives that make the world around them a better place.

ALICE WALKER & PEMA CHÖDRÖN
in Conversation:
Good World Medicine

CHAPTER
34

Buddhist teacher Pema Chödrön and novelist Alice Walker on how tonglen meditation practice opens our heart, expands our vision, and plants the seeds of love in our lives. From an evening of discussion at San Francisco's Palace of Fine Arts Theater.

Alice Walker: About four years ago I was having a very difficult time. I had lost someone I loved deeply and nothing seemed to help. Then a friend sent me a tape set by Pema Chödrön called "Awakening Compassion." I stayed in the country and I listened to you, Pema, every night for the next year. I studied lojong mind training and I practiced tonglen. It was tonglen, the practice of taking in people's pain and sending out whatever you have that is positive, that helped me through this difficult passage. I want to thank you so much, and to ask you a question. In my experience suffering is perennial; there is always suffering. But does suffering really have a use? I used to think there was no use to it, but now I think that there is.

Pema Chödrön: Is there any use in suffering? I think the reason I am so taken by these teachings is that they are based on using suffering as good medicine, like the Buddhist metaphor of using poison as medicine. It's as if there's a moment of suffering that occurs over and over and over again in every human life. What usually happens in that moment is that it hardens us; it hardens the heart because we don't want any more pain. But the lojong teachings say we can take that very moment and flip it. The very thing that causes

Alice Walker has been involved in activism since the civil rights movement in the 1960s. She is the author of the Pulitzer prize-winning *The Color Purple* (Harcourt, 1992) and other books. She has spoken for the women's movement, the anti-apartheid movement, for the anti-nuclear movement. www.AliceWalker.com.

Pema Chödrön became a Buddhist nun in 1974. She studied with famed Buddhist teacher Trungpa Rinpoche until his death in 1987. She is the author of *Practicing Peace in Times of War* (Shambhala, 2007) and many other books. She spends seven months of each year in solitary retreat, and is greatly respected as a teacher. www.PemaChodron.com.

us to harden and our suffering to intensify can soften us and make us more decent and kinder people.

That takes a lot of courage. This is a teaching for people who are willing to cultivate their courage. What's wonderful about it is that you have plenty of material to work with. If you're waiting for only the high points to work with, you might give up, but there's an endless succession of suffering.

One of the main teachings of the Buddha was the truth of dukha, which is usually translated as "suffering." But a better translation might be "dissatisfaction." Dissatis-faction is inherent in being human; it's not some mistake that you or I have made as individuals. Therefore, if we can learn to catch that moment, to relax with it, dissatisfaction doesn't need to keep escalating. In fact it becomes the seed of compassion, the seed of loving-kindness.

Alice Walker: I was surprised how the heart literally responds to this practice. You can feel it responding physically. As you breathe in what is difficult to bear, there is initial resistance, which is the fear, the constriction. That's the time when you really have to be brave. But if you keep going and doing the practice, the heart actually relaxes. That is quite amazing to feel.

Pema Chödrön: When we start out on a spiritual path we often have ideals we think we're supposed to live up to. We feel we're supposed to be better than we are in some way. But with this practice you take yourself completely as you are. Then ironically, taking in pain—breathing it in for yourself and all others in the same boat as you are—heightens your awareness of exactly where you're stuck. Instead of feeling you need some magic makeover so you can suddenly become some great person, there's much more emotional honesty about where you're stuck.

Alice Walker: Exactly. You see that the work is right ahead of you all the time.

Pema Chödrön: There is a kind of unstuckness that starts to happen. You develop loving-kindness and compassion for this self that is stuck, which is called maitri. And since you have a sense of all the other sentient beings stuck just like you, it also awakens compassion.

Alice Walker: I remember the day I really got it that we're not connected as human beings because of our perfection, but because of our flaws. That was such a relief.

Pema Chödrön: Rumi wrote a poem called "Night Travelers." It's about how all the darkness of human beings is a shared thing from the beginning of time, and how understanding that opens up your heart and opens up your world. You begin to think bigger. Rather than depressing you, it makes you feel part of the whole.

Alice Walker: I like what you say about understanding that the darkness represents our wealth, because that's true. There's so much fixation on the light, as if the darkness can be dispensed with, but of course it cannot. After all, there is night, there is earth; so this is a wonderful acknowledgment of richness.

I think the Jamaicans are right when they call each other "fellow sufferer," because that's how it feels. We aren't angels, we aren't saints, we're all down here doing the best we can. We're trying to be good people, but we do get really mad. You talk in your tapes about when you discovered that your former husband was seeing someone else, and you threw a rock at him. This was very helpful (laughter). It was really good to have a humorous, earthy, real person as a teacher. This was great.

Pema Chödrön: When that marriage broke up, I don't know why it devastated me so much but it was really a kind of annihilation. It was the beginning of my spiritual path, definitely, because I was looking for answers. I was in the lowest point in my life and I read this article by Trungpa Rinpoche called "Working With Negativity." I was scared by my anger and looking for answers to it. I kept having all these fantasies of destroying my ex-husband and they were hard to shake. There was an enormous feeling of groundlessness and fear that came from not being able to entertain myself out of the pain. The usual exits, the usual ways of distracting myself—nothing was working.

Alice Walker: Nothing worked.

Pema Chödrön: And Trungpa Rinpoche basically said that there's nothing wrong with negativity per se. He said there's a lot you can learn from it, that it's a very strong creative energy. He said the real problem is what he called negative negativity, which is when you don't just stay with negativity but spin off into all the endless cycle of things you can say to yourself about it.

Alice Walker: What gets us is the spinoff. If you could just sit with the basic feeling then you could free yourself, but it's almost impossible if you're caught up in one mental drama after another. That's what happens.

Pema Chödrön: This is an essential understanding of vajrayana, or tantric, Buddhism. In vajrayana Buddhism they talk about how what we call negative energies—such as anger, lust, envy, jealousy, these powerful energies—are all actually wisdoms in disguise. But to experience that you have to not spin off; you have to be able to relax with the energy.

So tonglen, which is considered more of a mahayana practice, was my entry into being able to sit with that kind of energy. And it gave me a way to include all the other people, to recognize that so many people were in the same boat as I was.

Alice Walker: You do recognize that everybody is in that boat sooner or later, in one form or other. It's good to feel that you're not alone.

Pema Chödrön: I want to ask you about joy. It's all very well to talk about poison as medicine and breathing in the suffering and sending out relief and so forth, but did you find any joy coming out of this?

Alice Walker: Oh Yes! Even just not being so miserable.

Part of the joyousness was knowing we have help. It was great to know that this wisdom is so old. That means people have had this pain for a long time, they've been dealing with it, and they had the foresight to leave these practices for us to use. I'm always supported by spirits and ancestors and people in my tribe, whoever they've been and however long ago they lived. So it was like having another tribe of people, of ancestors, come to the rescue with this wisdom that came through you and your way of teaching.

Pema Chödrön: I think the times are ripe for this kind of teaching.

Alice Walker: Oh, I think it's just the right medicine for today. You know, the other really joyous thing is that I feel more open, I feel more openness toward people in my world.

It's what you have said about feeling more at home in your world. I think this is the result of going the distance in your own heart — really being disciplined about opening your heart as much as you can. The thing I find, Pema, is that it closes up again. You know?

Pema Chödrön: Oh no! (laughter) One year of listening to me and your heart still closes up?

Alice Walker: Yeah. It's like what you have said about how the ego is like a closed room and our whole life's work is to open the door. You may open the door and then discover that you're not up to keeping it open for long. The work is to keep opening it. You have an epiphany, you understand something, you feel slightly enlightened about something, but then you lose it. That's the reality. So it's not a bad thing.

Pema Chödrön: No.

Alice Walker: But it's frustrating at times, because you think to yourself, I've worked on this, why is it still snagging in the same spot?

Pema Chödrön: That's how life keeps us honest. The inspiration that comes from feeling the openness seems so important, but on the other hand, I'm sure it would eventually turn into some kind of spiritual pride or arrogance. So life has this miraculous ability to smack you in the face with a real humdinger just when you're going over the edge in terms of thinking you've accomplished something. That humbles you; it's some kind of natural balancing that keeps you human. At the same time the sense of joy does get stronger and stronger.

Alice Walker: Because otherwise you feel you're just going to be smacked endlessly, and what's the point? (laughter)

Pema Chödrön: It's about relaxing with the moment, whether it's painful or pleasurable. I teach about that a lot because that's personally how I experience it. The openness brings the smile on my face, the sense of gladness just to be here. And when it gets painful, it's not like there's been some big mistake or something. It just comes and goes.

Alice Walker: That brings me to something else I've discovered in my practice, because I've been doing meditation for many years — not tonglen, but TM and metta practice. There are times when I meditate, really meditate, very on the dot, for a year or so, and then I'll stop. So what happens? Does that ever happen to you?

Pema Chödrön: Yes. (laughter)

Alice Walker: Good!

Pema Chödrön: And I just don't worry about it.

Alice Walker: Good! (laughter)

Pema Chödrön: One of the things I've discovered as the years go on is that there can't be any "shoulds." Even meditation practice can become something you feel you should do, and then it becomes another thing you worry about.

So I just let it ebb and flow, because I feel it's always with you in some way, whether you're formally practicing or not. My hunger for meditation ebbs but the hunger always comes back, and not necessarily because things are going badly. It's like a natural opening and closing, or a natural relaxation and then getting involved in something else, going back and forth.

Alice Walker: I was surprised to discover how easy it was for me to begin meditating many years ago. What I liked was how familiar that state was. The place that I most love is when I disappear. You know, there's a point where you just disappear. That is so wonderful, because I'm sure that's how it will be after we die, that you're just not here, but it's fine.

CHAPTER THIRTY-FOUR

Pema Chödrön: What do you mean exactly, you disappear?

Alice Walker: Well, you reach that point where it's just like space, and you don't feel yourself. You're not thinking about what you're going to cook, and you're not thinking about what you're going to wear, and you're not really aware of your body. I like that because as a writer I spend a lot of time in spaces that I've created myself and it's a relief to have another place that is basically empty.

Pema Chödrön: I don't think I have the same experience. It's more like being here—fully and completely here. It's true that meditation practice is liberating and timeless and that, definitely, there is no caught-up-ness. But it is also profoundly simple and immediate. In contrast, everything else feels like fantasy, like it is completely made up by mind.

Alice Walker: Well, I feel like I live a lot of my life in a different realm anyway, especially when I'm out in nature. So meditation takes me to that place when I'm not in nature. It is a place of really feeling the oneness, that you're not kept from it by the fact that you're wearing a suit. You're just in it; that's one of the really good things about meditation for me.

Judy Lief: I assume, Alice, that as an activist your job is to take on situations of extreme suffering and try to alleviate them to some degree. How has this practice affected your approach to activism?

Alice Walker: Well, my activism really is for myself, because I see places in the world where I really feel I should be. If there is something really bad, really evil, happening somewhere, then that is where I should be. I need, for myself, to feel that I have stood there. It feels a lot better than just watching it on television.

Judy Lief: This is where you bring together your private practice and your public action.

Alice Walker: Yes. Before I was sort of feeling my way. I went to places like Mississippi and stood with the people and realized the suffering they were experiencing. I shared the danger they put themselves in by demanding their rights. I felt this incredible opening, a feeling of finally being at home in my world, which was what I needed. I needed to feel I could be at home there, and the only way was to actually go and connect with the people.

Pema Chödrön: And the other extreme is when our primary motivation is avoidance of pain. Then the world becomes scarier and scarier.

Alice Walker: Exactly.

Pema Chödrön: That's the really sad thing—the world becomes more and more frightening, and you don't want to go out your door. Sure there's a lot of danger out there, but the tonglen approach makes you more open to the fear it evokes in you, and your world gets bigger.

Judy Lief: When you are practicing tonglen, taking on pain of others, what causes that to flip into something positive, as opposed to being stuck in a negative space or seeing yourself as a martyr?

Alice Walker: I think it's knowing that you're not the only one suffering. That's just what happens on earth. There may be other places in the galaxy where people don't suffer, where beings are just fine, where they never get parking tickets even. But what seems to be happening here is just really heavy duty suffering.

I remember years ago, when I was asking myself what was the use of all this suffering. I was reading the Gnostic Gospels, in which Jesus says something that really struck me. He says basically, learn how to suffer and you will not suffer. That dovetails with this teaching, which is a kind of an acceptance that suffering is the human condition.

Pema Chödrön: It is true people fear tonglen practice. Particularly if people have a lot of depression, they fear it is going to be tough to relate with the suffering so directly.

I have found that it's less overwhelming if you start with your own experience of suffering and then generalize to all the other people who are feeling what you do. That gives you a way to work with your pain; instead of feeling like you're increasing your suffering, you're making it meaningful. If you're taught that you should do tonglen only for other people, that's too big a leap for most people. But if you start with yourself as the reference point and extend out from that, you find that your compassion becomes much more spontaneous and real. You have less fear of the suffering you perceive in the world — yours and other people's. It's a lot about overcoming the fear of suffering.

My experience of working with this practice is that it has brought me a moment-by-moment sense of wellbeing. That's encouraging to people who are afraid to start the practice — to know that relating directly with your suffering is a doorway to wellbeing for yourself and others, rather than some kind of masochism.

Alice Walker: I would say that is also true for me in going to stand where I feel I need to stand. I feel I get to that same place.

I also appreciate the teaching on driving all blame into yourself. We need a teaching on how fruitless it is to always blame the other person. In my life I can see places where I have not wanted to take my part of the blame. That's a losing proposition. There's no gain in it because you never learn very much about yourself. You don't own all your parts. There are places in each of us that are quite scary, but you have to make friends with them. You have to really get to know them, to say, hello, there you are again. It's very helpful to do that.

Pema Chödrön: One of the things the Buddha pointed out in his early teaching was that everybody wants happiness or freedom from pain, but the methods human beings habitually use are not in sync with the wish. The methods always end up escalating the pain. For example, someone yells at you and then you yell back and then they yell back and it gets worse and worse. You think the reason not to yell back is because, you know, good people don't yell back. But the truth is that by not yelling back you're just getting smart about what's really going to bring you some happiness.

Judy Lief: The lojong slogan says "Drive all blames into one," that is, yourself. But there are definitely situations where from the conventional viewpoint there are bad guys and good guys, oppressors and oppressed. How do you combine taking the blame yourself with combating oppression or evil that you encounter?

Alice Walker: Maybe it doesn't work there. (laughter) Pema why don't you take that one. (laughter)

Pema Chödrön: Well, here would be my **Question:** does it help to have a sense of enemy in trying to end oppression?

Alice Walker: No.

Pema Chödrön: So maybe that's it.

Alice Walker: I think it's probably about seeing. As Bob Marley said so beautifully, the biggest bully you ever did see was once a tiny baby. That's true. I mean, I've tried that on Ronald Reagan. I even tried that on Richard Nixon, but it didn't really work that well.

But really, when you're standing face to face with someone who just told you to go to the back of the bus, or someone who has said that women aren't allowed here, or whatever, what do you do? I don't know what you do, Pema, but at that moment I always see that they're really miserable people and they need help. Now, of course, I think I would love to send them a copy of "Awakening Compassion." (laughter)

Pema Chödrön: It's seeing that the cause of someone's aggression is their suffering. And you could also realize that your aggression is not going to help anything.

So you're standing there, you are being provoked, you are feeling aggression, and what do you do? That's when tonglen becomes very helpful. You breathe in and connect with your own aggression with a lot of honesty. You have such a strong recognition in that moment of all the oppressed people who are provoked and feeling like you do. If you just keep doing that, something different might come out of your mouth.

Alice Walker: And war will not be what comes out.

Judy Lief: It seems to me that Dr. Martin Luther King had the quality of a tonglen practitioner. Yet he didn't ask us not to take stands.

Alice Walker: He was from a long line of Baptist preachers, someone who could really get to that place of centeredness through prayer and through love. I think the person who has a great capacity to love, which often flowers when you can see and feel the suffering of other people, can also strategize. I think he was a great strategist. I think he often got very angry and upset, but at the same time he knew what he was up against. Sometimes he was the only really lucid person in a situation, so he knew how much of the load he was carrying and how much depended on him.

As activists, it is really important to have some kind of practice, so that when we go out into the world to confront horrible situations we can do it knowing we're in the right place ourselves. Knowing we're not bringing more fuel to the fire, more anger, more despair. It's difficult but that should not be a deterrent. The more difficult something seems, the more it's possible to give up hope. You approach the situation with the feeling of having already given up hope, but that doesn't stop you. You said we should put that slogan about abandoning hope on our refrigerators.

Pema Chödrön: "Give up all hope of fruition."

Alice Walker: Right. Just do it because you're doing it and it feels like the right thing to do, but without feeling it's necessarily going to change anything.

Pema Chödrön: Something that I heard Trungpa Rinpoche say has been a big help to me. He said to live your life as an experiment, so that you're always experimenting. You could experiment with yelling back and see what happens. You could experiment with tonglen and see how that works. You could see what actually allows some kind of communication to happen. You learn pretty fast what closes down communication, and that's the strong sense of enemy. If the other person feels your hatred, then everyone closes down.

Alice Walker: I feel that fear is what closes people down more than anything, just being afraid. The times when I have really been afraid to go forward, with a relationship or a problem, is because there is fear. I think practice of being with your feelings, letting them come up and not trying to push them away, is incredibly helpful.

Question from the audience: Thank you both for being here and bringing so much pleasure to so many people tonight. I'm asking a question for a friend who couldn't come tonight. She was at Pema's three-day seminar and she left on Saturday feeling badly because she had got in touch with her anger and couldn't stay. Now she feels she's a bad Buddhist, a bad practitioner. I've been trying to tell her it's okay but I think she needs to hear your words.

Pema Chödrön: Well, tell her we're used to using everything that we hear against ourselves, so it's really common to take the dharma teachings and use them against yourself. But the fact is we don't have to do that anymore. We don't have to do that. It's just like Alice saying that the heart opens and then it closes, so she has to realize that's how it is forever and ever. She'll get in touch and then she'll lose touch and get in touch and lose touch. So she has to keep on going with herself and not give up on herself.

Question: This is really hard on her because you two are her favorite people in the entire world.

Alice Walker: And she didn't come?

Question: She's so broken-hearted.

Pema Chödrön: She didn't come because she was so ashamed of herself for not being able to stay with it...that's not true, is it?

Question: Yes, it is.

Pema Chödrön: Really. Wow. You should tell her that she's just an ordinary human being. (laughter) What's a little unusual about her is that she was willing to get in touch with it for even a little bit.

Question: My name is Margaret, and I have practiced Tibetan Buddhism for a number of years. About eighteen months ago, right around the time that for the first time in my life I fell in love with a woman, the Dalai Lama made a number of comments pointing out where the Tibetan tradition did not regard homosexuality as a positive thing, but in fact as an obstacle to spiritual growth. It reached the point that I left the sangha I was connected with and found a different part of the spiritual path that's working for me now. I have gay and bisexual friends who are interested in Buddhism but some of them have been stopped by what the Dalai Lama had to say and by the lack of coherent answers from other people. I think it would be a big service if you could address that.

Pema Chödrön: Well, listen. I have so much respect for the Dalai Lama and I think that's where people get stuck. I didn't actually hear those comments, and I heard there were also favorable comments. But aside from all that, as Buddhism comes to the West, Western Buddhist teachers simply don't buy that. It's as if Asian teachers said that women were inferior or something. I mean, it's absurd. That's all there is to it. (applause) It's just ridiculous.

Question: Let me ask you to say that often and loud.

Pema Chödrön: Sure! I go on record. And I'm not alone, it's not something unique with me. Western teachers, coming from this culture, we see things pretty differently on certain issues and this is one, for sure.

But the Dalai Lama is a wonderful man, and I have a feeling that if he were sitting here he'd have something else to say on the subject.

Alice Walker: You know, when he was here at the peace conference he was confronted by gay men and lesbian women and he readily admitted that he really didn't know. He didn't seem rigid on it.

But also, when there is wisdom about, we should have it! Wisdom belongs to the people. We must never be kept from wisdom by anybody telling us you can't have it because you're this, that or the other.

Question: I have a question about the connection between tonglen and joy. I kind of understood the moderator's question about when you breathe in so much suffering, how do you avoid becoming so burdened or martyred by it? What I'm understanding about tonglen is that there's something kind of transformative about it, when you breathe in suffering and then you breathe out relief and healing. I keep thinking about that prayer of St. Francis of Assisi about being an instrument of peace, and where there is hatred, let me sow love, and where there is despair, let me sow hope. I'm wondering if joy has a place in the ability to make that transformation.

Alice Walker: I think the practice of tonglen is really revolutionary, because you're taking in what you usually push away with everything you've got, and then you're breathing out what you would rather keep. This is just amazing. I mean, it really shakes you up.

PART SIX

New Medicine, New Psychology

LYNNE McTAGGART

CHAPTER
35

The Biology
of Intention

*T*he *Intention Experiment* rests on an outlandish premise: thought affects physical reality. A sizable body of research exploring the nature of consciousness, carried on for more than thirty years in prestigious scientific institutions around the world, shows that thoughts are capable of affecting everything from the simplest machines to the most complex living beings.[1] This evidence suggests that human thoughts and intentions are an actual physical "something" with the astonishing power to change our world. Every thought we have is a tangible energy with the power to transform. A thought is not only a thing; a thought is a thing that influences other things.

This central idea, that consciousness affects matter, lies at the very heart of an irreconcilable difference between the worldview offered by classical physics—the science of the big, visible world—and that of quantum physics: the science of the world's most diminutive components. That difference concerns the very nature of matter and the ways it can be influenced to change.

All of classical physics, and indeed the rest of science, is derived from the laws of motion and gravity developed by Isaac Newton in his *Principia,* published in 1687.[2] Newton's laws described a universe in which all objects moved within the three-dimensional space of geometry and time according to certain fixed laws of motion. Matter was considered inviolate and self-contained, with its own fixed boundaries. Influence of any sort required something physical to

Lynne McTaggart is an internationally recognized speaker on the science of spirituality and the award-winning author of five books, including *The Field* (Harper, 2003), which has been published in fourteen languages and inspired the wildly successful cult classic movie *What the Bleep Do We Know!?* Her most recent book is *The Intention Experiment* (Simon & Schuster, 2007). She is also co-executive director of Conatus, which publishes some of the world's most respected health and spiritual newsletters, including *What Doctors Don't tell You* and *Living the Field.* www.TheIntentionExperiment.com.

be done to something else—a force or collision. Making something change basically entailed heating it, burning it, freezing it, dropping it, or giving it a good swift kick.

Newtonian laws, science's grand "rules of the game," as the celebrated physicist Richard Feynman once referred to them,[3] and their central premise, that things exist independently of each other, underpin our own philosophical view of the world. We believe that all of life and its tumultuous activity carries on around us, regardless of what we do or think. We sleep easy in our beds at night, in the certainty that when we close our eyes, the universe doesn't disappear.

Nevertheless, that tidy view of the universe as a collection of isolated, well-behaved objects got dashed in the early part of the twentieth century, once the pioneers of quantum physics began peering closer into the heart of matter. The tiniest bits of the universe, those very things that make up the big, objective world, did not in any way behave themselves according to any rules that these scientists had ever known.

This outlaw behavior was encapsulated in a collection of ideas that became known as the Copenhagen Interpretation, after the place where the forceful Danish physicist Niels Bohr and his brilliant protégé, the German physicist Werner Heisenberg, formulated the likely meaning of their extraordinary mathematical discoveries. Bohr and Heisenberg realized that atoms are not little solar systems of billiard balls but something far more messy: tiny clouds of probability. Every subatomic particle is not a solid and stable thing, but exists simply as a potential of any one of its future selves—or what is known by physicists as a "superposition," or sum, of all probabilities, like a person staring at himself in a hall of mirrors.

One of their conclusions concerned the notion of "indeterminacy"— that you can never know all there is to know about a subatomic particle all at the same time. If you discover information about where it is, for instance, you cannot work out at the same time exactly where it is going or at what speed. They spoke about a quantum particle as both a particle—a congealed, set thing—and a "wave": a big smeared-out region of space and time, any corner of which the particle may occupy. It was akin to describing a person as comprising the entire street where he lives.

Their conclusions suggested that, at its most elemental, physical matter isn't solid and stable—indeed, isn't *anything* yet. Subatomic reality resembled not the solid and reliable state of being described to us by classical science, but an ephemeral prospect of seemingly infinite options. So capricious seemed the smallest bits of nature that the first quantum physicists had to make do with a crude symbolic approximation of the truth— a mathematical range of all possibility.

At the quantum level, reality resembled unset Jell-O.

The quantum theories developed by Bohr, Heisenberg, and a host of others rocked the very foundation of the Newtonian view of matter as something discrete and self-contained. They suggested that matter, at its most fundamental, could not be divided into independently existing units and indeed could not even be fully described. Things had no meaning in isolation; they had meaning only in a web of dynamic interrelationships.

The quantum pioneers also discovered the astonishing ability of quantum particles to influence each other, despite the absence of all those usual things that physicists understand are responsible for influence, such as an exchange of force occurring at a finite velocity.

Once in contact, particles retained an eerie remote hold over each other. The actions—for instance, the magnetic orientation—of one subatomic particle instantaneously influenced the other, no matter how far they were separated.

At the subatomic level, change also resulted through dynamic shifts of energy; these little packets of vibrating energy constantly traded energy back and forth to each other via "virtual particles" like ongoing passes in a game of basketball, a ceaseless to-ing and fro-ing that gave rise to an unfathomably large basic layer of energy in the universe.[4]

Subatomic matter appeared to be involved in a continual exchange of information, causing continual refinement and subtle alteration. The universe was not a storehouse of static, separate objects, but a single organism of interconnected energy fields in a continuous state of becoming. At its infinitesimal level, our world resembled a vast network of quantum information, with all its component parts constantly on the phone.

The only thing dissolving this little cloud of probability into something solid and measurable was the involvement of an observer. Once these scientists decided to have a closer look at a subatomic particle by taking a measurement, the subatomic entity that existed as pure potential would "collapse" into one particular state.

The implications of these early experimental findings were profound: living consciousness somehow was the influence that turned the possibility of something into something real. The moment we looked at an electron or took a measurement, *it appeared that we helped to determine its final state.* This suggested that the most essential ingredient in creating our universe is the consciousness that observes it. Several of the central figures in quantum physics argued that the universe was democratic and participatory—a joint effort between observer and observed.[5]

The observer effect in quantum experimentation gives rise to another heretical notion: that living consciousness is somehow central to this process of transforming the unconstructed quantum world into something resembling everyday reality. It suggests not only that the observer brings the observed into being, but also that nothing in the universe exists as an actual "thing" independently of our perception of it.

It implies that observation—the very involvement of consciousness— gets the Jell-O to set.

It implies that reality is not fixed, but fluid or mutable, and hence possibly open to influence.

The idea that consciousness creates and possibly even affects the physical universe also challenges our current scientific view of consciousness, which developed from the theories of the seventeenth-century philosopher René Descartes—that mind is separate and somehow different from matter—and eventually embraced the notion that consciousness is entirely generated by the brain and remains locked up in the skull.

Most modern workaday physicists shrug their shoulders over this central conundrum: that big things are separate, but the tiny building blocks they're made up of are in instant and ceaseless communication with each other. For half a century, physicists have accepted, as though it makes perfect sense, that an electron behaving one way subatomically somehow transmutes into "classical" (that is, Newtonian) behavior once it realizes it is part of a larger whole.

In the main, scientists have stopped caring about the troublesome questions posed by quantum physics, and left unanswered by its earliest pioneers. Quantum theory works mathematically. It offers a highly successful recipe for dealing with the subatomic world. It helped to build atomic bombs and lasers, and to deconstruct the nature of the sun's radiation. Today's physicists have forgotten about the observer effect. They content themselves with their elegant equations and await the formulation of a unified Theory of Everything or the discovery of a few more dimensions beyond the ones that ordinary humans perceive, which they hope will somehow pull together all these contradictory findings into one centralized theory.

Thirty years ago, while the rest of the scientific community carried on by rote, a small band of frontier scientists at prestigious universities around the globe paused to consider the metaphysical implications of the Copenhagen Interpretation and the observer effect.[6] If matter was mutable, and consciousness *made* matter a set something, it seemed likely that consciousness might also be able to nudge things in a particular direction.

In the past, neuroscientists imagined the brain as something akin to a complex computer, which was fully constructed in adolescence. Davidson's results supported more recent evidence that the "hardwired" brain theory was outdated. The brain appeared to revise itself throughout life, depending on the nature of its thoughts. Certain sustained thoughts produced measurable physical differences and changed its structure. Form followed function; consciousness helped to form the brain.

Besides speeding up, brain waves also synchronize during meditation and healing. In fieldwork with indigenous and spiritual healers in five continents, Krippner suspected that, prior to healing, the healers all underwent brain "discharge patterns" that produce a coherence and synchronization of the two hemispheres of the brain, and integrate the limbic (the lower emotional center) with the cortical systems (the seat of higher reasoning).[7] At least 25 studies of meditation have shown that, during meditation, EEG activity between the four regions of the brain synchronizes.[8] Meditation makes the brain permanently more coherent—as might prayer. A study at the University of Pavia in Italy and John Radcliffe Hospital in Oxford showed that saying the rosary had the same effect on the body as reciting a mantra. Both were able to create a "striking, powerful, and synchronous increase" in cardiovascular rhythms when recited six times a minute.[9]

Another important effect of concentrated focus is the integration of both left and right hemispheres. Until recently, scientists believed that the two sides of the brain work more or less independently. The left side was depicted as the "accountant," responsible for logical, analytical, linear thinking, and speech; and the right side as the "artist," providing spatial orientation, musical and artistic ability, and intuition. But Peter Fenwick, consultant neuropsychiatrist at the Radcliffe Infirmary in Oxford and the Institute of Psychiatry at the Maudsley Hospital, gathered evidence to show that speech and many other functions are produced in both sides of the brain and that the brain works best when it can operate as a totality. During meditation, both sides communicate in a particularly harmonious manner.[10]

If the brain cannot distinguish between a thought and an action, would the body follow mental instructions of any sort? If I send my body a mental intention to calm down or speed up, will it necessarily listen to me? Literature about biofeedback and mind-body medicine indicates that it will. In 1961, Neal Miller, a behavioral neuroscientist at Yale University, first proposed that people can be taught to mentally influence their autonomic nervous system and control mechanisms such as blood pressure and bowel movements, much as a child learns to ride a bicycle. He conducted a series of remarkable conditioning-and-reward experiments on rats. Miller discovered that if he stimulated the pleasure center in the brain, his rats could be trained to decrease their heart rate at will, control the rate at which urine filled their kidneys, even create different dilations in the blood vessels of each ear.[11] If relatively simple animals like rats could achieve this remarkable level of internal control, Miller figured, couldn't human beings, with their greater intelligence, regulate more bodily processes?

After these early revelations, many scientists found that information about the autonomic nervous system could be fed back to a person as "biofeedback" to pinpoint where a person should send intention to his body. In the 1960s, John Basmajian, a professor of medicine at McMaster University in Ontario and a specialist in rehabilitative science, began training people with spinal-cord injuries to use EMG feedback to regain control over single cells in their spinal cords.[12] At roughly the same time, psychologist Elmer Green at the Menninger Institute pioneered a method of biofeedback to treat migraine, after discovering that a migraine patient of his could make her headaches go away whenever she practiced a structured form of relaxation. Green went on to use biofeedback to help patients cure their own migraines, and it is now an accepted form of therapy.[13] Biofeedback is particularly useful to treat Raynaud's disease, a vascular condition in which blood vessels are constricted when exposed to cold, causing extremities to grow cold, pale, and even blue.[14]

During a biofeedback treatment, a patient is hooked up to a computer. Transducers applied to different parts of his or her body send information to a visual display, which registers activities of the autonomic nervous system, such as brain waves, blood pressure and heart rate, or muscle contractions. The audio or visual information fed back to the patient depends on the condition; in the case of Raynaud's, as soon as the arteries to the hands constrict, the machines record a drop in skin temperature and a lightbulb flashes or a beeper sounds. The feedback prompts the patient to send an intention to his body to adjust the process in question—in the case of Raynaud's, the patient sends an intention to warm up his hands.

Since those early days, biofeedback has become well established as a therapy for virtually every chronic condition, from attention deficit hyperactivity disorder (ADHD) to menopausal hot flashes. Stroke patients and victims of spinal-cord injuries now use biofeedback to rehabilitate or regain the use of paralyzed muscles. It has proved invaluable in eliminating the pain felt in a phantom limb.[15] Astronauts have even used biofeedback to cure motion sickness while journeying to outer space.[16]

The more conventional view of biofeedback maintains that it has something to do with relaxation—learning to calm down the fight-or-flight responses of our autonomic nervous system. However, the sheer breadth of control would argue that the mechanism has more to do with the power of intention. Virtually every bodily process measurable on a machine—even a single nerve cell controlling a muscle fiber—appears to be within an individual's control. Volunteers in studies have achieved total mental mastery over the temperature in their bodies,[17] or even the direction of blood flow to the brain.[18]

Although the power of intention is such that any sort of focused will may have some effect, the scientific evidence suggests that you will be a more effective "intender" if you become more "coherent," in the scientific sense of the term. To do this to greatest effect, or so the scientific evidence suggests, you will need to choose the right time and place, quiet your mind, learn how to focus, entrain yourself with the object of your intention, visualize, and mentally rehearse. Believing that the experiment will work is also essential.

Most of us operate with very little in the way of mental coherence. We walk around immersed in a riot of fragmentary and discordant thought. You will become more coherent simply by learning to shut down that useless internal chatter, which always focuses on the past or the future, never the present. In time, you will become adept at quieting down your mind and "powering up," much as joggers train their muscles, and each day find that they can perform a little better than the day before.

The following exercises are designed to help you to become more coherent and so more effective in using intention in your life and in our group intention experiments. These have been extrapolated from what has appeared to work best in the scientific laboratory.

Think of intentions in terms of grand and smaller schemes. Take the grand schemes in stages, so that you send out intentions in steps toward achieving the grand scheme. Also start with modest goals—something realizable within a reasonable time frame. If you are forty pounds overweight and your goal is to be a size eight next week, that is not a realistic time frame. Nevertheless, keep the grand scheme in mind and build toward it as you gain experience. It is also important to overcome your natural skepticism. The idea that your thought can affect physical reality may not fit your current world paradigm, but neither would the concept of gravity if you were living in the Middle Ages.

Developing Mindfulness in Your Daily Life

Even when you are not using intention, the evidence suggests that you will mold your brain to become better at it if you develop mindfulness in your daily life. Psychologist Dr. Charles Tart, one of the worlds experts on altered states of consciousness, has a number of suggestions of ways to do so:[19]

- Take periodic breaks during the day in which you have quiet time to be mindful of what is happening internally and externally.

- Whenever you feel your concentration flitting away in your daily activities, sense your breath—it will help to ground you.

- Be mindful of the most mundane of activities, such as brushing your teeth or shaving.

- Start with a small exercise, such as fetching your coat and walking, in which you stay focused completely on what you are doing.

- Engage in mental noting, in which you label an ongoing activity, for example, "I'm putting on my coat," "opening the door," "tying my shoes."

- Use mindfulness in every ordinary situation. When you are preparing dinner or even brushing your teeth, be aware of all the smells, textures, colors, and sensual feelings you are experiencing.

- Learn to really look at your partner and your children, your pets, your friends, and your colleagues. Observe them closely during every activity—every part of them without judgment.

- During some activity, such as breakfast, ask your children to be mindful (without speaking) of every aspect of it. Concentrate on the taste of your food. Look closely at the texture and the colors of it. How does the cereal crunch? How does the juice feel as it cascades down your throat? Become aware of the smells and sounds around you. While you are watching all this, how are the different parts of your body feeling?

- Listen to what your life sounds like—the myriad noises surrounding you every day. When someone speaks to you, listen to the sound of his or her voice as well as the words. Do not think of a reply until he or she has stopped speaking.

- Practice mindfulness in every activity: walking down the street, driving home, in the garden.

- If you are practicing these exercises and you happen to bump into someone, do not enter into conversation. Just greet the person, shake hands, and stay in the present moment.

- Use mindfulness when you are extremely busy or under a tight deadline. Observe what it is like to hurry or to be under the gun and what happens when you do. How does it affect your equilibrium? Be an observer of yourself in that situation. Can you stay in your body while you are working hard?

- Practice mindfulness while you are standing in line. Experience the feeling of waiting itself, rather than focusing on what you are waiting for. Be aware of your physical movements and your thoughts.

- Do not think about or try to work out your problems. Just deal with whatever daily problem solving is immediately in front of you.

Stating Your Intention

In your meditative state, state your clear intention. Although many people use the construction "have always been" — "I have always been healthy" — I prefer the present tense — of sending your intention to its "endpoint" as *a wish that has already been achieved.* For instance, if you are trying to heal back pain, you can say, "My lower back and sacrum are free of all pain and now move easily and fluidly." Remember to frame your intention as a positive statement; rather than "I will not have side effects," say, "I will be free of side effects."

Be Specific

Specific intentions seem to work best. Make sure to make your intentions highly specific and directed — and the more detailed, the better. If you are trying to heal the fourth finger of your child's left hand, specify that finger and, if possible, the problem with it.

State your entire intention, and include what it is you would like to change, to whom, when, and where. Use the following as a checklist (as news reporters do) to ensure you have covered every specific: who, what, when, where, why, and how. It may help if you draw a picture of your intention, or create a collage from photos or magazine pictures. Place this where you can look at it often.

1. For a complete description of these scientists and their findings, consult L. McTaggart, *The Field: The Quest for the Secret force of the Universe* (New York: HarperCollins, 2001).

2. The full title of Newton's major treatise was the *Philosophiae Naturalis Principia Mathematica,* a name which offers a nod to its philosophical implications, although it is always referred to reverentially as the *Principia.*

3. R. P. Feynman, *Six Easy Pieces: The Fundamentals of Physics Explained* (New York: Penguin, 1995), 24.

4. McTaggart, *The Field.*

5. Eugene Wigner, the Hungarian-born American physicist, who received a Nobel Prize for his contribution to the theory of quantum physics, is one of the pioneers of the central role of consciousness in determining reality and argued, through a thought experiment called "Wigner's friend," that the observer—"the friend"—might collapse Schrodinger's famous cat into a single state or, like the cat itself, remain in a state of superposition until another "friend" comes into the lab. Other proponents of "the observer effect" include John Eccles and Evan Harris Walker. John Wheeler is credited with espousing the theory that the universe is participatory: it only exists because we happen to be looking at it.

6. McTaggart, *The Field.*

7. S. Krippner, "The technologies of shamanic states of consciousness," in M. Schlitz and T. Amorok with M. S. Micozzi, *Consciousness and Healing: Integral Approaches to Mind-Body Medicine,* (St. Louis, MO: Elsevier, Churchill Livingstone, 2005).

8. M. Murphy, *Meditation*

9. L. Bernardi et al. "Effect of rosary prayer and yoga mantras on autonomic cardiovascular rhythms: comparative study," *British Medical Journal,* 2001; 323: 1446-9.

10. P. Fenwick et al., "Metabolic and EEG Changes during Transcendental Meditation: An Explanation," *Biological Psychology,* 1977; 5(2): 101-18.

11. M. E. Miller, and L. DiCara, "Instrumental learning of heart rate changes in curarized rats; Shaping and specificity to discriminative stimulus," *Journal of Comparative and Physiological Psychology,* 1967; 63: 12-19; N. E. Miller, "Learning of visceral and glandular responses," *Science,* 1969; 163: 434-45.

12. J. V. Basmajian, *Muscles Alive: Their Functions Revealed by Electromyography* (Baltimore: Williams and Wilkins, 1967).

13. E. Green, "Feedback technique for deep relaxation, "*Psychophysiology,* 1969; 6(3): 371-7; E. Green et el., "Self-regulation of internal states," in J. Rose, ed., *Progress of Cybernetics: Proceedings of the First International Congress of Cybernetics, London, September 1969* (London: Gordon and Breach Science Publishers, 1970), 1299-1318; E. Green et al., "Voluntary control of internal states: Psychological and physiological," *Journal of Transpersonal Psychology,* 1970; 2: 1-26; D. Satinsky, "Biofeedback treatment for headache: A two-year follow-up study," *American Journal of Clinical Biofeedback,* 1981; 4(1): 62-5; B. V. Silver et al., "Temperature biofeedback and relaxation training in the treatment of migraine headaches: One-year follow-up, *Biofeedback and Self-Regulation,* 1979; 4(4): 359-66.

14. B. M. Kappes, "Sequence effects of relaxation training, EMG, and temperature biofeedback on anxiety, symptom report, and self-concept," *Journal of Clinical Psychology,* 1983; 39(2): 203-8; G. D. Rose et al., "The behavioral treatment of Raynaud's disease: A review," *Biofeedback and Self-Regulation,* 1987; 12(4): 257-72.

15. W. T. Tsushima, "Treatment of phantom limb pain with EMG and temperature biofeedback: A case study, "*American Journal of Clinical Biofeedback,* 1982; 5(2): 150-3.

16. T. G. Dobie, "A comparison of two methods of training resistance to visually-induced motion sickness," presented at *VII International Man in Space Symposium: Physiologic adaptation of man in space,* Houston, Texas, 1986. Aviation, Space, and Environmental Medicine, 1987; 58(9), sect. 2: 34-41.

17. A. Ikemi et al., "Thermographical analysis of the warmth of the hands during the practice of self-regulation method, *Psychotherapy and Psychosomatics,* 1988; 50(1): 22-8.

18. J. L. Claghorn, "Directional effects of skin temperature self-regulation on regional cerebral blood flow in normal subjects and migraine patients," *American Journal of Psychiatry,* 1981; 138(9): 1182-7.

19. See C. T. Tart, "Initial application of mindfulness extension exercises in a traditional Buddhist meditation retreat setting, 1995, " unpublished, www.paradigm-sys.com/cttart.

SHARON BEGLEY

CHAPTER 36

Train Your Mind, Change Your Brain

No less a personage than William James, the father of experimental psychology in the United States, first introduced the word *plasticity* to the science of the brain, positing in 1890 that "organic matter, especially nervous tissue, seems endowed with a very extraordinary degree of plasticity." By that, he meant "a structure weak enough to yield to an influence." But James was "only" a psychologist, not a neurologist (there was no such thing as a neuroscientist a century ago), and his speculation went nowhere. Much more influential was the view expressed succinctly in 1913 by Santiago Ramón y Cajal, the great Spanish neuroanatomist who had won the Nobel Prize in Physiology or Medicine seven years earlier. Near the conclusion of his treatise on the nervous system, he declared, "In the adult centers the nerve paths are something fixed, ended and immutable." His gloomy assessment that the circuits of the living brain are unchanging, its structures and organization almost as static and stationary as a deathly white cadaver brain floating in a vat of formaldehyde, remained the prevailing dogma in neuroscience for almost a century. The textbook wisdom held that the adult brain is hardwired, fixed in form and function, so that by the time we reach adulthood, we are pretty much stuck with what we have.

Conventional wisdom in neuroscience held that the adult mammalian brain is fixed in two respects: no new neurons are born in it, and the functions of the structures that make it up are

Sharon Begley, science columnist for the *Wall Street Journal*, inaugurated the paper's "Science Journal" in 2002. Her books include *Train Your Mind, Change Your Brain* (Ballantine, 2007) and *The Mind and the Brain* (Harper, 2003). She was previously the senior science writer at *Newsweek*, covering neuroscience, genetics, physics, astronomy, and anthropology. She has won many awards for her articles. She is a frequent guest on radio and television, including The Charlie Rose Show, Today Weekend, and CBSs The Early Show. She also participates regularly in the Mind and Life foundation dialogs on science with the Dalai Lama.

immutable, so that if genes and development dictate that *this* cluster of neurons will process signals from the eye, and *this* cluster will move the fingers of the right hand, then by god they'll do that and nothing else come hell or high water. There was good reason why all those extravagantly illustrated brain books show the function, size, and location of the brain's structures in permanent ink. As late as 1999, neurologists writing in the prestigious journal *Science* admitted, "We are still taught that the fully mature brain lacks the intrinsic mechanisms needed to replenish neurons and reestablish neuronal networks after acute injury or in response to the insidious loss of neurons seen in neurodegenerative diseases."

The doctrine of the unchanging human brain has had profound ramifications, none of them very optimistic. It led neurologists to assume that rehabilitation for adults who had suffered brain damage from a stroke was almost certainly a waste of time. It suggested that trying to alter the pathological brain wiring that underlies psychiatric diseases, such as obsessive-compulsive disorder (OCD) and depression, was a fool's errand. And it implied that other brain-based fixities, such as the happiness "set point" to which a person returns after the deepest tragedy or the greatest joy, are as unalterable as Earth's orbit.

But the dogma is wrong. In the last years of the twentieth century, a few iconoclastic neuroscientists challenged the paradigm that the adult brain cannot change and made discovery after discovery that, to the contrary, it retains stunning powers of neuroplasticity. The brain can indeed be rewired. It can expand the area that is wired to move the fingers, forging new connections that underpin the dexterity of an accomplished violinist. It can activate long-dormant wires and run new cables like an electrician bringing an old house up to code, so that regions that once saw can instead feel or hear. It can quiet circuits that once crackled with the aberrant activity that characterizes depression and cut pathological connections that keep the brain in the oh-god-something-is-wrong state that marks obsessive-compulsive disorder. The adult brain, in short, retains much of the plasticity of the developing brain, including the power to repair damaged regions, to grow new neurons, to rezone regions that performed one task and have them assume a new task, to change the circuitry that weaves neurons into the networks that allow us to remember, feel, suffer, think, imagine, and dream. Yes, the brain of a child is remarkably malleable. But contrary to Ramón y Cajal and most neuroscientists since, the brain can change its physical structure and its wiring long into adulthood.

The revolution in our understanding of the brain's capacity to change well into adulthood does not end with the fact that the brain can and does change. Equally revolutionary is the discovery of how the brain changes. The actions we take can literally expand or contract different regions of the brain, pour more juice into quiet circuits and damp down activity in buzzing ones. The brain devotes more cortical real estate to functions that its owner uses more frequently and shrinks the space devoted to activities rarely performed. That's why the brains of violinists devote more space to the region that controls the digits of the fingering hand. In response to the actions and experiences of its owner, a brain forges stronger connections in circuits that underlie one behavior or thought and weakens the connections in others. Most of this happens because of what we do and what we experience of the outside world. In this sense, the very structure of our brain—the relative size of different regions, the strength of connections between one area and another—reflects the lives we have led. Like sand on a beach, the brain bears the footprints of the decisions we have made, the skills we have learned, the actions we have taken. But there are also hints that mind-sculpting can occur with no input from the outside world. That is, the brain can change as a result of the thoughts we have thought.

A few findings suggest that brain changes can be generated by pure mental activity: merely thinking about playing the piano leads to a measurable, physical change in the brain's motor cortex, and thinking about thoughts in certain ways can restore mental health. By willfully treating invasive urges and compulsions as errant neurochemistry—rather than as truthful messages that something is amiss—patients with OCD have altered the activity of the brain region that generates the OCD thoughts, for instance. By thinking differently about the thoughts that threaten to send them back into the abyss of despair, patients with depression have dialed up activity in one region of the brain and quieted it in another, reducing their risk of relapse. Something as seemingly insubstantial as a thought has the ability to act back on the very stuff of the brain, altering neuronal connections in a way that can lead to recovery from mental illness and perhaps to a greater capacity for empathy and compassion.

Richard J. Davidson, who would join the Mind and Life dialogues in 1994, was on the verge of seminal discoveries about patterns of brain activity that correspond to happiness and depression. Davidson also put out the word that he was in the market for Buddhist contemplatives, the people he calls "the Olympic athletes" of meditation practice. Matthieu Ricard, the French Buddhist monk at Shechen Monastery in Kathmandu, Nepal, who holds a Ph.D. in genetics, was both investigator and subject in these experiments, helping plan them as well as being tested himself.

All the Buddhist adepts who would eventually lend their brains to neuroscience had practiced meditation for at least ten thousand hours. One had racked up fifty-five thousand hours. All had gone on at least one three-year retreat, during which he lived apart from society and passed almost all his waking hours in meditation. For the most part, the adepts made a detour to Madison when they happened to be in the United States, usually for a speaking tour. That made for slow going. Weeks would pass before the next monk came through. But as time went by, Davidson methodically built up a unique database: recordings of the brain waves and brain-activation patterns of long-term practitioners of Buddhist meditation.

Davidson had been on a quest that much of modern neuroscience suggested was, to put it politely, quixotic: to discover whether states such as happiness, compassion, enthusiasm, joy, and other positive emotions are trainable. That is, do there exist techniques of mental training that can alter the brain in a way that raises the intensity of these emotions, makes them last longer, or makes them easier to trigger?

Take two data points. In the research that sealed his reputation for rigorous neuroscience, Davidson and colleagues discovered, in the 1970s, striking differences in the patterns of brain activity that characterize people at opposite ends of the "eudaemonic scale"—that is, along the spectrum of baseline happiness. That's fact one: there are specific brain states that correlate with happiness, as I'll discuss in greater detail below.

Second, brain-activation patterns can change as a result of therapy— specifically, as a result of cognitive-behavior therapy and mindfulness meditation, in which people learn to think differently about their thoughts. Jeffrey Schwartz showed that to be the case with patients beset by obsessive-compulsive disorder; Zindel Segal and Helen Mayberg showed it with patients suffering from depression. Thus, we have fact two: mental training, practice, and effort can bring about changes in the function of the brain.

From those facts, Davidson built his hypothesis: that meditation or other forms of mental training can, by exploiting the brain's neuroplasticity, produce changes—most likely in patterns of neuronal activation, but perhaps even in the structure of neural circuitry in the sense of what's connected to what and how strong those connections are—that underlie enduring happiness and other positive emotions. If that is so, then by exploiting the brain's potential to change its wiring, therapists or even individuals might restore the brain and hence the mind to emotional health.

Just to be clear, the goal is not merely the absence of mental illness, which seems to be all that psychiatric and psychological therapies strive for these days, but the enduring presence of robust mental and emotional health.

"That's the hypothesis: that we can think of emotions, moods, and states such as compassion as trainable mental skills," Davidson told the Dalai Lama. "For this to happen, the emotion circuits of the brain must be plastic. But there have been remarkable experiments showing that: we know that experience can induce changes in the structure and function of brain regions involved in regulating emotions. I don't think we have given this a fair shake, the possibility that there might be salubrious effects of mental training on the emotions."

Western psychology has never seriously considered such a possibility. The only research into whether enduring traits can be changed has focused on psychopathology, such as chronic depression, extreme introversion, phobias, and other mental illnesses. In contrast, "no effort has been invested in cultivating positive attributes of mind in individuals who do not have mental disorders," Alan Wallace, Davidson, and colleagues wrote in 2005. "Western approaches to changing enduring emotional states or traits do not involve the long-term persistent effort that is involved in all complex skill learning — for example, in becoming a chess master or learning to play a musical instrument." And why should they? One's baseline level of happiness, after all, is supposed to be as fixed as one's blood type.

The question of whether the brain can change, and whether the mind has the power to change it, is emerging as one of the most compelling of our time. This power ties in to a sea of change in biomedicine, neuroscience, and psychology.

If we score mental health on a scale that runs from very negative values (mental illness) through a zero point and then up into very positive values, the absence of mental illness is akin to the zero point. Science has always focused on the zeroth level and below, on people and conditions that are pathological, disturbed, or, at best, "normal." As a result, researchers have amassed quite a record when it comes to studying all the ways the mind and brain can go wrong. In its 943 dense pages, the latest edition of the bible of mental illness, *The Diagnostic and Statistical Manual of Mental Disorders,* covers everything from autism and Tourette's to schizophrenia, depression, masochism, and "feeding disorders of infancy." And no wonder it's so full. In the last thirty years, there have been about forty-six thousand scientific papers just on depression and an underwhelming four hundred on joy. When psychology researcher Martin Seligman became the president of the American Psychological Association, he drew attention to the field's onesided view of the human mind and urged researchers to investigate positive psychological states — happiness and contentment, curiosity and drive, engagement and compassion. "Social science," he lamented, "finds itself in almost total darkness about the qualities that make life most worth living."

There is a more practical effect, too. Virtually all of biomedical science focuses on getting people up to the zeroth level and nothing more. As long as someone can attain nonsickness, that is deemed sufficient. As Buddhist scholar Alan Wallace put it, "Western scientists have an underlying assumption that normal is absolutely as good as it gets and that the exceptional is only for saints, that it is something that cannot be cultivated. We in the modern West have grown accustomed to the assumption that the 'normal' mind, in the sense of one free from clinical mental illness, is a healthy one. But a 'normal mind' is still subject to many types of mental distress, including anxiety, frustration, restlessness, boredom, and resentment." All are considered normal, part of the vicissitudes of living. We call unhappiness a normal part of life and say "it's normal" to feel frustration when thwarted; "it's normal" to feel bored when the mind feels empty and nothing in our surroundings engages us. As long as the distress is neither chronic nor disabling, the mind gets a clean bill of health. "There are so many people who are sick in the same way that we accept that as being normal," Matthieu Ricard added. "In this case, 'being sick' means having a mixture of positive and destructive emotions. Because it's so common, we sort of feel this is natural, normal. We accept that and say, oh, this is life, this is how things are, we have this mixture of shadows and light, of qualities and defects. It's normalcy."

Tapping into the brain's powers of neuroplasticity offers the hope of changing the understanding of mental health. The growing evidence of the brain's ability to change its structure and function in response to certain inputs, combined with discoveries such as Davidson's on the power of mental training to harness that neuroplasticity to change the brain, suggests that humanity does not have to be content with this strange notion of normalcy, with the zeroth level of mental and emotional health. "Cognitive-behavioral therapy is primarily to get people up to normal, not to bring about exceptional states of compassion, of virtue," Wallace continued. "Buddhism is designed to heal the afflictions of the mind. Meditative practice — mind training — is designed to bring about exceptional states of focused attention, compassion, empathy, and patience."

As researchers probe the power of meditation and other techniques to alter the brain and allow it to function at the highest levels, we are therefore poised at the brink of "above-the-line" science — of studying people whose powers of attention are far above the norm, whose wellsprings of compassion dwarf those of most people, who have successfully set their happiness baseline at a point that most mortals achieve only transiently before tumbling down to something comfortably above depression but far from what may be possible. What we learn from them may provide the key to raising everyone — or at least everyone who chooses to engage in the necessary mental training — to that level. Neuroplasticity will provide the key to realizing positive mental and emotional functioning. The effects of mental training, as shown in the brains of the accomplished Buddhist meditators, suggest what humans can achieve.

In speeches around the world, the Dalai Lama has argued that humankind needs a new basis for a modern ethics, one that appeals to the billions of people who adhere to different religions or to no religion, one that supports basic values such as personal responsibility, altruism, and compassion. Yet a scientifically literate person — indeed, anyone who gives even a cursory glance at newspaper science stories — may well react to that message with some skepticism. For modern science seems to be offering a radically different view of human responsibility.

Critics call this view neurogenetic determinism. It is the belief, ascendant from the early 1990s and propelled by the mystique of modern genetics, that ascribes inescapable causal power to the genes one inherits from one's parents. Hardly a month went by in that decade without the announcement of another discovery of a gene "for" this or that behavior or mental illness, from risk taking to loss of appetite control, from violence to neuroticism — as well as discoveries linking a deficit of one neurotransmitter with depression and of imbalances in another with addiction. Each connection that neuroscientists forged between a neurochemical and a behavior, and that geneticists made between a gene and a behavior, dealt another blow to the notion of an efficacious will. The discoveries paint an image of individuals as automatons, slaves to their genes or their neurotransmitters, and with no more free will than a child's radio-controlled car. "My genes (or my neurotransmitters) made me do it" might as well be the current mantra. Invoking "a failure of willpower" to explain overeating or addiction or anger began to seem as outdated and discredited as applying leeches to the sick.

"Neurogenetic determinism argues that there is a direct causal relationship between gene and behavior," neurobiologist Steven Rose of the Open University explains. "A woman is depressed because she has genes 'for' depression. There is violence on the streets because people have 'violent' or 'criminal' genes; people get drunk because they have genes 'for' alcoholism."

The validity of this view is more than an esoteric argument raging within the academy. If the source of our happiness and our despair, of our compassion and our cruelty, lies in the twisting strands of our DNA, then it is "to pharmacology and molecular engineering that we should turn for solutions," Rose concludes. And if will is an illusion, then what is the basis for personal responsibility? If we are truly-slaves to our neurotransmitters and to the neural circuits laid down in childhood by our genes, then the concept of personal responsibility becomes specious.

I hope that this has shown that that *if* is empty. Instead, each step in that causal chain is far from deterministic. Because neuroplasticity and the power of mind and mental training effect changes in the very structure and function of our brain, free will and moral responsibility become meaningful in a way that they have not been for some time in the scientific West. The genes carried by Michael Meaney's baby rats are altered by the behavior of the mother rat who raises them, with the result that the babies develop a strikingly different suite of behaviors and "personalities" (or the rat version thereof). So much for genes determining supposedly inborn traits such as shyness and timidity. The visual cortex in the blind children trooping into Helen Neville's lab does not see but, instead, hears; so much for genes being the driving forces behind the structure and function of the developing brain. Something as slight as a reminder of someone who once loved and cared for them is enough to trigger a circuit, presumably involving both memory and emotion, so that the people Phil Shaver studied do not merely feel compassion but act on it to help a suffering person. Neuroplasticity and the ability of the brain to change as a result of mental training step between genes and behavior like a hero in front of a speeding locomotive. If the brain can change, then genes "for" this or that behavior are much less deterministic. The ability of thought and attention to physically alter the brain echoes one of Buddhism's more remarkable hypotheses: that will is a real, physical force that can change the brain. Perhaps one of the most provocative implications of neuroplasticity and the power of mental training to alter the circuits of the brain is that it undermines neurogenetic determinism.

The Buddhist understanding of volition is quite different from the notion that humans are tethered to their genes or to hardwired neural circuitry. In Buddhist philosophy, one's choice is not determined by anything in the physical, material world, including the state of one's neurotransmitters or genes (not that traditional Buddhism had any inkling that brain chemicals or DNA even existed). Instead, volition arises from such ineffable qualities as the state of one's mind and the quality of one's attention. The last of Buddhism's Four Noble

Truths also invokes the power of mind, arguing that although life is suffering, and suffering arises from cravings and desires, there is a way out of suffering: through mental training and, specifically, the sustained practice of meditation.

The conscious act of thinking about one's thoughts in a different way changes the very brain circuits that do that thinking, as studies of how psychotherapy changes the brains of people with depression show. Such willfully induced brain changes require focus, training, and effort, but a growing number of studies using neuroimaging show how real those changes are. They come from within. As the discoveries of neuroplasticity, and this self-directed neuroplasticity, trickle down to clinics and schools and plain old living rooms, the ability to willfully change the brain will become a central part of our lives—and of our understanding of what it means to be human.

Richard Gracer

Regenerative Medicine

Jeffrey Skoll, the first CEO of eBay and executive producer of the movie *Syriana,* had disabling back pain. So severe was his condition that he did business lying on a couch in his office. He could afford any treatment the world had to offer, and he consulted many specialists. The diagnosis he received was internal disc disruption (IDD). This diagnosis is given when the back pain the patient is experiencing is not related to direct pressure on a nerve root or the tissues covering it.

Jeffrey chose extensive conventional medical treatment at Stanford University Medical Center, but his condition did not improve. His doctors eventually told him he needed lumbar fusion, a surgery that joins the bones of the lower back, rendering the patient's lower spine permanently inflexible.

After researching the success rate for this procedure, however, Jeffrey came to the conclusion that it bore a major risk of leaving him worse off, rather than better. So he decided against the surgery. His research also left him wondering if the diagnosis of IDD might be wrong. But with no alternative, he went back to popping pain pills and working from the couch in his office.

There are millions of Jeffreys in the world. Back pain affects an estimated two-thirds of people in developed countries at some point in their lives. In Britain, back pain costs the economy an estimated 11 million workdays a year. The comparable figure for the United States

Richard I. Gracer, MD, is the founder and director of Gracer Medical Group. He is board certified in Family Practice and is a Diplomate of the American Academy of Pain Management. He was Assistant Clinical Professor of Medicine at UC San Francisco School of Medicine until 2005. He currently runs Gracer Behavioral Health Services, an innovative and comprehensive substance abuse program that stresses the reduction of cravings. He edited *Beating the Years* (Barron's, 2006), *Beating Sports Injuries* (Barron's, 2005) and *Beating Back Pain* (Barron's, 2003), and recently authored *A New Prescription for Addiction* (Elite, 2007). www.GracerMedicalGroup.com.

is 102 million workdays per year. Few of these people can afford care at the Stanford University Medical Center, and even for those who can, their chances of living permanently pain-free are poor.

Regenerative Medicine

I have believed for a long time that the best way to deal with many medical problems is to help the body take care of itself. If our bodies did not have their own systems of maintenance, it wouldn't be long before we would die. Small cuts wouldn't heal. Any infection would overwhelm us. As it is, our bodies maintain a specific body temperature, closely regulate the levels of many hormones, and keep us balanced on our feet. This is called *homeostasis,* the action of a system to maintain stability.

The name of the treatment philosophy that harnesses the body's own healing systems is *regenerative medicine.* It includes nutritional and hormonal treatments, as well as spinal and joint manipulation. We are just starting to learn how to harness and regulate the body's own healing processes to repair damage that up to now would lead to chronic pain and disability.

In contrast to this approach, Western medicine looks for the specific problem and tries to fix it. A cancerous growth is removed, irradiated, or poisoned. A worn-out hip is replaced. An infectious organism is killed with antibiotics. A blocked artery is bypassed, or a stent inserted. The problem with the Western scientific approach to new ideas is not that specific, reductionist discovery and treatment are not needed. It has helped increase longevity, and given us valuable treatments for trauma.

The regenerative approach seeks to engage the body's own biological systems in fixing the problem. It aims to restore the body to peak performance, giving us healthier, happier, and longer lives.

The Believing Is Seeing Disease

The conventional medical system is virtually impervious to change. It is run by a network of power brokers, from government bodies such as the National Institutes of Health in the US and the National Health Service in the UK, to big-dollar research institutes, universities, and massive multinational pharmaceutical companies. Medical experts in these institutions are mostly well intentioned, and certain that they are right. This results in the "Believing Is Seeing Disease." When you absolutely *know* that something is true, you interpret whatever you see in that light, even when the facts indicate otherwise.

To be accepted as efficacious, a treatment or strategy has to be proven in a randomized clinical trial or RCT. These studies often demonstrate the benefits of new treatments, or show the flaws in accepted ones. But the results are often "interpreted" by drug companies in ways that serve their interests. The recent debacles surrounding the drugs Vioxx and Avandia illustrate the cynical comment of one researcher: "Figures don't lie, but liars figure." In addition, small independent entities with potentially promising therapies don't have the millions of dollars required to launch such multimillion-dollar studies. The medical establishment thus epitomizes modern medicine's Golden Rule: "They who have the gold make the rules."

When information contrary to the established worldview turns up, it is invariably attacked; researchers dismiss the data as wrong or the study as too small, or charge that untested factors produced the results. Anomalies are dismissed in order to maintain a world that conforms to what current orthodoxy believes to be true. In the religion of medical science, fundamentalist beliefs about the world are bedrock, and heresies are punished or ignored. Getting new ideas accepted is very difficult, and this structure has been a major obstacle to proponents of regenerative medicine.

Help from Stem Cells

Like a rubber band that is stretched repeatedly, our tendons and ligaments can become lax over time. Normally, our bodies repair compromised tissue daily. But if immunity is compromised, if we're highly stressed by either emotional factors or actual threats to our survival, then the process of cell repair is interrupted. Injuries aren't repaired as fast or as well, and over the years tendons that were supple and taut can become slack and less able to do their job of holding bones and muscles together efficiently. These lax tissues are less able to cope with the strains of daily living, and certainly unable to cope with extraordinary stresses on the joints.

I have practiced musculoskeletal medicine for almost thirty years. Over time my conception of how to treat orthopedic problems evolved from the basics I learned in medical school to more sophisticated concepts that allowed me to make tissue diagnoses quickly and easily, usually without the need for expensive testing. This enabled me to help patients in chronic pain, many of whom had previously been told that there was no treatment for their problem, and to spot problems with slack ligaments and tendons.

Even with all of these tools, there were people who I could not get well. I realized that many of them had nutritional deficits and/or hormonal problems that kept their bodies from healing themselves. When I learned how to treat these problems, another large group of patients improved. The magic came from a therapy called Regenerative Injection Therapy or RIT. In RIT, a concentrated sugar solution is injected into weakened joints, producing a low-grade inflammation. This mild inflammation stimulates the healing process by prompting the body to produce new fibers of connective tissue, creating a matrix around which fresh new tissue can grow. Unless the structure has been damaged beyond the body's ability to self-repair—in which case surgery may be the best solution—the simple and low-tech technique of RIT is often able to stimulate healing. Like the frame of a new building, once a latticework of fibers is laid into the wound, the body has a structure on which to lay down the rest of the new tissue.

Jeffrey Skoll, after suffering through several more months of working from his couch, consulted a friend's uncle, Scott Haldeman, DC, MD. Dr. Haldeman is a medical school neurology professor who began his career as a chiropractor. This background gives him a special perspective on the biomechanics of the spine. He concluded that Jeffrey's pain came from his ligaments and sacroiliac joints, not his discs. He sent Jeffrey to an orthopedist who specializes in RIT. After treatment, Jeffrey's pain was essentially gone. He was able to get back to his normal activities without the surgery that conventional doctors had prescribed.

After this experience, Jeffrey went back to the doctors he had consulted at Stanford and asked them about RIT. They admitted knowing about it, but they didn't believe it was efficacious. He was upset by this answer, and eventually helped set up a nonprofit organization to study this type of treatment and help it gain widespread medical approval. Since the medication used is mostly sugar, no drug company is interested in supporting research in this field. It takes many millions of dollars to do the type of studies necessary to meet FDA approval. Now, thanks to Jeffrey and other like-minded philanthropists, this research is under way.

Similar exciting advances are revolutionizing medical practice, not only in the musculoskeletal area, but also in every aspect of medical science. A human embryo begins as a single simple cell. As the embryo grows, new and undifferentiated cells must change into specific shapes in order to form all the organs of the body, from the skin to the heart. The early cells of the embryo have the capacity to become any other type of cell. This is called *differentiation*. Some cells maintain this ability to "morph" in later years as well. These cells are called *stem cells*, and due to their ability to change into specialized cells required for healing, they are the subject of intense research.

In the musculoskeletal system, the most common cell of this type is the fibroblast. Fibroblasts are drawn to the site of injury or inflammation and create collagen, which forms the connective tissue needed for repair. Common forms of connective tissue are found in ligaments, tendons, cartilage, and scar tissue. If the stimulation is large and nonspecific, as after a wound, the fibroblasts will create a scar, which is made of collagen fibers arranged in random directions. If the stimulation is less intense, and if that area has specific stresses in specific directions, the fibers will line up. The result is a stronger, less painful, and more flexible structure.

Focusing on Whole Body Systems

More than five years ago, Jim came to my office with a serious back problem that had caused him to apply to Social Security for permanent disability. Jim was fifty-two years old and had suffered from severe low back pain for the past five years. He had seen several specialists who had told him that he could either have a multiple-level spinal fusion, which would "probably" help him, or learn to live with his severe pain. Needless to say, he was very depressed. He had been a bank manager making a good salary and had had a full life. When I met him, he was lying in bed most of the time. My examination showed that he had ligament problems and that his pain was not from the degenerative discs on which the other physicians had focused their attention.

As part of my evaluation I always look at the body system, not just the painful area. I found that Jim had metabolic syndrome and low testosterone levels. Metabolic syndrome is a group of symptoms that indicate increased risk of heart disease, diabetes, stroke, and degenerative diseases. People with this problem have a markedly increased level of inflammation in their bodies. This is the root cause of the problems associated with this all too common and destructive disorder. The treatment is to limit simple carbohydrates and take several nutritional supplements. Men who have this problem almost always have low male hormone levels. Treating Jim for his back pain without correcting these underlying abnormalities would be much less likely to restore his normal life and would leave him at a huge risk of heart disease and other problems.

I started Jim on injections of testosterone and he switched to a low-carbohydrate diet. He also started taking supplements, which gave him the building blocks to create new connective tissue and supported his metabolism. He began to feel better in just a couple of weeks. I then treated him with a series of regenerative injections (consisting of concentrated sugar and lidocaine), which reduced his back pain to a mild level. He was able to return to work and has been working since. Jim continues his nutritional program and I recently had to see him for a flare-up of his back pain, but overall, he leads a normal productive life with minimal pain.

The important point to learn from Jim's story is that successful treatment of his problems required that I not only correctly diagnose and treat his back problem (which had been missed by several other physicians), but also correct and support his healing system, using the principles in the nutrition chapter of my book, *A New Prescription for Addiction.*

Helping the Body Repair Itself

There are four basic elements that are needed for the body to repair itself. They are:

1. The *nutrients* from which the body builds new tissue
2. The specific *signal* that turns on the healing system
3. *Stem cells* such as fibroblasts
4. A *matrix* or scaffolding on which the body can create new tissue

We can help the body with each of these steps. The easiest way to understand the process of tissue repair is to work from the other direction, to examine what happens when an injury occurs. There are three phases of the process.

During the first phase, with trauma or inflammation, blood escapes from the blood vessels into the surrounding area around the cells. Collagen fibers that are usually organized and protected from direct exposure to blood are exposed. In addition, cells are damaged or ruptured, releasing powerful substances, called *cytokines,* into the bloodstream. This draws tiny cell fragments circulating in the blood, called *platelets,* to the wounded area. The platelets contain structures called *alpha granules.* These rupture and release growth factors that initiate and then maintain the healing process. This first phase of wound healing lasts a few days.

During the second phase, a matrix is formed that will be slowly filled in over time, as new tissue is grown. In addition, new blood vessels form to supply the needed nutrients.

During the third phase, which can last several months, the matrix is filled in and the extra blood vessels that were created in phase two decrease. It may take six months for this tissue to get back to its normal strength.

When ligaments or tendons become lax over long periods of time, the body does not recognize this gradual deterioration as a wound, and so the three-phase healing cascade is not triggered. At other times, the healing process begins but never quite completes itself. A third cause of ligament and tendon laxity is the use of anti-inflammatory drugs such as ibuprofen (Motrin, Advil) or naproxen (Aleve) directly after injury or surgery. These medications work by stopping the very process that starts and then maintains healing. Many surgeons are now telling their patients not to use such drugs after spinal fusions, and many physicians now know that use of these drugs can cause long-term problems after injuries such as ankle sprains.

Combining Treatments

RIT injections irritate the cells in the specific region that needs healing by introducing a concentrated sugar solution into the area. When a concentrated solution is placed near cells, the body tries to dilute it to match the body's normal concentration. This process, called *osmosis*, is like dropping a sugar cube into a glass of water. Initially, the water right around the sugar cube is much sweeter. But after a few minutes, the sugar concentration spreads throughout the water, making the whole solution uniformly sweet. The body's cells attempt to do exactly the same thing at the site of an RIT sugar injection.

In their effort to dilute the sugar, the cells give up their water and eventually rupture. This releases the messenger molecules that signal tissue damage and that initiate the healing process. In addition, sugar itself is a nutrient that the cells can use for energy. Other RIT treatments use other kinds of cell irritants, such as pumice powder or ozone, for different sites and conditions. Another enhancement uses a substance called Platelet Rich Plasma or PRP.

Because platelets, with their alpha granules, are so important to healing, researchers have been looking for ways to use them to accelerate healing. Recently, a way of quickly and easily concentrating the fraction of blood that contains the platelets has been developed for outpatient use. Blood is drawn from the patient and then centrifuged. The fraction of the blood that contains the platelets is then drawn off and injected into specific joints that need repair. Bone marrow, which is rich in stem cells, can also be concentrated into PRP. Our clinic is designing a study to see if bone marrow PRP has a measurable impact on degenerative disc disease. The combination of ozone and PRP has also been shown to increase cell repair.

Barbara is a 55-year-old married woman I met on a trip to Italy. She suffered from severe knee pain and was told that she needed a knee replacement. The outer aspect of her knee joint had degenerated to the point where she could barely walk, and stairs were a real problem. My examination and review of her MRI corroborated the diagnosis but also showed that the ligaments supporting the joint were lax.

Barbara had suffered a minor knee injury in her twenties. Although this healed quickly and was not painful, it left some of the ligaments in the knee slightly lax and unable to keep the joint on track. Over the years, these forces pulling at abnormal angles slowly wore away her knee cartilage. She was too young for a knee replacement, as it certainly would not last her whole life, and yet she was facing constant pain and limitation.

I treated her with RIT into the joint and onto the affected ligaments. Her husband is a physician, so I was able to teach him to continue the treatment after I went home to California. Her pain decreased steadily and she was soon able to resume normal activities, although she still had some pain, which would increase if she became too active. She recently came to California for a visit. Her exam showed that her knee was more stable and that her range of motion was only slightly limited. I decided to treat her with PRP into the knee joint and on the ligaments. After this treatment, her knee improved markedly. She now has only minimal pain and can participate in all normal daily activities. Though RIT helped her, it took the increased healing power of PRP to finish the job.

The Future

Medicine has long dreamed of a day when we can regrow new body parts and stimulate the body to repair anything that is injured or degenerating. With RIT and PRP, this is happening today. The use of bone marrow as a source of stem cells, along with ozone stimulation of growth factors, is making this dream a reality.

It is my hope that better, less expensive ways of assessing the efficacy of treatments will be developed and accepted by the medical mainstream. It is very difficult to carry out a randomized clinical trial, today's gold standard of proof, for treatments that affect whole body systems. It takes huge amounts of money and large numbers of patients to get valid results with this method. We must also change the attitudes of those in power to value holistic treatments, and recognize that there are many ailments that cannot be reduced to a single cause.

I am optimistic that medicine will redefine itself in this way, and that the medical experience of our children will focus on supporting the body's natural healing systems.

RAFFAELE FILICE

CHAPTER
38

The Power
of Presence

"Our deepest fear is not that we are inadequate. Our deepest fear is that we are powerful beyond measure."

—Marianne Williamson

One lovely autumn afternoon, I was blessed by a visit from a young child and her parents. They had heard of the opening of our new integrative health center and about the training I had done with Dr. Weil. The child had been diagnosed with a rare genetic biochemical disorder that had already begun to have deleterious effects on her neurological development. Actually, she had been regressing. I was faced with the juxtaposition of the child playing happily, yet oblivious to the reality of her condition, and her parents who were desperately seeking to find a remedy that would restore their precious daughter to full health. At that point, they had seen or been in touch with a range of practitioners, from world authorities on their child's condition to esoteric healers.

After the initial visit, I did much reflection, meditation, and research on the child and her family. Part of what I went through was an exercise to confirm something that I already knew: There is no effective treatment for this child's condition. The other part was determining what I could offer these parents to ease their suffering.

At our follow-up visit, I began by gently sharing with them that I, too, had no answers for their child's disease. I did, however, offer

Raffaele Filice, MD, completed his undergraduate studies and medical degree at the University of Western Ontario, Canada. He specialized in diagnostic radiology at McMaster University. Over time, Dr. Filice developed and nurtured an interest in natural healing and complementary/alternative medicine, and completed a clinical fellowship in integrative medicine at the University of Arizona under the direction of Dr. Andrew Weil. He now divides his time between diagnostic radiology and a consulting practice in integrative medicine and healing. He is an assistant clinical professor in family medicine at McMaster University. www.drfilice.com.

them a perspective — a spiritual perspective — on their situation. They listened respectfully to my offering that on a spiritual level I believed that their daughter was quite powerful, though on their faces appeared incredulous looks. I continued, pointing out how many people their daughter had "raised to arms." She had leading scientists working on finding a cure, world authorities and government officials trying to secure an experimental treatment, family and friends taking on fundraising activities to support her and her family, schoolmates and teachers sending their support, and on and on. The parents had shared with me that people, some of them strangers, were also expressing their support by offering prayers or making donations. I suggested that most of us can only dream of having that kind of influence in the world.

In the end, while they still felt compelled to keep searching for a cure, they were grateful and somewhat comforted by the broadened perspective on their situation. I trust that I was able to help them come to some level of acceptance and gratitude for their lives, to see the "silver lining" when all there seemed to be were clouds, to find some meaning or purpose in their challenges.

I should say that I see a distinction between being a physician and being a healer. As a physician, I am bound by rules, regulations, and countless expectations. As a healer, I am not. As a physician, I have a limited time to take a history of the presenting complaint; discover and document relevant information about the patient's past illnesses, social situation, and personal habits; make observations about the patient's state of mind; and examine any and all pertinent body parts. As a healer, I just sit and listen. I listen with my ears; I listen with my eyes and with my hands. Indeed I listen with my emotions, my heart, and all of the focused attention I can muster.

What is almost invariably revealed is more than the so-called chief complaint. I discover that the intractable indigestion stems from an inability to accept things and people as they are; that the irritable bowel stems from an incapacity to appreciate, acknowledge, and express strong emotions; that a conjunctivitis is related to tears that have not been shed. As a healer I have no agenda, no structure to my patient encounter, other than that I am there for that person and open myself up to appreciating what the human being before me is going through and what she is asking for. Sometimes this entails heroic measures such as a bone marrow transplant. Other times it simply means holding the person's hand and acknowledging his suffering. More often than not, it is the latter.

To help my patients find meaning in their illnesses and provide inspiration and possibility for healing is my prayer. The hard reality is that this requires time spent with the person in need. Fixing is expeditious. Healing is an involved process. It requires more from both the healer and the healee.

An acceptance that we are more than just physical beings is necessary to actualize healing in our lives. I believe miracles can be realized when all of me and all of the patient is present to the moment and when the illness is appreciated as a mind-body-spirit event and not just a physical disturbance needing to be fixed. If my integrative medicine training has taught me nothing else, it is that the mystery of healing is revealed when I look at that patient/person in front of me and see "all" of her: body, mind, and spirit.

To appreciate another in a holistic way requires that I bring this broadened perspective to bear with expanded awareness. Developing awareness is a lifelong endeavor. Our own life experiences, both personal and professional, are our greatest teachers. Personal practices such as meditation, spending time in nature, solitude, mindfulness, and yoga are ways and means to experience ever-expanding levels of awareness. All of these foster a greater capacity for focus, clarity, and the equanimity necessary to be fully present to another.

There is clear consensus about the importance of the mind-body connection. Today's sciences have begun to reveal just how deeply and inexorably connected the mind and the body are. The modern field of psychoneuroimmunology (PNI) has shown connections between our emotions and the molecules that course through our veins, between our beliefs and the expression of our DNA, and between our thoughts and intentions and our manifest reality. The time has come to integrate these revelations into our professional pursuits. In fact, many distinguished medical institutions around the world have established centers for mind-body medicine. I believe this is a necessary step in the evolution toward mind-body-spirit medicine.

The spiritual part of the equation remains the most contentious. It conjures up so many things for people; fear, judgment, cynicism, skepticism, ridicule, distrust, trust, hope, inspiration, purpose, meaning, fulfillment, conviction, peace. I have encountered all of these and more in my interactions with people challenged by illness. My own inclination and persuasion is that we most certainly have a spiritual or timeless aspect to our existence and that this is as fundamental to human experience as the body and the mind. Perhaps even more so.

The spiritual, however one relates to it, opens doctor and patient, healer and healee, therapist and client to deeper, more meaningful levels. Recently, a patient came to see me for chronic abdominal pain.

She wondered if she could have "candida" and wanted some testing and treatment for that. Among other things, I explored with her how her body responded to emotional upset. She placed her hands over her belly — the mind-body connection.

We conversed a bit more and she shared with me that she was now into her third marriage (this third and most recent one was a common-law relationship, as she was too reluctant to formalize the union). One of her greatest concerns was that her husband/partner was soon to retire and she feared what it would be like to spend so much time with him. She described her first two husbands as having been very difficult aggressive types, but her current mate as fairly laid back and *easier* to live with. There was no use of the "L" word. Could there be a connection between her chronic health problems and her compromise of her potential happiness, fulfillment, and continued personal and spiritual growth? How could there not be? I submit that in addition to the mind-body connection, the spirit-mind-body connections *also* affect change on the physical body and environment and quite possibly on all of one's manifest reality.

The body is a wondrous and mysterious creation. This applies as much to the functioning of a single cell as it does to the whole body. With each passing day, we discover more details about its intricate complexity. We know so much that we tend to lose sight of the startling fact that medical science has no theoretical construct whatsoever to explain how the body is able to do what it does or how it is that we are sentient. Even the most accomplished of researchers would acknowledge that we are still only scratching the surface. Furthermore, there are so many different ways of looking at the body and how it functions.

From the Western perspective, we see a myriad of biochemical, electrochemical, and biomechanical processes at work. The Eastern sees the body more as a functional unit, that in addition to the biophysiology that unfolds below the surface, there is an intricate connectivity to the external environment and that maintaining balance between the internal and external is the key to good health. The esoteric point of view takes this perspective even further, seeing the body-mind-spirit in quantum energetic terms; that is, consciousness/ spirit is primary and the visible, palpable, and measurable parts are the epiphenomenon. Acknowledging and, from time to time, looking at a human being from these different points of reference deepens our insight and understanding into what ultimately is an unfolding mystery.

Acupuncture is a prime example. Here is a modality that has been embraced in the West even to the point of being reimbursed by most health plans, yet it has no direct anatomical or morphological basis. The meridian system is well mapped out, reproducible from person to person, formulated by centuries of empirical use and observation, and based entirely on the idea of the flow of energy or *chi* through the body. Recent technological advances such as functional MRI have begun to validate connections between remote acupuncture points and the central nervous system that actually follow the non-anatomical channels detailed in the meridian charts.

Homeopathy is another therapeutic system that takes conventional scientists to the edge. They invariably ask the question: "How can a remedy that does not contain any of the parent substance from which it is made possibly have any efficacy?" How indeed? I usually refrain from adding the kicker, which is that the more you dilute the remedy, the more potent it becomes. There will surely be a Nobel Prize for whoever figures out how homeopathy actually works. Clearly, there are things happening in the body-mind-spirit on an "energetic" level that we don't fully understand. Countless such phenomena observed in the arena of health and healing have stimulated scientific research ranging from laboratory investigation of the emergent properties of water to studies on the survival of consciousness.

One phenomenon that I have both experienced personally and observed in my clinical practice is the "storage" or "holding" of emotionally charged experiences within the body. Chiropractors, massage therapists, and other manual therapists are quite aware that clients sometimes experience emotional "releases" when the practitioner manipulates specific body parts. Some osteopaths use a technique called somato-emotional release.

Energy psychology is an umbrella term encompassing an array of therapies that incorporate knowledge of the meridian and chakra systems with psychologically oriented techniques to facilitate and heal these emotional blocks. One of the original techniques developed by Dr. Roger Callahan is Thought Field Therapy (TFT). In the past two decades, there have been many refinements and iterations of this technique. Energy psychology is now widely practiced and has shown clinical efficacy in the treatment of phobias, PTSD, and depression and to enhance sports performance. I have had remarkable results applying some of the energy psychology techniques. The most gratifying aspects of applying these therapies is how quickly and painlessly patients are able to release/heal their emotional problems, some of which have plagued them for as long as they can remember.

As a medical doctor, I am "licensed" to touch my patients. This privilege, of course, carries with it great responsibility. Less appreciated, however, is the tremendous opportunity that it presents.

Early in my transformative journey, I took an introductory Therapeutic Touch class, which actually turned out to be an initiation. In practicing the technique with my fellow initiates, something (I later learned was my empathic sense) was awakened within me. I discovered that by simply passing my hands over a person's body and through their aura, I could obtain additional information about the person's concerns or condition, whether mental or physical. Sometimes the person was consciously aware of what I perceived, and sometimes not.

Over time, I have learned to trust these perceptions as right and appropriate for the moment in which they are realized. Those early experiences with Therapeutic Touch opened a whole new realm of healing practice for me. Some of the more recognizable approaches include Therapeutic Touch, Healing Touch, Reiki, Johrei, and Prana Healing. (I do not intend this list to be either inclusive or representative of the energy healing being practiced today.) My view is that whenever a healer is either in the presence of or has focused her attention on someone in need, energy is exchanged. The proximity to the patient only increases the amplitude of the effect. Touch heals. Intention heals.

One of the things about our modern clinical research methodology (the so-called randomized double-blind control trial) that I have difficulty accepting is that, by it's very design, it seeks to factor out any untoward influence the health care provider might have on the outcome! Then, in interpreting the outcome of the study, the focus is entirely on the difference between the control (non-treated) group and the treated group. Infrequently, researchers marvel at how many people get better without the treatment (placebo effect) or even more so at how it is that some of the non-treated subjects develop some of the same side effects seen in the treated group (nocebo effect). These phenomena require further attention and inquiry….but I digress.

Touch is primary. In the 1970s, a number of interesting animal experiments demonstrated how fundamental touch is to the healthy development of the psyche. Touch is comforting. Touch is nurturing and touch is therapeutic. The "laying on of hands" in healing dates back not hundreds but thousands of years. Today, however, health care providers have to be careful about how they "handle" their patients/ clients. This brings me back to the distinction between being a doctor and being a healer. In doing a hands-on healing session with one of my patients, the very least that happens is that they are comforted. Sometimes that is all that can be expected or desired. Besides potentially healing what is ailing my patient/client, it facilitates a deepening and an enriching of the therapeutic relationship. This form of healing demands a high level of authenticity and integrity on the part of the doctor/healer. It can also be more fulfilling for both practitioner and patient/client.

As I noted, license to touch another comes with great responsibility. On the personal, quantum or energetic level, what I believe this means is that practitioners must perpetually do their *own* inner work. On an energetic level, as well as on a more conscious psychological level, "do as I say and not as I do" is less than optimal. Like our patients/clients, we, too, are in need of healing. If we acknowledge, nurture, and evolve ourselves, we can be more available and effective not only for our patients or clients, but also for anyone (or anything) with whom we interact.

One of my most enjoyable activities is tutoring the medical students from my local university. The students are sent out to have an experience with a complementary/alternative medicine practitioner in our community. This can range from the relatively mainstream chiropractor to a traditional Chinese medicine (TCM) practitioner to a Reiki Master. The students report on their observations and experiences. As one might expect, their reactions are varied. Almost invariably, however, they are intrigued. Intrigued by how sticking needles in certain spots in the body can have generalized effects, how creating a tranquil atmosphere in an office seems to improve a patient's disposition, how "channeling" chi relaxes and soothes, and how the practitioner's *presence* facilitates the healing interaction. They begin to realize that they themselves are or can be as important to the healing process as anything they say, prescribe, or do.

One of our greatest challenges as healers is that there is simply no scanner for spiritual or emotional crises other than our empathetic selves. It takes time to create rapport and much patience and perspective to begin to unravel the deeper mysteries of "illness." Sometimes the body gives clues in the way it changes in response to situations, circumstances, and experiences. It is critical to appreciate this information at more than face value. Very often, if not always, the feelings and the experiences conveyed give even greater insight. The hopes and aspirations expressed betray that which is missing and what the soul and the person needs most. Being *fully present* and having a holistic approach that truly encompasses the body, mind, and spirit of the patient/client and practitioner, as well as their heretofore underappreciated interconnectedness, will open a path to health and healing of extraordinary proportions.

Bruce H. Lipton

Intelligence of Your Cells

U nderneath your skin is a bustling metropolis of 50 trillion cells, each biologically and functionally equivalent to a minia-ture human. Current popular opinion holds that the fate and behavior of our internal cellular citizens are preprogrammed in their genes, a notion derived from the now dated scientific concept known as *genetic determinism*. Since Watson and Crick's discovery of the genet-ic code, the public has been programmed with the conventional belief that DNA "controls" the attributes passed down through a family's lineage, including dysfunctional traits such as cancer, Alzheimer's, diabetes, and depression, among scores of others. As "victims" of heredity, we naturally perceive of ourselves as being powerless in regard to the unfolding of our lives. Unfortunately, the assumption of being powerless is the road to personal irresponsibility: "Since I can't do anything about it anyway...why should I care?"

Shattering Illusions

Just as the Human Genome Project got off the ground in the late 1980s, scientists began to acquire a paradigm-shattering new view of how life works. Their revolutionary research has become the foundation for a new branch of science known as *epigenetic control*, which has shaken the foundations of biology and medicine. It reveals that we are not "victims," but rather "masters" of our genes.

Bruce Lipton, Ph.D., is an internationally recognized authority in bridging science and spirit. A cell biologist by training, he taught anatomy at the University of Virginia, and later performed pioneering studies at Stanford University's School of Medicine. He has been a guest speaker on dozens of TV and radio shows, as well as keynote presenter for national confer-ences. His breakthrough studies on the cell membrane presaged the new science of Epigenetics, and made him a leading voice of the new biology. His book *The Biology of Belief* (Elite, 2005) quickly became a best-seller, and you can find him on the web at www.BruceLipton.com.

The conventional version of heredity still taught in schools emphasizes *genetic control*, or "control by genes." However, newly revealed *epigenetic control* mechanisms provide a profoundly different view of how life is managed. The Greek-derived prefix *epi-* means "over or above." Consequently, the literal translation of *epigenetic control* is "control *above* the genes." Genes do NOT control life—life is controlled by something *above* the genes. This knowledge of how life works provides the most important element in our quest for self-empowerment.

The new science of epigenetics recognizes that environmental signals are the primary regulators of gene activity. As described in my book, *The Biology of Belief: Unleashing the Power of Consciousness, Matter and Miracles*, cells read and respond to the conditions of their environment using membrane protein perception switches. Activated switches send signals to control behavior and regulate the activity of the genes—the hereditary blueprints used to make the body. Amazingly, epigenetic information can modify or edit the readout of a gene blueprint to create over 30,000 different variations of proteins—the cell's molecular building blocks—from the same gene. This editing process can provide for normal or dysfunctional protein products from the same gene. One can be born with healthy genes and through epigenetic processes express mutant behaviors, such as cancer. Similarly, one can be born with defective mutant genes and through epigenetic mechanisms create normal healthy proteins and functions.

The conventional belief that the genome represents the equivalent of a computer's "read-only" programs is now proven to be false. Epigenetic mechanisms modify the readout of genetic the code—which means that genes actually represent "read-write" programs, wherein life experiences actively redefine an individual's genetic expression. The "new" biology is based upon the fact that perception controls behavior *and* gene activity! This revised version of science emphasizes the reality that we actively control our genetic expression moment by moment throughout our lives. Rather than seeing ourselves as victims of our genes, we must come to own the responsibility that our perceptions are dynamically shaping our biology and behavior.

As organisms experience the environment, their perception mechanisms fine-tune genetic expression so as to enhance their opportunities for survival. The expression of a healthy or dis-eased biology is directly influenced by the accuracy of an individual's interpretation or perception of their environment. Misperceptions rewrite genetic expression just as effectively as accurate perceptions, yet with far graver, perhaps even life threatening consequences.

From the Microcosm of the Cell to the Macrocosm of the Mind

For the first three and a half billion years of life on this planet, the biosphere consisted of a massive population of individual single-celled organisms, such as bacteria, yeast, algae, and protozoa. About 700 million years ago, individual cells started to assemble into multicellular colonies. The collective awareness afforded in a community of cells was far greater than an individual cell's awareness. Since awareness is a primary factor in organismal survival, the communal experience offered its citizens a far greater opportunity to stay alive and reproduce.

The first cellular communities, like the earliest human communities, were basic hunter-gatherer clans wherein each member of the society offered the same services to support the survival of the community. However, as the population densities of both cellular and human communities reached greater numbers, it was no longer efficient or effective for all individuals to do the same job. In both types of communities, evolution led to individuals taking on specialized functions. For example, in human communities some members focused upon hunting, others upon domestic chores or child rearing. In cellular communities specialization meant that some cells began to differentiate as digestive cells, others as heart cells, and still others as muscle cells.

Most of the trillions of cells forming bodies such as ours have no direct perception of the external environment. Liver cells "see" what's going on in the liver, but don't directly know what's going on in the world outside of the skin. The function of the brain and nervous system is to interpret environmental stimuli and send out signals to the cells that integrate and regulate the life-sustaining functions of the body's organ systems.

The successful nature of multicellular communities allowed evolving brains to dedicate vast numbers of cells to cataloguing, memorizing, and integrating complex perceptions. The ability to remember and select among the millions of experienced perceptions in life provides the brain with a powerful creative database from which it can create complex behavioral repertoires. When put into play, these behavioral programs endow the organism with the characteristic trait of *consciousness*—: the state of being awake and aware of what is going on around you.

Many scientists prefer to think of consciousness in terms of a digital quality, an organism either has it or not. However, an assessment of the evolution of biological properties suggests consciousness, like any other quality, evolved over time. Consequently, the character of consciousness would likely express itself as a gradient of awareness from its simpler roots in primitive organisms to the unique character of *self-consciousness* manifest in humans and other higher vertebrates.

The expression of *self-consciousness* is specifically associated with a small evolutionary adaptation in the brain known as the *prefrontal cortex*. This is the neurological platform that enables us to realize our personal identity and experience the quality of "thinking." Monkeys and lower organisms do not express self-consciousness. When looking into a mirror, monkeys will never recognize that they are looking at them selves; they will always perceive the image to be that of another monkey. In contrast, neurologically more advanced chimps looking in the mirror perceive the mirror's reflection as an image of themselves.

An important difference between the brain's *consciousness* and the prefrontal cortex's *self-consciousness* is that consciousness enables an organism to assess and respond to the immediate conditions of its environment that are relevant at that moment. In contrast, self-consciousness enables the individual to factor in the consequences of their actions in regard to not only how they impact the present moment but also how they will influence the future.

Self-consciousness is an evolutionary adjunct to consciousness in that it provided another behavior-creating platform: the role of a "self" in the decision-making process. While conventional *consciousness* enables organisms to participate in the dynamics of life's "play," the quality of *self-consciousness* offers an opportunity to simultaneously be an observer in the "audience." From this perspective, self-consciousness provides the individual with the option for self-reflection, reviewing and editing their character's performance. The conscious and self-conscious functions of the brain may be collectively referred to as the *mind*.

In conventional parlance, the brain's conscious mechanism associated with automated stimulus-response behaviors is referred to as the *subconscious* or *unconscious mind*, for the reason that its functions require neither observation nor attention from the self-conscious mind. Subconscious mind functions evolved long before the prefrontal cortex; consequently, it is able to successfully operate a body and its behavior without any contribution from the more evolved *self-conscious mind*.

The subconscious mind is an astonishingly powerful information processor that can record and replay perceptual experiences (programs). Interestingly, many people only become aware of their subconscious mind's automated programmed behaviors when they realize they're engaged in an undesirable behavior as a result of someone "pushing their buttons."

The power of the subconscious mind lies in its ability to process massive amounts of data acquired from direct and indirect learning experiences at extraordinarily high rates of speed. It has been estimated that the disproportionately larger brain mass providing the subconscious mind's function has the ability to interpret and respond to over 40 million nerve impulses per second. In contrast, it is estimated that the diminutive self-conscious mind's prefrontal cortex can only process about 40 nerve impulses per second. As an information processor, the subconscious mind is *one million times* more powerful than the self-conscious mind.

As a tradeoff for its computational bravado, the subconscious mind expresses only a marginal creative ability—one that may be best compared to that of a precocious five-year-old. In contrast to the freewill offered by the conscious mind, the subconscious mind primarily expresses prerecorded stimulus-response "habits," such as walking, getting dressed, or driving a car.

Although the prefrontal cortex's ability for multitasking is physically constrained, the self-conscious mind can focus upon and control *any* function in the human body. It was once thought that some bodily functions—such as the regulation of heartbeat, blood pressure, and body temperature—were beyond the control of the self-conscious mind. It is now recognized, however, that yogis and other practitioners that train their conscious minds can absolutely control functions formerly defined as involuntary behaviors.

The subconscious and self-conscious components of the mind work in tandem, with the subconscious controlling every behavior not attended to by the self-conscious mind. Most people's self-conscious minds are rarely focused upon the current moment, since their mental processing continuously flits from one thought to another. The self-conscious mind is so preoccupied with thoughts about the future, the past, or resolving some imaginary problem, that most of our lives are actually controlled by programs in the subconscious mind.

Simple Insights...Profound Consequences!

Cognitive neuroscientists conclude that the self-conscious mind contributes only about 5 percent of our cognitive activity. Consequently, 95 percent of our decisions, actions, emotions, and behaviors are derived from the unobserved processing of the subconscious mind. This data reveals that our lives are not controlled by our personal intentions and desires, as we may inherently believe. Do the math! Our fate is actually under the control of the preprogrammed experiences managed by the *subconscious mind.*

The most powerful and influential programs in the subconscious mind originated during the formative period between gestation and six years of age. Now here's the catch—these life-shaping subconscious programs are direct downloads derived from observing our primary teachers: our parents, siblings, and local community. Unfortunately, as psychiatrists, psychologists, and counselors are keenly aware, many of the perceptions acquired about ourselves in the formative period are expressed as limiting and self-sabotaging beliefs.

Unbeknownst to most parents, their words and actions are being continuously recorded by their children's minds. Since the role of the mind is to make coherence between its programs and real life, the brain generates appropriate behavioral responses to life's stimuli to assure the "truth" of the programmed perceptions.

Let's apply this understanding to real-life behavior: Consider that you were a five-year-old child throwing a tantrum over your desire to have a particular toy. In silencing your outburst, your father yelled, "*You* don't deserve things!" You are now an adult and in your self-conscious mind you are considering the idea that you have the qualities and power to assume a position of leadership at your job. While in the process of entertaining this positive thought in the self-conscious mind, all of your behaviors are automatically managed by the programs in your more powerful subconscious mind. Since your fundamental behavioral programs are those derived in your formative years, your father's admonition that "you do not deserve things" may become the subconscious mind's automated directive. So while you are entertaining wonderful thoughts of a positive future and not paying attention, your subconscious mind automatically engages self-sabotaging behavior to assure that your reality matches your program of not-deserving.

Now here's the catch: Behavior is automatically controlled by the subconscious mind's programs when the self-conscious mind is not focused on the present moment. When the reflective self-conscious mind is preoccupied in thought and not paying attention, it does not observe the automatic behaviors derived from subconscious mind. Since 95 percent or more of our behavior is derived from the subconscious mind...then most of our own behavior is invisible to us!

For example, consider you intimately know someone and you also know his or her parent. From your perspective you see that your friend's behavior closely resembles their parent. Then one day you casually remark to your friend something like, "You know Mary, you're just like your mom." Back away! In disbelief and perhaps shock, Mary will likely respond with, "How can you say that!" The cosmic joke is that everyone else can see that Mary's behavior resembles her mom's *except* Mary. Why? Simply because when Mary is engaging the subconscious behavioral programs she downloaded in her youth from observing her mom, it's because her self-conscious mind is not paying attention. At those moments, her automatic subconscious programs operate without observation.

Consequently, when life does not work out as planned, we rarely recognize that we were very likely contributing to our own disappointments. Since we are generally unaware of the influence of our own subconscious behaviors, we naturally perceive of ourselves as victims of outside forces. Unfortunately, assuming the role of victim means that we assume we are powerless in manifesting our intentions. Nothing is further from the truth! The primary determinant in shaping the fate of our lives is the database of perceptions and beliefs programmed in our minds.

Where Did That Behavior Come From?

There are three sources of perceptions that control our biology and behavior. The most primitive perceptions are those we acquire with our genome. Built into our genes are programs that provide fundamental reflex behaviors referred to as instincts. Pulling your hand out of an open flame is a genetically derived behavior that does not have to be learned. More complex instincts include the ability of newborn babies to swim like a dolphin or the activation of innate healing mechanisms to repair a damaged system or eliminate a cancerous growth. Genetically inherited instincts are perceptions acquired from *nature.*

The second source of life-controlling perceptions represents memories derived from life experiences downloaded into the subconscious mind. These profoundly powerful learned perceptions represent the contribution from *nurture.* Among the earliest perceptions of life to be downloaded are the emotions and sensations experienced by the mother as she responds to her world. Along with nutrition, the emotional chemistry, hormones, and stress factors controlling the mother's responses to life experiences cross the placental barrier and influence fetal physiology and development. When the mother is happy, so is the fetus. When the mother is in fear, so is the fetus. When the mother "rejects" her fetus as a potential threat to family survival, the fetal nervous system is preprogrammed with the emotion of being rejected. Sue Gearhardt's very valuable book *Why Love Matters,* reveals that the fetal nervous system records memories of the womb experiences. By the time the baby is born, emotional information downloaded from the life experiences in womb have already shaped half of that individual's personality.

However, the most influential perceptual programming of the subconscious mind occurs in the time period spanning from the birth process through the first six years of life. During this time the child's brain is recording all sensory experiences as well as learning complex motor programs for speech, and for learning first how to crawl, then stand, and ultimately run and jump. Simultaneously, the subconscious mind acquires perceptions in regard to parents, who are they and what they do. Then by observing behavioral patterns of people in their immediate environment, a child learns perceptions of acceptable and unacceptable social behaviors that become the subconscious programs that establish the "rules" of life.

Nature facilitates the enculturation process by developmentally enhancing the subconscious mind's ability to download massive amounts of information. EEG readings from adult brains reveal that neural electrical activity is correlated with at least five different states of awareness, each associated with a different frequency level:

Activity	Frequency	Brain State
delta	0.5-4 Hz	sleeping/unconscious
theta	4-8 Hz	imagination
alpha	8-12 Hz	calm consciousness
beta	12-35 Hz	focused consciousness
gamma	>35 Hz	peak performance

EEG vibrations continuously shift from state to state over the whole range of frequencies during normal brain processing in adults. However, EEG vibration rates and their corresponding states evolve in incremental stages over time. The predominant brain activity during the child's first two years of life is *delta*, the lowest EEG frequency range. In the adult brain, *delta* is associated with sleeping or unconsciousness.

Between two and six years of age, the child's brain activity state ramps up and operates primarily in the range of *theta*. In the adult, *theta* activity is associated with states of reverie or imagination. While in the *theta* state, children spend much of their time mixing the imaginary world with the real world. Calm consciousness associated with emerging *alpha* activity only becomes a predominant brain state after six years of age. By twelve years, the brain expresses all frequency ranges although it's primary activity is in the *beta's* state of focused consciousness. Children leave elementary education behind at this age and enter into the more intense academic programs of junior high.

A profoundly important fact in the above timeline that may have missed your attention is that children do not express the *alpha* EEG frequencies of conscious processing as a predominant brain state until *after* they are six years old. The predominant *delta* and *theta* activity of children under six signifies that their brains are operating at levels below consciousness. *Delta* and *theta* brain frequencies define a brain state known as a hypnogogic trance, the same neural state that hypnotherapists use to download new behaviors directly into the subconscious mind of their clients.

The first six years of a child's life is spent in a hypnotic trance. Its perceptions of the world are directly downloaded into the subconscious during this time, without the discrimination of the dormant self-conscious mind. Consequently, our fundamental perceptions about life are learned before we express the capacity to choose or reject those beliefs. We are simply "programmed." The Jesuits were aware of this programmable state and proudly boasted, "Give us a child until it is six or seven years old and it will belong to the Church for the rest of its life." They knew that once the dogma of the Church was implanted into the child's subconscious mind, that information would inevitably influence 95 percent of that individual's behavior for the rest of his or her life.

The inhibition of conscious processing (*alpha* EEG activity) and the simultaneous engagement of a hypnogogic trance during the formative stages of a child's life are a logical necessity. The thinking processes associated with the self-conscious mind cannot operate from a blank slate. Self-conscious behavior requires a working database of learned perceptions. Consequently, before self-consciousness is expressed, the brain's primary task is to acquire a working awareness of the world by directly downloading experiences and observations into the subconscious mind.

However, there is a very, *very* serious downside to acquiring awareness by this method. The consequence is so profound that it not only impacts the life of the individual, it can also alter an entire civilization. The issue concerns the fact that we download our perceptions and beliefs about life long before we acquire the ability for critical thinking. Our primary perceptions are literally written in stone as unequivocal truths in the subconscious mind, where they habitually operate for life, unless there is an active effort to reprogram them. When as young children we download limiting or sabotaging beliefs about ourselves, these perceptions become our truths and our subconscious processing will invisibly generate behaviors that are coherent with those truths.

Acquired perceptions in the subconscious mind can even override genetically endowed instincts. For example, every human can instinctually swim like a dolphin the moment they emerge from the birth canal. So, why do we have to work so hard at teaching our children how to swim? The answer lies in the fact that every time the infant encounters open water, such as a pool, a river, or a bathtub, the parents freak out in concern for the safety of their child. In the baby's mind, the parent's behavior causes the child to equate water as something to be feared. The acquired perception of water as dangerous and life threatening, overrides the instinctual ability to swim and makes the formerly proficient child susceptible to drowning.

Through our developmental experiences we acquire the perception that we are frail, vulnerable organisms subject to the ravages of contagious germs and disease. The belief of being frail actually leads to frailty since the mind's limiting perceptions inhibit the body's innate ability to heal itself. This influence of the mind on healing processes is the focus of psychoneuroimmunology, the field that describes the mechanism by which our thoughts change brain chemistry, which in turn regulates the function of the immune system. While negative beliefs can precipitate illness (nocebo effect), the resulting dis-ease state can be alleviated through the healing effects of positive thoughts (placebo effect).

Finally, the third source of perceptions that shape our lives is derived from the self-conscious mind. Unlike the reflexive programming of subconscious mind, the self-conscious mind is a creative platform that provides for the mixing and morphing of a variety of perceptions with the infusion of imagination, a process that generates an unlimited number of beliefs and behavioral variations. The quality of the self-conscious mind endows organisms with one of the most powerful forces in the Universe, the opportunity to express free will.

Taking Personal Responsibility

We have all been shackled with emotional chains wrought by dysfunctional behaviors programmed by the stories of the past. However, the next time you are "talking to yourself" with the hope of changing sabotaging subconscious programs, it is important to realize the following information. Using reason to communicate with your subconscious in an effort to change its behavior would essentially have the same influence as trying to change a program on a cassette tape by talking to the tape player. In neither case is there an entity in the mechanism that will respond to your dialogue.

Subconscious programs are not fixed, unchangeable behaviors. We have the ability to rewrite our limiting beliefs and in the process take control of our lives. However, to change subconscious programs requires the activation of a process other than simply engaging in the usual running dialogue with the subconscious mind. There are a large variety of effective processes to reprogram limiting beliefs, which include clinical hypnotherapy, Buddhist mindfulness practice, and a number of newly developed and very powerful modalities collectively referred to as Energy Psychology.

Learning how to harness our minds to promote growth is the secret of life, which is why I refer to the new science as *The Biology of Belief.* As we become more conscious and rely less on subconscious automated programs, we become the masters of our fates rather than the "victims" of our programs. In this way we can rewrite old, limiting perceptions and actively transform the character of our lives so that they are filled with the love, health, and prosperity that are our true birthrights.

DAWSON CHURCH

CHAPTER
40

Your DNA is Not Your Destiny

Josephine Tesauro, though 92 years old, is in excellent spirits and good health. According to a story about her that appeared in the *New York Times* in 2006: "She is straight backed, firm jawed and vibrantly healthy, living alone in an immaculate brick ranch house high on a hill near McKeesport, a Pittsburgh suburb. She works part time in a hospital gift shop and drives her 1995 white Oldsmobile Cutlass Ciera to meetings of her four bridge groups, to church and to the grocery store. She has outlived her husband, who died nine years ago, when he was 84. She has outlived her friends, and she has outlived three of her six brothers."

Josephine's sister, though, is not in the same fortunate position. She suffers from senile dementia, and has had a variety of health problems, including incontinence, a degenerative disorder that has destroyed most of her vision, and joint degeneration.

The remarkable thing about Josephine and her sister is that they both have exactly the same genes. And I don't mean *similar* genes, I mean *identical* genes. This is because they are identical twins. The definition of identical twins is that the egg from which they were born, after having been fertilized by a sperm, split in two. This gave both halves of the egg the same genes. Josephine and her sister developed from the identical sets of genetic instructions. They've also lived their whole lives in the same location, with similar friends, upbringing and surroundings.

Dawson Church, PhD, has edited or authored many books, and collaborated with leading voices including Larry Dossey, MD, Bernie Siegel, MD, and Caroline Myss, PhD. His new book, *The Genie in Your Genes* (Elite, 2007, www.GenieBestSeller.com), pioneers the field of epigenetics, (control of genes from outside the cell), explaining the remarkable self-healing mechanisms now emerging from this research. It has been hailed as a brilliant breakthrough by leading scientists. He founded Soul Medicine Institute (www.SoulMedicineInstitute.org) to teach the healing techniques now emerging from epigenetic medicine.

Figure 1: Josephine Tesauro and her Sister

This disparity between identical twins is not the exception. According to James W. Vaupel, who directs the Laboratory of Survival and Longevity at the Max Planck Institute, one of the world's top research establishments, identical twins die more than ten years apart, on average.

The notion that our genes determine our longevity, health and quality of life is deeply engrained in our culture. This belief is called *genetic determinism,* and I give many examples in my book *The Genie in Your Genes.* In the media, genetic determinism is a bedrock assumption. Stories abound about genes for this and genes for that. In popular culture, the almighty gene has replaced an almighty deity as the dispenser of life and death.

The popularization of genetic determinism began soon after the discovery that the DNA molecule had the structure of a double helix, for which Francis Crick and James Watson received the Nobel Prize in 1962. In fact, genetic determinism has been an article of faith in the scientific canon for half a century; a famous paper by Sir Francis Crick in the journal *Nature* which enshrined the idea that DNA is the blueprint from which all the processes of life spring was entitled, "The Central Dogma of Molecular Biology."

From the structure of your tissues and bones, to the metabolic processes that drive your body, most of the molecules in your body are proteins. A gene is a length of DNA that contains the blueprint to build a particular protein. Your cells require these blueprints to tell them how to build proteins. Proteins are very large and complex molecules and there are more than 100,000 different proteins making up your body. Without the blueprint for protein-building contained in the genes, the body is unable to perform many of the functions of life. So the "primacy of DNA" or genetic determinism has seemed like a logical foundation of biology for most of the modern era.

378

DNA → RNA → Protein

Figure 2: The Central Dogma of Molecular Biology

There's only one problem with the Central Dogma. It's wrong. It's about as wrong as the medieval Papal bulls that decreed that the sun revolves around the Earth. And just as the discoveries of Galileo, Kepler and Copernicus ran counter to the established order, and despite the best efforts of the then-current orthodoxy at suppressing them, the evidence that our genes do not control our destiny is piling up so high and fast that Sir Francis's dogma is developing cracks that even its most ardent supporters are having trouble papering over.

The new heresy has a name: *epigenetics.* Epigenetics is the activation of genes by signals from outside the genome, sometimes even from the environment outside the body. Epigenetics now has its own journals and conferences. Someday, it will have it's own treatments; I've coined the term *epigenetic medicine* to describe therapies which act epigenetically to stimulate health and longevity in the body. There are many such therapies that simulate the whole body to produce positive genetic change; I list and describe many of them in the book *Soul Medicine,* coauthored with brilliant neurosurgeon Norman Shealy, MD, PhD. Researchers perform scientific research into these therapies at the nonprofit Soul Medicine Institute.

For it turns out that our genes are much more like sets of potentials than precise military commands. Which genes are in expression, producing which proteins, is a function of many epigenetic factors. And the best news of all is that *many of these epigenetic effects are under our conscious control.* Incredible though it may sound to minds steeped in genetic determinism, each of us has the power to activate or deactivate whole cascades of genes and proteins throughout our bodies. You are, in effect, a genetic engineer, influencing which sets of potentials are coming into actualization in your body, moment by moment. The turning on and off of groups of genes is called *gene expression.* I won't try and pack all the scientific evidence for what I'm talking about into this brief article. But you can rest assured that it's all based on mainstream science; there are over three hundred scientific studies referenced in *The Genie in Your Genes.*

One simple way of illustrating the reality of epigenetic intervention on gene expression is stress. When you're stressed, most of your body's systems respond, in the *fight or flight response.* When you're confronted with an external threat like a predator or crisis, your body has an immediate response. Picture a large vicious snarling dog running at you. If this happened in real life, your nervous system, digestive system, circulatory system, respiratory system, immune system, and musculoskeletal system would all undergo immediate changes. Your muscles would tense. Blood would rush from your gut and genitals to your muscles. Your immune and reproductive systems temporarily power down, to free up energy for the body's immediate needs.

Messenger molecules would course through your body. Nerve impulses would shoot through your nervous system. Electrical signals would flash through your electromagnetic body, traveling at the speed of light, to and from every last cell.

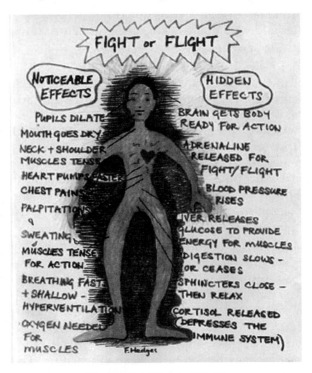

Figure 3: Fight or Flight

Immediate Early Genes (IEGs)

Groups of genes also express differently in response to stress. Genes can be classified in several ways, but the most relevant classification for the purpose of examining fight or flight is the speed of activation. We have some genes that take many hours to express. Others, like the clock genes that influence cycles or alertness and drowsiness during the day, are called intermediate genes, and they reach peaks or troughs of expression every two hours or thereabouts. The class of genes involved in fight or flight is called the Immediate

Early Genes or IEGs. IEGs can express in three seconds or less. A second or two after you see the barking dog, your IEGs have already got your body producing all the stress proteins required to deal with the crisis.

One of the primary stress hormones is cortisol. Our bodies produce cortisol as part of the stress response, along with adrenaline, norepinephrine, and other proteins that help us cope with stress.

Our bodies are well adapted to giving us a quick boost in these hormones when we need to get out of danger. However, our body is not equipped to deal with the effects of high cortisol production long term. It's like you drinking a cup of coffee to help you stay awake. That's fine once in a while, or perhaps once a day. But a constant diet of coffee all day long is going to take its toll.

What does your dog or cat do when faced with a crisis? Just what you do! All the same changes occur in other animals as well. The big difference is what your dog or cat does after the threat has passed. A cat might roll on its back and lick its fur. A dog might shake itself a few times then go and lie in the sun.

Unfortunately, few modern humans unwind as fast as their pets. We're more likely to replay the threatening dog image in our minds. We might start worrying about all dogs, not just barking snarling ones. We might even develop a phobia of dogs, or lie awake at night obsessively thinking about the experience for hours on end.

Guess what your body's doing when your mind is bombarding it with scary images of snarling dogs? It has no idea that the images are just in your imagination. It makes no moral judgment about the wisdom of your mental choices. It simply does what it's designed to do in the face of danger: make more cortisol. Cortisol is one of several hormones manufactured by the adrenal glands.

So while your cat very quickly breaks down the cortisol in its system and returns to normal physical function, human beings can keep their bodies on high alert for days, weeks or months. Your body is not designed to handle high cortisol for long periods.

Think of a vehicle manufacturing factory which has large stores of glass, metal, rubber, paint, and everything else required to produce vehicles. Your adrenal glands are the factory, and the materials are the precursors your body has available to it. Either the factory can produce battle tanks to destroy invaders, or it can produce construction equipment to build and repair its surroundings. It is capable of producing 100 % tanks, or 100 % construction equipment, or any percentage in between. A balanced body might be producing 15% tanks, just enough to stay out of trouble, but devoting 85% of its

energies to producing useful construction equipment to repair and restore your cells. On this sliding scale, you're here:

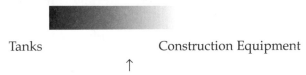

Tanks   Construction Equipment

↑

Figure 4: Relaxed Ratio

When you're in danger, epigenetic signals from your environment kick your IEGs kick on, and your body quickly responds by producing all the tanks required to defend you, like this:

Tanks   Construction Equipment

↑

Figure 5: High Alert Ratio

This response is perfectly adapted to what we need in that moment. Our cortisol production spikes, and when the threat is past, returns to normal. The manufacturing plant of our adrenal glands, after producing lots of tanks for a short while, starts using all the molecular resources available to produce construction equipment. And if cortisol is tanks, then construction equipment is one of the other main hormones produced by the adrenals, called DHEA. DHEA is the most common hormone in the human body, and is used for cell repair. High levels of DHEA are associated with health. When you stop needing those high cortisol levels to counter a threat, your body quickly breaks down those molecules and uses those same precursors to produce DHEA. The molecules even look alike, because they are so similar, though they stimulate your body in diametrically opposite ways.

If you're obsessing about all the bad things in your life, using your heart and mind to trigger the stress response in your body, you shift your genetic expression to produce more cortisol. All the resources your body was using to create DHEA are now grabbed to make cortisol. Suddenly, your cells are starved of this vital hormone they need to communicate and repair themselves. Over time, their repair capacities are reduced, and organs are not repaired as frequently or as efficiently as they might be. They are more susceptible to degeneration, which is why low DHEA levels are found in virtually every disease. When you choose your state of mind, you in effect grab the slider bar in Figures 4 and 5 and slide it in one direction or another. Either you nudge yourself to produce less DHEA and more cortisol with the available resources of your adrenal factory, or the reverse.

The effects of chronic high cortisol are not pretty. Here's a partial list, based on research from many sources.

High blood pressure

Reduced memory & learning

High blood sugar

Heart disease

Diminished cell repair

Accelerated aging

Slower wound healing

Reduced bone repair

Decreased circulating immune cells

Diminished immune antibodies

Death of brain cells

Reduced muscle mass

Decreased skin cell repair

Increased fat deposits around waist/hips

Osteoporosis

Figure 6: Chronic Cortisol Effects

So you definitely want to be grabbing your cortisol-DHEA slider and pulling it in the direction of health. How do you do this? That's where epigenetic medicine comes in. Epigenetic medicine suggests that we act more like our pets, quickly dissipating the effects of stress, and not worrying about imaginary problems and threats. We can fill up our minds with worry, projecting threatening and upset emotions on the television screen of our awareness. We can also use that same capacity of consciousness to project thoughts and feelings that pull us in the direction of DHEA and away from the stress response. Studies are giving us a clear picture of the kinds of practices that produce serenity and joy. Among these epigenetic interventions are:

Prayer

Optimism

Meditation

Energy Medicine

Positive Attitude

Nurturing

Energy Psychology

Positive Beliefs

Visualization

Spirituality

Altruism

Figure 7: Epigenetic Medicine Interventions

The effects of these epigenetic interventions is not small. Positive beliefs have been linked to a threefold improvement in immune function. Altruism correlates with cutting your risk of death by half. The parts of the brain associated with joy light up in meditators, and light up brighter the more years a meditator has practiced consistently. People with positive attitudes about aging have been found to live 7 ½ years longer than those with negative attitudes. Optimists have less than half the risk of death that pessimists do. People with lifelong patterns of hopelessness die, on average, 35 years sooner than positive ones. So if all these epigenetic interventions are so good for us, why don't we all do them every day?

If you've been a worrier all your life, it's quite hard to change. Rather than being addicted to worry, you might be addicted to dysfunctional relationships, or to drugs or alcohol. We've all met the person who complains bitterly about the abuse marriage they're in. They get divorced — then choose someone just as abusive for their next partner. And the next. Even when we're uncomfortable, we tend to repeat our old patterns. Change is pain.

One of our studies at Soul Medicine Institute examines Iraq war veterans with posttraumatic stress disorder, or PTSD. When recruiting volunteers for treatment in the study, we found that most veterans who had traumatic experiences in Iraq had a pattern of trauma that began long before they went to war. Their childhood homes were often combat zones, and in the Army they were often merely recreating the psychological and biological conditions they were used to living in.

If your body is used the mix of proteins associated with a high stress level, you cannot change the mixture without it *feeling wrong in every cell*. If you're used to having a cube of sugar in your tea, you'll spit out the first mouthful if someone hands you a cup of tea made with a cube of salt. The sum of the fluids inside our bodies are the same. We're used to living with a certain ratio, a comfort zone. Change the ratio, and it *feels wrong* inside, even when we're trying on a more healthy behavior.

Fortunately, most epigenetic medicine interventions are fast, effective, and cheap. Meditation costs nothing beyond a half hour in the morning or evening. You can choose to replace a negative image with a positive one in a moment. Whatever your religious orientation, you can chant the name of a saint whenever your mind strays to someone you detest. Energy Psychology, which uses touching, breathing and tapping various stress-reduction points on the body, takes less than five minutes. The Iraq vets with PTSD that Soul Medicine Institute is treating are getting a form of Energy Psychology called Emotional Freedom Techniques or EFT, and it is proving remarkably effective. Even multiple, long-standing traumas can be reversed, like this story of "Rich," a Vietnam veteran who had been incapacitated by his war traumas. Rich was treated by EFT originator Gary Craig:

"Despite seventeen years of psychotherapy for symptoms of posttraumatic stress disorder (PTSD) tracing back to the Vietnam war, Rich's insomnia was so disabling that he had checked himself in two months earlier for yet another round of inpatient treatment at the Veterans' Administration Hospital in Los Angeles. When he tried to sleep, any of more than a hundred haunting war memories might intrude into his awareness. He felt trapped in these overwhelming images, and every night was dreaded and interminably long. Every day was clouded with exhaustion and further anxiety. He could not function effectively. He also suffered from a severe height phobia that had developed over the course of some fifty parachute jumps he had made during the war.

"Rich was one of twenty patients treated by Gary Craig and his associate, Adrienne Fowlie, during a weeklong visit after a hospital administrator had invited them to demonstrate the effects of energy-oriented therapy on emotional trauma. Rich's treatment first focused on his height phobia. He was asked to think about a situation involving heights. His fear level shot up immediately. He was wearing short pants, and he pointed out that the hair on his legs was literally standing up. At the same time, as he brought to mind the terror of facing a height, he was directed to stimulate a series electromagnetically sensitive points on his skin by tapping them with his fingertips. Within fifteen minutes of using this procedure, Rich reported no fear reaction when imagining situations involving heights. To test this, Gary had him walk out onto the fire escape of the third floor of the building and look down. Rich expressed amazement when he had no fear response whatsoever.

"Gary then focused on several of Rich's most intense war memories, using the same tapping procedure. They, too, were similarly 'neutralized' within an hour. He still remembered them, of course, but they had lost their debilitating emotional charge. Gary taught Rich a technique for stimulating energy points that he could apply to his remaining memories outside the treatment setting. He complied with this homework assignment, focusing on several of the more intense memories. Eventually, there was a generalization effect in that, after a number of the traumatic memories had been neutralized, the others lost their overwhelming emotional charge. Haunting memories simply stopped intruding into Rich's awareness, even at night. Within a few days his insomnia had cleared, and he discontinued his medication. He checked himself out of the hospital shortly after that. At a two-month telephone follow-up, he was still free of the height phobia, the insomnia, and the intrusion of disturbing war memories.

"Most of the twenty V.A. Hospital patients that Gary and Adrienne worked with enjoyed near-immediate, readily observable results for PTSD symptoms that had in many instances resisted years of psychotherapy."

As you can see from this story, change does not need to be long or hard. In a study currently being done by Soul Medicine Institute, we looked at the effects of a half hour session on people with frozen shoulders and other shoulder joint limitations. Some of them had suffered with the same restriction for over ten years.

We measured the maximum number of degrees each shoulder could travel. We then sent the patients in for treatment. One group got EFT. The other got a visualization treatment. Both groups were then compared to a control group without treatment. The EFT group regained most of their normal range of motion, and the visualization group regained a significant amount. The results still held when the patients were re-measured thirty days later. Similar results have been reported for migraine headaches, irritable bowel syndrome, fibromyalgia, blood pressure, depression, anxiety, and even cancer. If a safe and non-invasive treatment lasting such a short while can make such a big difference, the time investment is well worth it.

Evidence suggests that if we practice these epigenetic interventions regularly, we *re-set our internal biochemistry*. We start to produce less cortisol and more DHEA. We then start to feel better, and when problems arise, we deal with them better, and like our pets, return to a serene baseline faster. These treatments have been found to help with releasing emotional trauma in many of the world's disaster zones, and are being used to help severely traumatized populations such as genocide survivors in Rwanda. In Guatemala, which went through a 35-year civil war which touched virtually every family in the country, the use of Energy Psychology has become widespread as survivors cope with the residual emotional impact of an enormous national horror.

**Figure 8: Energy Psychology in the
Mayan village of Solola, Guatemala**

Peak Vitality

Regular practice of epigenetic medicine interventions such as
those in Figure 7 can change the default settings on our cortisol-
DHEA slider. Every time we grab the handle and shift the ratio, we
are setting ourselves up for better health. Eventually, we become used
to a new mix of sugar in our internal biochemical tea. We discover
what it feels like to be normal, which can be a wonderful relief after
years of suffering.

But wait, there's more! What happens when you take very healthy
people and use the same techniques on them?

I recently performed a study with members of the Oregon State
University men's and women's basketball teams. These are not sick
people, but rather people in top physical and mental condition. I
wanted to find out *what happens when you apply these same treatments
to well people.* To control for the effects of players' expectations from
the treatment, and any bias of the experimenters, the players were
divided randomly into two groups based on how high they could
jump. We called one group Team X, and the other Team Y. One team
got EFT. The other got a sham treatment consisting of a reading of
inspirational tips and techniques written by a college basketball
coach. The players were not told which was the real treatment.
Besides their jump height, we also measured how many balls they
could throw accurately into the basket from a set point called the free
throw line.

We then gave each team a treatment lasting about fifteen minutes,
then measured their free throws and jump height again. The results

were sent for analysis to a statistician who did not know which team was which. The results were remarkable. The players who had received EFT got about 24% better free throw results after treatment than the group who had received the sham treatment. So even if you're healthy, epigenetic medicine can move you to new peaks of vitality.

Disease　　　Normal　　　Peak

Figure 9: The Vitality Spectrum

Here's my challenge to you: If these very brief epigenetic interventions can produce a huge boost in your physical performance, quell your anxiety, reduce your suffering from physical ailments, and move you to a biochemical set point that supports healthy cell repair, what are you waiting for? The days of hoping to be pain-free, or just "normal," can give way to a whole new horizon at living at peak day in and day out. There is a world beyond "normal" waiting for you to explore. You have no idea of how good your body can feel till you try it.

Consciousness → DNA → RNA → Protein

Figure 10: The Epigenetic Model of Molecular Biology

Best of all, it doesn't take money, advanced training, or lifestyle change to bring these epigenetic interventions into your life. Consciousness change is free. You can set your alarm clock a half hour earlier and start meditating tomorrow. You can find many Energy Psychology instruction sources with a five minute search on the web. Trying one out will take you all of ten minutes. You can change your beliefs with a snap of the fingers. You can replace your negative visualizations with positive ones starting this very second. You can stop yourself before you say anything negative, and replace it with a positive. You can pray about anything that bothers you, and hand the problem to God. You can join a social circle of optimistic, kind, positive people, and dump the others, starting this minute. None of this is going to cost you anything. But it's likely to improve your life, or even save it. And by embracing peak vitality, you become a force of nature, able to change the world in ways that are impossible when you're miserable, limited and sick.

PART SEVEN

Breaking Through Your Barriers

ANDREW WEIL

Attitude is Everything

Your thoughts, emotions, and attitudes are key determinants of how you age. Let me explain some of their influences on health and the aging process, then give you suggestions for moving them in better directions.

Thoughts (with a contribution from visual images) are primary sources of emotions, behavior, and (over time) of attitudes about ourselves and the world we live in. Most bad moods, most feelings of sadness and anxiety, are rooted in thoughts and habitual patterns of thought. We tend to be unconscious of the connection and untrained in ways to affect it.

The most common forms of emotional imbalance — depression and anxiety — are so common that they can properly be called epidemic. They affect people of all ages, including a large percentage of the elderly population, and certainly compromise quality of life and interfere with healthy aging. Doctors manage them with drugs, antidepressants, and anti-anxiety agents, the key word here being "manage." These drugs suppress depression and anxiety; they do not cure them or get to their roots. I support the use of psychiatric drugs for the short-term management of severe conditions, recognizing that depression can be life threatening and anxiety disabling, but I encourage both patients and doctors to be aware of alternative measures. The drugs can be toxic, can produce dependence, and may change brain chemistry in ways that increase rather than decrease the likelihood of emotional problems in the future.

Andrew Weil, MD, is an internationally recognized expert on medicinal herbs, mind-body interactions, and integrative medicine. He is a clinical professor of internal medicine, as well as the founder and director of the Program in Integrative Medicine at the University of Arizona, where he is training a new generation of physicians. Dr Weil also established the non-profit Polaris Foundation to advance the cause of integrative medicine through public policy, education, and research. He is the author of eight books, including the national bestsellers *Spontaneous Healing* (Ballantine, 2000) and *Eating Well for Optimum Health* (Quill, 2001).

Depression is often rooted in habitual thoughts of worthlessness and isolation, anxiety in thoughts of being out of control or incapable of responding to the daily challenges that life brings. As you age, susceptibility to this kind of thinking can easily increase. In a youth-oriented culture, older people often take on the belief that the worth of life declines with age and find themselves isolated with other old people. Inevitably, your aging body will fail you, forcing you to cut back on the activities of youth, leaving you less in control and more fearful.

I observe that old people often torment themselves with three general concerns: 1) they don't want to suffer; 2) they don't want to be burdens to others; 3) they want the remainder of their lives to be meaningful. These are real issues in later life, and they should be faced rather than obsessed over. The first one requires that you sit down with your doctors and with your family and discuss just what you want and do not want done for you in case you develop a life-threatening illness or are otherwise incapacitated. The decisions you come to should be put in writing and communicated to all who may be involved in your care. The second requires similar advance preparation, in this case with lawyers, family, and financial planners. The third puts more responsibility on you—to think about what activities might enrich your life and increase your sense of self-worth. It may be that service work of some kind or some form of creative expression will do it for you.

Instead of ruminating about the emptiness of life, find something to do.

Conventional psychotherapy can make people aware of the thought patterns that give rise to emotional problems but rarely helps people change them, hence the continued popularity of suppressive medications. I consider it important to learn how to change counterproductive thought patterns. If you do not, you remain at risk for depression and anxiety, both of which are obstacles to healthy aging. Depression can sabotage motivation to treat your body well; it interferes with eating right and getting proper physical activity and sleep, for example, and it can directly lower immunity. Anxiety is associated with increased activity of the sympathetic nervous system, which blocks the relaxation response.

Changing habits of thought requires conscious effort and practice and often outside help. The best sources of help I have found are innovative forms of psychotherapy and Buddhist psychology.

Cognitive behavioral therapy, or CBT, has become popular only in recent years. It traces its remote origins to the teachings of the Buddha and a Greek philosopher, Epictetus (about A.D. 55 to about 135), a former slave who developed a science of happiness. He taught people to live in accordance with nature, to unlearn the habit of judging everything that happens as good or bad, and to learn to distinguish what is within your power to change and what is not. "Make the best use of what is in your power, take the rest as it comes" is one quote attributed to him. Another, quite central to the subject matter of this chapter, is "The thing that upsets people is not what happens but what they think it means."

(A well-known expression of Epictetus's philosophy is the Serenity Prayer, attributed to the late Protestant theologian Reinhold Niebuhr [1891-1971] and much used by Alcoholics Anonymous and other self-help groups: "God, grant me the Serenity to accept the things I cannot change, Courage to change the things I can, and Wisdom to know the difference."*)

Five hundred years earlier, the Buddha taught his followers that unhappiness derives from the incessant habits of judging every experience as pleasant, unpleasant, or neutral and of trying to hold on to the pleasant ones while shunning the unpleasant. He talked much about the tyranny of the undisciplined mind, recommending meditation as a way of developing the ability to observe the process of thought without getting attached to it. Attachment to thought, in the Buddhist conception, leads to emotional imbalance and, in turn, to behavior that increases suffering.

But prayer and meditation are long-term strategies that only some of us are willing to stick with. In the 1970s, a "cognitive revolution" in psychotherapy incorporated the above ideas into modern psychology and inspired the development of practical methods of implementing them. The result is that technologies now exist to help people change their patterns of thought and the emotions and behavior that derive from them. (By "technologies," I mean therapeutic strategies like CBT, not the use of devices.) Moreover, these new forms of psychotherapy are effective—as effective as the latest psychiatric drugs in many studies—and they work quickly, not requiring the commitments of time and money that older forms of talk therapy do.

One prominent exponent of the new psychology is Martin E. P. Seligman, a professor of psychology at the University of Pennsylvania and author of the classic work *Learned Optimism.* Seligman studied differences between persons prone to depression following setbacks

---

*A friend recently sent me a relevant parody titled the Senility Prayer: "God, grant me the senility to forget the people I never liked anyway, the good fortune to run into the ones I do, and the eyesight to tell the difference."

in life and those who bounced back from them. He found the critical difference to be in "explanatory style" — how people explain rejections and defeats to themselves. Pessimists interpret them as confirmation of their own failings and lack of worth, while optimists do not see them as permanent and do not let them affect their sense of self-worth. Seligman's most important finding was that this difference is not just a matter of how people are but rather how people have learned to interpret their experience. Optimism can be learned. And optimists do better than pessimists in almost every aspect of life, including how well their immune systems function.

The process of learning to be optimistic begins with identification of self-defeating thoughts. This is most efficiently done with the help of a trained cognitive therapist. Once you are aware of habits of thought that lead to negative emotions, you can begin to substitute other ones. For example, whenever you notice yourself ruminating on a theme like *I am worthless and this latest setback just confirms it*, you can consciously substitute *This setback is just something that happened; I will get through it, because I am capable and resilient*. The theory behind this work is simple: it is impossible to hold opposite thoughts in mind at the same time, and the impact of a negative thought on feelings can be canceled by thinking a positive one. As you practice the substitution of positive thinking for negative thinking, it will gradually become the dominant habit. This is the cognitive part of CBT. Behavioral therapy can then show you how to change your behavior based on the new ways of thinking.

Psychotherapists, even those steeped in the new psychology, tend to pay more attention to thoughts than to images in the mind, but my experience is that images have at least as much power to call forth emotions and influence behavior and can be dealt with in the same way. That is, the impact of negative images can be neutralized by consciously calling up positive ones.

George Lakoff, a professor of cognitive science and linguistics at the University of California, Berkeley, has written about his experience of the terrorist attacks on the World Trade Center on September 11, 2001, in his insightful book *Don't Think of an Elephant!*:

> I now realize that the image of the plane going into South Tower was for me an image of a bullet going through someone's head, the flames pouring from the other-side like blood spurting out. It was an assassination. The tower falling was a body falling... The image afterward was hell: ashes, smoke and steam rising, the building skeleton, darkness, suffering, death... By day the consequences flooded my mind; by night the images had me breathing heavily, nightmares keeping me awake. Those symbols lived in the emotional centers of my brain.

This is a graphic description of the power of images in the mind and their link to emotions. I can think of many patients I have worked with who have needed to change images they retained, images that stirred up fear and blocked healing. One was a young man with autoimmune disorders that targeted his platelets and red blood cells, causing episodic anemia and bleeding problems. He became critically ill after a serious auto accident, a head-on collision in which an oncoming driver crossed into his lane. The patient felt that it was a suicidal act; the last thing he saw before the impact was the face of the other driver with a frightening fixed grin on her face. She was killed, and his passengers were injured. Although he came through relatively unscathed physically, the psychological trauma of the event — symbolized by that image — activated his autoimmunity with a vengeance. He was unable to erase the image from his memory, and whenever it came up he would relive the terror of the accident. It kept him in a state of mind-body imbalance that fueled his autoimmune disease.

This patient learned the hard way that you cannot get rid of a negative image by trying not to see it, any more than you can get rid of a negative thought by trying not to think it. (Hence the title of George Lakoff's book.) Trying not to focus on images and thoughts you do not want only puts more mental energy into them, making them stronger and more persistent. The only strategy that works is to put energy into their opposites, into images and thoughts that are incompatible with the undesired ones and that evoke opposite feelings. Through guided imagery training, my patient learned to call up an image of a place where he felt secure and happy whenever the visual memory of the accident started to intrude on his consciousness. He practiced this faithfully, and as the unwanted image and its linked emotions faded, his disease remitted.

Here are a few suggestions for managing this aspect of mind as part of a program for healthy aging:

- Learn to identify habitual thoughts and images that produce feelings of sadness or anxiety, particularly those about the process of aging and changes in your body and appearance. If you find this hard to do on your own, consider working with a cognitive therapist, even for just a few sessions. It can be an effective short-term strategy for improving mental health.

- Do not try to stop negative thinking or imagery. Instead, practice substituting positive thoughts and images that evoke feelings of happiness and security.

- Remember that it takes practice to change mental habits. Just keep at it.

Over time, mental habits create attitudes that characterize our ways of looking at life and interpreting our experience of aging. I want to call your attention to two attitudes that I associate with healthy aging: flexibility and humor.

I have already written about the desirability of cultivating flexibility of the body, by stretching or doing yoga, for instance. The more physically flexible you are, the less you will be bothered by the routine aches and pains of aging and the less likely you will be to suffer serious injury if you fall. There is an analogous quality of flexibility of the mind that can protect you from being thrown off balance by the changes of growing older.

Here is an example of what I mean. The older you get, the more likely you are to experience loss—loss of parents, of family, of friends, of mates, of companion animals, of youth and youthful attractiveness, of sensory acuity, of independence, of body functions, possibly even of body parts. Any loss can remind you of all losses, plunging you into grief and despair. But recall the fundamental teaching of Epictetus: "The thing that upsets people is not what happens but what they think it means." He is pointing to a truth of highest importance: we have a choice as to how we interpret our experience, as to what meaning we assign to it.

Buddhist psychology also directs our attention to this potential for choice. It aims to help us experience greater freedom in assigning meaning to what happens through the unlearning of old habits and the practice of new ones. I have watched the successful incorporation of one meditation technique derived from the Buddhist tradition, mindfulness-based stress reduction (MBSR), into medical settings to help the chronically ill improve quality of life and better deal with symptoms that medical treatment cannot change. MBSR is particularly effective with chronic pain, whatever its cause. As patients learn and practice the technique, they have the actual experience of increased freedom in interpreting their sensations. Even though they are experiencing pain, the mind can learn to regard it in a new and different way, one that decreases the stress and anxiety it generates. Then, as one is able to stop defending against the pain, the experience of pain often changes for the better.

This is the magic of which the mind is capable. Knowing it exists and knowing how to take advantage of it are most useful—I would say essential—for healthy aging.

Humor is a related attitude that helps reassign meaning to experience, one that my mother considered vital to graceful aging and maintained even through her final decline. It is a way of seeing the ridiculous side of life, the incongruities and absurdities that can make you laugh even in the midst of misfortunes, especially in the midst of misfortunes. Laughter may indeed be the best medicine and, like optimism, it can be learned. Dr. Madan Kataria, a physician from Mumbai, India, has recently started a practice called laughter yoga, in which large groups of people meet in order to laugh together as a form of physical and mental exercise. He has traveled around the world starting laughter clubs. In them, people laugh for no reason, using yogic breathing techniques at the start and not depending on jokes, comedy routines, or even a sense of humor. Soon the faked laughter turns into real laughter that goes on for fifteen to twenty minutes, leaving everyone feeling great. To be able to laugh at a bad experience—a loss, for instance— is the surest sign of healthy acceptance of it and adaptation to it.*

*One of the most affecting depictions I know of this potential of the mind is in an early (1957) film by Federico Fellini, *Le Notti di Cabiria (Nights of Cabiria)*, about a young prostitute in Rome who truly loses everything, including her life savings and love. Though devastated by what life has handed her, she is nonetheless able to find a different way of interpreting her experience and in a triumphant last scene recover her sense of humor and self-worth. Giulietta Masina, who plays the prostitute brilliantly, expresses this shift of consciousness without uttering a word—so brilliantly that many viewers regard that last scene as the greatest three minutes in the history of cinema. It is a very powerful expression of the philosophy I urge you to apply in your own life.

TOM AMBROSE

The Unknown Zone

"It is a basic principle of spiritual life that we learn the deepest things in unknown territory."

—Jack Kornfield

There are moments in our lives that we will never forget. Like where we were and what we were doing when President John F. Kennedy was shot, or where we were and what we were doing when those two airplanes crashed into the twin towers on 9/11. I remember where I was and what I was doing the moment my life changed forever.

I worked in the training department of a financial institution and was simply doing my job, a job I loved: delivering a training course to a group of colleagues. At one point, I gave the group an exercise to complete, and as they set about their task, I began walking slowly back and forth at the front of the room.

I was at that point in my life when, to the outside world, I "had it all"—loving relationships, third-level education, a job I was passionate about, my own home, and a nice car. I enjoyed a wonderful social life and frequent travel abroad. Yet deep within me, I was not happy. Now that I "had it all," I began to ask myself "Is this it?" I knew I was fortunate and privileged, yet I also knew that something was missing. In my quiet moments, I had begun to ask myself some soul-searching questions, like "Who am I?" and "For what purpose am I here?" As I

Tom Ambrose has worked extensively in training and development, human resource management, and consultancy in Ireland and in the UK. His work has spanned various industries in the private and public sectors. He is a life coach, specializing in anger management and domestic violence prevention. He holds a bachelor's degree in psychology from University College Dublin, and is a postgraduate of the University of Surrey, where he specialized in preretirement and midlife planning. He is a chartered member of the Chartered Institute of Personnel and Development (UK) and is an associate fellow of the Pre-Retirement Association (UK).

walked quietly back and forth, this last question raised its head again, but this time it was phrased differently: "What are you doing here?"

I answered immediately: "I'm helping these people to do their jobs well."

The question was repeated in my mind: "What are you doing here?"

I knew some of the people in the room, one of whom had just returned to work after having her second child. "I'm helping these people to do their jobs well so that they can pay their mortgages and feed their children" was my new response.

This didn't satisfy my interrogative mind either. I heard the question a third time: "What are you doing here?"

I stopped walking. I stopped playing mind games. I stopped in my tracks and answered despondently, "I'm helping a wealthy financial institution to become wealthier."

The game was over. The job that I loved suddenly meant nothing to me. I knew that something significant had happened in that moment of truthful response, but I did not know that this would mark the beginning of an amazing inner journey . . . and my entry into what I now refer to as the "unknown zone."

Without realizing it, I had become one of the "living dead." I was "dead" in my job, and in my life, and although I knew that something was over for me (that "the game was up"), like many people in this place, I continued to go through the motions of my life as if all was well.

But the questions persisted: Who am I? Why am I here? What is my purpose? What is the best way I can live my life in order to make a difference in the lives of others? These were not superficial questions. When I asked who I was it meant who was I apart from my family, the roles I have played, my traditions, my culture, my faith, my work, and my relationships? Who was I apart from all the outer influences to which I had adapted or conformed? Who was I apart from the masks I had donned to seek outer approval? Who was I at my inner core?

These questions were deeply unsettling for me. It is unsettling to realize that you don't know who you are. That you don't know what your purpose is. That you thought you did. But you don't, really. It was unsettling to consider letting go of the familiar and grasping the new (whatever that might be, because it was unknown). I wondered why everybody around me seemed to be able to get on with their lives, and why I seemed to be the only person with questions that haunted me. I felt lost. Bewildered. Afraid. Frustrated. Even though I was surrounded by family and friends, I often felt alone, feeling that nobody understood what I was going through. I didn't understand it myself. When I tried to explain to them what was going on in my life, although they could empathize with me, I felt that they did not really comprehend what was happening, as most of them had not experienced life in this strange place.

Later, I would learn that I was not alone, that there were others dealing with the same process, though some had come to this unfamiliar terrain by a different path. I came to the unknown zone through my work. Others arrive here through the breakup of a significant relationship, the death of somebody close to them, or an illness. Sometimes people arrive through a combination of these or other life challenges. The challenges presented in the unknown zone are unique to each of us, depending on our life path, and are designed to teach us the key lessons of courage and faith. Courage: to question, to ascertain who one is, and to *be* that person. And faith: to trust the process, knowing that it will lead to authenticity and inner peace.

I did not understand this at the time, however. I knew that something fundamental had happened in that moment of truthful response the day I stood before my colleagues, but I did not realize that life would never be the same again. At some level, I knew that obtaining the answers to the questions I was asking meant going within, into stillness and quiet, but I had always led a busy life, and this concept of stillness and quiet was not something that sat comfortably with me. I did not have the discipline of going into that place. Rather than choosing to work on this, or even look at it, I chose to bury myself in my job to escape the relentless questioning.

That is, until I became ill. I was struck with a mystery illness, an exhaustion that the battery of medical tests I underwent could not explain. I was forced by my physical state to take leave from work, which lasted for six months. Lying motionless in bed with an inexplicable illness, I thought about little else but the "big picture," asking myself "What is this illness about?" and "Am I going to die?"

I learned that the only certainty in life is death, and I sought to reconcile myself with it. This inevitably led me to look at questions about spirituality: What (if anything) happens after death? If I die, what will my life have meant? What *is* the meaning of my life? Why am I here? What will I do differently with my life if I ever recover?

There was no medication I could take for this illness. I was advised to rest — simply rest — to allow by body to heal, but I was so hardwired to do, to act, to make it happen that the concept of "doing nothing" was alien to me. I was determined not to give in to this illness. I was afraid that if I did, I'd be consumed by it. First, I tried to control it. But fighting the illness, trying to stay strong, didn't work. As time went on and I was not making progress, I came to the realization that I'd have to try another way. I decided to look for the gift in this illness.

I began to look at it positively. I was being given time off work. It was summertime. How cool was that! It also presented me with time to reflect on the questions I had been asking. I learned to be grateful for this illness, and I began to surrender to it. I started to trust in the unknown zone. The miraculous thing was that the moment I trusted in the unknown zone (the moment I surrendered to the illness), I began to recover. As I recovered, I learned to be grateful for my health. I planned to organize an event that would raise funds for a local charity and I decided to go on a world trip (something I had always wanted to do, but never gotten around to).

When I recovered, I returned to work, but I was now in a different state of awareness. I had become an observer of my life. Watching. Learning. Constantly looking at my reasons and motivations for doing whatever it was that I was doing at the time so that I could question the authentic truth underlying all my thoughts and actions.

"If a fairy godmother landed beside you and asked you what you would choose to do with your life (and she could make it happen regardless of education, finances, or any other considerations), what would it be?"

Ponder this question. It might change your life. It certainly changed mine when I heard it at a seminar I attended shortly after I returned to work. My response was the stark realization that, to satisfy me, work would have to express my soul's purpose, and I embarked on a journey to discover what that might be.

I took a year off and went traveling. I met people and lived in countries of varying cultural and spiritual beliefs. I learned about the difference between religion and spirituality. I read. My focus was now on material that offered insights on the broader questions I had been asking.

When I returned from my travels, the quest continued. I decided to become self-employed. I thought that by changing from financial services to healthcare (making a contribution in an environment motivated by care as opposed to wealth) I would satisfy my soul's purpose. Although I enjoyed this for a while, after a time I outgrew this, too. I went back to study, thinking that a change in career direction would satisfy me, but this didn't last either. I became more aware of seminars, workshops and courses that I had not previously considered and I eagerly attended these. I tuned in to radio and television programs and documentaries that covered any topic that could enlighten me in some way.

During this time, I learned about the chakra system. I learned how the chakras could be linked to certain illnesses, and how they could, in turn, be linked to emotional and spiritual aspects of our lives. I learned that my illness was linked to a search for spiritual meaning. And I also learned a new concept for me: that spirituality is intrinsically intertwined with sexuality.

I now understand that like many people (particularly men) who are in the unknown zone, I was focusing on work for answers to the question "Who am I?" but I was not looking at the two most fundamental topics that underlie our search for authenticity: spirituality and sexuality. I was already exploring questions about spirituality, but I had not stopped to consider questions of sexuality: Who am I sexually? Am I heterosexual or am I homosexual or bisexual or any of these? What is seeking to be expressed within? Is there an aspect of me that I have ignored, overlooked, or suppressed?

It was only when I began to explore the fundamental topics of spirituality and sexuality that energy began to shift, and I started to move deeper into the unknown and open to other possibilities that I had not previously considered or been open to.

I used to think the unknown zone was an event to be mastered, that when I had learned the lesson, or found my soul's purpose, or answered the questions, I'd never have to visit this place again. Given that I distinctly remember the moment I entered the unknown zone (that wonderful day in front of my colleagues), I was certain that I would experience a similar eureka moment that would herald my exit from it. How naïve I was!

I now understand that the unknown zone is a mystery school. It's like the collective gathering of all of the tunnels you drive through when traveling on a road through mountains. Most of the time, you don't know how long your drive through a tunnel will last. It's uncertain (unknown). When you are in it, you cannot turn back. You just have to trust the process, trust that at some stage you will emerge into brightness (the known) again, understanding that you will be five or ten miles further on your journey, knowing that this was a necessary, intrinsic part of the route. The unknown zone is an intrinsic part of the journey called life. The time spent in each unknown zone experience is unique to each individual. It takes as long as it takes! It depends on the issue(s) (whatever needs to be learned), the individual (how quickly or otherwise they rise to the challenges set out for them), and the Universe (sometimes we have to wait until the conditions are ready for something to happen).

And then, the unknown becomes known (we exit the tunnel) — until we meet the next tunnel (the next unknown). And sometimes there might even be several unknown entities in the one unknown experience. I am learning to live with this!

I now understand that the unknown zone is a way of life. The unknown zone *is* life!

I needed to experience the challenges I encountered (initially through work and later through illness) so that I could learn how to *be* in the unknown zone. So I could learn how to *be* in times of uncertainty. It took me a long time to realize that the key to the questions I was asking and the key to the peace I was seeking are not to be found by running around doing (as I did), but by *being*. By going *within*. And do you know how I go within? By breathing.

Recently — very recently — I've learned to breathe. Consciously. To be aware of my breath, my breathing. To experience the air making its way through my nostrils, into my lungs, feeling my stomach expand with this infusion of purity, and then making its long journey up through my body and out through my mouth. When I am aware of this breathing, I relax. It's a reminder that whatever is happening in my life at this time, I'm still here. Breathing. Present. Aware of my breath. Grateful for it. I am reminded that whatever situations have arisen in the past, I've always breathed! Just like I'm breathing now. I am reminded to trust. To trust my breath. To trust. To trust the process…

The unknown zone presents us with trials or challenges that show us how resilient we are when we have the courage and faith *to go within* at times when the path ahead is not clear or feels unsafe. I experience this resilience as a power, an energy — an intuitive awareness and a calm confidence — within me. I literally focus on my breath to get to this place. I know that my initial experience in the unknown zone (although unfamiliar, anxiety-producing, and confusing) was a training ground for me to be able to recognize and draw on this energy. And the lessons of the unknown zone have taught me that this energy, which is available to everyone, lies *within* us.

This energy that is within us is Divine. Divine energy. Divine power. The lessons of the unknown zone are arranged to teach us to know that in unknown times and situations there is a resilience (Divine power) operating within us. And that this Divinity is *real*.

The greatest movement that is happening in our time is an *inner* movement. It's a quiet revolution. It is greater than all the physical, external, global displays of power (the wars in the world) combined.

As in times past, when religious and great spiritual masters drew courage from their inner wisdom in the face of external strife, this inner wisdom is calling us to be the missionaries of its message—to allow the Divine in us to manifest—and to be strong in times of uncertainty (the unknown).

We live in an uncertain time. There will be challenges ahead. We know this. The unknown zone teaches us how to *be* in times of personal uncertainty. The beautiful gift of this lesson is that it also teaches us how to be in times of *global* uncertainty. How to be *in* it, but not *of* it. Like a doctor or a nurse in a hospital, who do their job tending to the ill without physically taking on the illness (they are *in* the illness, but not *of* it), we are shown how to *be* in times of chaos and strife, without succumbing to the malaise around us.

The individual challenges we encounter in the unknown zone are microcosms of the macrocosm. We are presented with challenges. We learn how to deal with these. We learn to live with the unknown entity during the learning (we learn how to *be* in the unknown), and we learn that it all works out. We learn to trust the process. The lessons learned in our personal unknown zone (the microcosm) teach us not only how to be in our own personal lives, but how to be in the unknown zone that is the world (the macrocosm) at this time.

There is no need to fear the unknown zone that is the world. We know that challenges lie ahead, but having gone through personal unknown zone experiences, we now know that we will be led into these challenges *divinely*. The caterpillar cannot become a butterfly, nor can the chick crack out of the egg without some kind of effort. It requires energy and stamina. We need to know that we have the energy and the stamina for the challenges ahead. We need to know that we have this energy and stamina *within* us.

We would not trust somebody to fly an airplane unless we knew they had prior experience and had passed some kind of test to demonstrate their capability. In the same way, the unknown zone presents us with tests to demonstrate *to ourselves* that we are capable. To show us that we have the energy and the stamina for the tasks that lie ahead. To make us aware of our power—Divine power. So that we know for certain that it is there. Within us.

We need to go through the unknown zone to confirm *to ourselves* that we have the endurance, the stamina, the backbone for the job. The job? To know how to be in an uncertain world. To find out who I am, for what purpose I am here, and then place myself in the best position to allow whatever is within me (the divine) to shine for the good of all, regardless of the challenges and uncertainties around me. Simply put, the job is for each one of us to ascertain where our individual piece fits in the great jigsaw puzzle of life! Writing this chapter is a part of my piece of the puzzle. I haven't figured it all out yet, but I trust the process. I'm happy and grateful to *be* in this unknown (now familiar!) terrain.

I've often heard it said: "This is life. It's not a dress rehearsal!" The curtain has gone back, the camera is rolling, we're on. This *is* life! Now. Is the unknown zone beckoning to you? In view of what you now know about the unknown zone, can you accept and welcome it into your life? Can you embrace the personal challenges it holds for you? Can you...trust the process?

STANLEY KRIPPNER

C H A P T E R

43

Searching for New Myths

A t the end of the twentieth century, a number of writers heralded the twenty-first century as one of untold possibilities and new guiding myths. These became known as "Millennium Myths" and portrayed a New Golden Age, the New Jerusalem, the Peaceable Kingdom, or the City of the Sun. In some of these mythic narratives, it was told that Heaven will come down to Earth, or at least that we would experience a kind of earthly Paradise. Other narratives foretold the arrival of the Messiah, the return of Quetzalcoatl, the appearance of Maitreya, or the emerging of the Goddess.

Joseph Campbell cautioned that one cannot predict the next mythology any more than one can predict the night's dreams. He was very clear, however, that if humanity was to survive, its dysfunctional myths must be transformed. Instead of looking at myth from a metaphysical and esoteric perspective, I prefer to define it within the context of common sense. A myth, then, can be seen as an imaginative story about an important, existential human issue that has behavioral consequences. Some myths, such as those held by most religions, are considered to be "sacred"; but the myths that guide our daily behavior are simply examples of "self-talk," even though they often have dimensions of which we are dimly aware.

As you can see, my definition contains words that are psychological in nature rather than esoteric. It encompasses personal myths, which give guidance for daily living, as well as cultural myths that involve

Stanley Krippner, PhD, professor of psychology at Saybrook Graduate School in San Francisco, is a fellow in three divisions of the American Psychological Association (APA) and former president of two divisions (30 and 32). Formerly, he was director of the Kent State University Child Study Center, and the Maimonides Medical Center Dream Research Laboratory in Brooklyn, New York. He is coauthor of *Extraordinary Dreams* (SUNY, 2002) and *Haunted by Combat: Understanding PTSD in War Veterans* (Greenwood, 2007), and coeditor of *Varieties of Anomalous Experience: Examining the Scientific Evidence* (APA, 2000).

gods and goddesses, spirits and demons, and various creation stories. The first part of this definition sees myths as imaginative narratives. Thus, a myth could be one sentence long or it could comprise an entire saga such as *Tristan and Isolde* or the *Odyssey*. These narratives are usually expressed in words, but sometimes they include pictures, architecture, sculpture, dance, or song.

Second, myths concern themselves with important, existential human issues. They are not about trivial matters, but about life and death, birth and rebirth, starvation and bounty, love and war. Myths confront us with the here and now: What do we do when we are in the middle of a crisis? What do we do if we want to make changes in our lives? What do we do when a moral choice is demanded of us? Whether we know it or not, we fall back upon personal, cultural, or religious myths to direct our behavior.

Third, myths have behavioral consequences. They are not just fanciful tales of fantasy, they impact the way we make decisions and live our lives. They play an important role in determining who we will marry, what work we will choose, the way in which we will raise our children, and how we will relate to God, the Tao, the Ground of Being, or whatever we believe to be greater than ourselves. For Carl Jung and other writers who saw the relevance of myths to contemporary times, mythology was of critical importance because it contained profound psychological insights essential to the art of "soul making."

Campbell and Jung both wrote about such critical concepts as the survival of humanity and the fate of the Earth. Yet when individuals think in these terms it can be overwhelming. "Global warming, social crises, and paradigm shifts are happening right now," we think. And then we ask, "What can I do in the face of such tremendous obstacles and such widespread dysfunction?" It is at this point that people need to feel empowered, to know that positive change is possible, and that their vitality—or inner energetic capacity—is the key to mythic change, on both the personal and the cultural levels.

Such cultural myths as the *Iliad* and the *Aeneid*, the Shiva and Shakti stories, and the Australian aborigines' Dreamtime, posed the same questions. These issues also are addressed by religious myths and are proclaimed in churches, temples, and mosques, often giving the worshippers contradictory messages. World leaders, when they make crucial decisions about war and peace, neglect the world of mythology at their peril.

In addition to personal, religious, and cultural myths, there are distinct family mythologies. Some families, for example, expect their children to marry within the same religion, and there is often a crisis if they don't. They reflect one's family mythology, one's cultural mythology, one's religious mythology—or the lack of it. Personal mythologies are derived from our biology, our cultural environment, our interpersonal relationships, and our transpersonal experiences. They are the microcosm of the macrocosm.

Why do I use the term "mythology" as opposed to "world view" or "belief system"? Beliefs are very intellectual; mythology is not only intellectual, it is attitudinal and emotional. Mythology combines the unconscious as well as one's conscious inclinations, and it involves symbols (such as mandalas and crucifixes) and metaphors (such as "running with the wind") in addition to straightforward language.

We can ask if a myth is "functional" or "dysfunctional." Does the myth support a person's life and well-being or does it lead to fanaticism, depression, or constant anxiety? A basic guideline could be that functional myths are those that enhance our vitality, while dysfunctional myths are those that hamper our vitality.

Functional myths will differ from person to person, yet even the most functional mythic structures continually evolve if they are to further a person's optimal adjustment and development. The symbols and metaphors that are inherent in our myths have the power to transcend polarities and unite opposites, fostering a transition from psychic conflict to the achievement of greater unity. Sometimes a superficial mythic structure is revealed by one's "persona," a term Jung adopted from the Greek word for "mask," which is basically a role that is enacted to adapt to the requirements of specific life situations. This persona can reflect deeper layers of the psyche or it can disguise what people actually feel, think, and believe. In other words, it may be a mask for the deep-set personal myths of the person wearing it.

Personal conflicts in one's inner life and external circumstances are natural markers of times of transition. A myth is a narrative, yet beneath the words and images there are feelings, there are convictions, and there are attitudes that we don't often put into words. A personal myth is more than intellectual; it has an emotional component to it. And in working to transform our personal myths, it is essential that we create new myths that pack an emotional punch. Many resolutions for the New Year are never carried out because they are simply words that lack the emotion, the intention, and the vitality to bring about a long-term behavioral change.

Year after year, Marie resolved to improve her habit of procrastinating, but by the end of January she had lapsed into her previous dysfunctional behavior patterns, telling herself, "It really doesn't matter if I put off an assignment or am late for an appointment; everyone else does it." A friend suggested that she add an exercise routine to her agenda. Marie discovered that half an hour of vigorous exercise five times each week provided her with a source of vitality she had ignored. For the first time, she was able to finish job assignments on time, appear punctually for appointments, and turn around the personal myths that she had used as an excuse for procrastination. Other people have enhanced their vitality through changing their diet, by setting aside some time each day for meditation or contemplation, or simply by getting an extra hour of sleep each night.

Personal myths that have been with us since childhood are very difficult to change. Something that is learned early in life is hard to unlearn later in life. We don't just stop what we are doing; we must learn to behave differently. Yet this is not how we commonly go about trying to make change. Instead, people who have the urge to keep doing something over and over again—like a compulsive sex or drug addict, for example—tell themselves, "When I have enough will power I will just stop." But the behavior does not stop because the verbal resolution does not reflect the deepest layers of the addict's psyche.

Embodying a new myth is one of the best ways to make a change. Our bodies usually tell us whether we are ready to make a beneficial change. Our bodies provide clues that inform us in our dreams, in our periods of meditation and contemplation, and in our bodily symptoms, or lack of them. Can we relax easily? Are we beset with aches and pains? If a medical examination can reveal no reason for bodily discomfort, we might look into our personal myths to see if there are some that are dysfunctional and not working on our behalf. Do we spend too much time with people who give us "a pain in the neck"? Do we have "gut feelings" that we ignore when making decisions? Physical vitality usually accompanies emotional vitality, intellectual vitality, social vitality, and spiritual vitality.

I learned a great deal from Albert Ellis, the founder of Rational-Emotive Behavior Therapy. Early in his career Ellis realized that what he was then calling Rational Therapy was not descriptive enough. He changed the name because he understood that it was necessary to bring emotions and behavior into the process. His books and those of Joseph Campbell are just a couple of examples of the many resources that provide access to wisdom on how to change our dysfunctional myths.

We in the "First World" have more options and choices than are available in developing countries. Even so, many people still suffer from depression and apathy. More often than not, this suffering is a part of a collection of dysfunctional personal myths, an insight that the Buddha grasped centuries ago. These men and women have imagined the way their world "should be." When the world does not measure up to their expectations, they suffer. Remember that I defined "myths" as "imaginary" narratives. If we have imagined the world in an unrealistic way, we can learn to imagine the world in a realistic way. And when we improve our mythology on the personal level, we will have an opportunity to change our interactions with people on the social and cultural level.

Jackie Robinson grew up in poverty, but wanted more than anything to play major league baseball. However, the cultural myths of the time told him that black athletes couldn't be baseball players. The best they could hope for was to get a decent job and play baseball on weekends, or perhaps participate in one of the so-called "Negro leagues" that consisted only of black athletes. Robinson started out by playing baseball in one of the "Negro leagues," where he was noticed by talent scouts such as Branch Rickey, a team manager for the Brooklyn Dodgers. Rickey courageously signed him up and that action changed the face (and the color) of baseball. Neither Robinson nor Rickey accepted the current mythologies. Together they made a paradigm shift—not in the world-at-large but certainly in the world of sports.

Jackie Robinson walked his talk, fighting for civil rights the rest of his life, even after he retired from baseball. When he and Rickey changed the mythology of the baseball community, that began to change the cultural myths about racial relations. In time, people began to see that if Jackie Robinson could excel in baseball, and if Duke Ellington could excel in music, and if Harry Belafonte could excel in movies, the cultural myths of the era were dysfunctional. Eventually, African American candidates for the presidency of the United States emerged in both the Democratic and Republican parties.

I am not an advocate of the one-person theory of history, nor do I hold that there is a simple cause-and-effect relationship between events. However, one person or a small group of people can initiate a change; if the times are ready for it the change very well might occur, especially if there are social supports in place to reinforce and to build upon the new cultural myths that have come into play.

But in order to accelerate this process, it would help each of us to know just what we want to do, and to establish a belief system that supports what we want and not what we don't want. One way to discover the belief system that underlies our current personal myths is by finding out the underlying intention that is running our mythology. Here are some myths that reveal various intentions: "I want peak vitality because I want to win every basketball game this season for my team." "I want peak vitality because I want to be a better sexual athlete in bed." "I want peak vitality because I want to live a long and healthy life." "I want peak vitality because my body is the temple of God." "I want peak vitality so that I can do all of my tasks and not be fatigued at the end of the day." "I want peak vitality so that I can be a role model for my children." "I want peak vitality so that I can maintain my mental and spiritual health."

We incorporate belief systems from many sources. Four sources of personal myths are: our biology, our culture, our interpersonal relationships, and our transpersonal experiences. Any of these, alone or in combination, can produce a personal myth. So, peak vitality will differ according to the person and also from gender to gender. Often, peak vitality relates to bodily health, as it is necessary to be in optimal condition if our intention focuses on athletics, on longevity, on sexual prowess, on spiritual development, or any number of other goals.

When I talk about physical vitality I take a very holistic approach, since physical vitality overlaps with emotional vitality, intellectual vitality, even spiritual vitality and social vitality. Vitality is all part of one piece as far as I am concerned. But its components can interact. Instead of complimenting one another they can conflict and interrupt one another if they are not synchronized and headed in the same direction.

When we discuss functional myths and dysfunctional myths, we need to relate them to brain functioning. Our awareness of myths comes in the form of a narrative, and language originates in the brain. But beneath those words, there are feelings, there are images, and there are attitudes that we don't put into words. They are grounded in the brain as well, but in different areas than words and language. So we use the total brain when we form and act out our personal myths. When there is a mythic conflict, there is also a neurological conflict because our neural networks are at odds with each other. This saps our physical vitality, and produces the "mixed messages" that we give ourselves and that we give others.

A person might make the statement, "I have the intention of being personally fit and vital until I am well into my 80s and my 90s." That intention sounds positive, but how deep does that intention go? It might come from the prefrontal cortex, but what is happening in the amygdala and other parts of the limbic system that are associated with emotion? A person may see a Twinkie and go for it because the pleasure centers of the brain are taking over. This part of the brain simply is at odds with the more rational parts of the brain's cortex that knows better.

Then there is the person whose stated personal myth is, "I know that to get through high school and college I have to be focused on my academic work and coordinate my social life accordingly." Once again, an invitation to a party stimulates those pleasure centers and the noble, high-minded intention is tested. Personal awareness and self-monitoring can help us regulate our behavior in ways that keep us focused on our goals, not distracted from them.

Something that is learned is very difficult to unlearn. Old myths die hard. In order to unlearn a dysfunctional personal myth, one does not simply stop in one's tracks and say, "I will better next time." One learns to do something differently by changing behavior, by diligently practicing the new behavior, and by surrounding oneself with people who will support the new behavior. It is not enough to say "When I have enough will power I will just stop." I have heard people apply this personal myth to smoking (and other addictions), to overeating, to gambling, and to procrastinating. The problem is that their will power never quite materializes. They have neglected feelings, emotions, intentions, and the practice that is needed to change a personal myth and to eradicate a harmful habit.

Your body is an excellent guide to finding your bliss. Do you feel good about what you are doing? Do you sense accomplishment when your task is finished? If you have been eating properly, exercising well, and getting enough rest and sleep, you can trust your body to help you make crucial decisions. But if your body is filled with aches and pains that a physician cannot explain, something is disconnected. Re-examine your personal mythology, your work situation, and your love life. Are they working together or are they at odds?

Physical vitality is the bottom line to connecting your bodily feelings with your personal mythology. If your life is synchronized, you will feel vital and energetic. Some exercise programs are designed to coordinate mind and body, feelings and intellect, your inner life and outer life. Yoga is one path, and the martial arts are another; for some people, aerobics is the key and for others, a daily run or swim produces results.

In his classic book called The *Nature of Things,* the Roman philosopher Lucretius discussed free will and how difficult it is to exercise it. He used the term "swerve," and gave several recipes to help people bring "swerve" into their lives. This is exactly what David Feinstein and I have been doing in our workshops and books about personal mythology. We have advised our workshop members and our readers to empower themselves, to take charge of those aspects of their lives where change is possible, and to direct their personal vitality in ways that will anchor those changes. We believe that personal vitality is not just a catch phrase. It is the product of an optimistic, life-affirming, compassionate personal mythology. It starts with the individual, spreads to that person's associates, and can even affect society at large. When enough people transform their personal mythology, there will be changes in family mythologies, cultural mythologies, and even religious mythologies.

The need for a new unifying mythic vision amidst the disorienting cacophony of competing myths presses on. Abraham Lincoln's Civil War-era plea is now more appropriate than ever. In a famous speech he observed that "the dogmas of the past are inadequate to the stormy present. As our case is new, so we must think anew and act anew." This is not inconsistent with the mythology of the North American Iroquois Indians who ask in what way the decisions we make today will affect the seventh generation that follows us.

As a result of studying Native American and other indigenous people's mythologies, some contemporary anthropologists and psychologists have proposed a number of strategies for implementing new functional mythologies:

1) "Learned Optimism" counters the tendency to believe that when something terrible happens to one's group or nation it will be permanent and pervasive.

2) "Subordinate Goals" are mutually beneficial outcomes that transcend the separate interests of conflicting groups.

3) "Synergy" leads to beneficial outcomes that transcend the separate interests of the group and the individual.

4) "Emotional Education" supplements reasoning and critical thinking with the development of children's ability to defer gratification, control their anger, cultivate insight about their own feelings, and develop empathy for others.

5) "Spiritual Enrichment" can clarify an individual's values and ethics, as well as those held by groups.

In conclusion, Joseph Campbell understood the importance of myth for our time, and he popularized this understanding through his books, his lectures, and his television series. Other scholars have reached the same conclusion even though they might use different terms than "mythology." But time is running out. We need to translate theory into action. A living mythology is more than belief, more than attitude, more than emotion. If dysfunctional myths and paradigms are going to shift, the new narrative needs to lead to new behaviors. Vitality is a canvas and we need different paints on our palette in order to create a beautiful picture. Every day, we are painting a self-portrait as well as a representation of our environment. It is naïve to claim that we "create" our reality. But it is accurate to state that we "construct" our reality. To cite Epictetus, a Greek philosopher, our life is determined not so much by what happens to us, but by our interpretation of what happens to us. Thus, our self-portrait is composed, in great part, of our personal myths. We need to select those self-statements, beliefs, attitudes, and behaviors that will keep us physically, intellectually, emotionally, socially, and spiritually vital. Indeed, we must think anew and act anew.

OLIVIA MELLAN

Money Harmony

CHAPTER
44

W e all have a lifelong relationship with money that is either in balance or out of whack. When the relationship is unbalanced, having more money won't help. If you're already an overspender, you'll just spend more. If you tend to worry about money now, you'll worry more when there's more money to worry about. If you're a hoarder, you'll find more reasons to deny yourself pleasurable purchases. You'll never have "enough" money to feel serene, secure, and confident because these feelings cannot be bought or traded on the stock exchange.

Only when you begin moving toward what I call money harmony—a state of being in balance with your money—will you feel free to use money in a way that reflects your deepest values and integrity. And only then will you be able to fully experience peak vitality.

Money Messages, Childhood Vows:

Many of us find it more difficult to talk about money than sex, death, or even childhood abuse. In fact, money may well be the last taboo in today's relationships. Whenever the topic comes up in my therapy practice, it's as though there are ghosts sitting around the room that nobody wants to acknowledge. We have all learned lessons in the past that still influence our present-day attitudes and behaviors toward money.

Olivia Mellan is a groundbreaker in the field of money psychology and money conflict resolution. She is the author of four critically acclaimed books, including *Overcoming Overspending* (Walker, 1997), and *Advisor's Guide to Money Psychology* (Investment Advisor, 2004). She writes a money column, "The Psychology of Advice" in *Investment Advisor* magazine. As a psychotherapist and money coach, she offers teleclasses, and sessions in person and by phone to individuals, couples, therapists, counselors, coaches and financial professionals. She has appeared frequently on Oprah and other media. www.MoneyHarmony.com.

The first step toward money harmony is to examine these haunting memories and experiences. As you think about your own life, how would you answer the following questions? To encourage deeper exploration, I would suggest writing down your responses in as much detail as you can.

1. What are your earliest memories around money?

2. What was your mother like with money? A spender? Saver? Worrier? Avoider? Did she seem relaxed around money? Did she fight with your dad about money?

3. What was your father like? Did he save, spend, worry, avoid, stockpile his money? Did he get along with your mom on financial matters?

4. Do you have any memories about money involving your grandparents or other relatives? Were any of them traumatized by money crises?

5. Were you given an allowance when you were growing up? What for? Any positive or negative memories about how it was handled?

6. Were you influenced by religious messages about money, such as the story of the prodigal son, the warning about rich men not entering heaven, or admonishments that "it is better to give than to receive" or "money is the root of all evil?"

7. Do you have any money memories involving your schoolmates? If so, what conclusions did you draw from their behavior?

8. Do you remember any societal money messages from your youth? Was it important to outdo the neighbors? To marry into money? To do good and not worry about money?

9. Are there any other emotional money memories that may still be influencing you today?

My own most powerful money memory goes back to when I was five years old. Waiting in a Brooklyn barbershop with my dad, I saw a young boy ask his father for a quarter. The father said no, and the child began to sob uncontrollably. I was so gripped by this scene that I vowed then and there never to let myself feel as deprived as that poor kid. Whether I had enough money or not, I told myself, I'd act as if I did. Years later, this vow fueled out-of-control spending that put me deeply in debt. Today I'm a debt-free "recovering overspender" — proof that awareness can lead to change.

By exploring your own money memories, you can identify old messages and childhood vows and compare them to your present attitudes and behaviors. Then, decide whether you need to make some changes to align your present money style with your adult values and the direction of your life.

Exposing the Deficit

Everyone has some aspect of their moneylife that they feel ashamed of, uncomfortable with, or afraid to share with others. Sometimes we even keep these secrets from ourselves. For example, I used to hide my credit card balances from myself, paying the minimum and never looking at the total amount I owed. Once I came to grips with my overspending, I could choose to make changes. And I have: For years now, I've been paying the balance in full every month.

So ask yourself: What money issues do I need to confront and change to feel more whole? What money secrets am I keeping? What's motivating me to keep them secret? Who can I risk sharing them with, to "blow air into the system"? If you follow the emotional, spiritual, and behavioral road map I'm about to outline, you will expose any areas of deficit and will be able to make changes to improve the integrity of your life.

And believe me, you'll feel the difference. Changing your attitudes and behavior will bring about a tremendous increase in self-knowledge, self-respect, self-love, and self-esteem. I see this particularly in women who have been raised to believe they can't handle money. The realization that they can be excellent stewards and managers of their finances has a greater impact on their life, and their access to vitality, than almost any other psychological or spiritual work they have done or might do.

Do Money Myths Rule Your Life?

Studying your memories and secrets can often reveal certain themes that have influenced you. For example, remembering my mother's limited ability to express her love except through buying me clothes, I realized I had learned that money was love—a common money myth.

Money myths are deeply held beliefs about the magical things that money can do for us. Although partly true, they are dangerous because they prevent us from making rational decisions about money.

When you review what you wrote down earlier, do you detect signs of any of the following myths? Which ones resonate with you as lessons you've come to believe?

Chapter Forty-Four

- Money = Happiness
- Money = Love
- Money = Power (whether to do good or to corrupt)
- Money = Freedom
- Money = Self-Worth
- Money = Security

If, say, you've always thought that you would finally be happy once you had more money, try debunking this myth by jotting down one or two activities that make you happy and how much they cost. You may be surprised to realize that some of the best things in life are indeed free (or at least pretty inexpensive).

Another way to shrink the power of a money myth is to look for real-life examples that belie it. For instance, if you believe that money equals security, consider the story of an elderly woman I knew who lived in a Florida retirement community. Although quite wealthy, she had made herself a hermit. She didn't know a soul who could take her to the grocery store or to the doctor's office. If she'd had a stroke, it might have been weeks before someone found her in her apartment. Only a debilitating illness at the end of her life made her reach out to others for the support she needed. Money certainly did not provide enough security for her.

By the same token, you can prove this money myth's weakness by thinking of people you know who feel comfortable and secure among their loved ones and their community, despite being far from wealthy.

As I say, all these myths are partly true. There's no question that financial security is very important. But it needs to be cultivated in a context of life balance and human connection. An obsession with amassing money in order to become more and more secure can hold you back in your quest for wholeness and happiness.

Opening Up Your Money Style by Practicing the Non-Habitual

In the next phase of moving toward money harmony, I'll help you identify your basic money personality. At the same time, I'm going to suggest that you infuse more openness into that personality, whatever it may be, by "practicing the non-habitual." I borrowed this expression from Moshe Feldenkrais because it reflects my belief that self-love and self-respect come from continuing to work on yourself throughout your lifetime. You develop and grow by doing what doesn't come naturally — by practicing new actions and attitudes that develop muscles you didn't have before.

In my work as a therapist, I've identified 10 money personality types. Most people are a combination of types: a spender/money avoider, say, or a worrier/risk avoider. See which of the money personalities listed below describes you best. With each type, I've proposed how to build new muscles to strengthen yourself.

• **Spenders** believe that money is love and/or pleasure. They hate to budget and save, and enjoy spending money for immediate pleasure. When spenders know they should say "no" to themselves (or even "no, not now,") one of two things happens: either they're unable to restrain themselves and spend anyway; or if they succeed in setting limits, they feel intensely deprived and upset or even angry. If you're a spender, you can develop a healthier relationship with money by practicing what is not habitual for you: in other words, by teaching yourself to be more mindful when you spend, by learning to save, and by avoiding places where you tend to buy compulsively or impulsively.

• **Hoarders** believe that money is security. They love to budget and save. To them, it seems wasteful and self-indulgent to spend money on anything they might enjoy right now. They often make good investors, but it's also possible that they keep their money in a cashbox in the closet or in a checking account, where it's close at hand but doesn't grow. Does this sound like you? If so, do what doesn't come naturally, starting with buying something "frivolous" for yourself or a loved one.

• **Money avoiders** don't know how much they spend, save, owe, carry around, or even how much they earn. They sometimes avoid money issues so completely that they're late filing their taxes. It may not occur to them to consult a financial advisor to make their money work harder for them. If they're induced to see an advisor, they prefer to hand over most of the responsibility for managing their money so they can keep on avoiding it. While it's fine to get help, avoiders need to keep educating themselves enough to know if their experts are serving them well. If you're an avoider, open up your awareness by taking on one money management task you usually avoid. (You may want to partner with a friend who's willing to coach you.)

• **Money worriers** worry about money to the point where they can't relax or trust anybody else. Many hoarders are also worriers. If you have this kind of money personality, you may benefit from working with a financial professional whose proficiency helps you worry less. But if you're still beset by anxiety about potential market crashes, bankruptcy, foreclosure, and other money catastrophes, one way to practice the non-habitual is to limit your worrying. When during the day do your worries usually peak? At that time every day, take 15 minutes to write down what you're worried about and what you will do if worse comes to worst. Then (this is the hard part) don't worry for the rest of the day. It may sound unlikely, but over time, choreographed "worry sessions" do help dispel compulsive worrying.

- **Money monks** think that money is dirty and will corrupt them. This group often includes old hippies, ex-activists, and certain spiritual or religious believers. Accumulating wealth is unimportant to them and may even be anathema. If forced to do something with a windfall, they tend to prefer socially responsible investments. To practice the non-habitual, a money monk should take a small amount of money and spend it on things he or she would consider "selfish" — for example, regular massages or a mini-vacation.

- **Amassers** are the folks you see trading investments on their laptops while the rest of the family is on the beach or the ski slopes. The phrase "The one who dies with the most money wins" makes sense to them, because they literally don't know when to quit. If you're an amasser, you're probably accustomed to checking your portfolio every day, if not every hour. To practice the non-habitual, spend an entire weekday without checking up on your money. Then make it two days in a row, and so on, until you can go for an entire week without seeing if you're up or down 0.005 percent. If you're brave enough to avoid money entirely for a period of time (on a spiritual retreat or an all-inclusive vacation, perhaps), it's very possible that your interpersonal relationships will improve exponentially.

- **Money mergers** want to combine all their money with their intimate partner's. However, it can be liberating for both parties to have some separate money to spend as they wish. For women, who often over-give in relationships, having some personal money helps foster healthy autonomy in the midst of intimacy. If you're currently a money merger, consider making an agreement with your partner to put aside a modest percentage of your individual incomes (or merged income) in separate accounts, to use as each of you wishes.

- **Money separatists** are people who don't want to mingle their money with their partner's. But combining money with a partner's can lead to stronger feelings of connection and closeness — especially for men, who by nature are less inclined to merge. If you're a money separatist, see how it feels to merge some portion of your funds for household expenses, savings, and/or an emergency fund.

- **Risk-takers** love the thrill of the ride. Men especially are hard-wired to enjoy the excitement of taking chances, both physical and financial. If risky investments make your eyes light up, expanding your money style to embrace less perilous choices could spare you a metaphoric crash landing. Practice the non-habitual by disciplining yourself to make lower-risk choices with part of your portfolio. This will feel constraining at first, and maybe depressingly tame. But as difficult as it may be, if you're in a relationship (especially with a risk avoider), it will open the door to a new alignment of goals and plans, and eventually to deeper intimacy.

- **Risk avoiders** like to play it safe with their money. New brain research indicates that women find risk actually painful to their nervous system, unlike the pleasurable thrill that many men derive from it. However, unless more women accustom themselves to taking calculated risks with their money, they may outlive their savings. If you're a risk avoider, practicing the non-habitual means taking a little more financial risk for the possibility of higher returns. Try this with only a portion of your savings at first. It may feel like putting on a blindfold and jumping off a cliff, but new choices and creativity will spring from your broadened money consciousness. If you're in a relationship with a risk-taker, the result of your new behavior may well be more closeness and a deeper connection.

Whatever combination of types you are, remember that each money style has both positive and negative qualities. The goal is to figure out which qualities are causing you trouble, either as an individual or in relationships. From there, you can design your own tasks of "practicing the non-habitual"; or, in a relationship, "walking a half-mile in the other's moccasins" — taking on non-habitual activities or attitudes that are more like your partner's.

After taking a non-habitual action, it's important to reward yourself in order to reinforce your new behavior. Also, your progress will be deepened if you write down how it feels to be different as well as your resistance to changing (which is normal, believe me). Eventually, opportunities to practice the non-habitual will become obvious to you. By committing to new behaviors, rewarding yourself for following through, and monitoring your progress regularly, I predict you will be able to anchor these positive changes in your moneylife.

Money Dialogues: Power Tools for Growth and Transformation

Since insight and awareness of past money scripts, present

limitations, and future possibilities can motivate dynamic change, I'd encourage you to continue your work by creating regular Money Dialogues. In my experience, these are the single most powerful tool for transformation and change around money. If you do these dialogues more than once, they will heighten your awareness of the past and present, and will illuminate how changing your attitude toward money can help you reach your life goals.

In your Money Dialogues, you're going to imagine that Money is a person with whom you've been having a lifelong relationship, and you'll talk with Money about how the relationship is going. (If you write down both sides of the conversation, you'll be able to refer to it to identify problem areas and monitor your progress.) Here's how it works:

1. Money walks into the room (or chat room). What do you say? What does Money say? Continue the conversation until it winds down of its own accord.

2. Invite the most influential voices from your past to comment on your dialogue with Money. The first two voices should be your mother's and father's or primary caregivers'. Then imagine the opinions of any other strong influences, such as a spouse or ex-spouse, a money mentor you've respected or feared, your minister or rabbi, a grandparent or godparent. Write down what they say. This is your Internal Commentary.

3. End the exercise with commentary from the voice of God, your Higher Power, or your inner wisdom. This voice will tell you where you need to go to heal and achieve more balance.

This isn't as difficult as it may sound. The way to hear these inner voices is to relax and open your mind to your intuition and imagination. Anyone can learn to do it with a little practice. As your awareness of your thoughts, feelings, fears, needs, and desires evolves, so will your Money Dialogues.

I invite the therapists, coaches, financial professionals, and counselors who attend my money harmony teleclasses to write a Money Dialogue every week. As time goes on, this dialogue often moves from their general money relationship to a more targeted topic—their career, say, or a specific financial decision. Often a dialogue begins with money and ends with another aspect of their life.

Dana, one of my teleclass participants, found her Money Dialogues to be especially revealing and inspiring. Here's an early dialogue she gave me permission to share:

Dana: How's it going, Money? It feels a little strange writing to you, though I know it's a good thing to do. So how have I been treating you lately?

Money: Well, you've been a tightwad, as usual. You walk around with fear all day long. You have no trust whatsoever. You treat me like you do your time. You rarely have time during the day to enjoy yourself, and you rarely have time to enjoy me. You're so darn serious!

Dana: That's because I don't believe you'll take care of me. I think I have to work my butt off to keep you around. I believe that all of this money stuff is supposed to be hard work. Actually, I believe life is supposed to be hard work...no time for fun and play. If I relaxed, I'd never get anywhere.

Money: Boy, for such a spiritual person, you sure are filled with ego and fear when it comes to money. Anytime you're feeling so much fear and tightness, it's a guarantee that you're not connected with spirit. You're coming directly from the ego.

Dana: Yeah, no kidding. Ego, ego, ego. It's hard to let go of it in real life. Easy concept to grasp, not so easy to live. What can I do to start treating you, and my life, differently? I'm so tired of trying to run my money, career, and life from my ego. Any suggestions?

Money: *Hello!* That's a no-brainer. Just lighten up and have some fun, why don't you? You know that what you really value most—more than me—is your time. You don't even have to spend more money to start having more fun. Start spending your time on yourself and your relationships, since you are craving that so much. Give yourself the gift of time for *you*. Instead of worrying about your career and about money so much, lighten up, relax, enjoy. Quit telling yourself that you don't have time for you.

Dana: Wow. I know you're right. Thanks for your wisdom and honesty. I truly appreciate it. It's just so hard to make time for me. But I will—I promise I will.

That's Dana's first Money Dialogue. We learn that she's a hoarder and a money worrier who doesn't take enough time to enjoy her money and her relationships. We also learn that she is longing for more time to relax and enjoy her life, but so far she has been unable to make this happen.

Next, Dana asked her past influences about this dialogue. What they "told" her helps explain where her workaholic and worrier tendencies originated, and why she might feel undeserving of quality time and abundance in all aspects of her life. Last, her take on how God would comment casts light on the past and offers hope for the future.

Mom: You really shouldn't spend any money on yourself, Dana. You know we don't have enough money for you. You'll just have to do without. I'm sure you'll grow out of your money needs anyway, just make do for the time being. And why spend time on yourself. If you shouldn't spend money on yourself, why bother spending time on yourself? It's not like you really matter that much anyway. The real purpose of your being here is to do the things I want you to do — not to do the things that you want to do.

Dad: Whatever you want to do is fine with me, Dana. I'm too busy dealing with my own life to care too much.

God: Dana, you are a very beautiful child. Can you see the gift that you are being given? This is your opportunity to learn how to love and to truly take care of yourself. Your mom was just trying to figure out her own life. She didn't mean anything personal against you. She was fearful. Her fear is your gift. And your opportunity is to learn how to love yourself and give yourself the things you need. You value time. Time is available to you right now. Just make a choice to take more time for you. Don't worry — I'll be there with you to walk you through it. I love you, and you have some incredible gifts to offer the world that will only shine all the more once you start taking time for you.

Didn't you breathe a sigh of relief when reading the empowerment and blessing of the God commentary in this Money Dialogue — especially after the painful and disparaging voices of Dana's mom and dad?

I've never read a Money Dialogue I didn't like. They are always moving, funny, wise, educational, and often deeply inspiring. They move us along the path to money harmony, as well as to other kinds of harmony in our lives. They give us energy, hope, and new directions to pursue in our journey of transformation.

If you create Money Dialogues of your own, I recommend doing them every week for a month to see how they evolve. Once you start, you can choose to do more specific money dialogues about asking for a raise or promotion, taking a new job, going back to school — whatever conflict or difficulty you may be facing. Sometimes Money will function a little like a Higher Power, inner wisdom, or God, and sometimes it will be neutral or even adversarial. But if you keep at it, your dialogues will help you identify stuck places from the past, the influences that helped create them, and possibilities for the future. As your awareness increases, you'll move toward more and more inner peace and vitality.

During the weeks of our class, Dana practiced identifying her money personality, practicing the non-habitual, and creating regular

Money Dialogues. In this process she experienced a palpable shift not only in her relationship with money, but also in other areas of her life. Money became a source of wisdom, urging her to trust herself and to connect more deeply with her spiritual center. This would give her more energy to put out the word about her work. With gratitude, she told Money that she felt "excitement and a quickening in (her) heart," and knew that Money was right.

One of the most interesting aspects of Dana's Money Dialogues was the evolution of her parents' voices. Here's how her last dialogue ended:

Mother: Dana, this is beautiful. I know you can trust yourself; you have so much wisdom. I'm sorry I was so controlling when you were younger. I only wanted you to be confident in yourself. I can see that my attempt to control you only caused you to doubt yourself and to not believe in yourself. Please know that I support your own internal guidance more than anything else. Even though I didn't know how to encourage you to listen to your internal guidance when you were a child, I love you and I'm proud of you.

Father: Dana, I'm proud of you too. I think you have so much to offer this world. You really do. I know I wasn't there for you when you were growing up. And sometimes even now, I don't know how to be there for you. But I'm trying to be different. Please know that I love you, and that I think you are a really special woman.

God: I can't tell you anything that you don't already know. You are powerful beyond belief. All you need to do is take the time to connect with me. I will always be here for you. You are surrounded by more support than you've ever dreamed of. More support than you are capable of comprehending. But know that even though you can't *see* this support, it is there, helping along your way—all the time.

If you follow the road map I've provided here—exploring your money messages and childhood vows, identifying your money myths and debunking them, exposing your money secrets to the light, and writing Money Dialogues to synthesize your past, your present, and your future—I guarantee that you will begin to enjoy the fruits of money harmony and find serenity in other areas of your life. The increased self-esteem and self-love that you'll experience will become a foundation for peak vitality.

Enjoy your journey toward money harmony. The more aware you are of your money as a tool to help reach cherished goals and dreams, the more boundless a source of energy it will become.

NANCY AUSPELMYER

Painting
Vibrant Lifescapes

Imagine preparing to travel to any given destination, whether in a familiar neighborhood or across the globe. What would be the likelihood of reaching the destination if the starting point were unknown? Even if the destination were clearly envisioned and committed to memory, we would have very little chance of reaching it without a road map, a plan. Any travel plan is contingent on at least two points: where we are starting from and where we are headed. With this information, we can effectively determine the best way to get there. We have become quite adept at choosing what we would like to be, where we would like to go, and what we would like to have, without clearly determining where we are in the present moment and what choices and changes will lead us closer to our intended destinations.

Life happens. We are born into families and situations that shape our beliefs, provide the framework for our life journeys, and establish the background against which our identities and self-images form. The expectations and needs of the people in our lives and the feedback we get from our actions often determine the next steps we take in our lives. We weave our life stories, drawing situations to us that substantiate and reinforce the beliefs we hold about ourselves at any given moment. Sometimes we are happy, and at other times, we just go along with what we feel is expected of us, meandering our way from one day to the next. At the mercy of external forces to provide us with validation and decide our fate, we set our sights on

Nancy Auspelmyer is a catalyst and facilitator for growth and change, offering insight and opportunities for healing and self-exploration. As a life coach, group facilitator, and energy healer, she offers individual sessions, classes, and group travel to promote healing and transformation. With thirty years of experience as an electromechanical designer and drafter, she is able to translate information from conceptual models into readily usable and understandable formats. She and Ling Chen developed and run Lifescape Services, providing services and tools for healing, well-being, and self-exploration. More at www.lifescapeservices.com.

goals and achievements that if met, urge us onward, and if not, leave us feeling frustrated and unfulfilled. We live in a world troubled by dissension, chaos, and the daily struggle for survival, where single events and natural occurrences can alter landscapes and impact lives without a moment's notice. The cohesiveness of our existence can be threatened when adversity strikes, presenting us with challenges and obstacles that have the potential to paralyze us with fear and misgiving. Caught up in a whirlwind of judgment and blame, we can easily become disoriented and distracted, living fretful and reactive lives, forgetting that we are souls incarnate, capable of purposeful and joyful living in a world we can consciously shape with our intentions, thoughts, and actions.

We are becoming increasingly aware of the effect the foods we ingest have on our bodies. Through conscientious choices and a regimen of exercise, we can promote physical stamina and cellular well-being. But we are more than physical beings, and physical balance is not enough to maintain health. Regardless of our level of awareness, through the choices we make, we create, characterize, and sustain our lives through our intentions, thoughts, and actions. Woven together, consciously and synergistically, in an environment conducive to growth and change, they can become tools of transformation in our pursuit of our personal and collective destinies. To achieve our goals, we must not only be decisive in our choices of direction, but determined and courageous, as well as willing to acknowledge our current point of reference and make the changes needed to lead us closer to our destination.

The course of our lives is dynamic, unfolding with every choice we make. The state of our present lives reflects choices we have already made. If we step back and look at the meanderings our lives have taken thus far, we will see that every new experience and opportunity we encountered was the result of some decision, some choice we made. With this realization, we may become concerned that we have the propensity for making wrong choices that will adversely affect our future. We may choose to postpone making the changes that will improve our lives, or choose to make no decision at all, content to maintain the status quo. It is not only us we affect when we do this, however. Opting for postponement or avoiding a decision is a choice for non-growth and non-change. Retreating to the safety and shelter of our own little worlds, wrapping ourselves in the illusion that we are safe there, free from harm and from doing harm, contributes to global disharmony by perpetuating separateness rather than fostering unity and cooperation.

The integrity and well-being of humanity is dependent on

each and every one of us. As individuals, societies, and a global community, we know things have to change, but we cannot begin to effect change in the world until we begin to work on ourselves. "You must be the change you wish to see in the world," Mahatma Gandhi told us. It is our responsibility, as individuals, to make honest assessments of our lives at any given moment to determine what changes we can implement that will lead us closer to experiencing personal peacefulness, joy, and fulfillment on a regular basis. It will take awareness, courage, and determination to consciously reshape ways of life that have become comfortable and familiar. We will be required to step into moments of stillness, rich in revelation, seeking to know more about ourselves. As Thomas Merton so aptly wrote: "In the last analysis, the individual person is responsible for living his own life and for 'finding himself.' If he persists in shifting his responsibility to somebody else, he fails to find the meaning of his own existence."

As we consciously choose to look objectively at various aspects of our lives, away from the cacophony of voices that scream our name and demand our attention, even for moments at a time, we may glimpse our authentic selves and evaluate our lives from new perspectives. Encouraged to find meaning, ponder possibilities, and stretch to new heights, even in the face of adversity, we will begin to sense the interconnectedness of events in our lives and understand that we are part of a greater pattern, written and woven by the choices we make.

Our ultimate goal is to be in alignment with soul, our authentic selves, living purposeful lives, in the flow of energy, where colors are more vibrant, relationships more meaningful, and our sense of Oneness is self-evident. In this place of authenticity, we will find an endless stream of creativity and the courage to nurture our dreams, utilizing the gifts and talents available to us to better our world. We will readily see the signposts at the crossroads in our lives, realizing, without any doubt, that the choices we make at any given moment determine the opportunities that present themselves to us in the next. In this place, we will also perceive challenges and obstacles as opportunities to know more about ourselves, to acknowledge what is no longer working for us, to help us grow in perspective and humility, and to be more creative in our choices and responses as we continue to sculpt our lives.

When we are out of alignment with a purpose that brings joyful fulfillment and an endless stream of energy, we are in discord, depleting our energy reserves. Soul patiently and endlessly seeks our attention, but are we listening? Do we leave the answering machine on to pick up and record the message, so we can give it our full attention at some point in the future when we have the time and the inclination? We all have things to do, tasks to complete, and obligations to fulfill. But we also have the responsibility to fulfill our personal destinies. What if we were to see the goal as one of transformation, of creating a workable plan to get into the flow of life-sustaining energy, living our lives centered in joy and peace?

The key to such transformation is to prepare the Lifescape, the magical, reflective world of mind, as dynamic as our thoughts and visions, and as individual and unique as its inhabitant. An energetic projection of our perceptions and thoughts, sustained by our reinforcing actions that determine the outcome of our intentions, it is the cyclic world of cause and effect. Defined by us, by the very nature of our thoughts, it remains attached to us through the energetic bonds that created it. Here, like seeds in a well-tended garden, intentions can thrive if nurtured by soul.

Tending the physical gardens or landscapes around our homes, we create peaceful places and areas of respite, central themes, and splashes of color. Through our efforts, the landscape becomes a reflection of our vision. The amount of effort applied to the landscaping process is evident in the results, and routine maintenance ensures the garden will continue to thrive as intended. When the season for growth has ended, we lovingly harvest the fruits of our labors and prepare the garden for the quietude of winter where we will, perhaps, dream the changes that will bloom in next year's garden. Although the gardens of our lives, bearing the fruits of our efforts, respond essentially the same, we have neither been willing to flow with the cycles nor as diligent in our efforts.

The conditions and climate of the Lifescape determine what and how much can grow there, much like in the landscape in our physical world. Intentions sown with care, in an environment conducive to growth and supported by authentic and focused efforts, will manifest in our lives as envisioned. We need only determine how to make the changes necessary to best nurture them.

Intention Is Not Enough

Energy follows thought. We may truly have every intention to complete a project, to reach a desired goal, to make lasting changes in how we live our lives; we may say mantras and make symbolic gestures to no avail. Our thoughts take on a life of their own, weaving their way in and around our intentions, energy following the thought to other thoughts and suppositions, distracting us from our original goals or prohibiting us from taking some actions while allowing others. If we can alter the course of our thoughts, in support of our intentions, we can change the direction of our lives. If we intend to plant a physical garden, but make and apply no effort, no energy to do so, no garden, regardless of how keenly we envision it, will materialize. The energy must follow the thoughts and intentions to bring the intentions into existence.

"We must make the choices that enable us to fulfill the deepest capacities of our real selves."

—Thomas Merton

Evaluating the Lifescape and the Nature of Soul

Since our ultimate goal is to be in alignment with soul, we must have a relative understanding of it before we can effectively create the Lifescape that will nourish it and allow it to flourish. Since we may be only vaguely aware of our soul-encoded potential, the expression of the authentic self, we can begin by recognizing signs that indicate its active presence in our lives. In addition to moments of peace and inexplicable joy, the authentic self is most easily recognized by contentment and anonymity in service. Without need for recognition, it quite accommodatingly slips into the background as ego-driven components of the personality vie for position.

Inactivated, the seeds of our perfected expression lie dormant, awaiting conditions conducive to their awakening. The Life Force Energy that frees the seed from the pod is the same that inspires us to reach our potential. With mind as the gatekeeper, we have the choice and opportunity to provide the environment that will nurture the growth and expression of our perfected selves.

Within any garden, elements compete for dominance. Weeds threaten to take over with flowers of their own, choking out the tentative growth of the delicate flower in the process. Contradictory and competing thoughts and intentions that demand our attention and dominate our time fragment our energies, delay, and sometimes prohibit the growth of soul's full expression. When the weeds and obstacles to growth are eliminated, our intentions can bloom like flowers in our well-intended garden. Recognizing and acknowledging the competing elements within us and distinguishing between ego-driven growth and authentic growth present a challenge, however.

Mind is the powerful gatekeeper, the filter through which all thoughts and intentions pass and from which the choices are made that govern the actions that will follow. Mind manages our perceptions, our perspectives, the flow of energy, and the use of our resources, and additionally has the ability to open channels to understanding and guidance from diverse sources, including soul. Mind is most likely to open to other possibilities when the ego-self is not threatened and when we value its learned and acquired skills and attributes as vital resources in soul-serving enterprises.

As we begin to explore the Lifescape and contemplate our choices, remember that the purpose of the tiny seed, encoded with all it needs to bloom to its greatest potential, is to become itself and it falls to us to provide the climate and conditions necessary to support its cycle of life.

Energetic Flow

Energy needs to flow freely through the body if we are to experience health, well-being, and clarity of thought. We depend on energy to transport much-needed cellular nourishment, fresh ideas, and inspiration. When we are tired, fatigued, and depressed or when our immune systems are compromised and we experience illness, energy is not flowing freely in the body, and it becomes extremely difficult to step aside from our physical needs in order to focus on our thoughts. Trapped in the body, the accumulating toxic and stagnant energies must find avenues for release so that health and balance can be restored. Similarly, mounting frustrations and conflicting personal agendas impose restrictions on the flow of energy and, unless cleared, make it challenging if not impossible to formulate viable plans for change and actualization, much less be attuned to soul.

In her book *Energy Medicine,* Donna Eden succinctly explains:

"When all your energies are brought into harmony, your body flourishes. And when your body flourishes, your soul has a soil in which it can blossom in the world. These are the ultimate reasons for energy medicine—to prepare the soil and nurture the blossom."

Energy clearing, centering, and balancing disciplines, of which yoga and energy medicine are but two, can help reestablish and maintain the energetic environment conducive for the flow of energy through the body, making it easier to maintain focus and achieve goals. Once we effectively balance the flow of energy, regular intervals of quiet and reflection can open other channels of energy so inspiration can flow and soul can begin to stir.

Authenticity

Once our energy begins to flow more freely, it becomes easier for us to assess the nature and condition of the Lifescape. If we planted artificial flowers in the garden, they might look lovely from a distance, all perfectly shaped and arranged, and unchanged by fluctuations in prevailing conditions. But they will never be more than they are at the time of the planting. Not being rooted, they can be easily dislodged; not part of a life cycle, they have no potential for growth. The same is true of efforts and endeavors not connected to our authentic selves. While some activities and pursuits may have some intrinsic value in our lives, if they do not support soul's expression, they are merely separate endeavors that distract and fragment our focus.

Endeavors that authentically reflect and embellish the nature of soul are nearly effortless, are creative and service oriented, and align us with the flow of an endless stream of energy. We always have the choice to determine where we will apply our efforts and to determine if they support or hinder the authenticity we hold within.

Gifts and Talents: Our Natural Resources

As complex, multifaceted beings with an enormous capacity for compassion, vision, and transformation, each of us has gifts, skills, and talents. Some we acquire through training and education, while others are inherently part of us. Together, they provide the toolkit of resources that we carry with us throughout our lifetime. As our personalities develop, based on the roles that define our place in the world, we learn to control the resources at our disposal to fulfill what we perceive to be our needs. They are reflected in the Lifescape, evident in what we do with our lives, although not always related to our livelihood. It is to be hoped that these resources are central to our daily activities, though we may not be consciously aware of them.

With soul come natural skills and talents that require acknowledgment and incorporation into our everyday lives, in the ways we express ourselves and make our statements in the world. Mind and soul become equal partners in the acquisition and utilization of our resources and our subsequent quest for fulfillment. Through mind, we decide what to learn, when, and from whom, while soul prompts, influencing our choices. When permitted to do so, soul will make subtle suggestions to us about complementary skills we could acquire to support those we already possess, as in instances when we are suddenly or inexplicably drawn to a teacher or teaching.

We all have the potential to live peaceful, integrated, and joyful lives. In each of our lives exists a central theme or focus that would benefit from our attention and the application of our energies. By altering our perspective, we can modify the perception we hold of ourselves and our true capabilities.

Perspective and Perception

Our perspective is predicated on the viewpoint we have at any given moment. Behind the scenes, soul is prompting while mind is interpreting through the filters of our perception. With mind alone in charge, and without living from the centered vantage point of soul, our viewpoints will change, depending on circumstances in our lives.

We are all products of our upbringing and environments. Though it may be challenging to step aside and view life from a neutral stance, it is not impossible. Energy is less likely to be diverted and blocked in this stance of neutrality, and we are more apt to perceive that not only are we the life we create with our thoughts, but we are also capable of consciously cultivating the gardens of our intentions. By consciously shifting our perceptions of the world and embracing new paradigms, we will decisively change our lives.

Typically, we tend to focus on what we do not have, what is missing, or how we lack some level of achievement we had set for ourselves, rather than on the blessings and riches to be found in our gifts, our skills, our talents, and the people that are close to us. Perhaps we depend on validation from external sources, unsure of our inherent capabilities, and move in directions that scatter the very life force that can deepen our relationship to ourselves. Ego, an element of mind that governs perspective, is extremely judgmental and competitive, focused primarily on its own comparative involvement in the secular world and orchestrating our priorities to satisfy its objectives.

With free will, we have the power to stop the cycles that keep us perpetually wanting. We can choose how we view the world and what we perceive to be truth. If we assume the perspective that we are blessed and that all things are possible, perhaps we will see that the stories of our lives are not yet complete, and that with effort we can embellish a central theme or premise. With every prayer of gratitude we offer, new blessings may find their way to us. If we begin to earnestly look at situations in our lives from new and different perspectives, we may glean new and valuable insights, different from what we first imagined.

We are far more attuned to the natural cycles found in our physical world. Do we walk away from the bud that takes its time revealing its potential in our garden, fearful it that might not be as beautiful as the full-blossomed flower in our neighbor's garden? Or can we believe that with care and nurturance, our own flower will bloom in colors that mirror our soul in its own season?

What we perceive to be the truth will determine how we perceive the world. If we trust that the gardens of our lives, planted with will and intention, will bloom when nurtured and tended with respect and care, then our efforts can be applied to keeping the garden free from clutter and the toxic contamination of thoughts gone unchecked. By becoming aware of our thoughts and projecting them as positive affirmations, we can effectively change the quality of our experiences by changing our perception of them.

The only time available to us is this moment. The moments of yesterday are a thing of the past and those of tomorrow have not yet arrived. By willingly tending to the energy of our thoughts as they materialize, pulling them like weeds from the garden when they threaten new and tentative growth, and with a bit of coaxing, we can transform our thoughts into the fertilizer that will encourage and nourish the developing shoots of the seeds we have sown.

We are organic beings living in an organic world, subject to and influenced by thoughts and beliefs, perceptions and perspective. Our bodies are 70 percent water, on average, according to Masaru Emoto, who has demonstrated and documented how thoughts influence the crystalline structure of water. If thoughts can change the structure of water crystals, then they have the potential to affect us in profound ways. The choice is ours whether we give them the power to harm us or to heal us.

If we want to affect our world positively, we must set goals to monitor our thoughts and to minimize nonsupportive behaviors. Through conscious effort, we can begin to live from an authentic perspective with the perception that all things are possible.

How Will We Know?

In unexpected moments of joy, we may realize that resistance, fatigue, and tension momentarily cease to exist. Inexplicably in the flow, where all things are suddenly possible, we are in touch with our creativity, tapping into our inner reserves. When we are in this mode, new opportunities unexpectedly appear and new ideas take root, transforming the Lifescape into one that is vibrant and full of promise.

Living from soul does not guarantee passage without trial, however, for it is through these trials that we cultivate strength of spirit, gathering insight and wisdom into the meaning of our experiences. There, we begin to see the connections between seemingly chance encounters and random happenings.

The journey into the coming age demands that we create and prepare the Lifescapes that will nurture our souls. Only then can we stimulate and sustain the fire of spirit within each of us to keep humanity moving forward in harmony and cooperation. Tomorrow's world is dependent on the choices we make today. Choosing to tend the gardens where intentions, thoughts, and actions impact our personal journeys makes it more likely that our collective journey will be richer and more meaningful. By honestly exploring and evaluating the Lifescapes in which we already live, we may come to know ourselves, perhaps for the first time, so that we can reshape and restructure our lives, in service and compassion, rather than seeking to have the world and the people in it comply and conform to our limiting personal view. It is a matter of choice.

"We shall not cease from exploration
And in the end of all our exploring
Will arrive where we started
And know the place for the first time."
—T. S. Eliot

Some Daily Suggestions to Enhance Your Lifescape

Before you put your feet on the floor as you get out of bed in the morning, affirm a soul-sustaining perspective by saying: "Today energy flows in me and through me as I seek soul's presence in all my endeavors."

Smile consciously and open your arms wide with the intention to receive the blessings that are all around you. Look at the positive aspects of a difficult situation that has occurred in your life. Then write down something positive about today.

Surround yourself with scents and sounds that promote a feeling of peacefulness.

Do some energy work of your choice to maintain the flow of energy, to foster change, and to support growth.

Set an achievable goal and evaluate whether your daily activities support your goal.

Become aware of your thoughts, writing them down in a journal to evaluate their relevance in your unfolding life story.

Find a "Gratitude Rock" and keep it in your pocket. Make a conscious effort to find something new and different to be grateful for every time you reach in your pocket and touch the rock.

Marianne Williamson

CHAPTER
46

Rituals for Rebirth

In the realm of human relationships, we participate in three distinct levels of interaction with each other, which I call "teaching assignments." The first, which I call the "casual relationship," may be as seemingly inconsequential as a smile exchanged in an elevator. The second, the "fairly intense learning experience," involves an ongoing interaction with someone that lasts for some period of time, say until you move to another city or change jobs. The third I dub the "lifelong assignment." These connections span a lifetime, such as relationships with family.

In all of our relationships, whether fleeting or enduring, one of our most important roles is to support the greatness of other human beings—to cheer each other on as we endeavor to become the people we are capable of being. Very few of us become our best without someone around cheering us on. Even in the most casual of encounters we can act as part of the cheering team for another. It's amazing how a passing comment or the kind smile of a stranger can create just the breakthrough we need.

The attack-and-defend mentality that predominates within our social fabric disallows healing in relationship and no ascension can occur. On the other hand, when we see forgiveness as our function, and relinquish all other goals we have invented for ourselves, relationship can serve the upliftment of all humanity. It really is that basic. This one imperative forms the basis of our capacity to be part of

Marianne Williamson is author of many books. One of her first, *A Return to Love*, (Harper Collins 1996), based on the teachings of *A Course in Miracles*, led to international renown. Her latest is *The Age of Miracles* (Hay House, 2008). In 1989, she founded Project Angel Food, a meals-on-wheels program that serves over 1,000 people homebound people with AIDS. She is president of The Peace Alliance, which supports legislation in Congress to establish a Department of Peace. In December 2006, a *Newsweek* magazine poll named Marianne Williamson one of the fifty most influential baby boomers. www.Marianne.com.

the cheering team and dedicate our relationship to the advancement of the whole. But how can we unlock our sense of unforgiveness when our judgments are so strong?

In ultimate reality, *everyone* is "like us." How can this be? Carl Jung posited the notion of the collective unconscious, wherein all humans are said to share certain mental images, or archetypes. *A Course in Miracles* takes this concept one step further, stating, "Our smallest judgment adds to war, and our smallest forgiveness adds to peace." And, "If you go deep enough into your mind, and deep enough into mine, we share the same mind." It's like the aspen trees in Colorado; they are actually all part of one root system. Since all minds are joined, conflict between any two of us contributes to war, and reconciliation between any two of us takes us to peace.

The illusion that we are separate is the source of all our pain. But how can we see the core humanity — the place where we all have the same needs and are part of the same family in a society that always jumps to attack-and-defend? Escaping the toxicity of our judgments, first within ourselves, and then in the world, takes a bit of Divine intervention, and that is what a true spiritual path offers – Divine help in shifting our thought patterns from fear and blame to love and blessings. A true spiritual path is a mind training in which we build the mental musculature to think in a different, more loving and more forgiving way.

We're constantly in situations where something isn't working the way we wish. We instinctively blame someone else, or at least some factor outside ourselves. Yet, *A Course In Miracles* says, "Only what we are not giving can be lacking in any situation." So to train your mind to think along those lines – "What am I not giving here?" "Who am I not forgiving?" "What am I not contributing?" "What is the goodwill that I am withholding?" – radically transforms where we dwell within a situation. And where we will dwell within a situation determines whether or not we have any transformative power there.

A journalist interviewed three people who lost loved ones at the World Trade Center. The reporter asked each one of them if they wanted revenge. None of them wanted revenge. All of them wanted the violence to stop. The only one who wanted revenge was the journalist! Heartbreak has a way of taking us back to our "right minds," and our realization of our oneness with other people. When war is theoretical – when someone else is fighting it, or when you can distance yourself emotionally from the horror of it – it's easier to commit to it. The closer violence comes to you, the more committed you become to try to transform it.

This is not to say that all is in Divine Right Order and all we have to do is accept things as they are. Slavery is not Divine Right Order; a holocaust is not Divine Right Order. But I do believe that every situation has the potential for Divine Right Order, because no matter where we go, God goes with us. The philosophy of *A Course In Miracles* is that, while we have freewill and can direct our minds away from Divine Order, God has placed the Holy Spirit in our minds to turn us back to the Divine when we ask Him to. In that sense, all things contain the seeds of Divine Right Order. If we can meditate on that idea and bring forth that reality, we can begin to make a difference in the world.

To begin the shift from separation to relatedness, we can visualize a golden light radiating from our hearts, which extends beyond our bodies and casts a light unto the entire world. I invite you to imagine a friend or foe standing next to you and to see the same light in them, and let their light merge with yours. It would be a very good idea for all of us to do this with the Moslem world in general.

On another level, this world in which things are not in Divine Right Order is itself a vast mortal hallucination because, in fact, only love exists as an eternal and ultimate reality. But that doesn't mean that we are to avoid the world or ignore it, or claim that it's in Divine Right Order. It's absolutely not in Divine Right Order and our mission on this earth is to claim it for that realm. When things are going well, we should perform rituals to praise God, and when things are going badly, perform rituals to call on your angels to help you endure.

So many times we don't want to look at the part that we're playing in keeping our lives stuck or creating this or that disaster. As *A Course In Miracles* says, "Only when you see the part you've played in creating a problem do you see that you can change it." Taking a good and honest look at ourselves is an important part of the true spiritual journey.

Live in continuous communion with God. Surrender every perception for His blessing and review. When we are radically available to Him, we will find Him radically available to us. I call these moments—when we allow our minds to dwell fully in the love of God and detach ourselves from fear-based thought forms—being in the Holy Instant.

We believe more in the limitations of the world than in the limitlessness of God. If we were to open up more to the limitlessness of God then any manner of miracles could be possible." We need to remember the first sentence in *A Course In Miracles*: "There is no order of difficulty in miracles."

Our interactions with God are not meant to be complicated. Life on earth is complicated; life in heaven is very simple. Our job is to bring the two together. Those of us who endeavor to walk a spiritual path have an opportunity to stand in the light of who we are and become the people we are capable of being. As I see it, we are "miracle workers" on this earth, and we have a sacred responsibility to grow into the fullness of our potential in order to take our place in God's plan.

God has a blueprint for creating peace on Earth, and pieces of that plan are ready to be downloaded by anyone who asks to receive his or her part. Rather than a specific call to action, the blueprint is more a spiritual illumination that is transmitted to those who are open to receive it. Prayer and meditation are keys to creating the stillness of mind and inner peace required to put us in a receptive mode. Such rituals are outer acts that realign internal forces, so that the plan can come into us and through us.

The most important goal is that we become the people God would have us be. We should ask how our thoughts and deeds can be so aligned with Him that our deepest desires just naturally unfold. We should let go of our personal agendas and be available to hear what God has in store for us. It's a natural law that when we are dwelling within the fullness of ourselves, in alignment with God, we become a conduit for the highest possibilities to come forth. Pray this beautiful prayer from *A Course In Miracles:* "Where would you have me go? What would you have me do? And what would you have me say, and to whom?"

Many of us would do well to rethink our rituals. We cannot meditate on peace when our minds are filled with fear and judgment. And we cannot become vessels of God's will if we talk to God as though we are giving him a shopping list. God is not the FedEx man, an on-call delivery service—"Please do this for me...and that. Amen." The highest level of prayer is where, rather than ask God for anything, we devote ourselves to Him and ask Him what we can do for Him.

We're the only generation in the history of the world that wants to reinvent society over white wine and brie. Great leaders like Mother Theresa, Martin Luther King, and Susan B. Anthony made supreme and noble efforts and made great strides for humanity, against seemingly insurmountable odds and without the benefit of technology to help them spread their messages. We need to prioritize our time for spiritual work. We always have excuses and we resist so often the things that are best for us. Whether it's physical exercise or spiritual exercise, there's a part of us that resists doing the things that would make our lives better.

God gives us opportunity after opportunity to practice forgiveness, and in every instance we either learn the lesson and become even better at forgiveness than we were before, or we postpone the lesson and it comes back around in a different form. What does this mean for individual relationships? If we didn't get it right with someone, we must pray about it, forgive, and just know that the lesson they represented will come around again. All who meet will someday meet again (although not necessarily in this lifetime) until their relationship becomes holy. A holy relationship is one in which we are able to find peace with each other because we radically accept each other as we are.

We need to think with so much love that fear begins to lose the false authority by which it rules the world. Think of a world in which there is only love and hold that thought for several minutes each day. Our thinking will lead to our acting to make it so.

PART EIGHT

Dancing With the Universe

ECKHART TOLLE

Enter Zen from Here

If you are not spending all of your waking life in discontent, worry, anxiety, depression, despair, or consumed by other negative states; if you are able to enjoy simple things like listening to the sound of the rain or the wind; if you can see the beauty of clouds moving across the sky or be alone at times without feeling lonely or needing the mental stimulus of entertainment; if you find yourself treating a complete stranger with heartfelt kindness without wanting anything from him or her... it means that a space has opened up, no matter how briefly, in the otherwise incessant stream of thinking that is the human mind. When this happens, there is a sense of well-being, of alive peace, even though it may be subtle. The intensity will vary from a perhaps barely noticeable background sense of contentment to what the ancient sages of India called *ananda*—the bliss of Being. Because you have been conditioned to pay attention only to form, you are probably not aware of it except indirectly. For example, there is a common element in the ability to see beauty, to appreciate simple things, to enjoy your own company, or to relate to other people with loving kindness. This common element is a sense of contentment, peace, and aliveness that is the invisible background without which these experiences would not be possible.

Whenever there is beauty, kindness, the recognition of the goodness of simple things in your life, look for the background to that experience within yourself. But don't look for it as if you were looking

Eckhart Tolle is the author of *The Power of Now* (New World Library, 1999), and *A New Earth* (Penguin, 2005). At the age of twenty-nine, a profound spiritual transformation virtually dissolved his old identity and radically changed the course of his life. The next few years were devoted to understanding, integrating and deepening that transformation, which marked the beginning of an intense inward journey. His teachings have helped thousands find inner peace and greater fulfillment in their lives. At the core of his teachings lies the transformation of individual and collective human consciousness. www.eckharttolle.com.

for something. You cannot pin it down and say, "Now I have it," or grasp it mentally and define it in some way. It is like the cloudless sky. It has no form. It is space; it is stillness, the sweetness of Being and infinitely more than these words, which are only pointers. When you are able to sense it directly within yourself, it deepens. So when you appreciate something simple—a sound, a sight, a touch—when you see beauty, when you feel loving kindness toward another, sense the inner spaciousness that is the source and background to that experience.

Many poets and sages throughout the ages have observed that true happiness—I call it the joy of Being—is found in simple, seemingly unremarkable things. Most people, in their restless search for something significant to happen to them, continuously miss the insignificant, which may not be insignificant at all. The philosopher Nietzsche, in a rare moment of deep stillness, wrote, "For happiness, how little suffices for happiness!...the least thing precisely, the gentlest thing, the lightest thing, a lizard's rustling, a breath, a wisk, an eye glance—little maketh up the best happiness. Be still."[1]

Why is it the "least thing" that makes up "the best happiness"? Because true happiness is not *caused* by the thing or event, although this is how it first appears. The thing or event is so subtle, so unobtrusive, that it takes up only a small part of your consciousness—and the rest is inner space, consciousness itself unobstructed by form. Inner space consciousness and who you are in your essence are one and the same. In other words, the form of little things leaves room for inner space. And it is from inner space, the unconditioned consciousness itself, that true happiness, the joy of Being, emanates. To be aware of little, quiet things, however, you need to be quiet inside. A high degree of alertness is required. Be still. Look. Listen. Be present.

Here is another way of finding inner space: Become conscious of being conscious. Say or think "I Am" and add nothing to it. Be aware of the stillness that follows the I Am. Sense your presence, the naked, unveiled, unclothed beingness. It is untouched by young or old, rich or poor, good or bad, or any other attributes. It is the spacious womb of all creation, all form.

Can You Hear the Mountain Stream?

A Zen Master was walking in silence with one of his disciples along a mountain trail. When they came to an ancient cedar tree, they sat down under it for a simple meal of some rice and vegetables. After the meal, the disciple, a young monk who had not yet found the key to the mystery of Zen, broke the silence by asking the Master, "Master, how do I enter Zen?"

He was, of course, inquiring how to enter the state of consciousness which is Zen.

The Master remained silent. Almost five minutes passed while the disciple anxiously waited for an answer. He was about to ask another question when the Master suddenly spoke. "Do you hear the sound of that mountain stream?"

The disciple had not been aware of any mountain stream. He had been too busy thinking about the meaning of Zen. Now, as he began to listen for the sound, his noisy mind subsided. At first he heard nothing. Then, his thinking gave way to heightened alertness, and suddenly he did hear the hardly perceptible murmur of a small stream in the far distance.

"Yes, I can hear it now," he said.

The Master raised his finger and, with a look in his eyes that in some way was both fierce and gentle, said, "Enter Zen from there."

The disciple was stunned. It was his first satori—a flash of enlightenment. He knew what Zen was without knowing what it was that he knew!

They continued on their journey in silence. The disciple was amazed at the aliveness of the world around him. He experienced everything as if for the first time. Gradually, however, he started thinking again. The alert stillness became covered up again by mental noise, and before long he had another question. "Master," he said, "I have been thinking. What would you have said if I hadn't been able to hear the mountain stream?" The Master stopped, looked at him, raised his finger and said, "Enter Zen from there."

1. Nietzsche, Friedriche, *Thus Spake Zarathustra: A Book for All and None* (New York: Viking, 1954), 288.

Brenda Sanders
What's Really Real

CHAPTER
48

Mysticism is an immediate, direct, intuitive knowledge of God or ultimate reality attained through personal experience. Wide variations are found in both the form and intensity of mystical experience... The mystical life is characterized by enhanced vitality, productivity, serenity, and joy as the inner and outer aspects harmonize in union.

On a Saturday in July 1997, my husband Ken and I traveled to the village of Primavera in the mountains of central Mexico to attend a week-long Tantra yoga workshop to rekindle the passion and intimacy in our marriage. We sat on the floor of the retreat center that first night among a dozen or so nervous couples, listening to well-known Tantra teachers Charles and Carolyn Muir, explaining that they were going to show us how our relationships could be revitalized and deepened through a daily Tantric yoga practice. I had no inkling at the time that, two days into the workshop, I would be split wide open to mystical states of consciousness, and that my fundamental view of reality would be turned inside out.

It started suddenly with an uncontrollable jerk, as I sat on a straight-backed chair in a small rustic cottage in Rio Caliente Resort. Then came a loud inner roar, like the sound of water rushing, followed by the searing image in my mind's eye of hot white light shooting up my spine, through my brain, and out the top of my head. The force was so strong that my head flew backward as my arms flung upward, fingers splayed, and palms raised to the heavens. Accompanied by a

Brenda Sanders, PhD. was a research scientist and Professor of Biological Sciences at California State University, Long Beach until her retirement in 1998. She co-founded a major environmental solutions startup company, and currently consults with similar enterprises. Her current passion is directed at understanding the true nature of reality, the evolution of consciousness and the role of personal transformation in global change. She lives with her family in Sebastopol, California, and is working on a memoir of her spiritual awakening which will be published by Elite books in 2008. Please visit her website at www.whatsreallyreal.com.

strong, hot, dry wind, the light drew me up and out of my body, to an expanded universe. This was a place where everything was vividly alive: conscious and interconnected. There were no boundaries. Time was the eternal moment. I was in absolute stillness and peace in a cosmic void. At that moment, life as I knew it — and the person that I believe myself to be — ended.

From some deep indwelling presence came the words I AM. It was pure consciousness, devoid of thought, meaning, and interpretation. There was a complete absence of emotion — particularly fear. I inherently knew that this expression was the essence of who I was. And as it was true for me, it was true for everyone and everything. In ecstasy and awe I breathed in this deep sense of wholeness and oneness with the universe.

At some point there was a separation from my complete absorption in their presence. I became aware of the presence of others - other souls blending together in a primordial soup of consciousness. As I merged with them, I accessed profound knowledge; everything there was to know, that was ever known, and would ever be known flooded into my being. As I dived in further, I found there were no specific facts, only an unformed type of knowledge composed of infinite potential, which I could shape at whim through thought. Then I became aware of an all powerful, all-knowing presence, which I knew to be the source of all things. Armed with a profound love, it threw daggers of ecstasy at my heart across time and space, shouting, "Love is the fabric of the universe."

Then came a strong contraction. Suddenly I felt intense pressure from all directions as the universe cracked and light spilled across the cosmos. The boundless became constrained. In my mind's eye, light and energy separated from the infinite, and with a loud crash I was slammed back into my tiny body. Stunned by the sheer pain of being in physical form again, and longing for the oneness I had experienced, I opened my eyes to find myself still sitting in that straight-backed chair with hands raised skyward. The room and everything in it sparkled with luminous white light. The air was thick, and the slightest movement of my hand created bioluminescent eddies of dancing light.

I began to recover my bearings. I was stunned realizing that I had been living my life, as Stephen Covey says, 'with my ladder on the wrong wall!' At the time I was a research biologist and university professor living comfortably with the notion that reality is only physical. Anything metaphysical was illusion or superstition. I believed that consciousness was generated by the brain, and that I was simply the sum total of my thoughts, hopes, and beliefs. There was nothing more. Yet with this new mystical insight, I knew that there was no separation. We are each really a facet of one seamless whole, and vitality — life, energy, vigor, exuberance — whatever you wish to call it — thrives to the extent to which each of us is aligned with the basic oneness of our nature. With this realization, the touchstone from which I had lived my life vanished, and was replaced by the direct experience of my own mystical nature. I had glimpsed what the Hindus call "the face of God," and in that instant everything about me changed.

It has taken me years to re-orient and realign my life to the knowledge that I am much more than my body, and that consciousness is not an awareness produced by my brain, but is instead the very stuff that creates the universe. I now know my brain is simply the instrument that I use to perceive this ultimate reality. Before this happened, I knew myself to be separate and distinct, an objective reality among objective realities. I saw life as a series of dichotomies: me versus you; yours versus mine; inside versus outside; and even good versus evil. Before that moment, there was me and there was everything else. I had a materialistic, self-centered worldview where events unfolded "out there" by cause and effect relationships according the laws of probability. The way I saw it, life was a crap shoot. It was also a zero sum game where the bigger your piece of the pie, the smaller mine had to be. Then, bam! In an instant, as I sat in that small rustic cottage, I found myself stark naked in the light of Spirit's passing glance.

Even now, ten years later, I can sit in stillness and re-experience this awakening. Much of it comes back to me as a cacophony of images, sounds, and sensations, mixed with the powerful emotions of rapture, wonder, and awe. Often it comes as a *gestalt*, a complete complex bundle of profound insight that can't be broken down in a linear fashion into smaller chunks. There is no specific sequence. Contradictions flow smoothly into insight. On the one hand, there are no boundaries. I am the observer and the observed. Yet on the other hand, the observer, the observed, and the very process itself are identifiable facets of an undivided whole. Underlying this whole, animating it, and orchestrating it all is the radiant life force powered by love, on an endless journey of self-expression.

For the first few days afterward I was unsteady and plagued by doubt about the validity of what had happened. Was this really a spiritual experience in which I glimpsed the true nature of reality, a reality made up of pure consciousness? Or was it the result of some kind of brain misfiring? My sanity seemed intact. I was assured by my husband that I was behaving rationally to an extraordinary event. A psychologist who was with me at the time of the awakening was also reassuring. He told me that I had had a "Kundalini" experience, and suggested that I read a book called *Spiritual Emergency* by Stanislav Grof to help me come to grips with it.

As I sorted through the many aspects of the experience, I couldn't shake the sense of sheer realness that I had felt — it felt more real to me than any other moment in my life. I also began to notice fundamental changes in the way my mind was working, as if my brain had been rewired in some way. Astounding insights — connections that I had never made before — flashed into my awareness almost daily. A strong voice of intuition screamed out at me almost as often. Unlike my previous life, which was consumed by science, cause and effect, and "just the facts," I had an insatiable curiosity to read and understand everything associated with consciousness and the true nature of reality. Over time other changes became apparent. I was more empathetic, more caring, and less materialistic. I had even lost my fear of death! Over time these changes stabilized into a different temperament and personality — a kinder, gentler me that remains to this day.

I quickly learned that my experience wasn't unique: more than forty percent of people in the United States claim to have had experiences that they define as mystical; and a National Institutes of Health study found that thirty-three percent of Americans have had an experience which they describe as "a divine and wonderful spiritual power." The author Arjuna Ardagh, who conducted over 170 interviews and 13,000 surveys for the book *The Translucent Revolution*, estimates that 3 to 4 million people worldwide have woken up to the realization that they are limitless consciousness, beyond birth and death. Ten percent of the general population has reported an out-of-body experience. In 1997 an estimated 15 million Americans had had a near-death-experience (NDE), another form of mystical experience that shares the same neurophysiology and biological mechanism as Kundalini awakenings.

It was the Hindus who first called the great force that cascaded up my spine that day *Kundalini*, the primal energy that created the cosmos. It is the life force itself, and the erotic energy that is the source of all creativity. Symbolized as a serpent coiled three and a half times around the base of the spine, it is known to many cultures, including the Native American Hopi, pre-Christian Gnostics, Buddhists, and the Kung bushmen of the Kalahari Desert. For Joseph Campbell kundalini was the driving force of evolution that underlies all underlying myths. For Sigmund Freud it was the libido. Carl Jung saw it as "the other face of God," while for Walt Whitman it was a metaphor for enlightenment.

And it turns out that while mystical experiences and spiritual awakenings have occurred for millennia, they are becoming more frequent in the West. They might even be the telltale signs of a massive shift in consciousness, catapulting us into the next stage in the evolution of our species. Some point to the development of advanced medical technologies which can bring us back from the brink of death as another powerful catalyst for evolutionary change. There is data to support this recent research conducted by a Dutch physician found that fully eighteen percent of patients who were brain-dead from cardiac arrests and then resuscitated, reported that they had an NDE. Upon recovery, most of these patients exhibited physiological and psychological changes similar to my own. As medicine becomes even more effective at bringing people back from close calls with death, it is creating a whole new class of mystics — people who, like me, have had a direct experience of oneness with the universe — and been transformed. In this way we are impacting the rate and direction of our own evolution.

While it was reassuring to find out that many others have had similar mystical experiences, I was still conflicted. I knew that I had experienced absolute reality — that knowledge was unshakable. Yet the scientist in me needed corroboration. I wasn't convinced that my experience was any more real just because it was shared with others. What I really wanted to understand was: Was there an objective basis for my perceptions? Or, more simply: How do we know what's really real? Looking back, I realize that underlying such a question is the naïve assumption that there really is some kind of objective reality "out there," an assumption that my own experience challenged. It assumes a Newtonian reality which just doesn't jive with brain science or quantum physics.

The similarity between my experience and those reported by others could easily be explained by our common neurophysiology resulting in similar but false perceptions. This latter explanation is often used to explain NDEs by suggesting that the person's perceptions were the result of oxygen deprivation or some pathology of the brain as a result of trauma or severe illness. I was left with two possibilities. I could either accept my experience at face value — I witnessed the true nature of reality — or I could consider that my perceptions were a consequence of brain malfunction. I set off to determine if it was possible to scientifically distinguish between these two options.

I found ample data in studies of the biological basis of mystical experiences. Two scientists in particular, Andrew Newberg and Eugene D'Aquili, have conducted seminal work in this area using as their subjects highly proficient meditators. The experiments were simple but provocative. The idea was to relate the subjective perceived reality of the meditator with specific patterns of brain activity at the moment of meditative unity. For example, one of their subjects, Robert, was a devout Buddhist and accomplished practitioner of Tibetan meditation, who described a spiritual awareness reminiscent of my own. He told how he felt as his meditation progressed toward spiritual climax: How as his conscious mind stills, a deeper part of 'himself' emerges. Robert believes that this inner self is who he really is and is what is most real. It is what is left after worry, fear, desire, and other thoughts of the rational mind are stripped away. He says that when this inner self emerges during meditation, he "suddenly understands that his inner self is not an isolated entity, it is inextricably connected to all of creation."

The researchers used state-of-the-art technology to obtain images of Robert's brain while he was in this meditative state. They found decreased activity in a small region nestled in the top rear section of the brain called the orientation association area, or OAA. The primary function of the OAA is to orient us in space. It helps us keep track of which end is up and to estimate the distance objects are from us in our environment. In other words, it helps us distinguish the boundaries of "self" from "other." At the same time during meditation, blood flow to another area of the brain, called the holistic operator, increased. The holistic operator, which is located in the parietal area of the right hemisphere, allows us to see the world as a whole — to distinguish the forest from the trees. It is the part of the brain that allows us to look at a nose, two eyes, and a mouth, and instantly recognize it as the face of a loved one — to assemble the big picture from the parts.

From these scans they determined that Robert's subjective reality was completely consistent with the activity of specific regions of his brain: At the very moment that he was experiencing "a connection to all of creation" — a state that recognizes the wholeness of all creation, while lacking any sense of separation from the whole — the holistic operator in his brain was highly active, and his OAA, that helped distinguish self from non-self, was depressed. The brain scans demonstrated that this mystical awareness was measurable. It corresponded to a series of specific, predictable neurological events within the range of normal brain function, and provided a biological basis for Robert's mystical perceptions.

With mystical insight I knew that everything is interconnected to one seamless whole — nothing is separate. I knew that this whole is made of pure untethered consciousness, which is the underlying foundation of all of creation — the God-stuff. I knew that the "I" of my awareness, when I was in this unity state, was not the "I" that I identified with in my everyday waking world. This was not a subjective I; Ken Wilber calls it the I-I. It exists beyond the brain, even beyond matter. It is the "I" of the one seamless whole. I knew that there really is a God and this was it, and that each of us is connected to this divine presence. I also knew that the implications of this insight would have a profound impact on how I was to live my life.

Usually, when we think of consciousness, we think of the consciousness of "something" with the tacit assumption that it springs forth from matter. Yet I experienced a consciousness that is the source of all matter — not the other way around.

If consciousness is generated by the brain, I reasoned that there could be no compelling evidence to the contrary. Yet in the last few decades, studies involving NDEs provide such evidence. The most clear-cut examples are the NDE case studies described by psychologist Ken Ring involving the blind. During their NDEs, they reported leaving their bodies, floating to the ceiling, and watching the medical team trying to revive them. Dr. Ring found that each was able to see and accurately describe in detail the events that were unfolding before them. Subsequently, they could provide details that were confirmed by doctors, nurses, and relatives who were in the room at the time. In a few cases, the person had been blind since birth, and during the NDE, experienced sight for the first time! If consciousness is indeed generated by the brain, how can we explain how a blind person could experience sight at precisely the moment his or her brain stopped functioning? This seemed like irrefutable evidence that consciousness cannot be a property that emerges from the brain.

I also knew that this mystical awareness felt more real to me than anything I'd ever experienced. It was as if the ego stepped away and the veil of judgment lifted — to reveal to me, for the first time, bare-ass-naked consciousness. It was vivid. It was authentic. It was unforgettable. It changed my life. Since the time of the Greek Stoics the central criterion for determining realness has been the "subjective vivid sense of reality," called *phantia catalyptica*. It is a compass pointing in the direction of wholeness, and vividness is the needle pointing us to the magnetic north of oneness and divine love.

I also finally understood that the question is not, "what is really real?" in some black-and-white sense of realness: this is real and that isn't. It's all real, but realness is a matter of degree. Everything we experience has a shade of realness in relation to that ultimate reality. Because we hold human form, each of our human experiences embodies spirit to some degree. No matter how tenuous, each experience holds a tinge of reality.

Each state of consciousness falls somewhere along the gradient between separation and oneness, with *vividness* indicating where on the spectrum it falls. For most altered states of consciousness, such as a dream, a psychotic episode, or an LSD trip, the experience is unhinged, and has only the flimsiest connection to oneness. Yet real it is, and is felt as such when in that state. Then it is immediately recognized as not real upon our return to day-to-day consciousness. Such experiences are less vivid, and therefore, less real.

Our day-to-day waking world is more lucid, and is what we normally think of as real. It encompasses a broad group of experiences along the continuum; at one end are such states as paranoia brewing in fear. Then a bit closer to oneness is depression with its overwhelming sense of separateness and alienation. Closer still is loneliness. We move closer to oneness as we connect with family, friends, and community, and closer still as we increase our sense of interconnection when we fall into romantic love or experience parent/child bonding.

The union felt during sexual climax may be on the borderline, bridging our everyday waking consciousness and those hyper-lucid states which we vividly sense as being more real than day-to-day consciousness, both during the experience and afterward. Cognitive psychologists call these *primary knowing states,* and suggest that they are the foundation from which all other states are derived. They lead us to our true north — to unity. They are how we experience increasing connection. The sense of being at one with nature is a start. Then we feel still a greater connection during certain trance states, peak experiences, visions, and lucid dreams. Near-death experiences are even more connected. And even closer to oneness, we enter the profound states reported in mystical accounts throughout the ages. Cosmic consciousness is described in the literature of every culture. It is the awareness of the interconnectedness of all things while still holding a separate identity. Farthest to the right on the continuum is oneness, the magnetic north of our internal compass, where there is no sense of time or space, or separation of subject and object.

As physical beings we tap-dance back and forth along this continuum of consciousness between separation and oneness, propelled by the choices we make every day — even moment by moment. The trick is to know where on the continuum we find ourselves, and if we are moving toward or away from oneness. How can we tell? Emotions are the key, as they are the barometer for sensing the changes in our inner landscape. They are fragile and volatile. They can be hijacked by thoughts of judgment, by regrets from the past, and worries about the future. All such thoughts take us out of present moment awareness, the only place where oneness can be found. Paying attention to what we feel allows us to understand where we are on the continuum. I can monitor what I am thinking, and change my thoughts to bring me closer to oneness.

Experienced meditators speak of the serenity and peacefulness within. Who could not see the joy and bliss reflected in the beaming face of the Dalai Lama? There is the rapture of St. Theresa of Avila, and the ecstasy of the Sufi poets. All of our emotions are really just hues of this divine love. It is the invisible fabric that weaves us together with the natural world. Vulnerable in their helplessness, pets, infants, and those at death's door might best pull us toward oneness. A puppy wagging its tail when its master returns; a young child being comforted in her mother's arms after a nasty fall; the last gaze of a dying parent — stark naked, God's love pours through their eyes and grabs our hearts. It takes our breath away. It is pure, unabashed, unconditional love!

So I remember to bring into each day and in each moment the eye-opening realization that the divine is fully present in every person and situation. With practice I have found this is easy when I am awed by a beautiful rainbow or when I look into the eyes of a newborn child. I've found it is much harder when I hear about the deaths of five young Amish girls gunned down in a country schoolhouse in Pennsylvania, reflect on 9/11, or try to comprehend genocide in Nazi Germany, Rwanda or Darfur. For while far from apparent at first blush, I know that these, too, must hold the divine. It is in these situations that I hold my faith tightly and use it to remind myself of my oneness, so that I can rise above simple judgments of good versus evil and hold the realization that we are all one, that that one is God and God is perfect.

From this place comes my sobering spiritual practice to live in present moment awareness and reframe my life as a perpetual search for the divine; to look beyond my judgments and straight through the faces of shock, horror, and disgust and ask, 'where is God in this?' Each time, I find that God shows up smack in the thick of it. It often appears under the guise of forgiveness but just under the surface is the essence of our life force — a steady stream of divine love which pulls us up out of the murk of blame, fear, and anger to glimpse the oneness.

In the Amish killings God's fingerprints are all over the place. At the very moment that the violence was taking place the killer's wife, Maria Roberts, was leading a prayer meeting for the community's schoolchildren. Emergency workers told reporters, "God was with us while we were taking care of these kids." Spontaneous prayer meetings sprouted all over Lancaster County. In their own grief, the

Amish people quickly recognized the suffering of the killer's family and reached out to them, bringing food to the home and attending the killer's funeral. And after the funerals of the slain girls, Maria met to console each of the families.

It's easy to assume that God was in Amish country because of the community's steadfast faith, but God doesn't play favorites. The divine shined through Al Braca as he led fifty people in a prayer circle on the 105th floor of Tower 1 of the World Trade Center (WTC) in the last few moments of their lives. Some believe God showed up in the form of a perfect twenty-foot cross found standing straight up, surrounded by smaller crosses amongst the rubble in the pile. "There's no symmetry to anything down there except those crosses," said an FBI chaplain. And a profound empathy brought together Phyllis Rodriguez, whose son Greg was killed when the WTC collapsed, and Aicha el-Wafi, whose son Zacarias was charged with conspiracy in connection with the attacks. "When I watched Zacarias at the trial, my heart was broken because I could not look at him as a stranger. He is the son of my friend," said Phyllis, glimpsing the oneness.

Only the power of divine love can forge these most unlikely reconciliations when families are torn apart by horrific violence. They are propelled by the longing for oneness that comes to the forefront when violence tears a swatch out of the cloth of wholeness leaving a gaping hole of pain and separation. This is how Amy Biehl's parents could employ two of their murdered daughter's accused killers in the foundation they founded in her name in Cape Town. And how Immaculée Ilibagiza forgave the Hutu friends and neighbors who hacked to pieces her family and friends as she holed up in a tiny bathroom with seven other women for three months. Hard as we might try to hold on to blame, fear, and anger, that gaping hole can only be filled by understanding, forgiveness, and compassion, the healing emotions that bring us closer to unity.

It is from this place that I know God as wholeness and realize that "to pray without ceasing" is to live in each moment — right here, right now — recognizing our divine nature. And I remind myself that emotions — beauty, rapture, delight, forgiveness, compassion — even sadness, anger, and despair — are all cues from God. They are bread crumbs leading us to gratitude, wonder, and awe — the feelings evoked when we recognize God in ourselves and one another. And as these emotions lead us to oneness, God responds. We are laid wide open to grace — that essential aspect of God which nourishes life and fuels expansion.

WAYNE DYER

Why Meditate?

CHAPTER
49

Why meditate? Many people have at one time or another considered this question and come up with all sorts of answers. Some of the many reasons for meditating include reducing stress, cultivating a sense of peace, eliminating fatigue, slowing the aging process, improving memory, finding clarity of purpose, and even healing. All of these are powerful motivators for beginning a meditation practice. Who wouldn't want the healthy, happy, and purposeful life that is the result of these benefits? However, all these reasons pale in significance to the realization that meditation is our way of making conscious contact with God.

The paramount reason for making meditation a part of our daily life is to join forces with our sacred energy and regain the power of our Source (God). Through meditation, we can tap in to an abundance of creative energy that resides within us, and a more meaningful experience of life, which enriches us permanently. By meditating, we come to know God, rather than know about God.

One quality that distinguishes our Source from the outer world is that it cannot be divided. Oneness defies being compartmentalized. For instance, our physical world is divided into dark and light, but the source of light, the sun, defies division. Or consider the nature of silence. It has been said that God's one and only voice is silence. No matter how you attempt to slice it up or cut it in half, silence is always silence. This indivisible root source of oneness is where the act of creation originates.

Wayne W. Dyer, PhD, is one of the most widely known and respected people in the field of self-empowerment. He became a well-known author with his bestselling book, *Your Erroneous Zones* (Harper, 1991), and has gone on to write many other self-help classics, including Getting In the Gap (Hay House, 2002), and The Power of Intention (Hay House, 2004). Despite a childhood spent in orphanages and foster homes, Dr. Dyer has overcome many obstacles to make his dreams come true. Today he spends much of his time showing others how to do the same. More at www.DrWayneDyer.com.

Indivisible oneness is the creative energy that turns a seed into a maple tree or a watermelon or a human being or anything else that's alive. It's invisible, omnipresent, and absolutely indivisible. We can't divide oneness. Meditation offers us the closest experience we can have of rejoining our Source and being in the oneness at the same time that we're embodied. This means that we have to tame our ego.

When we meditate, we begin to still the mind. As we get more and more adept at moving into inner silence, we come to know the peace of God in our entire being. We intuitively seek union with our generating source. Silence, or meditation, is the path to that center. We can make conscious contact with God, transcend the limitations of a dichotomous world, and regain the power that is only available to us when we're connected to the Source. This is what I call getting in the gap. It's where we create, manifest, heal live, and perform at a miraculous level. The gap is the powerful silence where we can access the stillness that may have been unattainable in other meditation attempts.

Our ultimate reason for meditating is to get in the gap where we enter the sacred space and know the unlimited power of our Source. Psalm 46:10 says: "Be still, and know that I am God." To know is to banish all doubt. Being still in meditation can take us to that awareness. But if you've tried meditation previously, what you're more likely to know is that your thoughts won't be still.

I find it helpful to think of my mind as a pond. The surface of the pond is similar to my mental chatter. On the surface of the pond are the disturbances. Here there are storms, debris, freezing and thawing, all on the surface. Beneath the pond surface, there is relative stillness. Here it is quiet and peaceful. If, as has been said, it's true that we have approximately 60,000 separate, often disconnected, thoughts during the day, then our mind is like a pond that's full of whitecaps from a choppy breeze. But beneath that surface chatter is the gap where we can know God and gain the unlimited power of reconnecting to our source.

Meditating is a way of quieting our chatterbox thoughts and swimming below the surface. This is where we can be still and know (not know about) God. If we have approximately 60,000 thoughts every day, then in all of our waking hours, it's unlikely that we ever get to the point where there's any space between our thoughts. How could we? With one thought leading to the next, either rationally connected or otherwise, there's simply no time or place to get into the gap between our thoughts. Yet it's precisely in that gap that magic and the infinite possibilities await us.

MICHAEL BECKWITH

Life as a Prayer

CHAPTER
50

Freedom's Testimony

I recently heard testimony from a woman whose history described her as a five-time felon confined to death row. Not surprisingly, she began to think about God, rather than the impending doom awaiting her. As her relationship with the Spirit deepened, it overtook her consciousness as being the Supreme Reality, and profound changes began to occur. At first, it was small things: she was allowed to exercise in the yard; she joined the prison choir and began to sing the good news about the Spirit. Eventually, her death sentence was reduced to a life sentence. Today she is free, and spends her time visiting churches singing and speaking about the empowering Presence of God.

The truth is that she became free the moment she turned to the Spirit within her own being as her refuge and strength. As she merged her mind with the One Mind, she sloughed off the sense of a self separate from the Essence of her life. Her union with God became so complete that she experienced a new incarnation right within this very lifetime. Divine Law responded, and everything around her conformed to a new birth in her true identity. She would have been free had she never left the confines of the prison cell because she was inwardly free already!

Michael Beckwith, one of the key figures in the movie *The Secret*, is a world leader and teacher in the New Thought–Ancient Wisdom tradition of spirituality. He is the founder of the Agape International Spiritual Center, which has a membership of some 9,000 congregants. He is also cofounder of the Association for Global New Thought, and the Season for Nonviolence, which are extensions of his vision of one human family united on a foundation of peace, based on the spiritual origin of every man, woman, and child. He is author of *Inspirations of the Heart* (Agape, 2004).

Many people give themselves death sentences served out in the prison of their own minds. They are prisoners of fear, jealousy, lack, limitation, greed and selfishness.

Today, examine the self-created prison into which you have confined yourself. Then, be willing to step into your God-consciousness without any thought of personal reward. Watch the shackles of your false beliefs, unwanted habits and negative thought patterns fall away as the revelation of your true Self unfolds. Desire freedom of the Spirit. Set your intention to live your life in the freedom consciousness that is already yours!

I claim the Truth that I was created free, born free and live in my true state of spiritual freedom. I feel, sense and know there is only a Law of Freedom and I am governed by it now.

Have Faith In Faith

When you have faith the size of a mustard seed and abandon yourself and all the details of your life to it, your greater-yet-to-be bursts forth. You will meet it everywhere. It will press itself against you and multiply around you! You will hear the Spirit whispering inwardly to you about why you are here and what you have come to do, revealing the agreements in your Divine Contract.

You don't have to wait for external circumstances to shift before such a transforming experience overtakes your life. Right now, on the ground on which you stand, you can breathe in the sublime, rarified atmosphere of the Holy Spirit. Then you will know absolutely that you live in a supportive Universe. There will be a tearing down of the strongholds of negativity. There will be the glory of the Living God moving through you in ways you can't even imagine. Be vigilant in your faith! It is your shield and your fortress.

Those who practice faith walk freely everywhere they go in this world. No mental barbs of negativity can penetrate their interior armor of conviction that God is the Source and Substance of their supply, their Sustainer, Provider and Comforter.

For the remainder of your waking hours this day, participate in this spiritual experiment: Every hour on the hour, stop, take a deep breath, and give thanks for your life. Then move back into your daily rounds of activity with an awareness of the Eternal beating in your heart. As you do this, you will notice that this form of discipline causes you to remember who and what you really are. With repeated practice, your faith in your true identity creates space for you to no longer live in the past or future. Instead, you will be available, awake and alive in the Eternal Now.

I have faith in faith! My faith is active, unconditional, and everything in my experience conforms to this truth.

Whole-Souled Devotion

Today, call forth the whole-souled devotion of your heart. Unleash it in your life! Live in the great mystery, in that sense of awe at the Infinite Possibilities that are right within you and all around you. Metaphorically fall on your knees at how healings happen, how insights and breakthroughs occur, how creativity expresses through you, how Grace moves through you, compelling you to intuitively do the right thing at the right time.

Be aware that when the scripture tells you to fear the Lord, it is saying to stand humbly before the magnificence, order and unconditional love of the Universe. Whole-souled devotion generates a purity that requalifies every thought form, directing your subjective thinking toward seeing the Face of God in every experience, walking through the feet of all humanity, smiling at you from within all creation. Devotion will do this for you.

You may think this is an impractical way to live, that it is more available to monks and yogis. Or, perhaps you see yourself as not inclined to mystical experiences. Such thinking is merely the hypnotism of the race suggestion into which you have been lulled by living too much on the surface of your consciousness. Contemplate the truth that not even your greatest human lover can give you the eternal love of God. They did not create you; God did. You came into this world alone and you will leave it alone, except for the Eternal Lover who leaves you never. Does this not make it worthwhile to cultivate an intimate and personal relationship with the One who is the Author of Love itself?

Contemplate the Eternality of the Spirit's love for you and it will transform every misery into a steppingstone to joy. God, God, God! You are God's hands and feet, serving Itself in all of Its human selves through you, loving Itself in all through your own heart. Can you imagine a life for yourself devoted to anything but the One who loves you so much It thought you forth into existence? Wake up today and cultivate whole-souled devotion for the All-encompassing Presence.

I surrender to the all-consuming Love of the Spirit. I am absorbed by this Divine Presence, so personal that it has personalized Itself as myself.

Living by Soul-Force

The more you live your life from a deep connection with the Spirit, the more you will experience and express your Soul-Force.

When Jesus said, "Blessed are the meek, for they shall inherit the earth," he was laying out an efficient blueprint for living and moving in the world. When you are meek, you are humble. When you are humble, you are in tune with your Soul-Force, you remain strong and secure in the Spirit. The need to pump up the false ego built by the surface mind simply falls away. You will then be free from running your rackets of defense mechanisms, pretense and fears that convince the little ego you will be annihilated if you don't heed its voice, if you don't cling to your personal history.

When with humility and sincerity you say "yes" to the still small voice speaking within, your Soul-Force takes over, and you step into your authentic identity as an individualized expression of the Living Spirit.

Today, ignite your Soul-Force by accepting that you are just as significant as the greatest saint who ever lived and was loved by the Spirit. Hear Its voice echoing within your heart, "You are my beloved in whom I am well pleased."

I offer myself as a humble instrument of the Spirit. I allow my Soul-Force to express in Its fullest form and all is well with my soul.

The Soul Aflame

Throughout this day, be courageous enough to not turn on your television or to participate in any outer distractions until you make contact with your soul. Be willing to say, "I'm not moving from this place until Divine Contact is made." When Buddha sat under the banyan tree, he refused to move until the mysteries of the Universe were revealed to him.

The Christian mystic Meister Eckhart said, "The eyes with which I see God are the eyes through which God sees me." When you set your intention to be serious about your God-Self, your God-Self will be serious about you. Mystical secrets will reveal themselves to you. What are those secrets? That you are now, always have been and ever shall be one with God.

Brother Lawrence, a humble monk, lived in the world as if only he and God existed. He performed every activity in the conscious company of Spirit.

There was no separation between his prayer time, meditation time and time of service. It was all one worshipful action of Divine Love. Living in this state of consciousness is the purpose of existence.

You see, when you make time for your soul to be enthralled with the Divine Presence, you are raised up to divine heights of oneness with the Spirit. But this doesn't come simply by saying or affirming it is so. No! You must be willing to give the Spirit more than a small percentage of your time.

Today, determine to practice spiritual discipline, which means consciously setting aside time to cultivate your relationship with the Spirit. Once you form this habit, I guarantee you won't want to miss your Divine Appointment with the Infinite.

God is first in my life. The beginning, middle and end is God. I live, move and have my being in the light of this recognition.

Thinker, Thinking, Thought

Thought is energy. The quality of your thought is reflected through your emotions, speech and behavior. The thoughts that pass through your awareness translate themselves into your experiences. That which you think reality to be is your experience.

In the Bible we read, "Hear this, O people, who have eyes, but do not see, who have ears, but do not hear." The metaphysical interpretation of this passage is that until you are fully awakened, you cannot directly perceive Reality, nor does it outpicture as the experience of your life. Instead, your understanding is processed through the limitations of your thinking about Reality, which then becomes the body of your affairs.

The survival level of mentality is reactive, unthinking. It is based on a mistaken mind-set from judgments based on input from the five senses and limitations of an unenlightened consciousness.

Through prayer and meditation, determine to shake off the dust of spiritual ignorance and free yourself from wrong thinking. As you commingle the self with the Self, your thoughts reveal the thinking of the Divine Mind that is within you. You move from thinking and analyzing to direct, intuitive perception of the Truth. Prayer facilitates your awareness of the Self; meditation expands your consciousness to merge with the Self. As the little self recedes and you touch Reality, thought becomes requalified, purified and aligned with the Original Thinker.

Today, begin to cultivate a hunger to live life at this level.

My whole consciousness is alive with the inspired thoughts of God. I am impregnated with Divine Ideas. I think directly from Spirit and let Divine Intelligence have Its way with me.

On Being Your Own Hero

In my estimation, true heroes and heroines are those who refuse to give up on the part they have been created to play on the stage of life. They go for their dream no matter what obstacles appear in their path. I am saying this to you: Don't give up on your vision!

When you go to bed late at night, or awaken early in the morning when all is yet still in your environment, I know you sometimes sense God's intention for your life. You see through the illusions common to the human experience. The thin veil of unseeing is rent asunder and you see God's idea for your life. It is then that you no longer cling to the conspiracy of human definitions that seek to convince you to give up, to believe there is not enough good to go around. You rise above all this and realize that you are surrounded by spiritual ideas. There comes a breakthrough, a recognition of the blueprint of excellence which is the Real Self! Then the prophets of doom and gloom take up no space in your mental household. You become a glorious agent of transformation in your own life and in the lives of others.

Today, continue to nourish your dreams. Hold fast to your vision and do something every day to bring it into manifestation. Everything is possible in God because God is the Infinite Possibility within everything. Know that you are God's beloved in whom God is well pleased. Never give up on yourself!

Awake in the Cosmic Dream, I fashion my life according to Spirit's perfect vision of me as Its individualized expression.

JONATHAN FOUST

CHAPTER

51

The Absence of Fear is Joy

L ike most of my generation I was in full-time pursuit of a better time than the one I was having. And like many boomers I
searched for it externally in the realm of relationships, drugs,
work, money, power, and my personal story dedicated to "fulfilling
my dreams."

We chase after vitality, energy, good feelings, good times, and
happy memories. This pursuit of what we think is happiness
appears to be a built-in drive, even sanctioned by the Declaration
of Independence. We are always on the run, though, chasing our
dreams and veering away from discomfort. We are often miserable,
constantly caught in a trap of comparing ourselves to others, doubting
our self-worth, reveling in how unfair life is. We spend most of our
time confined to believing we are not quite enough, that we are on
our way to becoming a better person but never quite arriving.

The Buddhist tradition speaks of the three poisons:

1. Greed, or simply wanting more of what we like

2. Aversion, or wanting to get rid of what we don't like

3. Delusion, or living in a story that has little to do with reality

If you watch what arises moment by moment, you may notice
that every experience is tinged with wanting more, pushing away,
and delusion or confusion. These three factors, unchecked, are the
source of great pain. Blaise Pascal said, "Most of the evils of life arise

Jonathan Foust, MA, is a founder of the **Mindfulness Training Institute of
Washington, DC,** and the former president and a senior teacher at **Kripalu
Center for Yoga and Health,** the largest center for yoga and health in North
America. Jonathan has studied numerous disciplines from both the Yogic
and Buddhist traditions and has been leading retreats, seminars and training teachers for over twenty years in residential, non-profit and corporate
settings. He is trained in numerous mind/body modalities and maintains a
private practice in the DC Metro area. You can learn more about Jonathan
at www.JonathanFoust.com and www.MindfulnessTraining.org.

from man's being unable to sit still in a room." When we rush to fix what we think is wrong, suffering inevitably follows.

I was lucky to have stumbled into a yoga class when I was in high school. I still remember that first class vividly: After taking us through a sequence of yoga postures the teacher led us into a deep relaxation. Lying on my back on the wrestling mat in the gym, feeling my breath gently flowing in and out, simply noticing parts of my body and letting them soften, I felt a remarkable experience of deep peace and at the same time, hyper-awareness of everything around me. Thoughts came and went, yet there was "something" watching this arising and passing away of sensation, thought, and feeling. I was floating in a euphoric cloud of well-being. I had never felt so free. At the end of the session I sat up, stunned at this peaceful inner world I had just visited. I wanted more.

For the next few days I would lie in bed and try to recreate that feeling of wellness. The sense of contentment and happiness eventually faded, but I never forgot the experience of such deep stillness and aliveness. A few months later I heard about a meditation training and immediately signed up. After learning my new mantra and settling into a regimen of twice-daily practice I felt an amazing sense of homecoming and, within a few weeks, a greater sense of stability, confidence, and creativity than I'd felt before. I was hooked. And I still wanted more.

Yoga and meditation became my passion and I dedicated my life to practice and study. I meditated every day through high school, college, grad school, and the Peace Corps. Everywhere I went I found some kind of group to help keep me inspired. I moved into a yoga ashram at 25, and stayed for 20 years. My wanting for more of this good stuff, I realized decades later, was a trap unto itself. There was something pure in my pursuit, yet my practice was suffused with grasping and wanting. For all the yoga and meditation I was doing, I was often far from any kind of true stillness.

The Invitation of Meditation

Spirit Rock Meditation Center in Marin County, California, is tucked up into a canyon and surrounded by hills, creeks, wandering deer and wild turkeys, supervised by hawks spiraling overhead in the clear coastal sky. The external beauty seems to hold a promise of what is possible.

It has been said that if meditation was a drug, it would be the miracle drug of this age. Up until this point, meditation had helped me maintain a hectic life. The last few years I had signed on to serve as president, primarily as a spokesperson, fundraiser and teacher. I was ill-prepared though, for what happened next. One administrative crisis after another pulled me from the role of spokesperson to the role of administrator and manager. We survived a fire that put us out of business for nine months. I had to dramatically cut back staff, firing people I liked and considered friends. There was infighting among the leaders and fear among the 300 staff members.

For years previous I had taught about how to work with stress. Now I learned about it from the inside out. I was stressed about my lack of management experience. I was stressed about raising the money we needed to keep the organization afloat. I was stressed about doing a good job for the Board of Directors and finally conceded to them that I was in over my head and burning out.

The scientific research on stress is clear. In the stress response, the brain interprets an event as life threatening. Stress hormones are released from the brain and your body moves into the classic "fight-or-flight" response. Blood is shunted away from the belly and out to the arms and legs. Capillaries dilate. The adrenals are activated. Supposedly, the body relaxes once the stressful situation goes away. That works perhaps if you're in the woods, see a bear, and the bear goes away. But in our culture, much of our stress is psychological. That was my problem.

Then one day I read a passage by Franz Kafka that called me to retreat:

> You do not need to leave your room.
>
> Remain sitting at your table and listen.
>
> Do not even listen, simply wait.
>
> Do not even wait, be still and solitary.
>
> The world will freely offer itself to you
>
> to be unmasked, it has no choice.
>
> It will roll in ecstasy at your feet.

Was this possible? If I sat still and waited, would the world offer itself to me? I was ready to finally learn.

Attachment and Suffering

Our inner practice for the month was to cultivate mindfulness. Jon Kabat Zin, the founder of Mindfulness Based Stress Reduction, the ground-breaking program based out of the University of Massachusetts, defines mindfulness as "paying attention in a particular way: on purpose, in the present moment, and nonjudgmentally." There is no "doing" in mindfulness. It is a quality of attention that simply recognizes what is happening and allows it to be, just as it is.

Most of our life is spent in reaction to what is happening. Even when we aren't aware of it, we lose ourselves in a trance of worry, fantasy, aggression, fear, depression, and doubt. Perhaps you are familiar with one or more of the five classical responses to discomfort or resistance, as described in the Buddhist tradition:

Anger and Aversion. You get irritated, judgmental and look for someone or something to blame.

Craving and Wanting. You start to fantasize about your future or anything that helps you feel good.

Restless. You lose your focus and become victim to the reactionary mind.

Sloth. You numb out to what you are feeling.

Doubt. You start to doubt yourself, your capabilities and your self-worth.

Meditation can stop this reactionary chain. Pausing allows you to see what is actually happening. Slowing things down can reveal the chain of events. Mindfulness allows us to re-inhabit a natural sense of spaciousness, clarity and balance. When Swami Satchitananda was asked if he was a Hindu, he paused and said, "No I think I'm an 'undo'." That's what my days at Spirit Rock Meditation Center felt like. I wasn't talking. I wasn't reading. I wasn't writing. I wasn't staying up late. I wasn't distracting myself with anything external.

What I was doing was bringing myself back again and again to the moment inside the moment around me: The breath in my belly. The fog flowing up the valley and hovering just above the ground. The wild turkey poking its head around the door to the meditation hall. The anticipation of lunch. The sound of breathing. My bare feet against the hot courtyard steps.

Two weeks into the month-long meditation retreat, however, I discovered that I was in serious pain. An amazingly angry knot constantly burned between my shoulder blades. Yet as tight and constricted as it was, it sometimes magically released when I moved, like I had received a chiropractic adjustment. Again and again I sat with my eyes closed, hands on my lap, and watched the pain grow. I'd shift a tiny bit to my right, and something would seem to let go. A crack-crack-crack would run up my spine from my sacrum to my neck and I would relax, almost discharged of pain...for about ten seconds. Then another wave of pain would set in. This went on for days. I tried to count each time I moved in just one mediation sitting and lost count after thirty. I was as restless as a twelve-year-old on espresso. Jumpy feet and jumpy mind.

I tried everything in my knowledge to get rid of this horrible discomfort, drawing on my decades of yoga training. I tried gentle yoga postures. I tried vigorous yoga postures. I tried breathing techniques to calm down and cool my system, running in place and shaking my body to throw off what felt like some ancient tension that wouldn't go away. Finally, I tried Tylenol to break the cycle of what felt like inflammation all through my upper spine.

Nothing worked. I was in unceasing agony. I felt trapped in this body and despair at the thought that I couldn't make it go away.

A New Approach

Twice a week during the retreat we would meet for interviews with a senior teacher. I had discussed my experience and my aversion to the pain and, so far, the coaching had been to stay with the practice as best I could. My teachers were empathetic and coached me to stay with it, to keep noticing. On the second or third interview, however, my teacher suggested that by giving into moving so much I might be dealing with it superficially and perhaps I could try not doing anything to fix it, but instead really investigate the sensations that arose.

I returned to my chair in the meditation hall committed to stay present no matter what. I was so frustrated and angry that I decided I'd die of this pain before I ran away from it. I determined to return to this essential practice of recognizing and allowing my experience to be just as it was without changing it in any way.

As the pain returned, I shifted my attention from the breath to the direct sensations and to the practice of noting or "labeling" what arose. This can be a powerful practice to enhance your moment-to-moment awareness, particularly when the mind is restless or powerful forces pull you away from the present.

I started to note the sensations along my back. "Burning pain." "Waves of pain." "Red hot pain." "Pulsing red hot waves of pain." As I sat with the sensations they continued to change and morph. Now the sensations felt like points of light. "Red hot points," I labeled. My concentration deepens and I actually become fascinated by these sensations which move and flow. "White hot points of pain" became "One hot point of pain."

I reminded myself again and again to let this be, just as it is. I softened the desire to shrink back or push anything away and did my best to rest my attention in the here and now.

"This feels like the point of a knife," I said to myself. "Now this feels like I'm being stabbed in the back."

As soon as I said those words, I instantly recalled a moment when I had felt utterly abandoned and betrayed by some former colleagues. The intensity of that emotion rushed through me and I broke out in a sweat. Anger and adrenaline flooded my whole body. I was enraged. I kept noting the emotions as they came into my awareness, struggling to stay open and make space for them. "Anger, anger," I said to myself, trying to stay present to the surging sensations as they morphed into feelings of betrayal and wanting revenge—to lash out. I watched and felt the burning in my gut, the sweating in my palms, my elevated pulse and breath, both fascinated and appalled by the intensity.

Eventually, betrayal and revenge fell away too, and under that lay feelings of hurt. Under hurt lay sadness. A flood of thoughts and stories accompanied the feelings: How could they have done this to me? Didn't they get how hard I tried? Why would they be so hard hearted? How did I get into this situation? Even under hurt and sadness there was more emotion, and now what arose were shame and humiliation. I was deeply embarrassed. But this, too, was impermanent and I realized that under shame and humiliation...there was a sense of quiet. I was soaked with perspiration, but I felt clean inside. I rested there, noting the heat in my body, my face flushed.

As long as we rely on our old strategies of reacting to stress, we remain identified and caught in a sense of the "small self". We tighten and, in fear, contract against the world. We block out what Deepak Chopra calls "the field of infinite possibility," the vastness of things and mystery of what is possible if we could drop our fears. When we let go of our reactivity, we discover our true nature. All that pain, the gush of emotions locked inside, I had no idea they were there and with such intensity. I felt as if a tsunami had passed through.

I felt light, spacious, and filled with a sense of kindness toward those around me in the meditation hall, wrapped in their blankets, so still and quiet. I thought about the memory of betrayal and, in a flash, understood that each person involved was afraid and doing the best they could. A surge of compassion for them flooded my heart. Who was that person hanging on so tightly? Was that me? I felt a wave of compassion for that guy who was trying so hard to do the right thing. I forgave and was forgiven.

From this new vantage point, the whole struggle seemed like nothing more than just a collection of stubborn, repetitive thoughts. The pain and struggle had been released into the morning sky. It was no longer me; who I was now was infinitely vast. I thought back to the Kafka poem. and the world did feel unmasked. In ecstasy I rolled with it.

Was this heaven?

The meditation bell rang. In keeping with tradition we all walked meditatively down the hill to breakfast, our eyes cast down and present to each step. I wanted to run! I wanted to skip and sing! The pain in my back was gone and I felt happy, clear, and at peace.

Our True Nature

All great traditions speak of our true nature. Yoga declares that your true nature is sat-chit-ananda: truth, knowledge, and bliss. Buddha declared that your true nature is made up of happiness, peace of mind, and freedom from suffering. Tibetans speak of "the natural mind," free from conditioning, free from greed, hatred, and delusion. Losing oneself in the love of Christ, Allah, Buddha, Krishna leads to a profound sense of wonder, presence, and aliveness.

The Buddha taught exclusively about this experience of losing oneself: "Nothing whatsoever is to be clung to as I or Mine. Whoever hears this teaching has heard all the teachings, who ever practices this teaching has practiced all the teachings…whoever realizes this teaching has realized all the teachings."

Perhaps the grandest illusion of them all is the belief that we are a wave cut off from the ocean. When we trust the ocean, we are not afraid of the waves.

The Art of Cultivating Presence

In that cathartic meditation I had been led to an insight about who I am in the absence of struggle and fear through a practice referred to in Buddhist circles by the acronym of RAIN. This helpful model for waking up in the midst of resistance allows us to break the cycle of constantly reacting to what we don't like and to find peace in the midst of turbulence.

- Recognize what is happening, just as it is. What do you feel in your body? What stories are arising? What emotion is present? You're not trying to change anything, but just naming what is here.

- Allow what is here to be here fully. You might give whatever you are feeling permission to get bigger, to move in any way it calls for.

- Investigate your experience. Does this feeling in your body seem permanent? Does it change in anyway? The story that's playing in your mind. Is it true? The emotion that is floating around in your body. Where do you feel it?

- Non-identification. Imagine you were a scientific objective observer of your body and mind. What is happening now? What if there was no clinging, no need to control what is next?

When you can stay with difficult emotions or obsessive thinking, riding the intensity of what arises, inevitably these states will shift, oftentimes leaving you feeling more relaxed, clearer, and perhaps with an insight into the experience. Oftentimes there is no deep insight, but simply a sense that something has passed through.

Recognizing what is here is the faculty of Wisdom. This wisdom allows you to penetrate through the stories to the fullness and truth of each moment.

Allowing cultivates the faculty of Compassion, your capacity to 'be with' the moment, whether it be comprised of joy or sorrow.

Basic Instructions for Mindfulness Meditation

While retreat is often an ideal scenario, it is by no means a requirement for meditation. All you really need is to set aside some quiet time when you won't be interrupted and find a posture that will support you to both relax and stay alert. You might take the first few moments to sweep through your body with the intention to relax. Soften and let go around areas of tightness and contraction, especially in the neck, shoulders, and stomach area. Let all the senses be awake: be aware of physical sensations, moods, sounds, and space in all directions.

Notice the movement of your breath. Feel where it is most predominant. You might like to focus the breath on either the rising and falling of the belly as you breath, in the nostrils, or wherever the breath feels the strongest. Once you decide where in the body to focus on the breath, let this be an anchor, a place you return to again and again when you notice that the mind is distracted from being present.

Bring full attention to the breath. You are making no effort to control or change how you breathe. Discover what the breath is actually like, moment to moment. If you notice that you are becoming tense, relax your body again and soften back into the breath. If your attention becomes too spacey or unfocused, bring more precision and clarity to the awareness of breathing.

Notice the aliveness of the senses. Feel the vibration of the sounds around you, the felt sense of your body. The purpose of this meditation is to bring attention to the changing flow of life without either clinging to what arises or resisting what is happening.

When a strong sensation, emotion, or thought arises, you might let go of the breath as the primary object of your attention and open your awareness to include the waves of experience that are arising. Notice what they are like as sensations in the body...and notice how they change. When you become aware of the mind wandering, simply return your attention to the breath and to the senses again and again. Let your intention be to neither resist what is painful nor grasp at what is pleasurable. Bring an unconditional caring presence that allows life to unfold without interference.

A quality of care, gentleness, and friendliness towards your experience is an essential part of meditation. Kindness allows you to relax and open, de-conditioning the tendency of the mind to resist and contract away from life. It is helpful to reflect on the intention of relating to experience in a gentle and kind way at the beginning of your meditation sitting (and throughout the day).

You might try this for five minutes at first. As you practice you can sit for ten, twenty, thirty minutes or longer. You may notice that no two meditation experiences are alike.

Meditation retreats are a wonderful way to step out of the everyday routine and break the habitual stress/reaction cycle. Even on retreat, though, you cannot help but bring your own mind to the meditation cushion. All the time, space, and intention in the world cannot spare us from the fundamental challenge of the practice itself.

While this unavoidable truth may seem daunting, it is also liberating because it means that we have everything we need to practice wherever we are. No matter how much — or how little — time or dedicated space we can afford at any given moment, it is in this moment to moment practice of mindful awareness that your true nature will reveal itself and, as Kafka wrote, the world will offer itself to you freely.

Caroline Myss

Living Mysticism

Mystics are what the word implies — people called to know the divine through its mysteries. Many people today want the mysteries and challenges in their lives solved and resolved quickly, but mystics know that we all have a deeper task: to accept that some challenges come into our lives in defiance of human reason, logic, order, justice, fairness, and even common sense. They know that underlying these challenges is a divine order and sense that may be revealed in time. It doesn't make sense, after all, to sit under a bodhi tree awaiting enlightenment without the promise that enlightenment will eventually come, but wait Gautama did, eventually to become the Buddha, a fully enlightened being. Nor does it make sense to sit for days, or weeks, or even months in positions that silence the body and free the spirit, and yet the first yogis did this over and over, showing the way to others.

You are unlikely to be called in this way, but your call may defy reason, too. In the Castle, you invite the sacred into your life; you learn to pray and to wait, to ready yourself for direction. Mystics know that their instructions will come along with the tasks God sets for them. The command, "Francis, rebuild my church," inspired the man who would come to be known as Francis of Assisi to rebuild a decaying church in a forest. Had he conceived that this command held a second, much greater meaning — to rebuild the Church of Rome — he may have run from the charge (although it would have caught up to him, inevitably, as our calls do).

Caroline Myss, PhD, is dedicated to creating educational programs in the field of human consciousness, spirituality and mysticism, health, energy medicine, and advancing the science of medical intuition. She has an international reputation as a renowned medical intuitive, and with C. Norman Shealy, MD, PhD, co-founded the American Board of Scientific Medical Intuition, which offers professional accreditation in this emerging field. Her book *Anatomy of the Spirit* (Three Rivers, 1997), was a *New York Times* best seller; her most recent book is *Entering the Castle* (Free Press, 2008). Full information is at www.Myss.com.

Some mystics wait just for the pure experience of grace and the divine. Grace is the word we give to the power of God that we recognize in our lives. We long to make this power so real that we can hold it in our hands, or feel it like heat running through our bodies. We want to know that this divine substance *is* real and that it protects us and heals us and flows down from heaven when we request it. Teresa of Avila's conversations with God, for instance, were even more real to her than her physical life. She felt grace around her and within her. She saw it manifest in visions and heard it in voices. One vision asked her, "Who are you?" and she replied, "I am Teresa of Jesus. Who are you?" "I am Jesus of Teresa," the vision famously replied. The sisters who saw her in her rapt states begged her to teach them the way into the presence of God, which she did in both *The Interior Castle* and *The Way of Perfection*.

As Martin Buber wrote, "living means being addressed." Once you are called, you have no choice but to follow. Perhaps once you are called, heaven has already made the choice for you and you can only surrender to this divine summons, even if that is the last thing you would consciously choose to do. The call awakens you to what is beyond.

The masters also reveal that we do have the strength and faith deep within our spiritual core to answer the call and embark on the journey into the beyond. "Yea, though I walk through the valley of the shadow of death, I will fear no evil. For thou art with me, Thy rod and thy staff they comfort me." Once you open yourself to God, once God shines a direct light within your soul, your life becomes a journey of faith. Mysteries will seem to fill you to overflowing, but faith and prayer will help you face both the known and the unknown.

Indeed, for the "Holy Anorexics"—Julian of Norwich, Hildegard of Bingen, and Clare of Assisi—their nourishment seemed to come only from their faith. Only the grace they received during spiritual experiences seemed to keep these divinely chosen few functioning where others would have collapsed from weakness, exhaustion, or madness. Their self-imposed suffering became the hallmark of the medieval mystic, an unnecessary extreme now, but, in their time, their example of fortitude in the face of suffering—endurance of bleak conditions and illnesses, poverty, and isolation—inspired thousands of people who also had hardscrabble lives. After all, pain and suffering comes to everyone; that's just life. If a mystic could suffer *that* much in poverty and privation and still have the generosity of spirit and the spiritual energy to heal others, found spiritual communities, write some of the most beautiful spiritual literature and soaring music in the world, and even become a conduit of miracles, then surely God was in his heaven and he would take care of other, ordinary human beings as well.

But what relevance is all this today? How can the experiences of cloistered mystics of four hundred years ago have any practical application to the stresses we encounter in our contemporary society? In fact, we do need their guidance now more than ever. So many people today are experiencing a dark night of the soul (as John of the Cross first defined spiritual alienation) that it qualifies as a spiritual epidemic. The beloved contemporary mystic Mother Teresa said that the real hunger in the West "is the hunger for the soul." No one has provided more precise, thorough routes for self-examination and psychological insight—as well as insight into what the divine expects of us—than the medieval mystics.

The mystics' time has come again. This second great mystical renaissance has been brewing for decades, as we've been asking the questions that bring the divine into direct contact with our souls: "For what purpose have I been born?" and "What is my spiritual path?" and "How can I receive clear guidance?" These are not ordinary questions. They are spiritual invocations, invitations for God to come closer. And when God hears them, God does exactly that.

What does divine intimacy feel like? How do you know if your soul is calling you to live a deeper expression of the divine for the rest of your life? Have you been called? How do you respond? You may find out when you enter the Castle.

You Are a Container for God in This World

Whenever societies have cycled through crises, mystics have arisen to address them. Like hidden angels of the divine, they emerge in every walk of life. Today, mystics without monasteries are wives and mothers, husbands and fathers, teachers and lawyers, bankers and doctors, soldiers and policemen, therapists and writers, social workers and salespeople. They are everywhere.

Mystics salvage the good of one culture and carry those treasures into the birth of the next. Mystics are not silent containers of God, make no mistake. Many are the loudest noisemakers. They wrestle with the great questions of life and death. They remind a people and a society of its principles and its vision. They inspire others through their example of living in accordance with their souls' direction, through their intensity and clearsightedness. Mystics recognize the signs that a society's soul is starving and has gone unconscious.

Mystics have the courage to see through common fears. They see beyond calls for destruction and violence as means for solving problems. They see the contradictions in others' statements—for instance, that war creates peace.

The one great difference between Teresa's time and ours is that God's new mystics are everywhere. And the new mystic should rightly be called a mystical activist.

Yet, the journey itself has not changed. There is no shortcut to God. Centuries may have passed since Teresa wrote her masterpiece, but her genius, wisdom, and guidance are as valuable today as in the sixteenth century.

It takes great courage to cross your drawbridge and enter your Castle. It is not easy to enter each room and begin a dialogue with your soul. It can be as painful as it is awesome and empowering. It is long and arduous. You have to be prepared to meet your shadow and to embrace your soul. Your life will change. But then, your life will change anyway. You are being called.

The divine will find you in your Castle. God will find you. And you must ask yourself, "Why does God want me? Why have I been called?" You are being called inward so that you will also be able to move out into the world.

Perhaps you have been called because you have that certain mystic's profile: strong, stubborn, independent, a silent (or loud) warrior type with a hot temper and a relentless will that's searching for something to serve. Perhaps your soul, a restless creature of eternity, is finally forcing you into the quest for your highest potential, after your many delays.

Something compels you to want to know more of the nature of God. This desire, this need, is what it feels like to be called. You don't necessarily want to withdraw from the chaotic influences of this world until the only voice you hear is that of the divine. In the middle of your earthly chaos, you discover a passion to follow that may even bring more chaos for the moment, but underneath it you will find a new order, a divine order.

Essential Guidance for Mystics Outside the Castle Walls

- **Maintain your work in the Castle.** Do not stay away from the interior work of your Castle for too long. Revisit the rooms that need the most attention, where you can finish only one exploration at a time. Add a room as you need to when a crisis arises in your life and then go into that room to resolve that crisis. This book is meant to be your companion for a lifetime—or for as long as you need before you feel God in the walls of your soul.

- **Practice illumination.** Do not treat your spiritual life as a hobby. Maintain the practices in the Castle, among them illumination. The mystic's life is not about showing up for a twenty-minute, close-your-eyes-and-listen-to-soft-music meditation. Mystical activism is proactive; it requires dedication and a soul with stamina.

- **Develop and share the gifts of your soul.** Do not keep your talents hidden from others. Do not be shy about your capacity to see a problem clearly and understand its symbolic message. Be available to bring illumination into another person's life, but be humble about it. Allow your inner guidance to alert you to act; if you do not receive that instruction, then remain silent and serve that individual through prayer. Always stay humble.

- **Keep alert.** Evil exists. And the greater the evil, the more difficult it can be to grasp, to see. Take refuge in your Castle, close the drawbridge, and enter into prayer. Insecurity and fear rule, but not within your soul.

- **Fly under the radar.** Never position yourself as an authority or presume that you are better than another. Never put yourself in a position to be criticized for your spiritual practices. Stay humble at all times.

- **Avoid power plays.** Your job is not to win arguments or prove anything to anyone. Power plays drain your soul and serve only the ego, and only temporarily.

- **Stop blaming others.** No other human being is responsible for your choices, even though that individual's choices may have affected your life, just as your choices have affected others' lives. Focus only on understanding the motivations behind your choices.

- **Don't use the word *deserve*.** To decide who deserves what in this world positions you as judge and jury over others. When have you ever had all the facts? Never. That is a cosmic position only. Believing you deserve something means that you think you are entitled. I am entitled to heal; I am entitled to guidance; I am entitled to an easy life. Entitlement is a self-inflicted form of suffering. Many times people use the word *deserve* as an excuse to buy or indulge in something special. As a result, their purchases land them in debt and sweet desserts make them gain weight. If you want something special, just get it. Leave out the game of "deserve." As Teresa wrote, never approach God with an expectation, either. You do not deserve to be healed because you prayed; you do not deserve to have your prayers answered because you are a good person. To believe in entitlement and divine obligation is to ask for self-inflicted suffering.

- **Let your first response in any situation be, "What can I do?"** You may not be able to build a house or repair a levee (although, to be frank, you don't know that). Sometimes you are called into action and sometimes that action is what you can do silently. You can change anything and everything with prayer and faith. You are never to assume a helpless posture. Inspire others with that truth *when appropriate.* You are not a preacher. You wait for your instructions to come through your soul to make you an invisible act of power.

- **Channel grace on a daily basis.** Understanding that you are a channel for grace is a core part of your identity as a mystic. Countless ways exist to channel grace; certainly daily prayer is a must. Make this a part of your daily practice—a priority, not a convenience. The length of time is not an issue, but daily devotion is required. Devote, for example, ten minutes a day to opening a channel on the cosmic grid.

- **Form a circle of grace with soul companions; such friends are essential to your well-being.** Soul companions support one another's spiritual journeys. The intent of a circle of grace is to empower every person in that circle. In a circle of grace you can channel grace for healing and for sharing higher guidance. You encourage one another's creative abilities, courageous decision making, and spiritual life. A book club can be part of a circle of grace, as you can also discuss the rich literature of the soul and spirituality. As you gather together, open the circle with prayer. If a member has a decision to make or an illness to heal, have him or her pose the dilemma or question. Open yourselves to the clearest guidance that you can bring to bear upon the questions. Pray for grace, and channel it to the person or situation.

- **Live congruently.** Make sure that your mind and your heart are in agreement with your soul in your actions, decisions, and thoughts. Mind, heart, and soul are your interior trinity. Keeping the integrity of your soul is extremely challenging, requiring serious introspection and inner work. This is a perfect theme for a group of soul companions.

- **Be devoted to truth.** Mystics are keepers of truth. No matter who you are or what you do professionally, a nonnegotiable devotion to truth is an essential life practice. A part of a mystic's task has always been to find new truths, to further intellectual pursuits, and to dismantle outdated, superstitious systems of thought. Nourish your mind and heart with reading material.

- **Stay active in the world.** Mystics are servants. Do not run and hide from this world. Violence, pollution, and war are challenges that require a response from you that serves the good of humanity. You cannot run and hide and expect others to make this world safe for you.

- **You are a source for healing.** Healing has many expressions. Prayer and the channeling of grace are the instruments of healing. You might find yourself in situations in which your help is needed; for instance, someone may want to confide in you who would normally not open up to anyone. In these moments, silently ask for a blessing and visualize grace flowing through you and into the person who is speaking to you. That is all you need to do. In rooms where there is tension, visualize grace flowing through you into the room, blessing and healing the atmosphere. Stay silent always about these actions.

- **Remain active in your Castle.** Use the visualization of the Castle. See yourself as safe within your Castle walls, surrounded by love and the blessings of other people. Animate the love in your life; do not always feed the idea that you must just protect yourself. Use your Castle as a source of positive replenishment. Make it a stronger and stronger psychic source of love and a field of creative and tranquil grace. See God in everything. Appreciate the presence of the divine in the details of your life every day.

Let your Castle become the sacred ground beneath your feet. Live the power of your soul. Listen to and follow the voice of your soul. You are not alone. No higher purpose in this life exists than to be called into a mystical relationship with the divine.

> Let nothing disturb you.
> Let nothing frighten you.
> All things pass away.
> God never changes
> Patience obtains all things.
> He who has God lacks for nothing.
> God alone suffices.
> —Teresa of Avila

JEANNE M. HOUSE

Belief *is* the Magic

"*W*ho *are we? Whence did we come? And why are here?*" I remember first asking these questions when my identical twin sister and I were five years old. We were still innocent and in touch with our *inner sense*. She was she and I was me, yet we both came from the very same womb, the very same "stuff."

No two people are exactly alike, of course. We are all unique individuals, yet at the same time, we are indivisible from our Source. Even at five, my sister and I understood that we each had our very own worthwhile purpose. To "us," anything was possible; yet to "them," that wasn't the case. Since we appeared exactly alike, most people tried to convince us that we actually were. So we learned very early not to mistake *appearances* for reality.

Joseph Campbell advises us to *follow our bliss*. Despite the efforts of the nuns in our Catholic school, that is exactly what we did! My sister took her most cherished desires outward and experienced them with all of their flying colors, *in action*. I experienced bliss in a more *inward way*. So even though we appeared exactly alike, we were actually polarities of each other. And this served our collective purpose very well. Whenever she needed a quick reading on her soul, she would check in with me. And whenever I needed to launch a brilliant idea, I would check in with her. My twin sister and I mirrored each other's opposites and yet, reflected back to one another our greatest strengths.

Jeanne House, MA, has helped head up the marketing and sales efforts of Elite Books and two book distributors, Summit Beacon and Associated Publishers Group. She previously held positions at NBC-TV and Miami University. She has a bachelor's degree in journalism and a postgraduate degree in consciousness studies, and is completing a second degree in transformational psychology. She is currently the president of Sol Communication. She is the associate editor of the award-winning anthology *Einstein's Business*. As editor of *Peak Vitality*, her focus is on bringing soul communication and conscious practices into everyday life. More at www.KiMoves.com.

Light shines through a crystal and suddenly a rainbow of color dances across my desk. Brilliant red, orange, yellow, green, blue and, finally, a violet hue shimmer all around me. This reminds me that each one of us is a perfect gem with our own unique color, frequency, and vibration originating from the white light that shines through the prism. As we radiate with that frequency, we contribute to this Great White Light. If we try on someone else's frequency, however, the white light would no longer exist; it needs every hue in the spectrum to be complete.

We are all authors of our own destiny and masters of our own circumstances. As children, most of us understand this and the world seems full of infinite possibilities. But by adulthood, we lose this wisdom and consciously or unconsciously give away our power, either to other people or to our outer circumstance. That is well and good for a time, but at some point we become fed up and seek to take the reigns back into our own hands.

Who are we? Whence did we come? Why are we here? When we start to ask ourselves these questions, it is usually a sign that we are about to embark on a journey of self-mastery. Once we get a taste of this magic in us, we are no longer satisfied to be enslaved by other people or the world around us. Our lives then become more vitalized, joyous, and adventurous. Outer judgments, appearances, and opinions cease to matter so much and we begin to focus inward, where we can imagine and believe in a whole new world.

Throughout history and around the world, people have felt the inner stirrings of dissatisfaction with even the "best" of day-to-day existence. This craving for more arises in those quiet moments when we know, deep down, that no amount of money or status, no credentials, career, or ideal mate can ever really fill us up or make us feel whole. Though it may be tempting to think of our discontent as some modern development—a kind of circumstantial *ennui* symptomatic of contemporary Western life—it is a basic aspect of the human condition. It was this very yearning that inspired the greatest stories and heroic journeys of all time. But the dissatisfaction is only the beginning. Recognizing and acting on it is the real adventure.

Back in the fifteenth century, a Spanish explorer named Juan Ponce de Leon grew bored with his material wealth. He began to fixate on a tale he had heard as a boy about the miraculous "Water of Life," an eternal wellspring that flowed unimpeded and never gave up! Assuming this to be a literal youth-rendering spring in a far-off land of plenty, Ponce de Leon launched an expedition across the Atlantic to the Americas. He searched high and low, holding fast to his dream, but to his great disappointment he found neither the fountain nor the salvation he sought.

The story of the Fountain of Youth lives on in our memories as a symbol of our hope for eternal life. It can even be viewed as the power of positive thinking over challenging circumstances or of rejuvenating our attitude to revitalize our minds and hearts. Yet, like Ponce de Leon, we often seek approval, success, and fame outside ourselves. After all, mirages are simply images that we mistake for reality. Whenever we draw near to an illusion, it simply disappears and reappears in the distance. We can save ourselves the trouble and wasted energy of deluded journeys by simply accessing the magic within us, instead of embarking on an elusive journey outside of us.

It is up to each of us to choose how we expend the natural resource of energy—of life—with which we are born. Whether we understand this gift as Aristotle did when he first coined the term "energy" to express the concept of "vigor of expression," or as a more spiritual, cosmic force as taught in the Mystery schools, each one of us is a unique aspect of the universal energy, personified. We express this energy through our thoughts, our feelings, our words, and our physical activities. In this way, the eternal wellspring flows unimpeded through our worlds. It is within our power to direct this fount of energy so that we can lift ourselves out of mediocrity and into true vitality.

There is magic in believing and hoping for a better tomorrow. We dissipate the magic when we doubt its existence and limit our focus to that which is external. Our *attitude* and our *attention* are our directors on the journey. Our focused attention is a sieve through which the pulp of life is pressed. What comes out in our day-to-day lives is molded by our own thoughts, feelings, and beliefs. Yes, we create our life circumstances from our very essence. It isn't something "out there," but "in here" that should matter to us most of all.

Energy and vibration, correctly applied, are as scientific as a radio or electricity. A live wire is a live wire, regardless of our opinions about whether it has a charge or not. We accept outside opinions because we have forgotten about our own energy source. But when opinions about who we are or what we do are destructive, they kill our higher aspirations. They clothe light with discord instead of harmony.

We can access our inner vitality at any time, without chasing after outer illusions by simply applying these principles to our lives. Concentrating on the *good* isn't easy. In order to do this, we need to remove the limitations of fear, doubt, and worry, then energy flows naturally through our lives and helps bring our dreams into manifestation. *Faith* is the key to what seems a mystery. We must concentrate on the good and not the bad that can happen. Of course, this takes work; it is not simply a mental exercise. It takes courage, stamina, and discipline to stay on course. Seeking after our ideals may take us on some unnecessary detours and a few wild goose chases.

It is essential, during these times of frustration and setback, that we remember the alchemists' Law of the One: *as above, so below.* Concentrating only on the failures, disappointments, and hurts of the past douses the inner flame of truth and vision. If we nurture this flame within us, the flow of energy and vitality will keep us youthful and vibrant. When we judge other people, our life circumstances, or ourselves, we tie ourselves to matter—instead of what really matters—and dam up the pure stream of our consciousness with con-dam-nation.

If we are experiencing inner poverty or inner bankruptcy, we should pay closer attention to which sticky point of our past is preventing us from moving forward in this otherwise fluid stream toward perfection. We may also want to carefully consider what compels us to journey to barren lands rather than the land of plenty. When we tune in to what the divine intends for us, we are free to drink of the Fount of Truth. We then realize that behind the appearance world lies an infinite world of masterful causes. We also discover that we matter in the great scheme of things and this fuels our journey, propelling us forward.

Attention is key to our victory. If we cultivate the art of attention, we solve the secret of mastering our moods and mental states. We can always choose to change our negative moods by deliberately focusing on something more desirable. Our will directs our attention and our attention affects our vibration. To change our world, we must change our consciousness. What we experience in life are finite ideas projected into materiality. Behind what we see is what spirit sees, and that infinite vision constitutes Reality.

The Attractor Factor

Energy moves through our consciousness and is either utilized *as is* or is altered according to our vibration and energy field. It is shaped by and shows up in the world according to our consciousness. In order to attract true abundance in our lives, we need to cultivate the *faith vibration.* At every turn on our journey, we must believe that we can take part in these masterful causes and not merely be blind instruments of our past actions. In order to do this, we can remind ourselves that no thing "out there" has any power over us, unless we let it.

The faith vibration attracts all that we have and experience. If our faith is pulsating to the "just getting by" frequency, then so, too, it is reflected in our world. If our faith is dialed in or set on insufficiency, there will *never* be enough. Our "All-seeing and All-knowing Self" sees no darkness; it only sees infinite possibility! It cannot want or it would not *be*. This pure thought energy is a mighty power that presses and radiates through our consciousness with unlimited supply, boundless prosperity, and overflowing abundance.

To maximize this force, we must watch our motives. Even if we are doing spectacular work for an outer cause, we might fail all of the time due to desire for power, place, and self-satisfaction. In order to reach the lost horizon, we need to proceed with wisdom and selflessness in every act. As we gain more faith muscles, the *Water of Life* flows at a more rapid speed and we enter a more purified stream of awareness that has a much faster vibration.

We need to guard our intent, because the journey gets perilous as we gain speed. We can fall as far backward as we have come forward. We need to make sure that we don't gain riches at the expense of others. The goal is self-dominion, not domination over people, nature, or the world around us. Only when we have learned self-mastery, when we cannot harm a single creature, can we master the elements of the world around us and gain our rightful inheritance.

This may have been where Ponce de Leon got caught up. If he had indeed found an actual fountain that ran with waters of youth and eternal life, his discovery may have served a "higher good" of bringing miraculous healing to humankind. But his focus was external, and his vision limited and ego-driven.

Tales of magic carpets, incredible voyages, glorious fountains, and wish-fulfilling lamps are eternal symbols of our yearning. As reminders of the reality of the *presence of perfection,* they give us hope when much of our daily attention is focused on distress and imperfection. But each time we deny this imperfection, we can refocus our journey upward in our consciousness—like the church spire pointing toward heaven, or our majestic mountain ranges, or the graceful pine trees swaying ever so slightly to and fro, (which are designed to remind us to look upward to the perfected realms of our own consciousness). When we do this, we are both renewed and refreshed.

The same building block of the Ageless Wisdom is contained in all these stories: the concept of *all-sufficiency.* The ancients knew how to release divine energy from within in order to transmute discord into harmony, ignorance into wisdom, fear into love, and lack into abundance. But the Secret of the Ages was not just given to anyone. It was only divulged to those who had eyes to see and ears to hear.

For century upon century, people have spent much of their vitality trying to discover the secret to lasting life. Different parts of the world have different concepts of that dream. Traditionally, the East has been the land of spirit and mystery, whereas the West has been characterized by the cult of the concrete, in which money, science, and machines are the idols worshipped.

While Aladdin's carpet is a magical means of transportation of spirit, we in the West, known for our material focus, have preferred our rugs on the cold, hard floor—beautiful at best, but by all means practical.

Western scientists, who have had the reputation of only believing in what they can touch and feel, have begun, however, to understand the unseen forces that make and mold the universe. They have discovered hidden laws and powers that lie beneath the seemingly manifest reality. And these same powers are within us.

At long last, the secret is revealed. The secret is: There is *no secret*. There is only law, the One Law of *Eternal Perfection*. We are perfect; we just forgot. Everything is simply vibrations and energies leading away from or to the Undivided One Source, which is Perfection.

If we just believed in our rightful inheritance and guarded that belief, riches could be ours, too. Ponce de Leon did not know *this secret*, or he would've realized that he was merely chasing after effects instead of tapping into his own Inner Fount, which we are all free to do at any time. We all have the power to choose at any moment where we place our attention: on poverty or abundance.

Each of one of us has the same potential for genius. Interestingly the common understanding of this word genius, "wit or talent," is in fact the third, most abstracted definition of the original Latin definition, according to the online etymology dictionary at www. etymonline.com. The first is *guardian deity* or *spirit* which watches over each person from birth, spirit, incarnation." Take into account the related word "genie" and it becomes clear that this magical spirit of our own potential is with us all the time, simply awaiting our recognition and command.

In the story of "Aladdin and the Wonderful Lamp," he discovers two genies: a genie or slave of the ring given to him by a conniving sorcerer who wants to use Aladdin for his own purposes, and a genie or slave of the lamp he discovers by accident.

This story is our story. The two genies illustrate that we can be the slave of our outer senses (like Ponce de Leon and represented by the ring) or we can embrace our own light source (represented by the lamp). We simply have to choose whom we will serve at any given time. We can either be a slave to our human desires, *wrapped* up in the enchanted treasures of our mental vision, or a Slave of the Lamp, so possessed and *rapt* with its extraordinary light that the boundary between self and Self fades and we become a vessel of Light.

It wasn't always easy for Aladdin to believe in himself. Once the sorcerer—the traitor within—had given him the ring, it seemed that Aladdin might get lost in the illusion of riches and shiny things. But he eventually transformed his own paradigm and reversed the negative spell by using the magical ring for more productive purposes. In this way, the ring within the story is a part of a greater tradition of rings or circles, resonating on three different levels with ancient esoteric meanings of this symbol:

1) *The Circle of Oneness:* Every time Aladdin acted on his one-eyed-vision of marrying the princess, he would see his one-pointed objective as good, real, and achievable. This automatically summoned the Genie of the Lamp—his inner sense or his sixth sense—to be at his command and fulfill his every rightful desire.

2) *The Ring-Pass-Not:* Aladdin also used the magical ring as a "ring-pass-not." He visualized a ring of light around himself that repelled all thoughts or beliefs from the outside that would tarnish his one-pointed vision of becoming a prince and ruling his own kingdom.

3) *The Circle of Necessity:* The copper ring emitted Aladdin's energetic frequency. Every time he was double-minded and couldn't quite see himself as royalty, he accessed the genie in the sorcerer's ring (his own conniving sorcerer within). The ring illustrated the principle of "what goes around comes around." As long as he chose the ring, his world was nothing but rounds and rounds of the very same thing.

Consciousness is the weapon of the master. It took Aladdin awhile to become conscious that the power of the lamp was actually the power that was hidden within him. All he had to do was acknowledge that he and the genie were one and the same. It wasn't until he lost the lamp by the cunning of the sorcerer who traded new lamps (and new paradigms) for old that Aladdin realized he would have to discover this very same power for himself.

The turning point in the story is when Aladdin is trapped beneath a cave and nothing from his past behaviors (the limiting conditions he placed on himself) can help him escape, so he prays, "I testify that there is no God save thy alone...thou art my Sufficiency and thou art my Truest of Trustees," and he is immediately transported to his home. This experience gave Aladdin a new way to behave. Now he knew to bow before this inner Light in order to remove his chagrin and to begin a new journey within.

Like a true hero, Aladdin (whose name comes from the Arabic *Ala' al Din*, or "nobility of faith") transforms himself in the course of his story, shifting his narrow outward focus within to find the magic of his own true nature. Compare this to his Western counterpart, Ponce de Leon, whose limited understanding of his own quest brought him nothing but frustration and failure. Of course, one of these figures is historical and the other metaphorical, but as in so many tales from cultures around the world, they share the common theme of a search for the elusive mystery that will lift them out of mundane "reality" and into bliss. What these heroes are really searching for is a state of being, entirely independent of physical locations or material things.

The Western logical mind is finally catching up with the Eastern adepts. Our scientists are teaching us that light is pure action, uncontaminated and perfect. It is eternally sustained, indestructible, self-luminous and comes in wholes. In *Scientific Autobiography and Other Papers*, Max Planck wrote that "the photons, which constitute a ray of light, behave like intelligent human beings: out of all possible curves, they always select the one which will take them most quickly to their goal."

Light Is Not Seen: It Is Seeing

This light is only part of what we see in our daily world. Sun shines through a prism and the invisible light rays show up as color, red light having a long wavelength and low frequency, and violet light a shorter wavelength and higher frequency. In the range from red to violet, the frequency of light doubles (one octave), according to Arthur Young. This reminds us that we are all vibrating at a certain frequency, but that we can change the speed of our frequency at any time. I wonder how it would be if we doubled our frequency?

If we aim the light carefully, we can transmute the red of our passions into the violet hue and become anew. By changing our feelings, we can change our attention. And by guiding our attention and governing our feelings, we can direct this living light to a greater height and, thereby, master our world. Remember, no thing or circumstance "out there" has any power over us unless we feed it our energy and give it our attention.

Like Aladdin, we can take a stand for our spiritual rights, regardless of what is going on in our lives. Each one of us determines our pathway, because when we use our minds and feelings in constructive ways, it is impossible for our ideals not to manifest in the physical world.

The nervous system is like a network of fine wires that carry the messages of our thoughts, feelings, attitudes, and beliefs throughout our body. It is only our discordant feelings that cause disintegration, lack of memory, and every other failure in our world. When we dwell on imperfection, especially in our feelings, which qualify our thoughts, we lower our vibrations and then we become prey to depression, poverty, ill health, and so on. When we focus instead on perfection, we don't subdue our emotions but simply transmute them into pure substance. And with this new energy, we can paint a new landscape.

True visualization helps us to bring perfection into our world. We can manifest any secret into life if we hold our attention unwaveringly. But we must acknowledge the Light within us as the doer. Because what we see, hear, taste, touch, and smell are our beliefs objectified; our experiences are merely effects. When we judge the effects, we believe "them" and give them power over us. Many of us find ourselves pondering: If I could only find my dream... A power greater than us surely put our dreams in our mind's eye to remind us that we are far from small and insignificant. We must believe that the power is within us because *the magic is in the believing!*

Even as children my twin sister and I instinctively believed in this magic and knew not to believe in *appearances*. After much seeking, we finally discovered the seemingly hidden "law of the contrary." She realized that being *in action* was fine, but it was better to *act on the I*. And I realized that *a goal is a dream with a deadline*.

A quick powerful change of attention can do wonders. To every negative thought, tie a positive one. Ponce de Leon and Aladdin would've discovered this ancient method of mastery sooner, if they had met. When we become masters of our mental and feeling states, instead of being servants and slaves to them, the universe will be at our command.

Julia Cameron

Heartfulness and Blessing

Life is a creative endeavor. It is active, not passive. We are the yeast that leavens our lives into rich, fully baked loaves. When we experience our lives as flat and lackluster, it is our consciousness that is at fault. We hold the inner key that turns our lives from thankless into fruitful. That key is "Blessing."

"My fathers house has many mansions," we are told. By counting our blessings, we name ourselves accurately as children of the universe, the richly dowried children of God, or, if you prefer, of "good." Focused on our good, focused on our abundance, we naturally attract more of the same. This is spiritual law. Our consciousness is creative. What we focus on, we empower and enlarge. Good multiplies when focused upon. Negativity multiplies when focused upon. The choice is ours: Which do we want more of?

In every event, in every circumstance, we have a choice of perspective. Faced with difficulty, we can choose between disappointment and curiosity as our mind-set. The choice is ours. Will we focus on what we see as lacking or will we look for the new good that is emerging? In every moment, however perilous or sorrowful it may feel, there is the seed of our greater happiness, greater expansion, and greater abundance.

It is easy to bless events that coincide with our perceived good. When things are going "our way," it is easy to experience faith and gratitude. To bless what might be called "contrary" circumstances

Julia Cameron is an active artist who teaches internationally. A poet, playwright, fiction writer, and essayist, she has extensive credits in film, television, and theater, and is an award-winning journalist. She is the author of the best-selling books on creative practice *The Artist's Way* (Tarcher, 2002), *Blessings* (Tarcher, 1998), and *The Vein of Gold* (Tarcher, 1997). She has been refining her methods for nearly two decades, inspiring people to pursue their creative dreams through her seminars at the Smithsonian, Omega, and Esalen. Creativity groups based on her books have formed in many countries. www.JuliaCameron.com.

requires more faith. Things do not seem to be going our way. In fact, the flow of events may actually run counter to our desires. In all times of such apparent difficulty, it is crucial to bless the flow of events as right and appropriate despite our reservations. The delays, difficulties, and disruptions we experience can in this way enlarge and enrich us. In short, we bless not only the road but the bumps on the road. They are all part of the higher journey.

It is easy, too, to bless people who are sunny and harmonious. It is easy to perceive such personalities as blessings on our path. When people are stormy and temperamental, when people are withholding, mean-spirited, greedy, or judgmental, it is more difficult to bless them, more difficult to perceive their positive contribution to our path. Faced with such unhappy individuals, blessing allows us to lessen their negative impact, to remember that they hold no real power over us. Blessing reminds us that our dignity comes from a divine source. That source is the wellspring of our self-valuing.

The key to practicing blessings is the willingness to accept the full value of each moment. As we are willing to allow each difficult moment to soften and transform into its inner potential, our hearts become hopeful, clear, brave. As we extend the tendrils of our faith above and through the walls of our resistance, our lives become green, verdant, affirming. We are the wild rose basking in the sun. As we cling to our conscious optimism, finding footholds of faith despite opposition, our lives become rooted in the soil of grace. We are nurtured, prospered, and blessed.

The act of blessing is a step into faith. Rather than stand blocked or stymied by circumstances that appear adversarial, we step forward, claiming the safety of our path, the firmness of the soil of God. We affirm, "This is to my benefit. This circumstance blesses my life; I am grateful to this difficult situation for the many gifts it carries. I accept my blessings as they unfold within me."

Counting every blessing is a small step in the direction of our dreams. We gradually perceive our lives on a safe and protected path. Every time we recognize a blessing, it increases our capacity to receive a blessing. As we expand our consciousness in gratitude, we become larger vessels for good. We can consciously and creatively choose to count and encounter our good. We can consciously and creatively choose to expand.

This is easier than it may sound—easier even in the face of very real and very human difficulties.

Blessing a difficulty is not simply accepting it. It is looking at it with new eyes, considering it from a higher, more open-minded perspective. To bless a situation is not to deny its sorrowful or challenging reality. To bless a situation is to claim its inner, hidden reality, a higher, finer working-out of good for all concerned.

To bless a difficult situation, we must soften our hearts to it. When we are in the pain of a difficult realization, we tend instead to wince and steel our hearts against acceptance. We feel the prodding of a pointed awareness and we recoil, fearing it is the point of a lance that will pierce us through.

Blessing is the scalpel of spiritual healing. It removes our poisoned attitudes of fear and constriction, causing the infection of self-importance to flow away, leaving us surrendered and open to the healing action of spirit, the cleansing power of grace. As we surrender resistance, we open our hearts. Freed to love again, they become full, expansive, and wise. We are no longer victimized by resentment and anger. A higher hand is at work.